FITZ

For my cousins in New Zealand
And in memory of my great-great-grandparents,
James Edward and Fanny FitzGerald

FITZ

The Colonial Adventures of
James Edward FitzGerald

Jenifer Roberts

OTAGO

Published by Otago University Press
P.O. Box 56 / Level 1, 398 Cumberland Street
Dunedin, New Zealand
university.press@otago.ac.nz
www.otago.ac.nz

First published in 2014
Text © 2014 Jenifer Roberts
Photographs © the photographers as named

ISBN 978-1-877578-73-1

A catalogue record for this book is available from the
National Library of New Zealand.

Back cover author photo: Gareth Williams

Publisher: Rachel Scott
Editor: Gillian Tewsley
Design/layout: Quentin Wilson & Associates
Index: Diane Lowther

Printed in New Zealand by PrintStop

Contents

Acknowledgements

I have received much kindness and help in New Zealand and made many new friends. I owe a large debt of gratitude to the many FitzGerald descendants who provided information and gave me access to papers and photographs, particularly Sally Astridge, Sue Blakely, Peter Budd, Robin Gilchrist, Ian and Pam Jackson, Dick Levin and Peter Levin. I should also like to thank Sally and Bruce Astridge, Sue and Jerry Blakely, Peter and Kalo Budd, Peter and Gael Levin, Clive and Debbie Roberts, and Lin Roberts and her partner Nick, for their generous hospitality.

Max Abernethy of the Cotter Medical History Trust provided information on Dr William Draper. Claire Le Couteur located and cleaned William Draper's grave in Lyttelton and carried out research for me in Christchurch. Stephen Barker provided copies of letters and photographs taken by his ancestor, Dr Alfred Barker. Neville Moar and Margaret Morrish of the Lincoln & Districts Historical Society guided me through the history of Lincoln. Jan Heynes of the Karori Historical Society met me in Karori and provided information and photographs. Jean Garner and Kate Foster of the Terrace Station Archive, Hororata, provided excerpts from the diary of Sir John Hall. Margaret Maynard and Dr Anne Mulcock provided information on the FitzGerald children. Colin Amodeo and Edmund Bohan gave much helpful advice. I am grateful to them all.

I should also like to thank the staff of the libraries and archives who sent photocopies halfway around the world and provided much support while I was in New Zealand. In particular, I should like to thank James Ashwell, Catherine Bisley, and the staff of the Alexander Turnbull Library in Wellington; Jo Drysdall and Richard Greenaway of the Aotearoa New Zealand Centre (Christchurch City Libraries); Joanna Condon, Michelle Lambert, and Kerry McCarthy of the Canterbury Museum in Christchurch; Jane Teal, archivist at Christ's College; David Murray of the Hocken Library/Uare Taoka o Hakena, University of Otago, in Dunedin; Liza Rossie of the Lyttelton Museum; and Caroline Etherington of the Christchurch office of Archives New Zealand. The Births, Deaths and Marriages Office at the Department of Internal Affairs and the staff of Archives New Zealand in Auckland and Wellington provided information swiftly and efficiently. I should also like to mention the Papers Past website, which is seriously addictive. It is easy to use and, with a little persistence, can provide an answer to almost any question.

In the northern hemisphere, Ansell and Anthony Hawkins allowed me to delve into Amy Levin's boxes of personal papers; and I should also like to thank them for their hospitality and good lunches. Lord Kilbracken showed me the treasures of the Godley family collection and lent me a large number of letters written by a FitzGerald grandchild. Viscount Cobham provided access to the Hagley Hall Archives. The staff of the British Library, Cambridge University Library and National Library of Wales were, as always, helpful and efficient. And a special thank you to Paul Skinner of the Philatelic Collections of the British Library for sending photocopies of a letter from Fanny FitzGerald, for which the Library had granted an export licence.

I owe a large debt of gratitude to Edmund Bohan, author of *Blest Madman: FitzGerald of Canterbury* (published in 1998), which guided me through FitzGerald's life and without which my task would have been more difficult. I also wish to pay tribute to two men who covered the same ground several decades earlier. W.J. Hunter and R.B. O'Neill researched FitzGerald with the intention of publishing biographies (Hunter in the late 1950s, O'Neill in the early 1960s). No books materialised but their research papers were donated to the Alexander Turnbull Library (Hunter) and the Canterbury Museum (O'Neill), and proved invaluable to my research.

I am immensely grateful to Rachel Scott of Otago University Press for having faith in this book, and to my editor, Gillian Tewsley, for her eagle eye and expert guidance. I should also like to thank Hilary Green, Professor Gareth Williams, and my husband Paul Beck for their helpful suggestions. Paul accompanied me on this journey through FitzGerald's life – we followed in his footsteps together; and without his support and unfailing good humour the book would never have been written.

Acknowledgements

...

I should like to thank the following individuals for permission to quote from original documents and reproduce illustrations: Sue Blakely, Peter Budd, Viscount Cobham, Robin Gilchrist, Ansell and Anthony Hawkins, Ian and Pam Jackson, Peter Levin, John Macalister and Geraldine Marriott. Permission to quote from original documents and reproduce illustrations has also been granted by Alexander Turnbull Library; Archives New Zealand/Te Rua Mahara o te Kawanatanga; British Library (London); Canterbury Museum; Fairfax Media; Hocken Collections/Uare Taoka o Hakena, University of Otago; Terrace Station Archives, Hororata; Karori Historical Society; National Library of Wales.

FitzGerald Family Tree

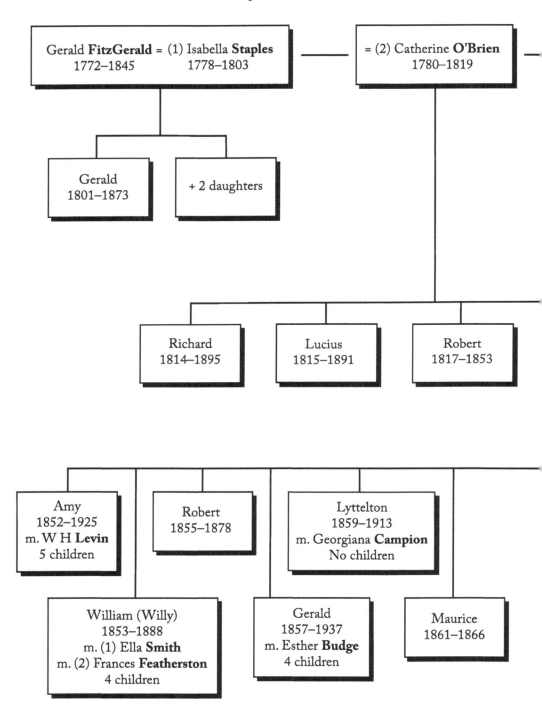

Gerald **FitzGerald** = (1) Isabella **Staples**
1772–1845   1778–1803

= (2) Catherine **O'Brien**
1780–1819

Gerald
1801–1873

+ 2 daughters

Richard
1814–1895

Lucius
1815–1891

Robert
1817–1853

Amy
1852–1925
m. W H **Levin**
5 children

Robert
1855–1878

Lyttelton
1859–1913
m. Georgiana **Campion**
No children

William (Willy)
1853–1888
m. (1) Ella **Smith**
m. (2) Frances **Featherston**
4 children

Gerald
1857–1937
m. Esther **Budge**
4 children

Maurice
1861–1866

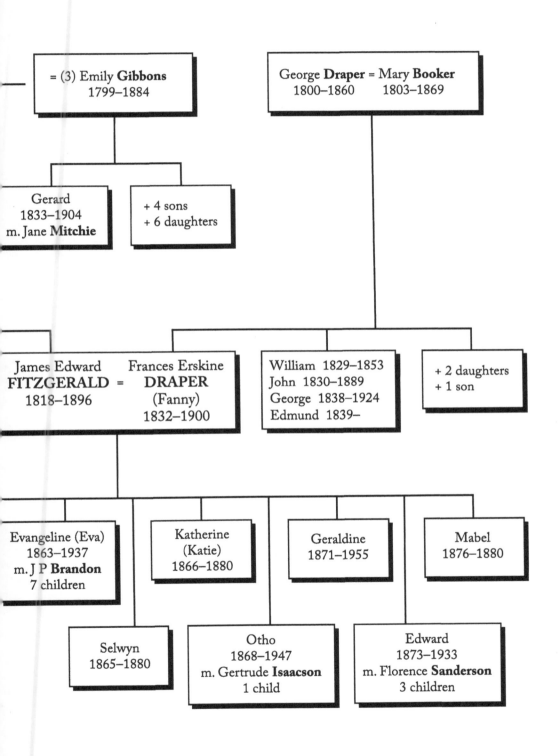

= (3) Emily **Gibbons**
1799–1884

George **Draper** = Mary **Booker**
1800–1860   1803–1869

Gerard
1833–1904
m. Jane **Mitchie**

+ 4 sons
+ 6 daughters

James Edward   Frances Erskine
FITZGERALD = **DRAPER**
1818–1896   (Fanny)
                 1832–1900

William 1829–1853
John 1830–1889
George 1838–1924
Edmund 1839–

+ 2 daughters
+ 1 son

Evangeline (Eva)
1863–1937
m. J P **Brandon**
7 children

Katherine
(Katie)
1866–1880

Geraldine
1871–1955

Mabel
1876–1880

Selwyn
1865–1880

Otho
1868–1947
m. Gertrude **Isaacson**
1 child

Edward
1873–1933
m. Florence **Sanderson**
3 children

Preface

*J*ames Edward FitzGerald – known to his friends as Fitz – was a politician, journalist, newspaper proprietor and civil servant. He was first superintendent of the province of Canterbury, first leader of the general government of New Zealand, and founder of the *Press* newspaper. A man of many talents – orator, writer, artist and musician – he was also renowned for his wit.

Friends revelled in his company, one writing that he was 'the jolliest, most amusing and sociable fellow in the world', another that 'no more delightful evenings were ever spent by me than those in his company'. The obverse of this coin was that he was also a most infuriating man. Described by one of his colleagues as 'unstable as water', he suffered from what is known today as bipolar disorder – periods of hyperactivity and depression which gave rise to the contradictions in his character, to his passionate changeability.

His wife Fanny was equally remarkable. Brave, intelligent and witty, she was a tiny woman (less than five feet tall) with steel in her backbone. Shortly after her eighteenth birthday, she defied a controlling father to marry a man almost twice her age; twelve days later, she set sail for a new life on the far side of the world. Described as 'just a schoolgirl' when she arrived in New Zealand, she entered into pioneer life with enthusiasm; and her marriage, as Fitz put it, brought an 'immense sum total of happiness' to them both.

'My father and mother were both brilliantly clever,' wrote their eldest daughter in her memoirs, 'a fact I never realised until I was married and away from them, when I began to think that all the people I met were very stupid. Of course this was not the case. It was just that other people were usual people and my parents were very unusual.'

These two 'unusual' people are remembered in New Zealand as among 'the best and bravest of the band of pioneers who came to a wilderness and founded a nation'. In doing so, they played their part in the expansion of the British Empire around the globe.

Colonisation is an arrogant concept in today's world – but ideas change over the decades: many of the things we do today will be shocking to future generations. We must judge people by the standards of their times and not by our own. The men and women who set out to colonise lands which they looked upon as nothing more than wide open spaces could not conceive how the imperialist ambition would be viewed more than a hundred and fifty years later.

Like most nineteenth-century pioneers, Fitz sailed away from his home country oblivious to the indigenous peoples of the land he had chosen to colonise. He arrived in New Zealand with his prejudices intact; ten years later, he had changed his mind. In a powerful speech in parliament in 1862, he proposed that Maori be integrated with Europeans 'into one united people', with 'a full and equal enjoyment of civil and political privileges'.

It was the colonisation projects of the mid-nineteenth century that spread the British Empire into so many corners of the world. How did such colonisation begin? How was it perceived by those who set out to begin new lives in a distant country? One of the reasons for writing this book was to find out. Another was to learn how legends grow down the generations.

More than a century has passed since Fitz's death. As his star began to fade in the New Zealand firmament, it burned even brighter among his descendants. I know this because he was my great-great-grandfather. He was adored by his wife and children, and this evolved over the years into a form of hero worship; for my mother and grandmother in England (with little knowledge of New Zealand history), the legend that Fitz was a great statesman – a hero of his times – became deeply rooted in family tradition.

I have, of course, discovered that legend is not truth. But the truth about James Edward FitzGerald is far more interesting and multifaceted than the legend. Having spent five years in his company, I have also learned much about nineteenth-century colonisation, the excitements and privations experienced by those early settlers, and the making and maturing of a nation.

...

Fitz arrived in Canterbury in December 1850 full of hope and optimism for the future. He and his fellow pioneers built a settlement on the plains which began with the construction of a few wooden houses and grew over the decades into a beautiful and thriving city – a city devastated by the earthquake of 22 February 2011.

The early pioneers did more than create a city. They forged a spirit of pride and independence, a legacy that was passed down the generations and lives on today in the people of Canterbury. Now it is their turn, for it is their hope and optimism that will overcome the disaster and build a new Christchurch.

Most statues have toppled off their pedestals but FitzGerald still stands, his gaze directed down Cashel Street where he and his family lived above the presses of his newspaper. Today he surveys a shattered city. Tomorrow he will see it rise again, even stronger than before.

Who would true valour see
Let him come hither;
One here will constant be,
Come wind, come weather.
There's no discouragement
Shall make him once relent
His first avowed intent
To be a Pilgrim.
— John Bunyan

PART I

Fitz finds a vocation

CHAPTER ONE

The Maternity

1818–1842

As long as it please God to spare your father's life, you shall never have a
guinea to *throw away*.

Gerald FitzGerald, 14 March 1818

My tutor thought I might be a good Wrangler if I had not been idle.

Fitz, 15 May 1840

he Georgian city of Bath was past its heyday when Fitz was born
here in 1818. Built of honey-coloured limestone, ringed by a girdle
of low green hills, it was a fashionable resort in the eighteenth century. The
upper classes arrived in large numbers for the summer season. They came to
mingle in society and take the hot spa waters which had attracted travellers
since Roman times. The city's popularity declined around the turn of the
century and by the time Fitz's father settled here in 1806, it had become a
haven for slightly faded gentry.

An Anglo-Irish landowner, Gerald FitzGerald held estates in Queen's
County (County Laois); he owned land, villages, farms and cottages but no
manor house, the ancestral castle having been destroyed by insurgents. His first
marriage to Isabella Staples in Dublin produced one son and two daughters
before Isabella died of tuberculosis in 1803. Gerald settled in Bath three years
later, acquiring an elegant five-storey house in St James's Square and falling
'wholly under the influence' of Hannah More, the writer and evangelist who
lived nearby in north Somerset. As a result, according to one of his sons, he
'gradually withdrew from society, all amusements were banned from the house,
and the only literature perused was Calvinist in nature'.

At this time, Bath was home to 'a number of residents from Ireland of
the upper class', with whom Gerald – despite his withdrawal from the rest of
society – was willing to 'maintain cordial relations'. One such resident was Lady
Ann O'Brien, widow of Sir Lucius O'Brien of County Clare, whose 33-year-old

daughter Catherine was considered too old for the marriage market. Widowed for ten years, Gerald was lonely; he wanted company as well as a stepmother for his children. He married Catherine in June 1813. During the next five years, four sons were born: Richard, Lucius, Robert and James Edward.

Fitz, the youngest son, was born in St James's Square on 4 March 1818. His mother died thirteen months later, after the birth of a stillborn child. 'In the midst of domestic enjoyments and blessings,' read an obituary in a local newspaper, 'this excellent lady was arrested by the hand of death and carried off after a severe illness of only five days.' She was buried in the nearby village of Weston – Gerald wrote the inscription for her tomb:

> Catherine FitzGerald, wife of Gerald FitzGerald Esq, died March 31st 1819, aged 39. Pious, prudent, affectionate, sedulous in the discharge of the duties of her station, she lived the servant of God, beloved by her husband and dear to her relatives and friends. Supported by the grace of God, she bore with patience and firmness the pains of dissolution and died in perfect peace, depending solely on the mercy of Christ.

…

Fitz was two years old when his father married for a third time. His bride was Emily Gibbons, a spoilt, childlike 21-year-old whose family owned a slave plantation in Barbados. Emily insisted that Catherine's sons refer to her as 'mother', but the boys were unenthusiastic. 'My stepmother,' one of them would later explain, 'has never done anything that calls on my part for gratitude.'

One of Emily's shortcomings, so far as Fitz and his brothers were concerned, was her fertility. She gave birth to eleven children in almost as many years and the house in Bath was filled with wailing babies, noisy toddlers, nurses, governesses and servants – referred to by Fitz collectively as 'the maternity'.

Descended from the earls of Kildare, Gerald instilled in his sons a fierce pride in their Irish ancestry. He was also a strict parent with a strong sense of duty. His sons called him 'the Governor'. Always careful with money, he was angry when his eldest son (aged sixteen) absconded from school to spend a day visiting 'a gentleman's place ten miles away, dining at an inn and not returning till eight o'clock in the evening'. This was, he wrote:

> very reprehensible conduct … boys do not fall all at once into habits of idleness and dissipation. They yield by degrees to one bad habit after another … If you would rather spend the little money you have got in eating and drinking at an inn … it would be vain for me to expect the growth of any generous feelings in your breast.

Remember (and I recommend you to keep this letter by you to help your memory) that as long as it please God to spare your father's life, you shall never have a guinea to *throw away*.

Shortly after his eighth birthday, Fitz was sent to a boarding school run by a clergyman in Wiltshire. It was here, in November 1830, that he witnessed the Swing Riots when farm workers, in protest against the introduction of machinery which threatened their livelihoods, rampaged across the countryside, smashing up threshing machines and setting fire to barns and hayricks. For the rest of his life, he would remember 'the mobs of poor men roving over the land, destroying and burning the machinery in all directions'. It was his first taste of politics.

After five years in Wiltshire, he joined his brothers at the Bath Grammar School, which catered for boys of the 'well-to-do class'.

Portrait of Fitz's father, Gerald FitzGerald (the Governor), painted by Fitz in St James's Square, Bath. 'All amusements were banned from the house, and the only literature perused was Calvinist in nature.'

Canterbury Museum (R.B. O'Neill manuscript collection, A995)

Under the headmastership of James Pears (chaplain to William IV), the boys were taught ancient languages – Latin, Greek and Hebrew – and learnt the Catechism on Saturdays. On Sundays, Gerald took his family to church in Weston, where Fitz would stand beneath the cedars and read the wording on Catherine's tomb, an inscription to a mother of whom he had no memory.

In the summer, the family spent 'a few weeks annually at the seaside'. The resort of choice was Weston-super-Mare (25 miles from Bath), where Gerald owned a house by the seafront. Here Fitz learned to swim, row and sail. He sailed back and forth across the Bristol Channel and painted the coastal scenery: fishing boats in rough seas, the light on the water, the wide expanse of beach at low tide.

...

While Fitz continued his education, his elder brothers moved out into the world. Richard read theology at Oxford before becoming a curate in Hampshire. He married an older woman from a lower class, without informing his family and much to their disgust. His father cut off all communication with him, and Robert told Fitz that it was 'a melancholy instance of *love in a cottage*, a thing which I detest and I know you do too. What a lamentable end for poor Richard!'

Robert – much against his father's wishes – enrolled in the military academy of the East India Company, where he was found to be 'remarkable for his strength of body and skill in sports, rather than for his taste for study or the restraints of discipline'. He sailed for Bombay, and wrote letters home about battles and skirmishes and shooting tigers from elephant back.

Lucius left home in the spring of 1835 to study law at St John's College, Cambridge. Fitz finished school two years later and spent the summer of 1837 on a walking tour, painting as he went. In June, he roamed through north Somerset. In July, he was in Wales, sketching Tintern Abbey and walking through Abergavenny, Crickhowell and the Brecon Beacons. In August and September, he was back in Somerset. He returned home in October and, a few weeks later, he joined Lucius at Cambridge to study mathematics at Christ's College.

He had learnt little arithmetic at school ('it was almost an unknown topic') but he showed an aptitude for the subject and was granted a scholarship in November 1838. This could have led to an academic career, but Fitz was impatient. He was bored with education and turned his mind to joining his brother in India. He wrote to Robert, only to receive a disillusioned reply:

> Don't come here if you can help it … A college education is a very great advantage. Read hard and make the best of the opportunity which will never fall to your lot again … You will see enough of the world bye and bye. Don't think the time heavy now, but prepare yourself with vigour for entering life, to pass through it with credit … You say you live in hope. By Jove, that time of hope is, take my word for it, the pleasantest time of a man's existence. That page turned and from manhood to second childhood you will meet with nothing but disappointment.

Despite this advice, Fitz failed to take advantage of his scholarship, preferring to spend his time outside the lecture rooms. His 'best and dearest friend' at Cambridge, John Ball (an Irish Catholic), introduced him to politics and chess and encouraged him to join the debating society. Here Fitz studied the principles of oratory and took his first steps in political debate, on one occasion opposing the introduction of the penny post.

He spent the summer vacation of 1839 in his father's house at the seaside. He told Lucius in July that he intended 'to become a perfect *blood* in Weston', and this he did, flirting with a Miss Seymour, taking her sailing in rough weather (until she was sick) and spending time with her alone. The gossip spread and her father wrote a stiff letter to ask his intentions. Lucius wrote too, a letter which Fitz answered with irritation:

> In good truth, my dear Lucius, if you find it necessary to avoid the company of women, or any one woman, for fear of committing yourself, you are very much to be pitied … I must inform you that, in plain terms, I do not and never shall intend to marry Miss Seymour and that she knows that as well as I do. Furthermore, I do not intend to enter into the matrimonial state with any woman who cannot pay for my board and lodging, washing etc.

…

Fitz was not only neglecting his studies, he was also living beyond his means. 'I want to have done with Cambridge as soon as I can,' he wrote to Lucius in January 1840, 'in order to set about making a livelihood. Every day spent at Cambridge after my degree, except to pay off debts, is time lost to my life as I do not intend to become a Cambridge don.'

In February, he won two medals ('value about £20'), one 'for reading in chapel', the other 'for best essay in English', an early indication of his two great strengths: oratory and journalism. It was a cold winter and he was suffering from a persistent cough and attacks of conjunctivitis, both of which were exacerbated by a week of making merry when John Ball, who had left Cambridge the previous year, returned for a visit in early March. 'Such a week of dissipation I never had,' he told Lucius, 'one of the most magnificent dinners … the wines first rate, and port, sherry, claret, champagne, the finest I ever tasted.' Other dinners followed, 'all of which combined to increase my cough tenfold'.

On 30 March, he complained of 'a long spell of illness, one of the most violent coughs I ever had and a very sore throat. I am better now but still taking lots of medicine and cannot open a book at night.' And he had changed his mind about an academic career:

> You must not breathe a word of this to any human being. I have received information indirectly that I have a chance of getting

Fitz's 'best and dearest college friend', John Ball, painted by Fitz in March 1840 when Ball returned to Cambridge on a visit ('such a week of dissipation I never had').

Private collection

the junior tutorship at Trinity Hall. If so, this will be glorious but you must not mention it to a soul. It may not be true, but I should not think it unlikely if I take a decent degree … At any rate, I am now certain of a fellowship here.

His optimism was short-lived – as was his enthusiasm to 'have done with Cambridge as soon as I can'. Cambridge undergraduates sat the Mathematical Tripos after three years, but Fitz soon realised that he had little chance of obtaining a degree without an additional year of study.

Although he would later assert that he was 'compelled through ill health' to postpone his degree for a year, a letter to Lucius in May 1840 is more to the point: 'I have written to the Governor to ask him to let me degrade into another year … My tutor thought I might be a good Wrangler[1] and if I had not been idle, I should not have wanted to degrade. I am persuaded that I could yet take a good degree if I read hard for a year.' Two weeks later, having taken the end-of-term examination, he wrote again:

> I am perfectly damned by fortune. After reading like mad for I don't know how many weeks, I have done next to nothing in the exam and shall not even approach the second optime. I don't care about it myself, because I know I could not get the first optime,[2] but I fear my father will be disgusted.

The summer vacation began on 6 June and Fitz travelled to London on foot, 'not being able to get a place by any coach'. He stayed with Lucius in his

---

1 Student who passed the Mathematical Tripos with first-class honours
2 First (senior) optime: equivalent to second-class honours; second (junior) optime: third-class honours

chambers in Lincoln's Inn, before attending a house party in Surrey. In July, he returned to London and, a few weeks later, took a train to Warwickshire where he hoped to find 'a bed *free of expense if possible*, food I can do without'. This he found in a farmhouse in Atherstone, where he paid for his accommodation by painting portraits of the farmer and his pigs.

...

Fitz sat the Mathematical Tripos for the first time in January 1841, six weeks after an attack of conjunctivitis. 'All the fires of hell have been sent forth to torment me,' he told Lucius on 22 November. 'Just at the last moment, when I have so much to lose, I have one of the most violent inflammations in both eyes I ever had, which will prevent my looking at a book for weeks. I'm half blind and can't write more.'

The Tripos examination was held in the Senate House, an elegant but unheated building which resembled a Greek temple; in cold winters, the ink had been known to freeze in the inkwells. The examination lasted for six days – an ordeal for Fitz, whose eyes were still encrusted and painful. And as he predicted, he failed.

In the summer of 1841, he visited friends in Brighton ('capital French cook, excellent wine') and spent time with his family in Bath, making the journey there for the first time by train. The Great Western Railway had recently arrived in Bath with the opening of the Box Tunnel five miles east of the city. This was a major feat of engineering: thousands of men worked day and night for two and a half years to drive the tunnel through two miles of hillside.

Many passengers, believing they would be 'stifled and deafened' by the pressure, left the train at the tunnel mouth and travelled over the hill in horse-drawn carts. Fitz remained on board, thrilled by the shriek of the whistle as the train plunged into the hole in the hill, the minutes spent puffing through darkness, the sudden re-emergence into the bright light of day.

The house in St James's Square was too full to accommodate him (there were now ten children in 'the maternity', together with eight domestic servants and a governess), so he took rooms around the corner in Park Street, where he enjoyed his freedom away from his father's strict views about social pleasures. This allowed him to make new friends in the city, including the poet Walter Savage Landor, who had taken lodgings in St James's Square.

Landor had a powerful personality and would 'often roar with laughter till the whole house seemed to shake'. He was many years older than Fitz, but he enjoyed his young friend's company. Fitz found himself on the periphery of a circle that included the lions of literary life: Dickens, Browning and Thackeray all spent time with Landor in Bath.

In January 1840, Fitz had given up smoking (which 'suited neither my pocket nor my health'), making a bet of 'twenty sovereigns to one that I would not smoke again till I had taken my degree'. He found this difficult – particularly in Landor's smoke-filled rooms – and after his return to Cambridge, he began to experience a recurring dream in which he was smoking a cigar. In this dream, he was:

> much distressed, for in those days twenty pounds were not only
> scarce but non-existent with me. I used then, in my dream, to say:
> 'Where the dickens am I to get twenty pounds from? Well, it will
> cost no more to smoke two cigars than one, so I will light another.'
> So I did – in my dream.

For the next few months, he worked hard at his books and after retaking the Mathematical Tripos in January 1842, he 'walked straight from the Senate House to a tobacconist's shop, and smoked, prouder I think of having won my bet than having got my degree'.

The results were posted on 21 January. Fitz had won second place in the senior optime, having failed to become a Wrangler by just a few percentage points.

CHAPTER TWO

Pride and Poverty

1842–1844

My father continues to give broad hints that he intends me to
provide for myself by monogamy.

Fitz, 23 November 1842

I am sadly distressed and perplexed in mind.

Fitz, 16 May 1843

*F*itz left Cambridge at a time of recession and high levels of unemployment. The upper classes were affected too. 'Even gentlemen of the first station,' said a member of parliament, 'find difficulty in knowing what to do with their younger sons. We hear every day of the sons of gentlemen entering occupations from which their pride in former times debarred them.'

Fitz was proud to call himself 'a gentleman', proud of his aristocratic connections, but as a younger son he had few prospects. On his father's death, the family estates in Ireland would pass to his eldest half-brother, while Fitz expected to receive the sum of £1500 from his mother's marriage settlement. Although this would give him a small private income, it was not large enough to provide what was known as an 'independence'. He would have to marry into a rich family or work for a living, a situation he found demeaning. He described this dilemma as 'the struggle between pride and poverty'.

The effort of taking his degree left him listless and depressed; his enthusiasm to 'set about making a livelihood' had faded. He visited friends and relatives in the country and, in June, accompanied his family to Weston-super-Mare where his eyes flared up again in the warm weather, 'threatening me with a violent attack'. The doctor treated him with lotions and advised him to 'to keep very quiet'. This he did until September when he attended a house party given by the Gollop family in Dorset ('nothing could be more agreeable – everyone does as they choose … I take my pipe in the shrubbery morning and sometimes night, smoking till two o'clock').

Portrait relief of Fitz as a young man, Walter Savage Landor's 'handsome friend'.

Private collection

Back in Bath for the winter months, he returned to his old rooms in Park Street and assessed his financial situation. 'I have paid £140 of debt today and dismissed all my pressing creditors,' he wrote to Lucius on 30 November:

> I owe only one man in Cambridge now and the tailor in London. The Governor has been more generous than I expected and I never intend asking him again for money. I am to have £25 the first week in January, my allowance beginning from 1 November. Another £25 is to come on 1 May. I can then get rid of the London tailor and shall do pretty well.

Fitz's father had been generous. At the same time, he continued to give his son 'broad hints that he intends me to provide for myself by monogamy'. When entertaining a titled relative, he turned the conversation to 'some friends of Miss Peters, two girls who are rich', before giving Fitz a meaningful look and saying, 'if I was a *bachelor*, I know what *I'd* do'.

So Fitz began looking around for suitable young women. 'Love in a cottage' was too expensive a luxury and (as he told Lucius) he did not intend 'to enter into the matrimonial state with any woman who cannot pay for my board and lodging'. He even joked that he would marry the ugliest woman in the world if she was rich enough to provide him with a living.

At a party in December, his eye alighted on 'a *very* pretty agreeable girl. I talked to her a good deal and was informed that her father was a squire of high degree with a *very good* fortune. She was a real beauty. Whether she has brothers I know not. I shall enquire tomorrow. Would to God she be an heiress.'

She was not an heiress so Fitz continued his search, mixing in society and cutting a dash in the streets of Bath. 'I have,' he wrote to Lucius, 'grown a grand pair of moustaches.' Extrovert and entertaining, handsome and elegant in his dark-blue frock coat, he was an asset at dinners and balls, a much sought-after guest. Introduced to the wealthy Paynter family by Walter Savage Landor, he was soon 'almost living at the Paynters of an evening'. And stimulating evenings they were too. As their daughter Rose wrote in her memoirs, 'there was seldom an evening that Walter Savage Landor did not visit us for an hour's conversation or music. He often brought friends who had stopped at Bath on purpose to see him – Dickens, Thackeray, Forster, Kenyon, etc. They all worshipped him.'

Rose Paynter was the belle of Bath society; her portrait was published in *Heath's Book of Beauty*. She was intelligent and spirited, she wrote poetry, and Landor adored her. Rose had brothers; she was not an heiress, but Fitz – encouraged by Landor who referred to him as 'our handsome friend' – was entranced. 'I have been drinking tea with Miss Paynter *alone*,' he wrote breathlessly in June 1843. 'What an agreeable woman she is!'

He also became friendly with one of Rose's brothers, a captain in the army. 'Howell Paynter is one of the best fellows I have met for a long time,' he told Lucius. 'He comes to Park Street almost every night and we smoke together

Rose Paynter, engraving from an oil painting by William Fisher, 1840. Three years after this portrait was published in *Heath's Book of Beauty*, Fitz drank tea 'with Miss Paynter *alone*. What an agreeable woman she is!'

Walter Savage Landor, *The Letters of Walter Savage Landor, Private and Public*, 1899. © The British Library Board. All rights reserved (W1/2296 DSC)

from eleven to one. He smokes his cigar and I my pipe. He is full of amusement and is quite a gentleman, an amazing relief after the monotony of the ordinary run of Bath society.'

During these smoking sessions, Fitz boasted of his brother's triumphs in battle. Robert, now second-in-command of the Scinde Horse, had fought in the battles of Meanee and Hyderabad, and received a commendation from General Sir Charles Napier ('the Scinde Horse took the enemy's camp, from which a vast body of their cavalry retired fighting. Lieutenant FitzGerald pursued them for two miles and slew three of the enemy in single combat'). This despatch was printed in the London newspapers, and Lady Napier wrote that Robert was 'one of the great heroes of the day'.

Fitz was proud of his brother, but Robert's success made him aware of his own lack of direction. He was still feeling unwell, still under doctor's orders to remain quiet. 'I am sadly distressed and perplexed in mind,' he wrote. 'I do not know that I ever felt more singularly uncomfortable than at the present moment.'

There was no physical reason for this malaise. Fitz suffered from what his friends referred to as 'intermittent energies', the mood swings of a bipolar disorder which began during his years at Cambridge. Periods of hyperactive energy and boundless enthusiasm were followed by lethargy, depression and perceived ill health. Fitz experienced these emotional ups and downs for most of his life, writing about 'hard work and the depression which follows it' and 'the lassitude which follows over-excitement'.

In June – a few days after 'drinking tea with Miss Paynter *alone*' – Fitz returned to Weston-super-Mare with his family. He disliked the seaside town and 'to make Weston liveable at', he bought a 'nice cheap boat which I can sell again at no loss'. Escaping to Bath for a few days in July, he told Landor at a dinner party that he planned to sail down the Bristol Channel and around the coast of south Wales.

'Now for the first time my poetry deserves the greater part of a smile from you,' Landor wrote to Rose Paynter a few days later. 'On Thursday our friend (rather fond of causing occasionally a slight trepidation) desired, in a laughing way, that I would write his epitaph in case he happened to be lost in the Bristol Channel … I wrote on the spot four Greek verses.' He translated one of them:

> Beloved by all FitzGerald lies
> Where the sea waves for ever moan;
> The dear delight of maiden eyes
> Is now embraced by Nymphs alone.

One of five illustrations for 'A Galopade' by G.T. Gollop, drawn by Fitz in September 1842 when he was staying with the Gollop family in Dorset. The (not very poetic) stanza for this illustration reads:

> I mounted my horse to get rid of my grief
> I rode into far distant lands for relief
> But perch'd on the crupper and clung to me close
> Grief gallops with Gollop wherever he goes.

Substitute the word 'depression' for 'grief' and the drawing gives a good impression of Fitz's mental state at the time.

Private collection

Fitz left 'the horrors of Weston-super-Mare' a few days later, 'going from port to port in an open boat' until he reached Tenby in south Wales. On his third evening in the town, he attended 'a dance at a friend's house' where he stayed until three o'clock in the morning. The alcohol made him reckless: with no thought for the weather, he decided to leave immediately for home.

He rigged his boat and set sail in the moonlight, reaching the far side of the bay shortly before sunrise. As he rounded the headland, he met the full blast of a strong westerly wind. The sea was rough and the little boat was tossed about in the waves:

> Had the boat broached-to with the sail I had on her, a capsize would
> have been tolerably certain, and careful steering was a necessity ...
> I was so tired that I kept falling asleep at the helm ... As the boat

flew round, as each sea overtook her, the pressure of the tiller on my hand awoke me instinctively, with a start, and I was in time to put the helm hard up. This happened repeatedly; and each time … as I dropped off asleep again as each sea passed under the boat, I dreamed a fresh dream.

He was wakened by the sun rising in the sky. Chastened to think that Landor's epitaph might have proved prophetic, he reefed the mainsail and arrived safely in Weston-super-Mare – where his father continued to chastise him about his idleness.

···

Over the years, Fitz toyed with a number of ideas for employment before casting them all aside. In March 1840, he had hoped – briefly –to be offered a fellowship at Cambridge, a position which would have given him a permanent stipend in return for a little tuition.

Two months later, he gave thought to astronomy: 'I am trying to get Challis[1] to take me on at the observatory. If he would, I do not think the Governor would disagree … I spent a considerable portion of last night looking at Jupiter, Saturn and the moon through the great telescope.'

Then he thought of joining Lucius in the law: 'I become more inclined every day to go to the Bar, and if so, the Irish Bar will have the honour of counting me among its number. I shall make you tutor me for nothing.'

A year later, he received a letter from Robert in India:

> More congenial … to my taste and I hope more suitable to your own wishes were you in some gallant Dragoon Corps, to which I am certain you would be an ornament, and better would you look leading the fiery charge of a squadron of cavalry than … receiving either compliments or fellowships from a pack of rusty old dons. Such however are not the sentiments of our good father.

He suggested that Fitz should 'enter the army if you can get a commission, but especially if there is a European war, and fight your way into notice or perish as many a noble lad has and many doubtless will'.

What Fitz thought of perishing in battle is not recorded, but later in life, he spoke of being turned down by the Royal Engineers because of weak eyesight. It is more likely that he dismissed the idea or failed to persuade his father to buy him a commission. The Governor disapproved of the military; he had opposed Robert's ambition to join the East India Company and only relented

---

1   James Challis, director of the Cambridge observatory

because his son could never stop talking about soldiers and battles. Fitz had no such vocation.

His next idea was to produce smoked salmon in Norway, a speculation inspired by Howell Paynter. 'The coast of Norway abounds with small rivers full of the finest salmon,' he told Lucius:

> and you would no doubt be allowed to fish there for very small sums. If one were to take out fishermen from the north of Ireland and a person skilled in smoking the salmon ... you could undersell the market for Scotch salmon ... What I want you to do is to obtain every information about the salmon market in town ... If there is a chance of clearing £100 or so, I shall lay it before the Governor and ask for money to take a tour up the coast of Norway ... Now keep *the most perfect silence* about this for the idea is quite new and everything depends on being first.

In May 1843, hoping to put his knowledge of mathematics to better use, Fitz wrote again to Lucius:

> I want you to make enquiries for me in London as to the steps taken by young men wishing to become civil engineers. I want to know what premium I should have to pay to a first-rate man and how long it would be, taking into consideration my knowledge of mathematics and drawing, before I could expect to make a living ... I have serious thoughts of taking to that profession.

A month later, his mind turned to the colonies:

> Now *entre nous*, Mr Paynter is going to write for an accurate account of the prospects for young men in Canada and whether a visit of two months or more might promise a good chance of obtaining a permanent situation there ... If the account is at all favourable, I shall go out in August or September. I shall then demand of my father £1000 instead of my allowance and any bequest at his death – in short to get rid of me *in toto*. He surely will not deny me this. I am quite determined on going out there if there is any prospect of success.

By the autumn, he had decided to stop flitting from one idea to another:

> I am at last quite sick of doing nothing and, with returning health, feel a return of some of the energy I once possessed and which I have been without now for years ... I begin to fret at the idleness of

this place dreadfully and am quite determined it shall not last much longer. I will bring matters to a crisis somehow.

In October, he sold his boat ('I don't know whether I am more sorry or glad') and took up fencing ('which, like billiards, requires constant practice to keep the hand in'). Four weeks later, he received a letter from John Ball about a position in Dublin. As he explained to Lucius:

> The Keeper of the museum in Trinity College is ill and wants someone to assist him in his duties on the *promise* of his place at his death. It is £200 and rooms. The assistant is to get *nothing* until the Keeper dies … If I could get this place, it would be worthwhile to read for the Botanical Professorship. As there are no young botanists in Dublin, I might have a *very* good chance of getting it in a few years' time. It is worth £700 a year.

He took this suggestion no further but Ball's letter gave him an idea. In December, he learned of a vacancy in the department of antiquities in the British Museum. The pay was twelve shillings a day, leading to an annual salary of 200 guineas after five years. At the time, there was 'a somewhat extraordinary' method of making appointments at the museum: they were handled exclusively by the Archbishop of Canterbury, who received details of all vacancies and dealt with the applications. Soon 'letters were flying on all sides' to ask for testimonials. One of Fitz's aunts wrote to Archdeacon Wilberforce and the Bishop of Winchester; friends of the family wrote to other influential contacts.

'The moment I get my testimonials,' Fitz told Lucius, 'I am going to bring them up to London *myself* and procure an interview with the electors, especially the Archbishop.' He asked his brother to 'look out for a very cheap bedroom' and find out if the archbishop was in residence at Lambeth Palace.

At his interview on 8 February, Fitz's intelligence and charm won over the electors. Sixteen days later, he left Bath for a new life in London. 'Dearest James left us this morning,' wrote one of his more pious half-sisters in her diary that night. 'May God in his own good time raise him from the death of sin to a life of righteousness for Christ's sake.'

CHAPTER THREE

Coins and Catalogues

1844–1845

James is going on comfortably at the British Museum and I am happy to
think is a great favourite with everyone.

Gerald FitzGerald, January 1845

Is it possible that I appeared to you sad and sorrowful on
your wedding day?

Walter Savage Landor to Rose Paynter, 15 March 1846

*F*itz began work at the British Museum on 26 February 1844,
warming his hands in his pockets as he was shown around the
enormous halls with their vast range of exhibits. He was 'powerfully moved'
by the Assyrian and Egyptian sculptures ('strange monuments ... preserved
... for more than two thousand years, by being buried in the warm and dry
sand of the desert') and by the Elgin marbles from the Parthenon in Athens
('the hard and brittle material vanishes from sight as you gaze; now melting
into the softest flesh ... now ossifying into bone; here quivering in a muscle,
there palpitating in a vein').

Given special responsibility for the museum's collection of coins and medals,
he learnt to distinguish the progress of ancient civilisations from the quality of
craftsmanship on these miniature works of art. He also began a long friendship
with William Vaux, who also worked in the department of antiquities. The two
men spent many evenings in Vaux's lodgings in nearby Gate Street, evenings
(as Fitz described them) 'of pipes and cocoa, coins and catalogues'.

Fitz was an imposing young man, six feet tall with a patrician profile, light
brown hair worn long over his ears, and penetrating eyes of the palest grey.
With his flamboyant personality and irrepressible sense of humour ('a special
gift for repartee'), he was entertaining company, 'a great favourite with everyone'
according to his father. Soon he and Vaux were hosting soirées in Gate Street,
sending out invitation cards twelve inches square: 'Fitz & Vaux at Home'.

Several men who made their mark in intellectual life came to these soirées:

Charles Newton, excavator of the mausoleum at Halicarnassus; Fitz's university friend John Ball, who was making a name for himself as a glaciologist; the writer Charles Kingsley; and the art critic John Ruskin, with whom Fitz indulged in a lengthy argument about the optical nature of shadows on water.

Mingling with these men, enjoying their company, Fitz became fascinated by the world around him. He discovered an interest in politics, philosophy, architecture, ancient history, music and opera, painting and sculpture, literature and poetry. He joined debating societies and honed the use of his pen, speaking and writing on a wide variety of subjects. He played the guitar and, as the wine flowed in Gate Street, he entertained his guests with Irish songs.

In the summer of 1844, a consignment of Lycian marbles arrived at the museum: statues, temples and tombs from the Mediterranean shores of Turkey. Props were installed under the floors to take their weight and there was 'an immense sensation' when they opened to the public. On 20 July, Landor wrote to Rose Paynter that he had visited the museum twice, 'and found our handsome friend in excellent health and spirits, full of Lycia and colonisation'.

In October, Fitz and Lucius took lodgings together in Great Russell Street, close to the museum. A few weeks later, the Paynter family arrived in London for the winter season. Fitz spent many evenings in their house, and he and Rose soon fell deeply in love. In January 1845, he wrote happily to Landor in Bath. Rose wrote too and received an opaque reply:

> I had lately a delightful letter from your friend, James FitzGerald, but it was written before yours. Whatever is amusing to you is interesting to me – for which reason I am confident you will always let me hear this much, leaving the rest to my powers of divination. The ancients were assisted in this art by certain birds, great and little. We have only birds.

Later in life, Fitz wrote a chapter of a romantic novel in which he referred to two young lovers who 'walked together, and sketched, and read to each other, as all lovers do, and looked forward in happy dream to the time when his independence might be the means of realising their brightest hopes'.

Rose's father, meanwhile, preferred a suitor with a private income. And waiting in the wings was Charles Graves Sawle, the eldest son of a baronet, who would provide Rose not only with a title but also with a stately home and plenty of inherited wealth.

···

In the spring of 1845, Fitz and Lucius received a summons from Bath. Their father had been 'very frail' for some years, suffering from chronic bronchitis and heart disease. Now he was dying. The house in St James's Square was filled with fifteen of his children – ranging in age from four to 51 – and Emily hovered about the sick room. 'I was his only nurse,' she wrote:

> nor could he bear me out of his presence. 'Is your mistress there?' I would hear him say if the servant was in sight and I not. And I can truly say it was sweeter to me than the sweetest music to hear him say that his dear wife was not only the best nurse in Bath, but the best in all Europe.

'It has been observed,' she continued, 'that the ruling feelings and thoughts of a man are clearly seen on his deathbed. I can bear testimony to the truth of this remark, for so it was with my dearest husband, the care of his soul first, then particularly to his accounts.'

The Governor died on 8 April. Seven days later, he was interred in the tomb he had built for Catherine in the churchyard at Weston. Under his will, the estates in Queen's County passed to his eldest son Gerald, while the house in Bath (which formed part of the residuary estate) was ordered to be sold. This may not have been his intention – the clause was vaguely worded – but Emily had no choice but to take her children to live in Weston-super-Mare.

The clause about Gerald's marriage settlement with Catherine O'Brien was more specific. The four sons of the marriage were each entitled to one quarter of the sum of £6000, plus accrued interest. Under the terms of the will, they were ordered to put this inheritance into the residuary estate, into the common pot to be shared equally with the children of Gerald's third marriage – of whom there were nine still living. As the will made clear:

> None of these four sons shall be entitled to any

Fitz's eldest half-brother, Gerald FitzGerald, painted by Fitz in St James's Square on 18 May 1842. Gerald was sixteen years older than Fitz.

Private collection

share of my residuary estate unless or until he shall bring his portion of £6000, to which he is entitled under the provisions of the marriage settlement, into entrepôt and distribution with the children of my third marriage.

Most of the residuary estate comprised lands in County Louth that Gerald's father had acquired on his marriage in 1766, lands which could only be sold after the death of several three-life tenancies (each individual tenancy lasting for three successive lives). So not only was Fitz's inheritance smaller than he had expected, he would also have to wait a long time to receive it.

He still clung to the hope that he and Rose would be allowed to marry. But at the end of the year – 'after long demur' – Rose decided to play safe; she agreed to marry Charles Graves Sawle. 'Who can describe the parting scene between those who love?' Fitz wrote in his chapter of a novel:

> Those short broken sentences, that painful beating of the heart, the oppression we feel at every syllable spoken, that sad, mournful intonation of the voice, that swimming, tender glance that seems to combine and speak every look of love … if the reader has ever loved and ever parted from one whose heart responded to his own, he will pardon my silence now.

Last page of Fitz's chapter of a romantic novel, written in manuscript. The young man is sailing away in his boat while his lover's aunt 'waited till she saw that her niece was on her way homeward, when she turned and with a deep sigh sought the cottage'.

Canterbury Museum (R.B. O'Neill manuscript collection, A995, item 58)

Landor attended the marriage ceremony on 18 February 1846. 'Is it possible,' he wrote to Rose a few weeks later, 'that I appeared to you sad and sorrowful on your wedding day?'

…

Fitz grieved for Rose. He was angry at his reduced financial prospects; even an increase in his daily wage did little to raise his spirits. He threw himself into work, writing a paper on a twelfth-century coin from Cyprus, an article published in the journal of the Royal Numismatic Society. In his spare time, he arranged the manufacture of two purpose-built steam engines. His brother Robert, now in command of the Scinde Camel Corps, was building a steamboat and he asked Fitz to have the engines made in London. He also wanted a gun purpose-built for mounting on camelback.

Negotiations with the engineers took eighteen months. And while Fitz received nagging letters from India ('It is damned odd if one can't get what one wants made in London … For God's sake, put the business into somebody's hands and send them out sharp to Bombay … Why the devil have my engines not started; do like a good chap send them off'), his thoughts returned to the colonies and he wrote to his brother about opportunities for trading on the Indus River. Robert's reply was discouraging:

> You must not think of coming out to India on a wild goose chase.
> You little know what it is pushing your way in the world with
> nothing to fall back upon if you fail … no trading in that way or
> colonisation would ever succeed in India, particularly in Scinde …
> Do not refuse my advice.

This letter arrived in London in January 1846 – by which time Fitz's mind had turned to other matters. The Irish potato famine had begun.

CHAPTER FOUR

The Colonial Microbe

1845–1849

There is a deep and active conviction awake, that the great task of this
generation allotted to the English race is *Colonisation*.

Fitz, August 1848

I know not what language to use to urge upon my countrymen the
wisdom, the necessity, the glory, of this course.

Fitz, 25 September 1848

*N*ews of the failure of the potato crop, the only food available to
the Irish peasantry, arrived in London in October 1845. The
leaves of the plant were turning black, the potatoes rotting as soon as they were
lifted from the soil. The government organised a programme of public works
and put in place a few – insufficient – relief measures.

Fitz's family had been Irish landowners for generations; the soil of Ireland
provided the wealth on which his family depended, and he put his mind to ways
of alleviating the distress. The following October, when the potato crop failed
for a second time, he published a pamphlet titled 'A Letter to the Noblemen,
Gentlemen and Merchants of England'. 'My Lords and Gentlemen,' he wrote.
'The Irish await your verdict. Shall we or shall we not interpose between four
millions of our fellow creatures, and starvation?' He proposed that subscriptions
be raised and the money spent on 'rye from Europe, Indian corn from America,
rice from India'. He referred to 'the urgency of the danger – the necessity of
immediate action ... Whilst I am writing, starvation is stalking abroad; the
convulsion of society is commencing – the plague has gone out amongst the
people – death has begun.'

As he later admitted, this pamphlet 'went unheeded, was read by only a few
and laughed at by some', but it was a turning point. Fitz had been obsessed
with the idea of colonisation for several years. The Irish famine politicised him
and he became, as a colleague would later remark, 'infected with the colonial
microbe'. Believing that emigration was the answer to the problem of food

supply in Ireland, he began to think about a place of settlement, not just for the working class but for all sections of Irish society.

The British had recently signed a treaty with the United States settling the border of the Oregon territory and awarding the whole of Vancouver Island to British Canada. The Hudson Bay Company (which had built a trading post on the island) was lobbying the Colonial Office for a charter to occupy the island, but Fitz had other ideas. He began to plan in some detail the administration and financing of a new colony. In May 1847, he printed a leaflet titled 'Proposal for the Formation of a Colony in Vancouver Island on the West Coast of North America'. In June, he wrote to the Colonial Office outlining his plans.

In November, he travelled to Dublin to meet John Ball, who was acting as assistant poor law commissioner. Having told the museum that he was 'detained in Ireland because of serious illness', he and Ball travelled southwest to Kilkenny to investigate the famine for themselves. This was the first time Fitz had set foot in his ancestral homeland and he was horrified to see 'the shocking distress, the appalling starvation, the revolting disease ... the languor, and dejection, and suspicion, depicted on every face'. Large numbers of people were dying of hunger, while tenants were forcibly ejected from their cottages and hovels. Packed into so-called 'coffin ships', they were emigrating in great numbers to the United States and Canada, many of them dying on the voyage. It was an unstructured migration and Fitz returned to London determined that his scheme for Vancouver Island would provide a better alternative.

In February 1848, when the government seemed likely to grant the island to the Hudson Bay Company, Fitz wrote a second letter to the Colonial Office asking whether it would consider other types of colonisation. In a reply received on the 24th, he was informed that the colonial secretary would 'be ready to consider any practical plan which may be submitted to him for these purposes, provided it be supported by parties of respectability, and possessing sufficient means to make success probable'.

This was enough for Fitz, who sprang into action. He lobbied for his plans, gave lectures at debating societies, and wrote articles for the *Colonial Magazine* extolling the natural resources of the island. 'England ought to know something about Colonisation,' he explained in his first article:

> She has made greater Colonies and spoilt greater Colonies, kept
> greater Colonies and lost greater Colonies, than any other nation in
> the world. And yet ... our whole system, up to the present moment,
> has been little better than a succession of experiments ... But a
> change is approaching; on all sides a muttering of many voices is

heard: the mass is thinking and speaking everywhere of *Colonisation* … that is, of making Colonies, and governing them when made. There is a deep and active conviction awake, that the great task of this generation allotted to the English race is *Colonisation*.

In early July, he approached a number of prominent politicians. He wrote to Lord Lincoln, who invited him to 'call upon me on your way to the British Museum on Wednesday next'. He wrote to William Gladstone (colonial secretary in the previous administration), who replied that he would 'be glad to see Mr FitzGerald as soon after four o'clock tomorrow as he can make it convenient to call'.

Fitz was persuasive at both these meetings. On 13 July, Lord Lincoln raised the matter in the House of Lords, asking whether a charter would be granted to the Hudson Bay Company without reference to parliament. Five weeks later, Gladstone spoke for two hours in the House of Commons, denouncing any plans to transfer the island to the company.

In September, when it was clear that the Irish potato blight was returning for a third year, Fitz took leave of absence and took the train north to drum up support from the merchant community. He wrote to Gladstone from Manchester:

> I have been working to get up a scheme which shall supplant that of the Hudson Bay Company and which shall offer sufficient inducements to colonists to go out to the island. At the same time, it seems to me that some inducements must be offered to merchants to persuade them to advance the capital … required for the final outlay … I find by enquiry that there is great difficulty in getting merchants to come forward but I do not despair … If I am not obliged to return to London, I shall go on to Liverpool where I hope I shall find some merchants of sufficient enterprise.

Gladstone replied that Fitz's ideas were 'sound and judicious'. He referred to 'the most palpable fault and weakness in modern colonisation, namely the want of a variety of persons of a superior cast who may form something of a natural aristocracy in an infant state'. He spoke eloquently in parliament about Fitz's plans for the colony.

Lord Lincoln was less optimistic, warning Fitz that he was being 'over-sanguine' in assuming the government would turn down the company's proposal. 'I think the grant will be made,' he wrote, and he 'greatly doubted' that the company would allow independent emigration. Fitz, fizzing with energy and enthusiasm, disregarded the warning.

On 25 September 1848, he published a letter titled 'Irish Migration', addressed to the member of parliament for Limerick. He pointed out that, in his pamphlet of 1846, he was 'the first person in England who called the attention of the public ... to the necessity of making a subscription to alleviate the Irish distress'. Since then, the landed gentry had been forced to take responsibility for famine relief, the cost of which was forcing many landlords into debt:

> What is to become of them? What new positions in life can be found for all those who are about to be driven from their former station in society, and to be reduced to work for their subsistence? How will they be able to secure their independence without a humiliation from which their pride will revolt, and without labour for which they are unfitted? I see no prospect in this country. But if I saw a land in which the labour, here regarded as a mark of poverty and inferiority, were esteemed honourable; in which exertions, here looked upon as the badge of fallen fortunes, were considered the surest promise of wealth and honour, – I should say 'That is the land to which these Irish landlords ought to go'.

Colonisation was the answer:

> The great emigration which must sooner or later take place from Ireland ought to be the formation of a new state – a New Ireland ... it should be headed by the gentry in person, going out in a body, along with all their servants and retainers who might be willing to follow them, to some new land, there to carve out for themselves new destinies, new names, and new fortunes ... I am not supposing any partial emigration. That which I contemplate should be the *migration* of a nation – of a race. From the noble to the serf; from the peeress to the peasant girl, all should join, – all for *the New Ireland*.

In October, when the government seemed minded to grant the island to the company, Fitz wrote another article for the *Colonial Magazine*:

> The enterprise of young men who would have gone out and planted the English name and power on those shores is trammelled and shackled by the mystery and obscurity of the Government in Downing-street ... It may not be too late for merchants of respectability to petition the Privy Council to pause before this Charter is signed – to come forward and say we will undertake the colonisation of this country.

Hoping the government might still change its mind, he took more time off work and travelled to Northern Ireland to publicise his scheme. In late November, he was given a review copy of a book eulogising the Hudson Bay Company. 'The Company's purse has stimulated the author's brain,' he told Gladstone. A review would not be sufficient. He must write another pamphlet.

He worked at speed in the evenings and weekends. 'I am getting on with my reply to Mr Martin's book,' he wrote to Gladstone on 10 December, 'but the small time I am able to devote to this work is a great drawback.' Over the next four weeks, he continued to work late into the night, straining his eyes and risking another bout of conjunctivitis, as the pamphlet grew into a 300-page book complete with pull-out map.

At the same time, the company was lobbying the Colonial Office with several political – and persuasive – reasons why its possession of the island would be of benefit to the British government. And on 13 January 1849, it received title to the whole of Vancouver Island for the princely sum of seven shillings a year.

Fitz published his book three weeks later. It was dedicated to Gladstone and included a postscript:

> This work was on the point of going to press when … the public were informed that the Charter granting Vancouver Island to the Hudson Bay Company had been signed. One of the objects of this publication was a full statement of the reasons why that grant ought not to have been made; to dwell upon this subject now the Charter has been issued would be, perhaps, a waste of time.

…

Fitz was no longer working in the department of antiquities. He was employed in the secretary's office, where Josiah Forshall, secretary to the museum trustees, had asked for an assistant on account of 'a great increase in business'. Forshall was a sick man, having returned to the museum in late 1847 after an absence of five months. The business of his department had not increased; the work was simply too much for him. So when Fitz took up the appointment of assistant secretary in January 1848 (with a salary of £200 a year) he had plenty of time on his hands. This allowed him to immerse himself in his scheme for Vancouver Island and travel around the country to raise support for his plans.

Meanwhile, a royal commission was at work, enquiring into 'the constitution and government of the British Museum … with the view of ascertaining in what manner that Institution may be made most effective'. For two years between July 1847 and June 1849, witnesses were called and questions asked on all aspects of the administration.

By February 1849, Forshall was once again 'in a very feeble state of health'. He was replaced as secretary by Sir Henry Ellis – a man whom Fitz would later refer to as 'that sneaking old witch'. Ellis was interrogated by the commission on 7 June. The Lord Advocate asked the questions.

> *Lord Advocate*: Have you found the duties of secretary very onerous?
>
> *Ellis*: On the days of a meeting of trustees, and for about three days afterwards, the work is heavy in preparing and sending out minutes, in writing letters which they order, and in making payments as directed by the board. In other respects it is extremely light. As regards correspondence, there is but little of that. I am perfectly surprised sometimes to find that three or four days pass without a single letter.
>
> *Lord Advocate*: How often are the days of meeting of the trustees?
>
> *Ellis*: The ordinary meetings are once a month but, upon average, you may take three weeks for the interval of their meetings of one kind and another.
>
> *Lord Advocate*: Is the assistant secretary fully employed?
>
> *Ellis*: I cannot say that he is.
>
> *Lord Advocate*: If there are no letters and it is extremely light for one party, it must be extremely light for the other?
>
> *Ellis*: He renders every assistance I could wish from him; but sometimes both he and I have very little to do for the whole day.
>
> *Lord Advocate*: For several days?
>
> *Ellis*: I have known for three or four days very little to be done.
>
> *Lord Advocate*: Would you have thought, under the circumstances, of applying for an assistant secretary for yourself?
>
> *Ellis*: If I had been secretary, I certainly should not have applied for an assistant secretary.

This interview spelled the end of Fitz's career at the British Museum. As the report of the commissioners explained:

> Mr Forshall has stated the nature of the duties which it is the object of the secretary and his staff to discharge … but he failed to convey the impression that these duties, as they now exist, are so laborious and extensive as to justify the present position of that office, or the staff which is annexed to his department.

The report recommended the abolition of the post of assistant secretary, followed a little later by the abolition of the entire secretary's department. At a meeting of the board of trustees in December 1849, 'the Principal Librarian reported that the engagement of J.E. FitzGerald as Assistant Secretary would terminate on 25th instant, and felt it his duty to add that the services of this gentlemen were not wanted in the Secretary's office'.

Fitz had been aware for some time that his job was at risk. 'If I thought that Vancouver Island were not utterly lost,' he had written to Gladstone in October, 'I would try to wait for the chance of being useful there.' But since there was 'very little hope of seeing anything done there at present, I turn all my attention to the best colony at present existing. New Zealand.'

CHAPTER FIVE

A Slice of England

1849–1850

A daguerreotype miniature of England, complete in every respect.
The Times, *5 December 1850*

If the scheme succeeds, it is to FitzGerald that it will be due!
Charles Wynne, 29 March 1850

One of Fitz's friends in London was John Robert Godley, brother-in-law to one of his cousins. Son of an Irish landowner, four years older than Fitz, Godley was a tall angular man with a serious expression. He congratulated Fitz on his work on the Hudson Bay Company ('I am not flattering you when I say that I *never* read a book more thoroughly satisfactory. It could not have been better done – argument, taste, everything, equally good') and, by the time Fitz's plans for Vancouver Island failed, he – together with Edward Gibbon Wakefield – had devised a remarkably similar scheme for New Zealand.

At this time, British dominions overseas were used mainly as penal settlements – a policy to which Wakefield was firmly opposed. Instead, he urged that colonisation be used to relieve overpopulation and poverty at home. He had formed the New Zealand Company, giving birth to settlements at Wellington, Nelson and New Plymouth; and written a book proposing the establishment of colonies formed from different religious groups.

Godley had acted as poor law commissioner for County Leitrim during the early years of the famine. He too had proposed mass emigration from Ireland to Canada. After moving to London in 1847, he wrote letters to the *Spectator* on Irish affairs, and became a leader writer on the *Morning Chronicle*. This brought him to Wakefield's attention and, in November 1847, he received a letter: 'I have a suggestion for your consideration, a very pleasant colonising object which I fancy you are likely to embrace.'

The two men formed the Canterbury Association, with the aim of establishing a Church of England settlement in the South Island of New Zealand. Land was reserved from the New Zealand Company, and the scheme attracted a number of heavyweight supporters: bishops and archbishops, members of parliament, aristocrats and landed gentry.

The association rented offices at 41 Charing Cross in London. The first meeting took place on 27 March 1848, and the prospectus was published in June. One passage was particularly relevant to Fitz:

> There is in a colonial life an absence of pretension, a universal
> plenty, a friendship of social intercourse, a continually increasing
> demand and reward for every kind of labour and exertion, which to
> those who have been suffering from the struggle between pride and
> penury, and whose minds are continually filled with anxiety about
> the future, is very pleasing and enjoyable.

Fitz met Wakefield early the following year. The older man was charming on first acquaintance. Fitz soon fell under his spell and, in late August 1849 (a few weeks after Henry Ellis's interview with the commissioners), he gave thought to becoming a Canterbury colonist himself. Wakefield was unimpressed. 'I don't fancy your project at all,' he wrote on 3 September. 'Without a specific object, a man of your qualities would be lost in a colony like New Zealand ... Sooner or later something will occur to suit you. Meanwhile patience!'

Fitz ignored this advice. He wrote of his idea to Gladstone, who replied on 15 September that, if he did become a colonist, 'we shall have to repent your loss, both as a member of society at home and as an ally in the matter of Vancouver's Island ... But I can hardly grudge you or any body to New Zealand.' He suggested that Fitz read the published journals of George Selwyn, Bishop of New Zealand ('I should much wish you to become acquainted with his views on colonisation ... before you finally commit yourself to any particular plan').

Fitz wrote again on 3 October. He had 'read the Bishop's journals with very great interest' and was considering his options:

> There is no doubt more to be done by *colonisers* in this country
> than in a colony. Nor would I willingly resign the advantages which
> London offers for helping in my own humble manner the move-
> ment which is taking place towards the more complete solution of
> the colonial question. But if circumstances which are beyond my
> control deprive me of the position of independence which I enjoy, I
> think I could do more as a colonist than by remaining in England.

On 27 November, he spoke in the debating society, proposing the motion 'that the recent attempt to force convicts on the Cape Colony is tyrannical and unconstitutional' (adding a note to his written draft that his speech was 'spoken word for word – *nearly*'). He attacked 'the evils inflicted on the Empire' by the colonial secretary, and referred to 'the tide of young and lusty nations which are rising like genie out of the Southern Ocean', colonies which would 'fulfil their destinies in spite of Colonial Secretaries'.

On 13 December, Godley sailed for New Zealand, having accepted the post of resident agent in Canterbury. He suffered from tuberculosis and chronic laryngitis, and had been advised to spend the winter in a warmer climate. Twelve days later, Fitz was out of a job. 'The museum ... let me drop off at Christmas,' he wrote. 'I made no row because I think it better not to attack and I am too busy.'

He was 'too busy' working as secretary of Wakefield's newly established Society for the Reform of Colonial Government. He accepted the post on 15 December and was, as he put it, 'running a great risk ... for I see no symptoms of pay at all'. With several high-profile members, the aim of the society was to achieve self-government for the colonies, which were, in Gladstone's words, 'simmering with discontent'.

At the end of the month, Fitz wrote an article on colonial reform which was published in *The Times* on 2 January and 'much talked about in the clubs of London'. He referred to 'a despotic and irresponsible central power in Downing Street' and explained that:

> The town of Manchester has lately voted £450,000 for the purpose of supplying itself with water. They consult no one but themselves when they do so. The Governor of a colony cannot lay out the tithe of so many pence without the sanction of a Secretary of State who lives at a distance of half the globe ... British colonists say they will not be taxed without their consent – and why should they? They say they will not obey laws to which they have not given their consent – and why should they? They will not be kept in doubt whilst a ship circumnavigates the globe as to what is to be law or what is not.

During the next few weeks, he spent many afternoons in Wakefield's cottage in Reigate. It was here that he drafted the society's manifesto, explaining the aims of colonial reform and referring again to the 'great evil' of colonial rule from London. Years later, he would remember 'the rare enjoyment of an evening spent in the company of this remarkable man ... seated by his own fire, with his magnificent bloodhounds at his feet'.

...

Fitz had lost his job at the museum, as well as his financial independence, at a time when the middle and upper classes were affected by increasing levels of unemployment. 'Let anyone put an advertisement in a morning paper offering £100 a year to a gentleman with a good education,' wrote a member of the Canterbury Association:

> and in two days he will have 500 applications … Sons of noblemen are going to the Bar, some are becoming architects … but in the colonies a man may work by the hand without disgrace and there is less need of equipage and style than at home. You will have intelligent men – men of family – going out in the first ships; they will become the leaders of the humbler classes.

With little chance of alternative employment, Fitz made his decision in January 1850. He would sail for Canterbury with the first body of colonists. 'It is true I am very poor,' he wrote to Godley (with more than a little exaggeration):

> poorer I suppose than a man who ever yet threw himself on the world but have never a moment's doubt or hesitation as to the result … there will be much to go through but all this is nothing compared with the unsatisfactory struggle between pride and poverty one has to maintain at home … Goodbye, my dear Godley. I had rather be making artichokes than articles and corn than constitutions.

Once again, Wakefield was unimpressed. He deplored Fitz's 'sudden resolve to give up colonial reform for emigration, which has disturbed and fretted me on your account'. Hoping to find a man of wealth and status to lead the colonists, he had come up with Captain Bellairs, son of Sir William Bellairs, who was willing to invest £70,000 in the scheme.

When the captain withdrew in early February, Fitz (who had infinite self-belief when his mood was high) sensed an opportunity. He wrote 'very earnestly' to Wakefield with the suggestion that he should become leader in Bellairs' place. He had supporters among the colonists but, as Wakefield put it, he lacked 'some of the essential qualifications'. Fitz had 'uncommon abilities, is a very good fellow, and I like him very much', but as 'a younger brother without property … he has not position enough in this country'. Fitz was summoned to Reigate on 26 February and informed that, because of his lack of financial prospects, he was 'quite unfit to be leader'. Three days later, he received a conciliatory letter:

> I am really anxious to make out some way of promoting the success of your emigrating project. But the idea of last week is not

reasonable ... Can you think of anything else that would meet your objects, except taking what was intended for Bellairs? ... I wish you would tell me *precisely* what your objects are, and what you require or desire. I am sure that all Godley's friends, and none more than myself, would be glad to see you embarked in a good career. Neither can they doubt that you have talents that might be of great service to the colony.

On 6 March, it was agreed that Fitz should be employed as emigration agent, screening working-class migrants and spending long hours in the 'hurry-skurry' of the office in Charing Cross. Thirteen days later, he was elected to the management committee. 'The "aid" of an earnest, active, very clever man, like FitzGerald,' Wakefield had written on 15 March, 'is much needed in [the] Committee of – what shall I call them? – delightful *amateurs*.'

Fitz became a committee member in time to avert a major disaster. The New Zealand Company had reserved two and a half million acres for the Canterbury settlement, but only on condition that sales worth £100,000 had been made by the end of April 1850. The sale price had been set at £3 an acre (ten shillings to reimburse the company, the balance to pay for further emigration and the building of infrastructure, churches and schools). It was proving difficult to persuade buyers to pay this price because great tracts of land elsewhere in the colonies could be obtained for ten shillings or less. By late March, sales were standing at just £2100. The whole scheme was at risk: the reserved land was in danger of reverting to the New Zealand Company, and the chairman of the association, John Hutt, showed no desire to rescue the situation. On 21 March, Fitz and another committee member, Charles Wynne:

> had a conversation with Hutt on the means to be adopted to save the game. We pressed on him the certainty of failure as matters stood ... We pressed him hard, and he lost his temper and allowed the truth to escape him – that he has for some time considered the thing as gone, and that he ... did not intend to make any attempt to save it. We were both aghast at the discovery.

Fitz now acted on impulse. 'After a long conversation' with Wakefield, he took a late train to Brighton to see Lord Lyttelton (an eminent member of the association), 'appearing before him suddenly at eleven o'clock at night'. The result of this dramatic appeal was a turning point. 'His Lordship came up at once to London and took charge of the affairs of the Association', while Hutt resigned ('*professedly* on the score of ill health and occupation, *really* of course on finding us acting independently of him').

This happy result had much to do with Fitz's high levels of energy and enthusiasm. 'If the scheme succeeds, it will be to FitzGerald that it will be due!' wrote Charles Wynne on 29 March. 'He first sounded the alarm – and of his exertions during the last week I can give you no idea.'

During the next few days, Wakefield persuaded the New Zealand Company to remove the minimum level of sales from the contract. At a committee meeting on 9 April, it was agreed that the association would provide a financial guarantee for the shortfall, with Wakefield, Lyttelton and two other members 'jointly and severally liable for £15,000'. 'It is settled that the colony goes forward,' wrote Wakefield that evening. 'The first body of colonists will *positively* sail for their destination this coming autumn.'

Eight days later, a public meeting was held in St Martin's Music Hall in London to publicise the scheme. 'We have perhaps been rather late in coming before the public,' explained a committee member, 'but we kept in scrupulous retirement till the whole scheme could be placed before you in a perfect state.'

The first ships were intended to sail for Canterbury no later than the first week in September, to allow emigrants to house themselves before the onset of winter, so there was less than five months to complete the arrangements. William Bowler was put in charge of shipping contracts, and Fitz wrote to influential people to publicise the scheme and ask for help in finding emigrants. The letters explained his own reasons for becoming a colonist:

> The Canterbury colony will open a new principle to the public
> mind, viz. how to form a colony in which the *higher classes* may take
> part … The kind of persons to whom this colony will be valuable are
> the sons of noblemen and gentlemen with no particular prospects or
> professions and not sufficient capital to maintain that station in life
> in which they have been educated.

By this time, the association had rented larger premises at 20 Cockspur Street and provided a meeting room in Adelphi Terrace, where 'gentlemen intending to emigrate as founders of the settlement meet daily, from ten till five o'clock, and will be happy to receive and co-operate with those who may wish to join them'. Here prospective colonists discussed their plans and listened to lectures on colonial life. The room was furnished with maps, charts, engravings, and books about Canterbury, including the *Hand-Book for New Zealand*, which provided information about the knowledge and skills required in the colony.

As soon as the departure date was announced, the colonists in Adelphi Terrace set up a formal body: the Society of Canterbury Colonists. The inaugural meeting was held on 25 April. Fitz was appointed to the committee and a young Irishman, Edward Ward, took on the role of secretary. Ward was, according to Godley, 'one of the best of our colonists, a nephew of Lord Bangor from County Down, very pleasing and industrious and, it seems, pretty well off'.

Wakefield disparaged the new society. 'The colonists have attempted a kind of self-organisation,' he wrote. 'It is not very real, but on the contrary partakes largely of the character of make-believe … playing at organisation and the exercise of authority.' But Fitz was thinking ahead. He drafted a constitution (unanimously adopted on 27 June) by which a council of colonists would be set up in Canterbury, 'entrusted with the conduct of all negotiations on the part of the colonists with the Association and the government'. This would, he explained to Godley:

> place the Society on such a basis that when we arrive in the colony
> you shall instantly have a definite body representing the colonists
> with whom you can communicate officially … The moment we land
> a council will be called; and as soon as possible, a general meeting of
> all the body.

Although he had been acting as emigration agent since March, there was little Fitz could do until the selection criteria for working-class emigrants were finalised at a meeting on 13 May. It was agreed that the emigrants should be under 40 years of age, in good health, with a letter from their vicar (countersigned by a JP) confirming that they were 'sober, industrious, honest and amongst the most respectable of their class in the parish'. He was to give preference to 'farm servants, shepherds, domestic servants, mechanics and artisans', and the fare for a passage in steerage was set at £15; the association would pay two-thirds of the cost for farm labourers and their families.

Fitz placed advertisements in the daily papers, as well as the weekly and religious press, and set off on a tour of East Anglia in search of emigrants. In Cambridge, he invited members of the university 'to meet and discuss the Canterbury settlement'. At the meeting on 18 May, he described the scheme to an audience of masters of colleges, librarians, fellows, tutors and undergraduates, 'illustrating his remarks by means of a large chart which was laid upon the table'.

Twelve days later, he was at a public meeting in Ipswich attended by a duke, a marquis, three earls, two viscounts, seven lords, nine bishops and several members of parliament. After a number of speeches, Fitz informed the audience that they had found in Canterbury 'a spot peculiarly favoured; no climate in any part of the world affords greater facilities for the increase and prosperity of the English races'. The object of the association, he continued:

> is to make the settlement attractive to the higher orders of people …

> We do not go to this colony to live there for a few years, merely to grow rich and return in old age to enjoy those riches in England. No, I say it, and I say it thankfully, we go out to take up our abode for ever on this new soil and to make it our home.

Further meetings were held elsewhere in the country, but recruitment of working-class emigrants remained below expectations. This was partly because the selection criteria were too strict; partly because the association refused to use a system of paid agents; and partly, perhaps, because Fitz was spending too much time on other aspects of the scheme. On 10 July, he appealed for help from the land purchasers:

> It is within your power to render the most valuable assistance to the colony by attracting the attention of working men in your neighbourhood to the nature of the Canterbury settlement, and to the prospects it holds out for the labouring classes; and I shall be greatly obliged if you will place me in communication with any families or individuals who are likely to become valuable settlers and who have any wish to go to the colony.

The association arranged a banquet – a 'farewell breakfast' – to be held on the *Randolph*, one of four ships being fitted out at the East India Docks at Blackwall. The ships were due to sail a few weeks later and 'the very smell of the pitch', as Wakefield put it, 'will help to give reality to what most people still consider only a pretty dream'.

Almost 350 colonists and friends paid 10/6 a ticket to attend the banquet on 30 July. The ships were 'gaily dressed' with flags. Tables filled the main deck of the *Randolph*, laid out with an 'elegant *déjeuner à la fourchette*' prepared by the London Tavern. The band of the Coldstream Guards played on the poop deck.

The banquet was followed by speeches: toasts to the queen, the royal family, the army and navy, and the departing colonists. Fitz then rose to his feet and 'with great pleasure' proposed a toast to Lord Lyttelton, to whose 'influence and exertions we owe the position we now occupy … and for the exertions of that noble Lord, the colonists and my colleagues on the Committee … owe him a deep debt of gratitude'. Lyttelton responded with generosity: 'There is no one that I would rather do me the honour of proposing that toast than Mr FitzGerald. Both the Canterbury Association and the colonists are deeply indebted to the energy, integrity and activity of that gentleman for his exertions on their behalf.' The final toast was 'Success to Canterbury!' after which the proceedings concluded with a rousing chorus of 'Auld Lang Syne' and dancing on the poop deck.

Two days later, Fitz attended a meeting of the Society of Canterbury Colonists at which it was agreed to establish a weekly newspaper in the colony. He offered to be its first (unpaid) editor, and arranged a meeting with Ingram Shrimpton, printer to several architectural and archaeological societies. Shrimpton was enthusiastic. He donated a printing press, together with supplies of type, ink and paper, and persuaded his sixteen-year-old son John to sail for Canterbury to work the press on arrival.

Fitz was firing on all cylinders – but his relationship with his mentor had begun to sour. Wakefield was increasingly annoyed by Fitz's efforts to involve himself in all aspects of the administration, as well by his role in the Society of Canterbury Colonists, which Wakefield perceived as insubordination. He had a habit of turning against his protégés after his initial enthusiasm faded, and his personality – described as 'intriguing and without scruple', 'Machiavellian', 'satanic' and 'sulky' – led to massive feuds with erstwhile colleagues. He and Fitz would soon become the fiercest of enemies.

'I am getting nervous about filling the ships at last with *good* emigrants,' Wakefield wrote to Fitz on 2 August. 'Unless the good be obtained early – before there is any pressure for time – the rubbish is taken up at last for want of better. The whole number ought to be booked before … the 15th of this month.' When Fitz replied that he was still 300 below target for the first ships, Wakefield was dismayed. 'Your letter … is alarming,' he wrote back the same day:

> Not an hour should be lost … It would be a terrible thing if the ships were detained for [lack of] emigrants; and you … as Head Emigration Officer, would have to stay for the last ship. If all the ships were not full, there would be a loss and an outcry. The hasty picking up of rubbish would be worse than all. I am very anxious about it.

Fitz's mood was spiralling out of control. In the space of seven months, he had lost his job in the museum and resolved to start a new life on the far side of the world. He was failing as emigration agent, a role in which he had expected to do well. He was involving himself in too many details of departure, as well as working 'ten or twelve hours a day' in the office in Cockspur Street. He was due to sail for New Zealand in early September. And on top of all this, he was about to be married.

CHAPTER SIX

Just a Schoolgirl

1850

She is such a good-natured merry little thing.
Charlotte Godley, 30 January 1851

I've lain beneath the feet
Of the blushing bride,
And heard her heart beat
With maiden love and pride.

Fitz, 'The Flower', July 1888

*W*akefield believed it advisable for young colonists to marry before leaving for New Zealand. 'There are no hardships in colonising nowadays,' he wrote to one young man:

> I have known most of the ladies who emigrated with the first colonists, ladies brought up in luxury and ease, and I never heard of a serious complaint from one of them, especially those of the highest rank who entered cheerfully into the spirit of the thing and enjoyed the *roughing* for a few weeks … the roughing is *a sort of lark*. To go unmarried is a misery … to go married to a *nice* girl is the best means you can adopt to make sure of happiness and prosperity.

Fitz's dreams of marrying into a rich family had faded with the loss of Rose Paynter. Instead, he was seeking a woman willing to sail halfway around the world with him and *rough* it in a distant colony. And he found her close to home, just a short walk from the British Museum.

…

Fanny Draper was born in Odessa in March 1832, the eldest daughter of a merchant trading with Russia. Her father, born into a family of leather workers in the east end of London, was apprenticed to a merchant house trading in leather and furs, after which he set up in business in the free port of Odessa, the largest seaport on the Black Sea.

Fanny's mother was born in Cronstadt, the deep-water port for the city of St Petersburg where her father, John Booker, worked as British vice-consul.

The firm of John Booker & Son was one of the largest merchant houses in St Petersburg, the family had lived in Russia for generations, and Mary Booker grew up in splendour in a large four-storey house by the waterfront, referred to as 'the best house in the town … the very temple of hospitality'. In years to come, she would tell her daughters about sleigh rides through snow; dinners and balls in the homes of Russian aristocrats; the long winter nights when the port of Cronstadt was ice-bound for months at a time.

A self-made man with a London accent, George Draper was not John Booker's choice of husband (he had married one daughter to a German aristocrat; another to a vice-admiral of the imperial Russian navy), but George had a powerful personality; he was not easily deterred. He and Mary married in September 1828, then travelled south to Odessa before winter set in – an overland journey of almost a thousand miles.

Three children were born in Odessa before George brought his family to London. In 1840, they moved abroad again, this time to Italy, where George extended his business dealings into the Mediterranean. They returned to London in 1842. George took a house in Woburn Square in Bloomsbury and became a regular visitor to the British Museum. He became friends with William Vaux and, when Fitz began work in the department of antiquities, Vaux introduced him to the Draper family, to a house bursting at the seams with eight children, a governess and three domestic servants.

Fanny was twelve years old when Fitz first came to Woburn Square. A tiny, intelligent, vivacious child, she spoke French and German fluently, Italian reasonably well, and knew a few words of Russian. She was also a talented musician with a beautiful singing voice ('far beyond the average amateur'). She took her music seriously, accompanying herself at the piano as she sang oratorios and cantatas in five different languages.

Despite an age difference of fourteen years, she and Fitz shared a sense of fun. They spent hours together, playing jokes, telling stories, making music. He told her about the Irish potato famine and his ideas for colonisation. He talked of art and ancient history; he taught her musical theory; and would soon congratulate himself on 'having in some measure helped to educate her mind'. And he watched (as he described it in his chapter of a novel) 'the timid lively child of twelve change into the thinking woman of seventeen'.

As Fanny matured, she blossomed into a 'pretty, witty, fascinating little creature'. She began to wear low-cut gowns at dinner that revealed her neck and the swell of her breasts. Fitz was startled by their beauty. 'Nothing,'

A rather disconcerting portrait (by an unknown artist) of Fanny aged about sixteen. Years later, Fitz would describe how he watched 'the timid lively child of twelve change into the thinking woman of seventeen'.

Private collection

he wrote, is 'more graceful in the female form than the delicate curvature by which the nervous and mobile lines of the neck sink as it were into the repose of the shoulder and the bust.'

In December 1849, he transcribed a passage from a book of sermons by John Henry Newman as a Christmas gift for Fanny with a hidden message. It was an extract from a sermon about music, associating 'those mysterious stirrings of the heart and keen emotions and strange yearnings after we know not what' with the 'outpourings of eternal harmony in the medium of created sound'.

In January 1850, he persuaded 'my friend Draper' to buy land in Canterbury. On 21 March, he arrived in Woburn Square to celebrate Fanny's eighteenth birthday. Three months later, after his return from East Anglia, he asked her to marry him, to sail with him to a new life on the far side of the world.

Fanny had idolised Fitz for six years now. She had listened to his talk of making a fortune in New Zealand, the 'incalculable profits' that would flow from any venture he undertook in the new colony. She worshipped her tall handsome suitor and was more than willing to make a new life with him in a distant country – but she was still a minor, unable to marry without her father's consent.

Fitz raised the subject one evening after dinner, asking his 'friend Draper' for Fanny's hand in marriage. The response was alarming. George became incandescent with rage. He railed at Fitz for having no money, for proposing to take his daughter to a colony where there was no bed for her to lie in, no roof to cover her head. The rows were so violent that Fitz would soon write of his former friend that 'nothing should ever induce me to speak to or hold any communication of any sort whatsoever with that man again', that 'nothing shall prevail upon me ever to meet him in this world … I would see him in [hell] before I would go into the same house with him'.

While Fanny stood up for herself, her mother kept a low profile and her father accused her of disrespect. She held her ground until he relented, agreeing to the marriage but refusing to allow her to accompany Fitz on the voyage. Instead, she should travel a few months later, after a house had been prepared for her to live in.

'I am at this moment in a great struggle,' Fitz wrote to Godley on 1 July. 'Her family won't allow her to come with me – they want her to follow in November … I shall do all I can to bring her.' His letter continued with praise for his 'little girl … one far dearer to me than anything in the world':

> I think her not only so far superior to the rest of women-kind as to wish to have her to wife but look up to her as the only woman I ever met whom I could ask to share my doubtful fortunes and present poverty. I look forward with a pleasure I cannot describe to the pleasant evenings we may enjoy together … My little girl is a grand musician and sings very sweetly so your pianoforte shall be in constant use.

Four days later, under determined pressure from Fanny, George relented once again. That evening, Fitz added a postscript:

> All my own troubles are settled. Fanny comes out with me … I must now ask you to get some shed for us to put our heads in. Anything will do till the house is built, but if you will keep us off the ground I shall be deeply obliged. I am naturally anxious that my little wife shall not be more exposed than necessary, though she cares for nothing of that kind …
>
> How much we shall have to talk about when we meet. How all the world will be changed – at least to me. The responsibility of a wife in the new land certainly makes one serious and sober, but I cannot say I ever doubt for a moment of success and prosperity. I am indeed very thankful for being permitted to live and die in a great cause and to find a brave and gentle heart to share one's struggles, hopes and triumphs. But I get sentimental and sentiment will hardly keep for 15,000 miles.

On the same evening, Charles Wynne also wrote to Godley: 'FitzGerald is engaged to be married to a Miss Draper … I report very well of her so far as I have seen ... without being positively beautiful, hers is one of the most interesting countenances I ever saw.'

...

Now that the marriage was agreed, Fitz was 'very anxious to get out first as I should like to help in getting the emigrants provided for as soon as possible'. During the next few weeks, he continued to work at full speed on emigration matters and in the Society of Canterbury Colonists. There was much to arrange. Livestock was being transported to Canterbury; an organ, church bell and oak panelling for the first church; scientific apparatus for the future college; books for the library; and Shrimpton's printing press, together with sufficient materials to print a newspaper once a week for several months.

During the first few days of August, he received increasingly ill-tempered letters from Wakefield about the shortage of emigrants, one of which suggested that Wakefield's brother Felix (who was in charge of land sales in Canterbury) be enlisted to recruit more settlers:

> I am pretty well satisfied that he can use with effect for this purpose the agency for land-selling which he has established in numerous places, and without *paying* any body for emigrants ... but the time is very short. If you choose to let him go to work, decide promptly and give him the requisite authority and papers, with a clear account of *exactly what you want* in point of numbers, sex, calling, etc, etc ... But his hands are already quite full of business, and he can only spend odd hours and a day now and then ... It will be sharp and difficult work at best.

At a committee meeting on the 5th, Fitz made a passionate plea to be allowed to use 'paid agents' around the country. This was rejected and, the following day, he wrote an almost incoherent letter to Lord Lyttelton. The use of Felix Wakefield's land agency was, he wrote, 'absurd ... I cannot be held responsible for filling the ships if my hands are tied at the most critical moment ... It is said that paid agents would only get in bad and disreputable emigrants. I reply that is my business.'

The selection criteria had been relaxed at the meeting – 'except as to character and religion' – and additional free passages were on offer. But there was still a shortfall and, on 8 August, Fitz wrote again to Lord Lyttelton (now in residence at his country house):

> The ships may be filled easily enough if we have a machinery large enough to do it, but one man sitting in a room with one clerk can't

do it ... I have friends working in all parts of the country and have told them I would pay expenses out of my own pocket ... Could not your Lordship find some man, some honest bailiff, and tell him he must go round your neighbourhood and get good families ... Such an agent set to work earnestly in your neighbourhood could pick up eight to ten excellent families.

Lyttelton replied on the 14th. He hoped to hear 'of some suitable emigrants' through the local board of guardians, 'but I must not be depended on as it is a function which I am very ill suited for.' He was unsure how far the rules had been relaxed. He asked Fitz 'whether *any* stout able-bodied people will do ... whether there is any other restriction as to health (for instance, I have heard of an excellent labourer with a *wooden leg*)'.

The ships were filling by this time, partly because of Fitz's mobilisation of his friends, partly because Felix Wakefield had recruited emigrants in Kent, and partly because of an appeal to the Catholic-run Family Colonisation Loan Society (which did not discriminate on grounds of religious faith).

Following the usual pattern of his behaviour, Wakefield had now completely reversed his opinion of Fitz's talents. He complained to Lord Lyttelton that his preoccupation with 'politics and government' had led to neglect of his emigration duties, resulting in them 'breaking down entirely'. Fitz was, he wrote, '*all* imagination and *no* action – an immense promiser ... *ready* to undertake everything, but for performance, except in writing or talking, singularly feeble and heedless'.

The association wanted to replace him as emigration agent but Fitz clung on; when William Bowler was asked to take over the work, he merely welcomed him into the office as an assistant. And as the days passed, the stress levels in Cockspur Street and Woburn Square continued to rise.

...

Fitz married his 'little girl' in St George's church, Bloomsbury, on the afternoon of Thursday, 22 August. Unable to compromise, even at this last moment, George Draper forbade his family from attending the wedding. Treating the occasion as a funeral, he told his household to change into mourning dress and, despite the warm summer weather, he ordered the servants to close and shutter the windows and drape them with black cloth.

Fanny and her father walked past the British Museum to the church, where they waited until Fitz rushed in, having hurried through the streets from the final meeting of the Society of Canterbury Colonists ('the best we have ever had, with capital speeches, the room full to overflowing'). Only six people attended the ceremony: Lucius, William Vaux, two of Fanny's friends, and two members of the association, who had accompanied Fitz from Adelphi Terrace.

Fitz stood tall at the altar rail; Fanny barely reached his shoulder. They were both in turmoil. He was exhausted by his battles with Wakefield and George Draper. She was bruised by the rows in Woburn Square and further distressed when her father stalked out of the church after his part in the ceremony was over. The marriage was a culmination of enormous levels of stress and, after the service, when Fitz had kissed his bride and accepted the congratulations of his friends, he too wandered out of the church and disappeared alone into the streets of Bloomsbury.

Fanny was eighteen years old. She had left her family, possibly forever, and was about to sail to the far side of the world. She needed Fitz beside her on her wedding day. Instead, his mind fizzing with the details of departure, he had left her in the church, just as her father had done halfway through the ceremony. So it was Lucius who took her to the lodgings in Great Russell Street before setting out in search of the missing bridegroom.

Fanny sat anxiously by the window. And when Fitz made his way home a few hours later, she 'ran out and brought him in'. He claimed to have lost his memory – although it is more likely that he returned to Adelphi Terrace or his office in Cockspur Street to involve himself in further last-minute preparations.

…

While Fitz was making his marriage vows in Bloomsbury, Wakefield was writing a letter to William Bowler:

> The only difficulty about getting the whole emigration matter placed under your sole direction, is that you have let FitzGerald expect that you would help him *as a helper*. As long as he hopes that you may undertake the work under him or subject to his interference, he will not give it quite up: but when he finds that you will not undertake less than the whole – power, responsibility and all – he will be glad to give up altogether: and this will be done tomorrow if you stand firm.

Next morning, as the landlady in Great Russell Street brought in the breakfast, Wakefield wrote another letter:

> I am tempted to urge the need of settling the FitzGerald-Bowler business tomorrow, and not later. For on Monday morning the whole emigration business ought to be taken in hand … The happiest thing for FitzGerald, whose time is nearly up, would be to take his wife out of town. If he is on the spot, he will be mortified,

or will meddle and spoil all: and it would be mortifying to him to *see* the work going on in other hands. Did he not seem to like the idea of having a leave of absence? That would be best for everybody.

Fitz had no intention of taking leave of absence. Emigrants were arriving in London and his duty was to receive them and load them into the ships in the East India Docks. This was, according to Wakefield, 'a difficult job, requiring particular order and patience', and Fitz was complicating matters by issuing 'wild and changeful orders'. On 24 August, two days after his marriage, the committee finally persuaded him 'to resign the whole matter into Bowler's hands'. Fitz took this as a 'great injury', writing to Lord Lyttelton to complain of 'interference about the ships'.

Left out of the final formalities, he reread his copy of the *Hand-Book for New Zealand*. Apart from mathematics ('absolutely essential') and agriculture ('how to shoe a horse, and kill and clean a hog or a sheep'), a colonist should have knowledge of chemistry, botany and geology, and hone his carpentry and cooking skills. He should learn surgery, 'how to bleed, set a broken or dislocated limb, and bind wounds. If he can learn how to amputate a limb, so much the better; a short attendance at the demonstrations at Guy's Hospital will impart this knowledge.' He should study land surveying, civil engineering, mechanics, architecture and navigation. He should know how to drain land and build fences, build and rig a ship, cure and smoke meat and fish, tan leather, and drive horses. Colonists should also understand the principles of political economy. In this at least, Fitz felt confident.

During the final days before departure, he spent his time buying furniture and equipment. He was taking 'all the farming tools' needed to cultivate 500 acres of land, wheels and springs for a dogcart, and a 'Sussex' grate which burned both wood and coal ('you can make as small a fire as you please and it always burns brightly'). He bought beds, tables and chairs, having been advised to 'take that which fills the least space in proportion to its usefulness'.

He bought tree guards and fruit saplings, packed in wooden cases with glass tops. He bought books and maps, and packed up his library on ancient civilisations. He arranged the transport of a piano, a wedding gift from members of the committee ('well-earned by his service to Canterbury; with the exception of Lord Lyttelton, there is no one to whom the scheme owes so much'). He packed watercolours and paper, and tools for woodcarving. And he was taking a Durham milch cow, 'a thoroughbred cow of the best kind', which would travel free in exchange for milk for the cabin passengers.

There were farewell letters to write to friends and relatives ('God bless you,

Daguerreotype portrait of Fitz at the time of his marriage in August 1850. He was hyperactive at the time, 'up and down like the steam-engine piston'.

Private collection

Daguerreotype portrait of Fanny taken at the same time. 'Without being positively beautiful, hers is one of the most interesting countenances I ever saw.'

Private collection

my boy,' replied Lord Naas, a distant cousin, 'I have no doubt your career will be profitable to yourself and a credit to auld Ireland'). There were photographs to be taken, daguerreotype miniatures of Fitz and Fanny to mark the occasion of their marriage. Fanny sat quietly with a gentle expression and serious eyes; Fitz strained every sinew to remain still during the long exposure, his hair combed close to his head, his pale eyes staring intently at the camera.

Fanny was busy, too, reading the advice for women in the *Hand-Book*. She provided herself with 'strong useful clothing, plenty of broad-brimmed straw hats, thick shoes with cork soles for walking on the wet deck, and a good stock of boots'. Despite the advice that 'finery is superfluous; an outfit or two of dress clothes lasts a long while in a colony', she packed crinolines and petticoats, bonnets and cloaks, and her favourite riding habit, all carefully folded into tin-lined trunks. She bought cookery books, sewing materials, knitting needles, and shanks of wool to knit a curtain during the voyage to stop draughts during the cold Canterbury winter. She ordered large quantities of soap and several cases of Jones's patent flour, 'which makes excellent bread without yeast or any preparation, very useful when you are busy'.

William Bowler completed the embarkation of the steerage passengers and, on 31 August, the four ships were 'hauled out' of the East India Docks and towed downriver to Greenwich. The following morning, the colonists – now known as the Canterbury Pilgrims – were blessed by the Archbishop of Canterbury in St Paul's Cathedral, at a service attended by 'an immense body of persons'. The colonists, said the archbishop, were like the children of Israel setting out for the Promised Land.

A song in four-part harmony, specially written for the occasion, was sung by the congregation. Fitz sang lustily in his rich bass voice; Fanny beside him sang with elegance and soaring notes:

> Heaven speed you, noble band! Linked together heart and hand,
> Sworn to seek that far off land, Canterbury Pilgrims.
> Heaven speed you! Brothers brave. Waft you well by wind and wave,
> Heaven shield you; Heaven save! Canterbury Pilgrims …

> Fresh the soil and fair the clime, lightly touched by toil or time,
> Scarcely tinged with care or crime, Canterbury Pilgrims.
> Go then, cheerfully, go forth. Hasten to replenish earth
> With Old England's honest worth, Canterbury Pilgrims …

On 2 September the ships, now anchored at Gravesend, were 'gaily decked with signal colours' and, shortly after midday, the steerage passengers were ferried ashore in boats and made their way to a marquee where Lord Lyttelton presided over a farewell dinner. To the accompaniment of the marine band from Chatham, several hundred men, women and children sat down to a meal of 'good old English fare': roast and boiled beef, plum pudding and beer.

Most cabin passengers were joining the ships at Plymouth, but Fitz had decided to sail with the emigrants from Gravesend. He and Fanny arrived on 3 September to embark on the 730-ton *Charlotte Jane* ('the fastest ship in the fleet' according to Fitz). Their trunks were loaded into the hold, their bags and a few items of furniture delivered to the cabin. The ship's surgeon, Alfred Barker, arrived in the afternoon with his wife Emma and three small sons, the youngest still a baby.

That evening, Fitz sat in his cabin and wrote a brief note to Lord Lyttelton:

> We sail at daylight tomorrow morning. I cannot depart without once more expressing in the warmest terms my sense of your Lordship's kindness to myself personally and of my gratitude, in common with all the Canterbury colonists, for your exertions in our behalf. I hope, though at the opposite corner of the world, I may still be esteemed.

Early next morning, the ships took advantage of a falling tide. 'We awoke very early,' wrote Barker in his diary, 'to the noise made by weighing the anchor, and when I got on deck I found we were already two miles from Gravesend in tow of the Black Eagle steam-tug. We saw Chatham at a distance and came the same day off Ramsgate about four miles distant … In the evening saw lights of Hastings.'

Fitz remained on deck for most of the day, watching the shores of England slide past in the distance. Beneath his feet, Fanny was sorting out the cabin. It was the best cabin on the *Charlotte Jane*, under the poop deck at the rear of the ship. It had its own toilet, built outside the hull and accessed through a narrow door. Lined with wood, the cabin was a tiny space (nine feet by eleven), with sloping windows above a wide sill with luggage lockers beneath. Fanny arranged the furniture – a bed with a cane back, a writing desk, a cowhide-covered trunk; and behind a canvas screen, she stacked up a nest of folding chairs, a deckchair and an iron washstand.

Next morning, the Isle of Wight came into view; and, in the afternoon, the coastline of Dorset. The *Charlotte Jane* was closely followed by the *Randolph*. On the morning of the third day, Fitz went below to collect his paper and paints. Sitting on the poop deck, he painted the *Randolph* in monochrome sepia, the sails filled, a still sea, the glint of sunlight on the water. That evening, after 'a lovely sail' along the Devonshire coast, the ships passed through the breakwater and dropped anchor in Plymouth Sound.

William Vaux and several members of the association had travelled to Plymouth to bid farewell to the colonists. They came on board next morning, after which Fitz and Alfred Barker went ashore to deal with several last-minute matters. There was a funeral to arrange for a child who had died in steerage; and sheep to buy to replace those which had perished on the voyage from Gravesend.

This last day in England was 'beautifully fine', but Fitz and Barker were anxious not to stay too long ashore. They re-embarked at midday, ready to greet the passengers who were joining the ship at Plymouth, including Edward Ward (secretary to the Society of Colonists in Adelphi Terrace) and his two younger brothers.

There was 'dire confusion' during the afternoon as cabin passengers arrived with their luggage and furniture, as the steerage passengers huddled together on deck, 'hungry and cold' as the ship 'rolled about'. At six o'clock, the captain received orders to sail. After an hour's delay while the replacement sheep were brought on board, the *Charlotte Jane* weighed anchor – at which point the captain realised that he had left the ship's papers in Plymouth and returned ashore to collect them.

As night began to fall, a yacht passed under the stern of the *Charlotte Jane*, then put about and came alongside. It was the Earl of Mount Edgecumbe, whose house overlooked the sound. Greetings were exchanged, the words 'God Speed!' shouted into the gathering gloom.

It was dark when the captain reappeared at ten o'clock. The pilot guided the ship through the breakwater, then William Vaux, who had remained on board, embraced his friend and returned to shore with the pilot. The sails filled and the *Charlotte Jane* began her long journey to New Zealand. As she passed astern of the *Sir George Seymour*, also headed for Canterbury, the two ships 'gave and received three hearty cheers'.

The bustle on deck died down, the lights of Plymouth receded into the distance, and the passengers fell quiet under the weight of their great adventure. 'Sternly real did I feel my position then,' wrote Edward Ward, 'the sails filling for my new country, not to stop or stay till we should arrive there. This feeling of reality was sudden as thunder.'

PART II

Fitz starts a new life

CHAPTER SEVEN

The *Charlotte Jane*

1850

Whilst our ship her path is cleaving
The flashing waters through,
Here's a health to the land we're leaving,
And the land we are going to.

Fitz, 'The Night Watch Song of the Charlotte Jane', 1 November 1850

ost passengers remained on deck until the lights of Plymouth blended with the darkness. The *Charlotte Jane* passed the Eddystone Light at midnight and, as the lighthouse fell astern of the ship, Fitz and Fanny retired to their cabin and tried to sleep. They had a restless night, disturbed by the motion of the ship, the jolting of the rudder post (which ran down between the two rear cabins), the thump of footsteps on the poop deck overhead, and the howling of the Barkers' baby, who was teething at the time.

At first light, Fitz joined Barker on the poop deck. They peered at the horizon to see the last of England, 'a light cloud in the distance [that] was pointed out to me as Land's End'. When this faded from sight in the morning haze, they felt – in Barker's words – 'that we were really cut off from the old country and our friends'.

Breakfast was served in the cuddy (the communal dining room for chief cabin passengers), after which everyone assembled on deck for the first Sunday service of the voyage. The chaplain stood at the capstan surrounded by emigrants from steerage; cabin passengers were ranged on the poop deck. 'They all seemed to feel the impressiveness of the scene,' wrote Edward Ward in his diary that night, 'and nearly all were in tears.'

Twenty-three adults occupied the chief cabins at the rear of the ship. They took their meals with Captain Lawrence in the cuddy, served by three men from steerage who acted as stewards. They had already met in Adelphi Terrace and, at midday on 8 September, they sat around the table for the first meal of the voyage. It was several days before most of them reappeared, unable to think of food as the *Charlotte Jane* made her way south through the Bay of Biscay, 'a long rolling swell sending the ship from side to side in a most distressing manner; the ladies all in a dreadful state, lying about the deck refusing to be comforted'. Emma Barker complained that the ship was sailing through 'hills of water', that she and her children were 'thrown about in all directions'. At first, Fitz joked about the motion. He was, according to Edward Ward, 'one of the bravest ... of the sea-sick', but even 'the cock who crowed so loud at first' eventually succumbed and retired to bed.

Most passengers found their sea-legs on the fifth day and settled into the daily routine of the voyage. They ate well in the cuddy: each adult had been allocated 'one sheep, one pig and a dozen head of poultry', and the galley was provided with 'spices, curry powder, salad oil, herbs and celery seed, sauces, preserved fruits, tamarinds, apples, macaroni and dried yeast for making bread'. On 13 September, they ate 'roast beef and fat beef steak for breakfast, and soup, hot-boiled beef, cold mutton, fowl and duck, hot apple pie and macaroni pudding for dinner'. Later in the voyage, when the livestock had been consumed, preserved meat and fish were sometimes augmented by freshly caught shark ('which smelt savoury and looked dangerous') and dolphin ('delicious').

The pigs and poultry were kept in crates on the foredeck, the sheep confined under an upturned longboat, and Fitz's milch cow was tethered in a makeshift cow-house. Cages of 'linnets, robins, thrushes and other small birds' were on their way to Canterbury, as well as partridges and pheasants to provide game for shooting. Edward Ward kept his dog in a kennel under a longboat and brought him onto the poop for exercise.

The poop deck was reserved for cabin passengers; here they took exercise and enjoyed the fresh air. The women read and sewed; the men took part in shooting contests, aiming at bottles suspended from the rigging, or at seabirds in flight. They dangled a hook and line from the stern and caught albatross in the Southern Ocean, one of which, according to Fanny, was nine feet wide between wingtips. Every day before breakfast, the men were doused with pails of salt water as the sailors washed the decks. The women had no such privilege; they were given a pint of water a day for washing, water described as 'most horrid, the smell beyond everything bad'.

To pass the time, the passengers played cards, chess, games and puzzles. The captain taught them shovelboard, 'a sort of deck quoits or bowls', and Fanny started a glee club (for singing unaccompanied part songs) in the cuddy. There was serious music too, with Fitz and Fanny, Edward Ward and Emma Barker singing choruses from oratorios.

In the evenings the younger passengers made merry on the poop deck, while older passengers sat in their cabins and complained about the 'great noise' overhead. At first they danced to the accompaniment of their own voices, 'to the tune of various choruses which our party could furnish', but soon a fiddler from steerage was invited to join them. His instrument had 'only three strings all the same size' but he could play country dances, reels and polkas, and Fitz and Fanny, delighted with their new life and with each other, danced happily in the moonlight.

Fitz had failed in his ambition to be leader of the Canterbury Pilgrims, but he could place himself at the head of this small band of cabin passengers and – he hoped – be the first Pilgrim to set foot in the new country. He was known on the ship as 'the prime mover of all'. On 12 September, he offered to edit a weekly newspaper, handwritten and 'published' by appearing on the cuddy table on Saturday afternoons.

The paper was titled *The Cockroach* – a tribute to the insect that infested the ship in large numbers ('to feel a cockroach crawl over us in the night is not pleasant'). Fitz painted a sepia image of a cockroach for the cover. He wrote the editorials and passengers submitted contributions, including a poem published in the first edition:

> I am no less than a cockroach bold,
> Creeping and crawling from deck to hold,
> Hunting each cabin and hammock and bed
> Under the pillow where rests your head,
> Under the tablecloth, up the chair,
> I run up your sleeves and I crawl through your hair …

Every week, the paper was read aloud in the cuddy 'amidst roars of laughter'. 'Captain Lawrence is so delighted with the *Cockroach*,' wrote Fanny. 'He is having the whole of every number copied out.'

The ship was now in the trade winds, 'careering along with every stitch of canvas set over a lovely sea as blue as indigo'. As they sailed south, the weather became warmer, the balmy nights tempting Fanny and the other women to remain on deck after the dancing. One night, the men gathered in the darkness to play 'a round of rhyme impromptu', some of the verses 'better suited to the hour of midnight than to the ears of ladies'. They thought they were alone on deck but, 'to our horror', they became aware that two women 'were sitting in a dark corner not far off'.

Mortified that their risqué ditties had been overheard, they spoke to Captain Lawrence, who hinted in the *Cockroach* that ladies should not remain on the poop deck after ten at night. It was, he wrote, most unseemly behaviour. His hints became stronger in later editions as the women continued to enjoy the warm night air. Eventually, the men resorted to hosing down the decks at half past ten, 'the last means of keeping below the ladies who persist in refusing to take the hint that it is very improper to stay late on deck'.

As the *Charlotte Jane* entered the tropics, the temperature began to climb. On 22 September, the wind was 'blowing dead aft, making the vessel roll and pitch uncomfortably, but as it kept the deck cool and tempered the tropical sun, we considered ourselves fortunate'. Next day, the wind dropped and the heat became 'most oppressive, the passengers lounging about in uneasy postures, like a fever hospital'. During the evening, 'some of the gentlemen took off their coats, waistcoats, shoes and stockings, sitting in a circle making poetry'.

On 24 September, the thermometer read 85 degrees Fahrenheit at breakfast. It was even hotter at ten o'clock, when the chaplain performed his first funeral. A child had died in steerage and, as the little bundle dropped into the sea, 'a huge school of porpoises appeared, playing abreast of the ship opposite the porthole where the body was lowered down'. That evening, the heat was 'so suffocating as scarcely to be endured'. 'We have left off all flannels and in fact everything in the way of clothing possible,' wrote Emma Barker. 'The gentlemen have abandoned their waistcoats and some their cravats and many wear white muslin jackets.'

Four days later, they were woken at six in the morning by shouts of 'close the scuttles, a squall is coming up!' The carpenter secured the cabin windows and the ship began to roll, 'the waves came high, the wind whistled, thunder and lightning, the captain's voice heard above all, sailors racing about, *all* noise'. This sudden storm was followed by a dead calm, 'the vessel rolling, the sails rattling'. That evening, Fanny led a female chorus on the poop deck, 'singing until very late'.

The ship was still becalmed on 30 September when Fitz and Edward Ward were lowered in the gig to row themselves around the ship in the late afternoon. Fitz took paper and paints, and he sketched the *Charlotte Jane* in sepia as the sun dropped low in the sky. 'Utter loneliness seemed the characteristic of the ship,' wrote Ward in his diary that night, 'so small did she appear in the middle of the vast ocean.'

After darkness had fallen a few days later, a display of phosphorescence lit up the sea, 'golden billows, indescribably glorious'. The passengers peered into the water as the *Charlotte Jane* seemed to 'plough her way through molten silver' and a school of dolphins played around the ship. 'We saw as it were fiery serpents running from under the vessel from all directions,' wrote Alfred Barker, 'and tumbling over each other ... disturbing the phosphorescence animalcules as they rushed through them, left long lines of light on their track.'

The ship was due to cross the equator on 9 October. Apprehensive about the legendary crossing-the-line ceremony, the passengers assembled on deck on the evening of the 8th to sing 'Home Sweet Home'. Next morning, they peered out of the cuddy door to watch the preparations. 'Do you think they will really shave us?' they asked nervously as they ate their midday meal. As soon as the meal was over:

> A wild shout was heard, and from behind a tarpaulin ... rushed the most motley group ... About a dozen grotesque figures suddenly appeared surrounding a gun carriage, which they dragged rumbling and creaking to the poop stairs. On the carriage was seated Neptune, clothed in a sort of tunic, botched and streaked into a fantastic pattern with tar and paints, red, blue and black. He wore a hideous mask of the same colours and was armed with a long sword and a speaking trumpet. Through this he kept continually shouting hoarse orders which we could not understand.

Accompanied by his 'secretary, barber and surgeon', and a sailor dressed in a sheepskin to represent a bear, Neptune climbed the ladder to the poop deck to collect 'tribute' from the cabin passengers. He then descended to the main deck and 'the motley group' made its way to 'Neptune's Easy Shaving Shop', a makeshift construction on top of the shed that housed Fitz's milch cow:

> On the top of the cow-house was placed a little dog-kennel on the brink of a large sail filled with water to the depth of about five feet. The barber and barber's assistant – the former with a razor of notched hoop, and the latter with a tar brush and a pot of tar grease and stinking filth, stood ready on the stage to receive the customers, and the bear stood in the sail below to duck them after the operation.

The first victim was one of the cuddy stewards. He was captured, blind-folded, and led to the cow-house, where he was met by the 'surgeon':

> who felt his pulse and ordered him some salts – which were immediately thrown over him in two or three buckets of salt water – lent him a smelling bottle – the cork being filled with pins. After this, and being tripped over a rope, he was led up the ladder to be shaved, amidst a shower of buckets from every quarter. Seated on the dog-kennel, he was lathered with the tar and grease, which was com-pletely scraped off with the hoop, the operator formally stropping

his razor between every few strokes upon an enormous black bone. After he had been well scraped, the unlucky victim was pitched, still blindfold, backwards into the sail, where he was received by the bear and well worried and ducked.

Fanny was enjoying this. She watched several men undergo the same treatment before Neptune turned to the poop deck and shouted through his trumpet: 'Pass the word to give the poop a raking fire.' On this command, there was 'a general throwing-about of water' as 'sailors began to pitch bucketsful of water from the main deck upwards'. The captain ordered the women and children below. Most of them fled to the cuddy where they locked themselves in for safety, while a few braver ones remained on deck and were thoroughly soaked as the men joined in the fun:

> Every one that could provided himself with a bucket and poured it over every one who came near him, sailors and passengers pell-mell, now rushing up the poop and deluging the people there, now in playful duels, surprises and ambuscades among themselves. Everyone on deck had their dress wetted through and through before they went down – Captain and all. The Captain was at one time seen scrambling up the rigging and chase given him from below.

All this lasted for more than two hours, before the decks were washed and dried, and a measure of rum distributed among the sailors, 'some of the gentlemen joining in'.

…

Three days into the southern hemisphere, the *Charlotte Jane* encountered an American ship on her way from Angola to New York. A 'mail bag was soon made up and despatched by the Chief Mate with a sack of potatoes and half a dozen of bottled porter'. The mate returned with a bag of oranges, some bottles of rum and a jar of preserved ginger. The men held a shooting contest for the ginger jar (Fitz was eliminated in the first round) and Fanny spent the afternoon in the galley, baking a cake for Hamilton Ward, Edward's youngest brother, to celebrate his sixteenth birthday.

The weather now began to cool and, by 20 October, many of the passengers were suffering from sore throats. A stove was lit in the cuddy, and was used to make toast and toffee. There was a great bustle as trunks were brought up from the hold and passengers changed from summer to winter clothing and put extra blankets on their beds. It was no longer warm enough to sit on deck. Edward Ward wrote in his diary that 'everything seems quite changed, as if we were beginning a new voyage or a new life'.

On the 28th, an unusually large number of birds congregated around the ship, 'flocks of albatross, cape pigeons and silver petrels, the sea covered with them afloat, the air filled with them on the wing, thickening the atmosphere like gnats on a summer evening'. The following day, the ship was hit by a severe gale. Sails were furled, the cuddy windows boarded up. No one slept that night because of 'the tremendous rolling of the vessel ... Two or three heavier rolls than ordinary seemed to bring every smashable article on the ship down at once'. Fitz and Fanny lay in bed listening to crashes and bangs, 'boxes, casks and heavy things giving way in every direction and people striking lights and looking timidly after their lives and their properties'.

The gale battered the *Charlotte Jane* for two days. It was difficult to move around the ship but 'the laughter occasioned was very great'. Meals were particularly eventful:

> Dinner was an awful scramble, plates and dishes falling about, of course, but that was the least. You were as likely to find your neigh-bour in your plate as your plate in your neighbour's lap, or your lap in your neighbour's, as any other arrangement. Thus, part of my dinner was eaten on the floor and part on the table – you must eat what you can get and for small dishes must exercise the art of harpooning ... as potatoes, salt and bread etc, come swimming past.

The second night of the storm was as noisy as the first, with 'doors slamming and knocking about, the sea roaring, the wind whistling, creaking, children crying, and us in our beds going from one side to the other, the sea dashing through the scuttles and through the planks'.

The gale was still blowing on 1 November when Fitz bet the captain at dinner, in bottles of champagne, that they would not reach Canterbury within 98 days of leaving Plymouth. That evening, he wrote a drinking song, 'The Night Watch Song of the *Charlotte Jane*', which was published next day in the *Cockroach*:

> 'Tis the first watch of the night, brothers,
> And the strong wind rides the deep;
> And the cold stars shining bright, brothers,
> Their mystic courses keep.
> Whilst our ship her path is cleaving
> The flashing waters through,
> Here's a health to the land we're leaving,
> And the land we are going to.

First sadly bow the head, brothers,
In silence o'er the wine,
To the memory of the dead, brothers,
The fathers of our line –
Though their tombs may not receive us,
Far o'er the ocean blue,
Their spirits ne'er shall leave us,
In the land we are going to …

But away with sorrow now, brothers,
Fill the wine cup to the brim!
Here's to all who'll swear the vow, brothers,
Of this our midnight hymn –
That each man shall be a brother
Who has joined our gallant crew;
That we'll stand by one another
In the land we are going to.

Fill again before we part brothers,
Fill the deepest draught of all,
To the loved ones of our hearts, brothers,
Who reward and share our toil –
From husbands and from brothers,
All honour be their due –
The noble maids and mothers
Of the land we are going to!

The wine is at an end, brothers,
But ere we close our eyes,
Let a silent prayer ascend, brothers,
For our gallant enterprise.
Should our toil be all unblest, brothers,
Should ill winds of fortune blow,
May we find God's haven of rest, brothers,
In the land we are going to.

After the women had retired to their cabins, the men sat around the cuddy table, glasses in hand, singing their way – more than once – through the six verses of Fitz's song. The weather was still 'very boisterous', the swinging lamp cast shadows on the walls, and Fitz at the head of the table sang loudest of all.

As the ship made her way south, every day was colder than the last. The *Charlotte Jane* was sailing deep into the Southern Ocean, well to the south of the Cape of Good Hope, down to the extreme cold of Latitude 52°36'S which they reached on 5 December. This was known as 'great circle sailing', a route which shortened the voyage by several weeks but proved an endurance test for passengers and crew.

First came 'a dreary drive of three weeks in cold and rain, with strong gales and no perceptible change in the sea, the sky, or the cape pigeons in the wake'. On 19 November, the thermometer in the cuddy read 33 degrees; most of the passengers remained in bed to keep warm. On the 27th, 'it came on to blow a whole gale, with snow and unendurable cold'. Three days later:

> The ship ... is taking us to more cold – more we can hardly bear now. It is utter misery – what between the cold of the windy deck, the smoke of the stove in the cuddy, and the darkness of our little cabin, we have positively no place to go. Everyone in their misery and discomfort rendered ill-tempered, is making everyone else ten times more uncomfortable.

They suffered this Antarctic cold for three weeks. They were on the lookout for icebergs (but saw none) and even Fanny – a brave and hardy soul – referred to the weather as 'very severe'. There was snow and hail, the decks were icy, the cabins cold and damp, and the cuddy stove produced an evil-smelling smoke. The men no longer washed on deck and the caged birds ('which up to this time had continued healthy and lively') died from exposure, 'a grievous loss' to the prospect of shooting game in the new land.

Fitz wrapped himself up and sat on deck, painting a quick sketch of the mountainous seas. On the morning of 28 November, after heavy snow had fallen during the night, he began a snowball fight with Captain Lawrence, who joined in with enthusiasm. The two men hurled snow at each other until Fitz slipped and crashed to the deck, giving his knee 'a very hard blow'. Alfred Barker applied a bandage and confined him to bed, where he lay cursing this 'great inconvenience' when he was 'so anxious to walk about and see everything'. To pass the time, he painted a view of the cabin, lying in bed with his sketchbook propped against his good knee. And he carved a gift for Barker's four-year-old son, 'a beautiful little boat, all complete with sails and masts, and painted – more fit for the mantelpiece than for child's play'.

The *Charlotte Jane* now turned northwards, towards New Zealand, and the days became warmer. It was 'much milder' on 7 December and two days later, on 'a beautiful morning', the deck was 'crowded with happy faces, everyone cheerful at the prospect of even *seeing* land, which the captain expects to do on Wednesday'. On the 11th, the captain 'looked out anxiously into what he called "the loom of the land". The expression was soon in everyone's mouth, and "looms of land" were seen in all directions.'

At five o'clock that afternoon, Edward Ward spotted a shadow beyond the bowsprit. At his eager shout of 'Land ahead!' a swarm of men climbed into the rigging; others ran to the foredeck where they 'vied and jostled with the emigrants' for a better view. It was Stewart Island, the southern tip of New Zealand. Fitz hobbled out of his cabin with paper and paints. The sea was 'covered with a vast number of albatross', and soon – 'to welcome us to our new home' – there was 'the most beautiful sunset we had ever beheld; indeed neither tongue nor pencil would give the slightest idea of its splendour'.

By nightfall, the *Charlotte Jane* was abreast of Stewart Island and Fanny, standing on deck, thought it looked 'beautiful in the moonlight'. During the next few days, the ship tacked into a headwind, sailing well out to sea and back again towards the coast. Every time she approached the land, Fitz painted views of the new country and Fanny 'delighted' in what she saw. 'There were no trees,' she wrote, 'the mountains covered with grass to the very tops. The sky was lovely with the most glorious sunsets.' And the weather had returned to early summer: 'The air is mild and fresh and, when the sun comes out, positively luxurious.'

At midday on 15 December, the 98th day of the voyage, Banks Peninsula came into view. Fitz claimed his champagne from the captain, which he shared out in the cuddy. In the afternoon, he painted the heads at Akaroa. During the night, the ship continued to tack to and fro until, early next morning, she made her final approach. The passengers were up at first light, crowded onto the decks. 'The land we passed was most beautifully situated,' wrote Edward Ward, 'high and wooded, with glades of grass running up through the forest here and there. We were all enchanted.'

The *Charlotte Jane* sailed into Lyttelton harbour, 'through high brown hills with not a speck of life upon them to be seen. Till at last we saw a line of road, sloping upwards across one of the hills.' As the ship moved beyond a small headland, 'there at the bottom of a shallow bay, lay snugly ensconced the pretty town of Lyttelton. We can scarcely imagine a more picturesque spot for a town. Its beauty caused an involuntary shout of delight from all our passengers.'

At ten o'clock, the captain gave orders to furl the sails and 'down into the depths of the water went the anchor with a thunderous din'. The emigrants were packed together on the foredeck, the cabin passengers on the poop, but the excitement was too much for Fanny. She suffered from migraine and now, on the first morning of her new life, she was felled with a particularly bad attack. As she retired to bed in the cabin, Fitz put two shillings and sixpence in his jacket pocket. He wanted to boast – when he had made his fortune – that he had landed with just half a crown in his pocket.

The *Charlotte Jane* was the first of the four ships to arrive in Lyttelton. There was a frustrating delay before the first boat arrived from shore. This brought the customs officer, Harry Gouland, 'a fussy, methodical red-tapeist'. The passengers were under the impression that they could land all personal goods free of import duty; Gouland now informed them that duty would be charged on every new and unused item, 'even on our outfits and cooking ware'. This gave rise to 'great alarm' and, while the passengers engaged in a flurry of anxious conversations, Fitz and Barker embarked in the customs boat to accompany Gouland as he returned to shore.

Barker, who had boasted that he would be the first passenger to leap ashore, took a seat in the bows. Fitz sat quietly behind him. As the boat approached the beach, he shouted 'Oh, no you don't!' and leapfrogged over the doctor's back. Pain knifed through his knee as he landed in the shallows but he limped ashore triumphant, the first Pilgrim to set foot on Canterbury soil.

CHAPTER EIGHT

The Cabin on the Hill

1850–1851

… How gladly then,
Sick of the uncomfortable ocean,
The impatient passengers approach the shore,
Escaping from the sense of endless motion,
To feel firm earth beneath their feet once more …

Robert Southey, quoted in Lyttelton Times, *11 January 1851*

Preparations had been underway in Lyttelton for fifteen months and the town now boasted several wooden houses, an immigration barracks, two hotels ('no more than small grogshops'), three commercial stores, several warehouses, a long sturdy jetty and a weatherboard customs hut. Behind the town, the Port Hills – the rim of an extinct volcano – rose steeply above the harbour to a height of some 1500 feet. Patches of low bush grew in the folds of the hills, and a track, 'almost as steep as the roof of a house', wound its way to the top and down the other side.

Godley and his wife Charlotte had arrived in New Zealand in March, and spent several months in Wellington before moving to Lyttelton in November to await the arrival of the Pilgrims. They were living in the only two-storey house in the settlement, a gabled house with a deep verandah and an English lawn. It was, according to Charlotte, 'tolerably furnished but rather short of chairs'.

The town was taken by surprise when the *Charlotte Jane* was seen rounding the headland. The ships had not been expected so soon. Godley set off for the waterside and, as he approached the shore, he saw an unlikely figure limping up the road from the harbour. Wearing a blue shirt, green plush jacket and 'immense straw hat', Fitz was unsteady on his feet after more than three months at sea, his appearance 'so altered … by very hollow cheeks, a ferocious moustache, and a lame leg … got in snowballing the captain in a gale' that, at first sight, Godley failed to recognise him.

As the two men came together under the hot midday sun, Godley was 'so overcome as hardly to know whether to laugh or to cry, and ... ended by doing both'. It was, he would later remember, 'the most affecting moment of both our lives'. They threw their arms round each other and the words came spilling out ('you may imagine the questions, etc, and the excitement of the whole morning').

Talking at a furious pace, Godley took Fitz to his house and introduced him to the governor, Sir George Grey, who had arrived on a visit three days earlier. Grey was described by Charlotte as 'tall and plain, with a rather red tip to a rather long nose'. She found him 'very stiff and not *very* agreeable, though you see at once that he is quite a clever man'.

Conversation flowed during the midday meal. 'Mr FitzGerald dined with us,' wrote Charlotte, 'and we talked as fast as we could, and that was not fast enough, and kept our eyes steadily fixed on his face, in the delight of seeing a real face, and hearing a voice, that we had seen and heard in England, a year and five days since we left it!' When Godley described the Canterbury Plains, which could only be seen from the top of the Port Hills, Fitz ached with desire to see his new homeland and it was soon agreed that he and Grey should set off up the track – known as the Bridle Path – that afternoon.

It was a climb of more than 1100 feet – described by Fitz as 'a mile and a half of almost perpendicular walking' – through low bush and clumps of yellow tussock grass. They stopped from time to time to rest his injured knee and, as the harbour receded into the distance behind them, the two men discussed colonial politics, the work (as Grey put it) of 'founding new nations and creating new governments'. And when they reached the top of the track, as they climbed the last few feet, the Canterbury Plains came into view, 'stretching away to an infinite distance'.

Covered in tussock, the plains appeared 'very brown and flat', with 'three large rivers meandering through them'. To the right lay the Pacific Ocean, 'the curve of the line of white breakers along the sea shore diminishing into obscurity'. Fifty miles in the distance, on the far edge of the plains, stood the Southern Alps, 'the great backbone of the island, a ridge of snow-capped mountains of exquisitely lovely appearance'. The view took Fitz's breath away and it seemed to him that his hopes and dreams lay spread out before him like the grass-covered plains he had come to colonise.

...

Meanwhile, Fanny had felt well enough to join the other passengers for the midday meal. As soon as they had taken their seats at the cuddy table, the mate put his head around the door. 'A large vessel in sight!' he said.

It was the *Randolph*. The ship tacked up the harbour and, as she approached the *Charlotte Jane*, the passengers 'gave and received three hearty cheers'. And when the *Randolph* dropped anchor, they stood to attention to give a rousing rendition of 'God Save the Queen'.

The arrival of the second ship gave rise to 'the most extraordinary excitement' in Lyttelton. The Godleys were 'full of wonder', and Fitz's enthusiasm increased as he descended the Bridle Path. He hobbled into Lyttelton and, an hour later, accompanied Godley and Grey on board the *Charlotte Jane*.

After supper in the cuddy, Edward Ward drafted an urgent petition to the governor about the import duties. The colonists had, he explained, 'provided themselves with the necessary implements for settling themselves in the colony and for cultivating the land', and were disappointed to learn that 'duties must be paid upon these goods at a time when all their resources are required to meet the difficulties of an entirely new settlement'.

At ten o'clock next morning a third ship, the *Sir George Seymour*, dropped anchor in the harbour. Three of the four ships that had set sail from Plymouth within hours of each other had arrived at the far side of the world – within hours of each other. This was a rare event in the days of sailing vessels and it led to much delight among the colonists, as well as putting pressure on the arrangements made to receive them.

Fitz, who had spent the night on board with Fanny, disembarked at first light and was hard at work when the *Sir George Seymour* tacked up the harbour. He was making arrangements for the first wave of settlers to move into the immigration barracks; and he was also finding an office for the printing press.

At midday, Ward presented his petition to the governor and, after a quiet word from Grey, Gouland agreed to interpret the regulations more leniently. As Fanny wrote to her mother, the governor 'made a great many little arrangements for us and did away with customs duties upon things the people declared to be personal property'.

Fanny went on shore for the first time on the 18th. It was a hot day in Lyttelton, the temperature climbing above 90 degrees, 'the dust most disagreeable'. The governor left that morning for Wellington, so there was room for Fitz and Fanny to stay in the Godleys' house, sleeping on a mattress on the floor of Godley's dressing room. That evening, the two couples talked over the teacups and Fanny took her place at the piano. 'I sang a good deal because Mr and Mrs Godley are very fond of music,' she wrote to her mother. 'Mr Godley understands German and appreciates all my songs.'

Charlotte Godley had been a lady of fashion in England. She was unaccustomed to 'roughing it', but she had a gaiety of spirit and was entering into pioneer life with enthusiasm. She took an immediate liking to Fanny:

She is such a good-natured merry little thing, just what you may call a *school girl*, and sings and plays so beautifully … I scarcely ever heard anyone say their words so well, and she sings, and understands, French, Italian, German, and Russian; and English best of all.

During the next two weeks, Fanny helped in the house and played with Charlotte's three-year-old son Arthur. There was no stove, so meals were cooked over an open fire. The rooms had to be swept every few hours to remove the dust that came in through the windows and doors. 'Our house is open all day and all night to everyone,' wrote Godley, 'large tea parties every evening with lots of music, talking and laughing, and very few cups or chairs.'

The Pilgrims attended their first church service in the new country on the morning of 22 December. It was held in the loft of a warehouse, accessible only by ladder and filled with 'sugar barrels, flour barrels, tar barrels, tar tarpaulins, coils of rope and what not'. There were no windows, 'only a wide opening at the seaward

J.R. Godley's house in Lyttelton (photographed before demolition in 1944). Fitz and Fanny stayed here for almost three weeks after arriving in Canterbury on 16 December 1850.

Fairfax Media

end, where a windlass protruded for lifting barrels and heavy goods'. Planks supported on boxes provided seating and another pile of boxes served as the lectern. 'Strange was it to see,' wrote one of the immigrants, 'the bright summer costumes, the pink and blue ribbons of the Pilgrim mothers and daughters, contrasted with those rough planks and cases and that dingy cobwebbed roof.'

'We have been here a week exactly,' wrote Fanny the following day, 'and I am perfectly well pleased with the whole place and all the preparations.' On the 24th, Charlotte decorated the house with 'a few greens' and Christmas Day dawned '*so hot*, even when we went to the early service at 7.30'. At midday, when the thermometer read 93 degrees, Charlotte served 'roast turkey, beef, peas, potatoes and a plum pudding'. Edward Ward joined the party and, in the afternoon, they took a rowing boat across the harbour. Then it was 'back to tea with Mr Godley, the piano was put in requisition by Mrs FitzGerald, followed by a pleasant civilised evening dinner party'.

Boxing Day was 'much cooler' and Fanny planned an expedition 'to gather *toi toi* grass[1] for pillows and mattresses'. On the 27th, the fourth ship, the *Cressy*, arrived in the early afternoon. Next day, Fitz and Fanny visited a sheep station on the far side of the harbour and on the 29th, Fitz's knee now fully recovered, he and Edward Ward set out to walk to Sumner, a coastal settlement on the far side of the hills.

They followed the line of road they had seen from the *Charlotte Jane*, which sloped upwards from the town, 'following the outer edge of a line of rugged and precipitous rocks, sometimes over gullies and ravines where bridges and walls had been constructed', until they reached a massive wall of rock known as Sticking Point. This was the end of the road to Sumner, unfinished because of lack of funds. Beyond lay 'innumerable obstacles – rocks, cliffs and gullies … Many places were actually dangerous to climb along … [but we] struck on to Sumner where we got an excellent luncheon of mutton chops, ale and cheese.'

After returning from Sumner, Fitz took Fanny for a walk along the shore, first on the beach, then 'clambering over rocks' until they met a party of Maori. 'One or two were beautifully tattooed,' she wrote to her mother:

> They were playing at draughts, of which game they are very fond. They were so very amiable as to get some oysters off the rocks and, opening them, they offered them to us. I begin to see that some of the men are very handsome; they have dark sort of Spanish and Italian faces, like Murillo paintings.

Next day, a party of Maori arrived at the house and squatted down to watch

---

1   Toetoe, a native grass, *Austroderia* spp.

Charlotte and Fanny at work. Fanny felt nervous but Charlotte reassured her, 'so I shook hands with them and said *tenakoe* (pronounced like Italian)[1]. They admired my blue brooch very much and afterwards they all gathered round to hear me sing and play.'

...

Fitz was once more in a hyperactive mood. 'Mr FitzGerald is not at all the same man that we knew in London,' wrote Charlotte, 'though he sings just as well ... he has plenty to do just now, and with all his private anxieties and businesses, about which he never can make up his mind, or remain two days in the same way of thinking, he has no time left to make himself agreeable.'

At the end of December, he bought a property from an Irish squatter, 'a mud cabin 18 feet by 12', situated 600 yards uphill from the jetty 'in a most inaccessible place'. It was, according to Charlotte, 'in a very pretty situation, close to a little bush of 120 acres'. Having bought the cabin, he was unable to make up his mind what to do with it. 'At first he thought it perfection,' wrote Charlotte:

> then his goods were very troublesome to carry up and he would build down below, in the town ... then the hill was to be preferred, and a well dug there to supply water, and a garden made where the soil is good, by the bush, and his fortune made by selling vegetables; then he would go down the hill again, and then up, and each time contrary lists of orders to his wife of things she was to do, and goods to be carried up, till I was quite tired of him, and I think she was too.

It was an uphill scramble to the cabin; the site, as one of Fitz's colleagues put it, was 'perfectly inaccessible except by a crane'. There was a ravine to cross, 'difficult when the water is rushing down and the nights are dark', and all provisions had to be carried up from the town. But Fanny was delighted. 'Mrs Godley says that I am a "public reserve" and must not leave them for a long time yet,' she told her mother, 'but as soon as possible I shall go into our cabin on the hill. It is the most prettily situated house here and quite out of the dust.' On New Year's Day, she and Fitz climbed the hill and spent the day 'putting the cabin to rights'. The move was, according to Fanny, 'much against Mr and Mrs Godleys' wishes but I think it is better to try and get things to rights myself'.

Two days later, Bishop Selwyn sailed into the harbour, 'standing at the helm of his schooner, guiding his little vessel into port with his tall athletic figure and his long bishop's coat'. He slept on board that night and arrived at

---

1   Tena koe: hello in Maori

the Godleys' house next morning to breakfast on oatmeal porridge. 'His fine face was stern in repose,' wrote one of the Pilgrims, 'but his smile was like a gleam of sunshine.' After breakfast, the bishop ('dressed in hat, apron and knee breeches') set out to visit the new arrivals in their huts and shelters, while Fitz and Fanny carried their possessions up the hill. Fanny cleaned the cabin and arranged the furniture, and because Selwyn was due to visit in the afternoon, she unpacked the silver tea service.

Fitz enjoyed talking with the bishop, whose journals he had enjoyed so much in London. Fanny made the tea and, when the visit was over, she accompanied Selwyn to the Godleys' house, where a party of Maori had gathered to meet him. She watched him hold 'a long conversation with them in their own language from the drawing-room, the Maoris poking their heads in at the windows'. In the evening, when she sang German songs, 'he declared that I did it to revenge myself for his talking a language I could not understand, by singing in one equally incomprehensible to him'.

During the next two days, Fitz and Fanny became 'comfortably stowed in the cabin; the stove is up and we make the best bread in town'. Fitz began building a lean-to ('the servants' room and a back kitchen for cooking in') and employed two immigrants from the *Charlotte Jane*, John and Elizabeth Horrell, to occupy the lean-to with their infant son. They were, wrote Fanny, 'a very nice couple. The woman was a schoolmistress but understands dairy work, dressmaking etc. The man can build, understands agriculture, and is by trade an implement maker.'

Fitz was proud of the 'very special cow' he had brought with him from England. 'He had not been five minutes in the house, before he was telling me all about her,' wrote Charlotte, 'and I was warning him of a plant which grows about here called toot ("*tutu*" native), of which cows are excessively fond, and when they get to it after a long voyage they eat such a quantity that, in their weak state, it kills them.' The *Hand-Book for New Zealand* had also warned about tutu: 'Imported cattle are more liable to this danger than those which have become acclimatised … It staggers about, soon falls, and death ensues in a very short time.'

Fitz's cow had been 'safely landed' from the *Charlotte Jane* on the morning of 2 January. Two days later, he led her up the hill to the cabin. It was almost three weeks since he had listened to Charlotte's advice and even longer since he had read the *Hand-Book*. His mood was hyperactive, his mind surging ahead with plans for the future. He forgot about the dangers of tutu. The following day he left the cow free to roam all night, 'eating what she pleased'. Next morning, she was in great distress. Fitz called two men to help and together they cut her veins to release blood, they held her mouth open to pour water into her stomach, they pushed implements down her gullet.

Inside the cabin, unaware of the drama outside, Fanny was writing a letter to her mother: 'It is great fun contriving and managing to make things do. At first we had only a foot-pan to milk the cow into. Captain Lawrence is coming to drink tea with us, so I have sent to the store for some teacups. We have only two teaspoons.'

In the evening, when the captain arrived with Edward Ward, they were surprised to find the cow lying on her side 'dying of the "toot" poison – she was far gone and had been dying the whole day, groaning as if in great pain'. They were equally surprised to find Fitz 'in his mud house and earthen floor with a splendid silver teapot and service laid out. They said it was the only one they had.'

This was a farewell visit for the captain; the *Charlotte Jane* was sailing for Sydney early next morning. The anchor was raised at first light. 'I felt quite melancholy as I saw her stand away,' Ward wrote in his diary. 'She seemed the last link between us and home.'

CHAPTER NINE

A Bigger Fish

1850–1851

It is only colonists who have any idea what rough is. It is ill-suited for any
but the young, strong and active.

Georgiana Bowen, 12 March 1851

There is plenty of roughing it here, but with the exhilarating climate and
such a wife as I have, London life is despicable in comparison.

Fitz, February 1851

Charlotte Godley's irritation with Fitz was coloured by a letter from Wakefield to her husband, which arrived on the *Charlotte Jane*. Not only had Wakefield written a venomous letter to Lord Lyttelton ('it was absolutely necessary to speak this truth to him, though I think it must have hurt him greatly: for he had got to trust in FitzGerald, and the disparagement was all news'), he also spilled out his venom to Godley. Fitz had, he wrote 'been up and down all along like the steam-engine piston':

> He is nearly the most provoking man I have ever had to do with:
> for he combines with great and quick ability in writing and talking,
> and very agreeable companionable qualities, a perfect incapacity for
> doing business. He is immensely presumptuous, believing himself
> that he can do everything better than anybody; and when it comes
> to the *doing*, he is a very child.

The letter, which ended in the pot calling the kettle black ('his worst behaviour has been the endeavour to instil his own jealousy and dislike of me into others'), failed in its purpose. Fitz and Godley remained friends. Fitz was appointed immigration agent at a salary of £300 a year, and on Godley's recommendation the governor also gave him the temporary appointment of sub-inspector of police. As Godley explained, 'the union of these two offices will give great weight and authority to his management of the immigrants'.

Fitz worked six hours a day as immigration officer, boarding the ships as they arrived in the harbour and supervising the barracks, which were 'only large enough to take in a set of immigrants for a week before they are turned out and another set housed for a week and so on'. He was particularly busy, with 'a most tremendous bustle and much inconvenience', in mid-December when the first three ships arrived within hours of each other. And when the *Cressy* arrived on 27 December, he had no choice but to order all single men to leave the barracks to make room for newly arrived families.

Almost 800 immigrants arrived in the first four ships. By 10 January, more than two-thirds of them had been accommodated in the barracks. Men and women who had spent three months in the cramped conditions of steerage were reluctant to leave the relative comfort of the barracks to camp out on the Lyttelton hillside or make the arduous climb over the hills in the midsummer heat, so there was, as Godley put it, 'some little dissatisfaction'. Fitz had to harden his heart – and some families held a grudge for years.

As the settlers built cabins and shelters, roofing them with bundles of toetoe and fern, the slopes above the town came alive with huts, tents and other temporary dwellings. The men enjoyed themselves ('who can ever forget that delightful and exciting time'), but some of the women were less enthusiastic. 'It is only colonists who have any idea what rough is,' wrote one of the wives who travelled in the *Charlotte Jane*. 'It is ill-suited for any but the young, strong and active. I could make you cry with a recital of the various shifts and difficulties that colonists have to encounter.'

Hundreds of men, women and children were toiling to the top of the Bridle Path carrying bundles of luggage and with pots and pans strung around their necks. Having reached the top, they scrambled down the other side through a wilderness of tussock. They crossed the Heathcote River on a ferry punt, then walked five miles over swampy ground, often wading knee deep in the marsh, to the site of Christchurch, the future town on the plains.

The Bridle Path was the only overland route to the plains. The sea route around the coast to the Sumner estuary, which gave access to the Heathcote and Avon rivers, was equally impractical. The bar was dangerous: shallow and shifting, pounded by surf and with strong rip currents, it could only be crossed by small vessels in calm weather and at high tide. Ships sometimes had to wait several weeks before they could enter the estuary – and many were wrecked in the attempt.

During Fitz's first year as immigration officer, nineteen ships carrying 3000 immigrants arrived in Lyttelton. He was optimistic about their prospects:

Anything like continued discomfort really does not exist. Hardship in the proper sense of the word is unknown. I think many of our settlers grumble because they are not miserable enough. I verily believe that more will get on here, and fewer will be ruined, than in any colony yet formed. You could not credit how rapidly this place grows up. Every time I go out in the harbour, it looks twice the size from the sea.

Fitz was also working as unpaid editor of Canterbury's first newspaper, the *Lyttelton Times*, published weekly on Saturdays. John Shrimpton was young but he knew the business. He set up the printing press in a temporary building on the waterfront, and his knowledge and skill enabled Fitz, 'under great difficulties in a shed by no means weatherproof', to bring out the first edition as early as 11 January. Fitz's leading article was stirring:

> It probably never before happened that a resolution was formed to print and publish a weekly journal upon the shores of a bay situated at the remotest corner of the globe, when … the surrounding country was a desert, and where scarcely twenty human habitations were in existence. Yet these were the circumstances under which our Journal was proposed, and in the face of which the necessary machinery and staff were transported at great expense from one side of the globe to the other.

Fitz worked on the newspaper in the evenings, 'a work of great labour, reading piles of English papers, selecting, correcting, and so on'. Immigrant ships arrived with English newspapers, and copies of the *Lyttelton Times* were sent to London to provide 'a continuous narrative from week to week, a complete history of the colony from its earliest foundation'.

Towards the end of the year, Fitz was cheered by an endorsement from *The Times* in London. Having explained that 'a slice of England cut from top to bottom was despatched in September last to the Antipodes', a leading article written in July 1851 congratulated Fitz on the prompt publication of his newspaper: 'It is difficult to glance at the first number of the *Lyttelton Times* and associate its existence with a community not a month old … So far from being ashamed of our namesake, we are positively proud of his acquaintance.'

…

The third string to Fitz's bow was the Society of Canterbury Colonists, now renamed the Society of Land Purchasers, which claimed the right to represent the colonists in all dealings with the association in London. The first meeting was held in the barracks on 20 December. A second meeting was held eleven days later, when it was agreed that committee members should submit themselves for re-election. At a special meeting on 7 January, Fitz was elected to the council of the new society. Now he could act the big fish in a small pond. His position as editor of the *Lyttelton Times* gave him a forum in which to express his political opinions. And the most important of these was colonial self-government.

Sir George Grey, who was answerable to the Colonial Office in London, ruled New Zealand with the help of three crown-appointed officials. He was an autocrat who believed the colonists would 'for a long series of years, cheerfully see vested in the hands of the Crown that power which it alone can exercise for the good of all'.

As a result, despite their amicable walk up the Port Hills, Fitz soon perceived Grey as an enemy. In the first edition of his newspaper, he wrote that he would 'never cease to oppose the continuance of the present form of government in New Zealand, and to insist upon the introduction of a constitution such as that under which we and our fathers have lived'. Grey's administration, he wrote three weeks later, was 'despotic ... the inhabitants of New Zealand have no voice whatsoever in the administration of public affairs, and no control whatever over the expenditure of the public revenue, or the appointment of public servants'.

On his part, Grey was an enemy of the Canterbury scheme. From Government House in Auckland, he wrote dismissive letters to London, complaining – among other things – about the high price of land in the Canterbury block ('it did not appear to him – at a time that so large a portion of the population of Great Britain were in such distress ... that the poor of the earth should have closed against them ... so large a tract of fertile country').

On 14 August, a public meeting was held in the Mitre Hotel, at which Fitz and Godley gave lengthy speeches. Godley defended the high cost of land in Canterbury and referred to 'the blighting and ruinous effect of distant government'. Fitz described the power structures in Britain and America and explained how similar structures could be achieved in New Zealand. He ended with the words: 'This government will not, cannot, must not last [loud cheers] ... If we are to have a representative of the Crown, let us at least protest against his being dependent upon instructions from clerks in an office on the far side of the world.'

This was 'the first political demonstration in the colony', a demonstration which – according to Fitz – had taken 'no little trouble and anxiety to organise. It went off most brilliantly, not a dissentient voice and tremendous cheers. We are now committed to the most decided hostility towards Sir George Grey who has attacked us most fiercely.'

The meeting was reported verbatim in a five-page supplement to the *Lyttelton Times*. Fitz sent a copy to Lucius in London: 'You will see that I have been engaged in political agitation. The government here is enough to disgust any human being. I am determined to overthrow it.'

…

In addition to his busy workload, Fitz was braving the summer heat to paint scenes of his new country. He sketched the view from the cabin, and rode over the Port Hills to paint the Canterbury Plains and the embryo town of Christchurch. Fanny organised the house and helped Elizabeth Horrell with the washing and cooking. Raised in a wealthy family, Fanny had never prepared a meal; she had lived in London since the age of ten, and had never fed a farm animal or dirtied her hands in the soil. But she learned fast, and her new life was – as Wakefield predicted – 'a bit of a lark'.

She started a glee club for the 'ladies and gentlemen' of Lyttelton, which practised on Wednesday and Friday evenings. Fitz sang Irish ballads at tea parties, and he and Fanny sang duets and solos from oratorios, particularly from Mendelssohn's *Elijah*, in which Fitz took the title role, Fanny sang the soprano solos, and together they sang the famous duet, 'What have I to do with thee, O man of God?' Their musical prowess became well known in Lyttelton, one colonist commenting that 'we have heard no very remarkable performances here, except for duets by Mr and Mrs FitzGerald'.

The glee singers held their first recital at a 'grand ball' on 4 February 1851, singing 'in exquisite style'. Most of the December arrivals had departed for Christchurch and the next ships had not yet arrived, so four rooms in the barracks were available for the occasion, looking 'very pretty hung with flags (procured from the ships in the harbour), evergreens and calico draperies'. Two interconnecting rooms were used for dancing, a third room served as a cloakroom ('ornamented with pink muslin dressing tables'), and refreshments ('a very large amount of tea, coffee, and cakes … with some huge joints of meat, ham, chicken, pie, etc, and sherry') were available in the fourth.

Female guests unpacked the ball gowns they had brought with them from England; male guests dressed in their best evening suits. Dancing began at ten o'clock on a 'cool, calm night' – and ended five hours later in the midst of a gale. 'The wind rose in gusts,' wrote Edward Ward, 'and one filled the rooms with such a cloud of street-dust as perhaps was never before seen in a ballroom.'

This 'boisterous sou'wester' blew in through the weatherboard walls until the guests 'could hardly open our eyes or draw a breath'. Everyone hurried home but found it impossible to sleep; the wind made the wooden houses 'shake and creak like ships at sea'. Fitz and Fanny struggled up the hill in the dark, fighting against the wind and picking their way across the ravine. The gale blew all night and they lay in bed listening to it howling round the cabin, lifting the wooden shingles on the roof.

In the morning, the hillside was in chaos, 'tents in every state of collapse, blankets, *toi toi* and fern careering madly through the air'. And the wind raised so much dust in the town that, from the vantage point of the cabin, 'it looked like a village on fire'.

Later that day, the wind changed to the northwest, 'a hot, stifling wind which raised the thermometer to 94 degrees in the shade, our highest degree of heat yet'. It was even hotter on 7 February (the wind 'like the breath of a fiery dragon … fowls, dogs and men lay gasping about, unfit for work') when a fifth ship, the *Castle Eden*, arrived in the harbour at midday.

Fitz went on board as soon as she dropped anchor. Not only did he have immigration duties to perform, but one of his half-brothers, seventeen-year-old Gerard, was on board, together with Fitz's piano and another pure-bred Durham cow, which arrived 'in a condition fit for a cattle show'. The piano was unloaded a few days later and lugged up the hill by a team of twelve men. It had survived the voyage 'in most perfect order, not a scratch of any kind, and really as well in tune as it was in Erard's shop in London, a quite extraordinary example of success in packing'.

Gerard found his brother much improved in appearance. Although Fitz had lost weight – he now weighed just over twelve stone – he had weathered in the sunshine. 'He has grown more wonderful than ever,' wrote Charlotte:

> His hair is all brushed and shaved away from his face, except for a very long moustache, and on hot days he used to wear the most frightful long brown Holland blouse, left very open, with a belt and turn-down collars, and on wet or cold days he sallied forth in the celebrated green plush shooting jacket.

Fitz's moustache served a useful function in the hot midday sun. As Fanny explained, 'every gentleman who comes out here should wear a moustache. All those who have not done so have suffered very much from sore lips.'

…

Two weeks after the 'grand ball' in the barracks, the first land selections were made in Christchurch. It was 17 February and Fitz left Lyttelton at first light to ride over the Port Hills to the plains.

The building of Christchurch had begun just nine weeks earlier and it was growing fast, with 'habitations of every variety: tents, houses of reeds, grass, sods, lath and plaster, boards, mud, and dry clay, a few that are merely pits scooped in the bank of the river, and one or two consisting of sheets and blankets hung on poles.' There were food shops and stores, and the streets were 'busy with bullock drays, horses and innumerable dogs of every conceivable breed'.

The Canterbury block (between the Waipara and Ashburton rivers, from the mountains to the sea) had been surveyed and divided into sections. The colonists had already explored the area, and they made their selections in the Land Office, the first permanent building in town. Still unfinished, it stood two storeys high with gabled windows, brick chimneys and a long verandah. A Union Jack flew from the flagpole. The colonists who had gathered for the day sat on the verandah or lounged about in the heat.

Alfred Barker had constructed a temporary home opposite the Land Office, a tent made with a large studding sail from the *Charlotte Jane*. It boasted a brass plaque at the entrance, reading 'Barker, Surgeon'. Throughout the day, he kept open house in 'Studding Sail Hall'. A caterer set up a trestle table nearby, serving 'joints of beef and mutton, bread, butter, tea and coffee'.

The selections were made on a 'first applied, first served' basis. Land purchases had been numbered when applications opened in London; these numbers were now called out in order. According to Barker, 'we each went in our turn and pointed out on the map the spot we wished, and if no one before us had chosen the same it was laid out at once on the map and our name inscribed in the Association's book as the owners of it'.

When his own turn came, Fitz made two selections: 200 acres on the Heathcote River and 150 acres in Purau Bay on the far side of the harbour. Both these blocks of land were owned in partnership with his father-in-law, 'so I am not quite certain where my own 50 acres will ultimately be'. And for each rural block selected, land purchasers in the first four ships could select a town section in Lyttelton or Christchurch.

The five-acre section on which Fitz's cabin stood was the first to be selected: it was acquired for a widow in England to endow the future Christ's College with a scholarship. So Fitz was in possession of his house, but not the land on which it stood. As a result, he was 'building on land which does not belong to me and for which I can get no legal title for a year. But I am promised a lease and there is no real doubt that I shall get one.'

On his return home that evening, Fitz dismounted near the Heathcote River, 'walked over my property with my gun and shot a duck'. This he carried over the Bridle Path and presented to Fanny for the pot.

Although he described himself (with his usual exaggeration) as 'the poorest man in the colony', he was having a splendid time. As he wrote to Lucius:

There is plenty of roughing it here, but with the exhilarating climate and such a wife as I have, London life is despicable in comparison … I wish you could eat the lump of home-baked bread I eat every evening, and smoke your excellent cheroot in the easy chair, looking at an indescribable sunset over the most splendid scenery.

The Irish squatter had 'walled in with a good sod wall two sides of above an acre of ground' near the cabin. Fitz was busy completing the work, 'and soon I shall have a walled garden of an acre and a half'. He was making plans for 'fowls and pigs and, next year, a paddock with cows'. He was also building a two-room cottage to replace the cabin, a house with sod walls and a shingle roof. 'My house is nearly ready,' he wrote on 23 February:

and has a most lovely view. The climate is perfect, at least in the summer, and I have experienced not one hour which could detract from my happiness. It is true I am living in a mud cabin but, in a week, I shall be in a good house – and perhaps not so happy as I have been in the cabin.

He and Fanny plastered and whitewashed the rooms, and when they moved into the cottage, they found it 'very cheerful, although the mess is indescribable'. Fitz acquired a guard dog, 'an excellent brindle bulldog cross, a male dog called Dido', which he kept chained in a barrel outside the door. Bulldog crosses were normally used for hunting wild pigs and Dido was, according to Charlotte:

horribly ferocious … it bites you as you pass, and if you take a stick, it flies at you at once. You are obliged to wait at a distance till your voice, and its barking, can bring out one of the inmates, who sits against the mouth of the barrel while you pass. It will bite anyone but Mr FitzGerald, and I think ought to be shot.

CHAPTER TEN

The First Winter

1851

It requires pluck to be a colonist. It is real hard work and no mistake.

Fitz, 20 February 1852

It was a fearful risk to bring a young wife so far and to such a life, but I
much under-rated the character of the wife I chose.

Fitz, 5 July 1851

The last day of February 1851 was 'another calm and cool day,
delicious weather', but the autumn rains began in earnest during
the night of 1 March. Down in the town, the Ward brothers lay awake in their
mud hut, 'trembling for the fate of our sod walls, hearing the rain pouring
through the roof and dripping in puddles on the floor … half of our floor was
a pool of water – the other half soft mud, almost ankle deep; and the water
roaring fast in a stream past my bed.'

The rain continued all next day and into the night. The sun reappeared on
the 3rd, providing a few days of fine weather to dry bedding and household
goods. The rains returned on the 12th and, by the following day, the water was
'flowing down the hillside in torrents; several mud houses have been swept
away'. Dry gullies became rushing streams, and roads became seas of yellow
mud; and Fitz and Fanny slipped and slid on their way to and from the town.

The rain also threatened to wash away their new house. 'It was quite
disheartening,' wrote Fitz on the 14th, 'to see my beautiful whitewashed walls
giving way under the rain and literally melting.' As a result, he was forced to
add weatherboards ('a great expense which I hoped to avoid'), while Fanny
mopped up the torrents of water that had poured through the roof and turned
the earthen floor into a sea of mud.

Fitz was now 'exceedingly thin, quite like a skeleton … and with a slouch
straw hat and large moustache, I look more like Don Quixote than anybody
else'. Winter was approaching. Firewood was in short supply but Godley had

imported coal and, when the rains abated at the end of the month, he and Fanny were 'very comfortable' in their new house, the fire in the Sussex grate keeping them warm in the evenings. 'Our books are all in shelves covering one wall of the room completely,' Fitz wrote to William Vaux on 29 April:

and in ten days more we shall have the whole room panelled with the beautiful woods of the country. We have such a fire place and chimney piece as you never saw for magnitude except in a farmhouse. And though one room is very small I am certain in a week more it would do no discredit to a noble lady in Park Lane – as a boudoir.

He was constructing a terrace in front of the cottage and had excavated into the rock behind the house to make space for a backyard, 'so all the mess has gone aft'. He had improved the access, with 'a good road winding up to the house and a rustic bridge over the ravine'. He had planted 'dozens of fruit trees', was digging two acres of land for potatoes, and had begun 'to look around for pigs and poultry … Next year, when I have no building to do, I shall cultivate my five acres which are certain to yield a good return in vegetables … Living here does not cost one half what it does in England.'

The first April in Canterbury was mostly bright and warm with clear blue skies. By the end of the month, it had become 'very cold, as cold as winter in England, only exquisitely clear and bright'. While snow lay on the hills and ice formed in the puddles, the sun continued to shine from a cloudless sky and the nights were 'brilliant, the snow lying thick on the mountains on the far side of the harbour which looked grand with the moon shining on them'.

Every morning, after practising her music, Fanny walked down to the town and ambled on the beach with Charlotte Godley and her son, collecting shells and looking for oysters (Fitz told William Vaux that she was becoming 'as brown as a Maori but is furious when I tell her so'). She was expecting the arrival of the *Duke of Bronté* with her eldest brother William (her 'favourite of all the family') on board as ship's surgeon. Newly qualified as a doctor, he was travelling to Canterbury to remain close to Fanny and to look after his father's land.

The *Duke of Bronté* had sailed on 10 January and was five weeks overdue when a regatta was held on 24 May to celebrate Queen Victoria's birthday. There was no wind, so the races were confined to rowing. The first was for five-oared whaleboats manned by Maori. 'The sun was very hot,' wrote Charlotte, 'and the sea like glass, and the boats full of brown figures … with bare arms and shoulders; such eager faces watching Mr FitzGerald, who stood by the great ensign on the jetty, with a gun, which was fired for the signal to start.'

The next race was for four-oared boats. Edward Ward entered the yawl he had built, which he rowed himself with three of his workmen, 'dressed exactly alike in white jersey and trousers, and a red handkerchief round their heads. He won very easily, and it was really quite exciting to see him come in, in the midst of "tremendous applause" from the jetty.'

After the races, several hundred Maori performed a haka. This was followed by 'long speeches', after which Fitz and Fanny joined the Godleys for lunch. There were games in the afternoon – 'a soapy pig, a greased pole and a wheelbarrow race' – and a tea party for the children. Fanny made the tea 'in the boiler of a small furnace we have for washing', while 'order was preserved by our schoolmaster, a very tremendous gentleman who rather took away from our joviality'. Fitz joined the glee singers, who performed until dark, when the children were entertained by a magic-lantern show, 'each new slide received with shouts of delight'.

The party continued on board the *Travancore*, an immigrant ship which had arrived in Lyttelton a few weeks earlier. Dinner in the cuddy was followed by 'frantic and uproarious' dancing on deck. 'Such a merry evening I certainly never passed,' wrote Ward in his diary. 'I shall never forget the whirlwind of animal spirits let loose at that dancing party. Thorough, genuine enjoyment was in everybody's face.' Fitz and Fanny disembarked shortly before midnight, and walked uphill to their cottage through the starlit night.

…

Fitz was up early next morning; he was leaving for a visit to Pigeon Bay on Banks Peninsula. Godley had asked him to inspect the fledgling farms in the area, to assess the demand for agricultural labour. He travelled around the coast by boat ('sometimes sailing, sometimes rowing'), a journey which took half a day.

He stayed with the Sinclair family, who had settled in Pigeon Bay in 1843. Captain Sinclair drowned three years later but his family continued to live there, providing hospitality to visitors. Charlotte described them as 'very nice simple people, excessively Scotch, and old-fashioned, and live a regular colonial life … plenty of cows, and milk, and butter, and cream, and doing everything for themselves'. Their house was 'in a most lovely spot; it is in a little bay near the head of the harbour, which they have quite to themselves'. A stream ran under the windows, 'with cold clear water'; the garden was filled with flowers; and the hills behind the house were covered in 'thick bush, with fern trees, and birds singing so loud that they almost wake you in the morning'.

Fitz spent three days in the area. He returned to Lyttelton on the evening of the 28th with a present for Arthur Godley: a model ship ('a magnificent topsail schooner … three feet high') made by a whaler captain who had married into the Sinclair family. He arrived at the Godleys' house straight from the jetty, surprising the family at supper. Godley 'crept upstairs … and brought down Arthur in his nightgown and nearly asleep. He was in perfect raptures at finding himself the owner of a vessel with a rudder, several blocks and eight sails!'

The wet weather returned a few days later, with strong winds and hard frosts at night. In early June, when Fitz was suffering from 'one of his old winter coughs', he set off to inspect the farms on the plains. He visited 30 farms: he reported on the acreage prepared for cultivation and the crops planted ('potatoes, barley, oats, some wheat and maize, garden vegetables'), and found a 'great want of animals, particularly bullocks and horses'.

Fanny was staying with the Godleys when news arrived on the morning of 6 June that a ship had entered the harbour. The *Duke of Brontë* was now more than eight weeks overdue and Fanny was 'greatly excited'. She and Charlotte walked out along the unfinished road to Sumner, and 'spent a good deal of a very cold day to watch her beating up the harbour against a biting south-easter, all the high hills round covered with real snow … We watched her till the anchor was dropped just before sunset.'

It had been 'a long and arduous voyage' on the *Duke of Brontë*, particularly for William, a diffident young man who had never practised medicine before. And to Fanny's surprise, he was accompanied by George, one of their younger brothers, who had celebrated his thirteenth birthday on board ship. What upheavals in Woburn Square, she wondered, had given rise to this last-minute decision?

Fitz returned from the plains the following day. He visited the *Duke of Brontë*, where he found a woman in steerage in some distress. Elizabeth Waller's husband had been killed while the ship was loading at Blackwall and she had travelled alone to Canterbury with two small children, 'aged five and two and very naughty'. Fitz and Fanny were about to lose their servant – John Horrell had sailed for the newly discovered goldfields in Australia; his wife was leaving to open a school in Christchurch – so Elizabeth Waller and her children moved into the lean-to at the back of the cottage.

She proved to be an unsatisfactory servant, unable to cook and – the last straw for Fitz – placing his new hedging plants 'to dry on the stove'. When he could bear it no longer, he found her alternative work in a laundry and employed Mary Coster in her place, an efficient young woman who would soon become a valued friend.

Another immigrant ship arrived on 9 June and Godley accompanied the ship's surgeon to Fitz's cottage, where they dined on 'fried boiled beef and a mess of Maori cabbage and potatoes'. That night, the winds increased to gale force ('quite a hurricane'); and on the night of the 10th, 'a dreadful storm blew, rain, hail and sleet against the house, and thunder'. The storm lasted all the following day, 'the wind dashing the rain – and even the hail – through the shingles and weatherboards'. It was 'wretchedly cold'. Fanny complained of chilblains; Fitz suffered from his persistent cough.

The storm began to abate on the 12th, which was Arthur Godley's fourth birthday. Fitz and Fanny had promised to arrive for tea but the rain confined them to their cottage, 'so we lost our music, and Arthur the great excitement of seeing Mr F draw a ship, which, in consideration of the birthday, he had promised to do, if Arthur could be allowed to sit up'. Fitz was a favourite with the little boy: 'He draws ships … every part accurately, talking to the child … and Arthur is quite beside himself with delight … Mr F has only drawn for him twice, but the mere idea of his coming again is hailed with intense happiness.'

…

Edward Ward was now living on Quail Island on the far side of the harbour, where he and his brothers were building a house. On 21 June, he sailed his yawl across the harbour to dine with Fitz and Fanny (on 'roast beef – a great treat'). In the afternoon, Edward and Fanny walked down to the waterside, Charlotte joined them and they took the boat to a sheltered bay to collect mussels. On the homeward journey, it was agreed that Fanny and Charlotte should picnic at Quail Island three days later.

On the morning of 24 June, the two women took a boat across the choppy waters of the harbour. The weather was cold and blustery, 'blowing tolerably hard, very threatening for rain, the tops of the hills enveloped in clouds'. Planning to cook lunch on the beach, they had brought 'a clothes-basket of food', but Edward and his brother Henry were not at home. They had set out in the yawl the previous morning to collect firewood from the head of the harbour and had not returned. Hamilton, the youngest brother, asked to borrow the boat and he set off with two workmen, leaving Fanny and Charlotte alone on the beach. 'Our dinner-party was rather small and it was very cold,' wrote Charlotte:

> but we sat under shelter near our fire, and got a few shells on the beach, and then began to wonder why they did not come back. It was very rough for the little boat; the wind, too, against us going home; and I, who never like going in one if I can help it, was getting a little unhappy.

They stayed on the beach all afternoon. The wind increased towards evening but still the boat did not return. Then, 'just as it was getting dark, they came, the poor boy crying, and the men, who were extremely fond of their master, almost as bad'. They had found the yawl upturned on the beach, one of the oars nearby, the other floating some distance away, the gathered firewood 'all strewed about'. There was no sign of the brothers.

It was a sorrowful party that returned across the harbour that night, bringing Hamilton Ward to stay with the Godleys. Three days later, Edward's body was found washed ashore, on a day when Lyttelton was hit by the worst storm the infant colony had yet encountered, 'the wind blowing a perfect hurricane'. The gale continued for two days, stranding four ships and sinking two more. It was not until the 29th that the weather was calm enough to collect the body.

Edward was buried the following day, in the cemetery a few yards above Fitz's cottage on the hill. Henry's body was found two months later, recognisable only by his clothes. As Fitz wrote in the *Lyttelton Times*, the loss of the brothers was 'the saddest event' in the life of the colony, throwing 'an indescribable gloom over the whole settlement'.

...

It was now midwinter, with 'pouring wet weather and such muddy roads, very unfavourable for slipping about in the dark up and down these muddy hills'. When a ball was arranged in the store on 31 July, Fitz and Fanny declined their invitation 'on account of the terrible state of the hill up to their house'. Charlotte climbed the hill with 'a long stick (without which you must not expect to be able to stand upright anywhere but on level gravel)' and told Fanny that 'as dancing ladies were very scarce, she ought to consider it a sort of duty to attend … and that she could come down by daylight and dress and sleep at our house, and so it was arranged'.

Fitz and Fanny were late arriving ('he is almost always late') and 'came sliding in' at seven o'clock. It was still pouring with rain and 'there was a great deal of groaning as the time approached for the start'. At eight o'clock, the two couples 'splashed through the mud' carrying a lantern. 'The flags of all the ships tapestried the … ballroom,' wrote Charlotte. 'We had loads of evergreens, and calico roses, pink and white; and a good many candles, and a tolerable boarded floor.' Music was provided by a schoolmaster on the piano, and a policeman 'played alternately on the flageolet and violin'.

Winter came to an end in early September, with 'a warm summer wind and threatenings of dust'. At the end of the month, a ship arrived with copies of the *New Zealand Journal*, a newspaper published in London on 7 June, which included transcripts of Fanny's letters to her mother. This caused 'great and general excitement' in Lyttelton, but Fanny was 'very much annoyed at having little incidents, which she had only repeated to let them know exactly how her life passed here, exhibited to the public'. She told Charlotte that she felt 'very foolish', particularly when Godley teased her about it.

CHAPTER ELEVEN

Sheep, Sheep, Sheep
1851–1852

I cannot overstate the advantages of going into sheep farming
immediately on as large a scale as possible.
Fitz, 2 September 1851

I am the father of a female girl.
Fitz, 20 February 1852

Fanny was now four months pregnant – the child conceived towards
the end of May (about the time of the high-spirited party on the
Travancore) – and she and Fitz were comfortably settled in their cottage on
the hill, having 'spent a great deal upon it'. They had made 'a beautiful garden'
and, now it was spring, they could sit outside in the evenings, watching the
hills on the far side of the harbour glow red from the setting sun.

Fitz had found a new obsession. He was convinced that sheep (arriving in
large numbers from Australia) were the answer to his financial problems. 'The
next step in the progress of the colony,' he wrote in early September, 'will be
filling up the whole country with *sheep – sheep – sheep*.' Sheep farming was,
he continued, the only route to riches: 'money may be literally coined in that
trade.' He was also attracted to the lifestyle:

> I long to be off to a sheep station in these most splendid plains. I
> cannot conceive a more glorious life … It is eminently the profession
> of a gentleman. The sheep farmer may have his comfortable house
> and gardens and a little farm producing all he requires, but his
> personal task is to ride about the country inspecting his vast flocks
> and giving directions for their management.

A sheep station required an injection of capital, estimated by Fitz at a
minimum of £2000. During August and September, he fired off letters to
Lucius, William Vaux, his brother in India (who replied that he was in debt

104

and had no money), and Henry Selfe, a friend and relative by marriage whom he had persuaded to buy land in Canterbury:

> It is very cruel that I must sit still with a meagre and precarious income and see all this done and not be able to join in it. I am writing to everyone I can think of to try and raise £2000 to get a station ... I could readily afford to pay ten per cent for the money and pay it all off in four or five years. But if I do not get it soon, all the valuable runs in the country will be taken up ... It is the most disgusting thing in the world to be compelled to sit by and do nothing as a duty government official when real prizes are in the market ... It is melancholy to see others reap the profits of this settlement when I have toiled so hard for its foundation.

Planning to enter into partnership with William Draper, and hoping his letters would produce sufficient capital, Fitz and William set off in late August 'to look for runs'. William had been licensed to work as a doctor in Lyttelton but, nervous and fearful of the responsibility, had given up medicine and was living on his father's land at Purau Bay, 'where he means to keep cows and sheep'. His young brother George was with him, 'cleaning the knives, fetching wood, and otherwise making himself useful'.

By early September, Fitz had persuaded William to join him in taking 'one of the finest runs in the country, containing everything, about 50 miles inland. It is large enough for him and for me too.' So he wrote again to Lucius: 'Now you really must get your wits to work to beg, borrow or steal £2000 for me.'

An old acquaintance of the Draper family, a Mr Jackson, now arrived in Canterbury with capital to invest. William enlisted him into the scheme and, on 15 October, a licence for a 20,000-acre station at Easedale Nook was issued to Jackson and Draper in partnership. Two days earlier, when Fitz and Fanny dined with the Godleys, Fitz had spoken enthusiastically about the project – but the Godleys were unimpressed. 'We are very angry with Mr FitzGerald,' Charlotte wrote next morning:

> He has, I believe, quite settled to go off in the wildest possible way and join a sort of picnic sheep station. He is always ... after something new, and now feels behind-hand because he cannot dive into all the barbarity of a station, for the mere fun of it ... the whole party are to live up at the station together ... and the ladies are to help in the work, all as uncomfortable as possible. Conceive living in the rough, in that way, under other people's command. Mr Jackson will be *en chef*, and Mrs FitzGerald, who has known [him] since she was a

child … says he is a most disagreeable man to deal with … I am quite
vexed about it for her, but her husband will hear no reason … It is a
most foolish plan, and, of course, falls most hardly upon her.

On 23 November, Fitz and William rode across the plains to inspect the
station at Easedale Nook, travelling northwest up the banks of the Waimakariri
River towards the foothills of the Alps. It took two days to reach the run,
which lay at the base of the foothills. Fitz stopped from time to time to paint
the views, and they spent the nights at sheep stations. They returned home in
early December.

On the 16th, there were great celebrations for the first anniversary of the
arrival of the *Charlotte Jane*. Crowds of people made their way to Christchurch
to enjoy cricket matches, races and wrestling bouts. It was 'a hot day, with a
good deal of dust and blow', so Fitz and Fanny stayed home and Fitz painted
a view of the cottage in the midsummer heat, an anniversary painting. Three
days later, he wrote to Gladstone:

> I venture to hope that, amid all your important and pressing busi-
> ness, you have not forgotten my name … Although you never took
> any part in Canterbury, you will, I know, be pleased to hear from a
> resident colonist the complete success of the settlement, so far as
> its physical advancement is concerned … I would not change this
> colony for any I have read of or imagined. I rest convinced that, of all
> the English Colonies, this will see the greatest destiny. It is the most
> glorious country. It is perfectly adapted to the English race.

No offers of money had arrived from England and Fitz was becoming
impatient. 'If you could help with Lucius and devise any means of getting me
£2000 or £3000,' he wrote to Henry Selfe on 19 January 1852, 'you would do
the wisest thing you could for the lenders as well as myself. I was going up to
a run with William Draper but I cannot manage it till I hear from England
at all events.'

In the past, Fitz had referred to his brother-in-law as 'a capital fellow, a
most useful colonist in every way'. Now he was changing his mind. 'My own
movements are again undecided,' he wrote to William Vaux on the 23rd:

> I find [William] so undecided, so utterly unfit to manage the affairs
> of a settler's life that I have withdrawn from the affair. He is always
> dissatisfied with everything he does and would not take my advice.
> He takes six persons' opinion in one day and wants to act upon all
> together … and is still quite undecided what to do. I am therefore

waiting till I hear from you and others … to see if I can raise means to start a sheep run myself.

He was having problems with William's family too. Almost every ship from England brought letters from Woburn Square, 'begging' Fitz and Fanny to apologise to her father. Fitz expressed his anger in a letter to William Vaux:

Nothing should ever induce me to speak to or hold any communication of any sort whatsoever with that man again … Nothing shall prevail upon me ever to meet him in this world, let him be dead as far as we are concerned. I have no doubt and never had any that he would torment himself to death about my marriage … With respect to Fanny I have told her I shall not permit her ever to write to her Father in reference to what is past. Should he wish to hear from her as though nothing had happened, of course I shall not think it right to keep father and daughter separate, but I shall not permit her to acknowledge that I or she have done anything wrong.

She entirely agreed with me in this view as indeed we agree in everything. It is not possible for two persons to [be] more completely of one mind in everything. Will you therefore suggest to the family that no more letters must be written to Fanny at all on the subject of the scenes before her marriage: I should be deeply distressed to stop all correspondence between her and her family, but I will not allow this subject to be a matter of any further communication.

This was not so easy. Fanny's mother continued to write long letters, 'all about the old story', and Fanny's brother John wrote a 'violent and impertinent' letter explaining that he would never write to Fanny until she had made amends with her father. John's letter arrived in early February 1852, after which Fitz wrote two letters.

The first was to Fanny's mother, informing her that 'any further allusion to the subject must conclude Fanny's correspondence for ever with her family'. The second was to William Vaux:

As for me, until he has made reparation on his bended knees for all his insults to her … I would see him in [hell] before I would go into the same house with him … If I can't prevent him making his own home wretched I will take good care he shall not pollute mine … No man shall interfere with my family. I would shoot him like a dog before I would allow it to be inoculated with the blackguardism of the scenes in Woburn Square.

Fanny's pregnancy was now close to full-term. Fitz wrote that she was 'very well', although she was finding it difficult to walk uphill in the midsummer heat. He thought it best 'to keep her moving about until the last moment' and she was still 'doing a great deal' on 18 February. Two days later, Fitz wrote another – triumphant – letter to William Vaux:

> Go to, thou Patriarch. I am the father of a female girl … Nurses and friends persist in pronouncing it a most beautiful child whether from an acuter perception of the merits of newly born infants than I can boast of, or to win the regard of credulous parents, I know not. I can simply pronounce that it is as fat as a Dutch Alderman … It eats voraciously, drinks hugely, and sleeps immeasurably – to which I may add that it snores like a tipsy guardsman … Fanny is … wonderfully well and will I have no doubt be up and about in a week. So here we are; one joy, and one care more in the world.

…

The Godleys were spending the summer months at Riccarton, two miles west of Christchurch. The area was settled in 1843 by two Deans brothers from Scotland, who built a homestead and farmed the land. William Deans drowned in July 1851 on a voyage to Australia to buy sheep; John left Canterbury six months later on a visit home to Scotland. So the Godleys had Riccarton to themselves and, soon after Fanny's confinement, they sent Charlotte's servant, Mary Powles, to inspect the new arrival. 'Tell Mrs FitzGerald,' Godley wrote to Fitz on 24 February, 'that Powles says hers is the "loveliest baby she ever saw".'

In March, Sir George Grey arrived in Lyttelton and Fitz entertained him to dinner. The two men were political enemies but Grey's behaviour was, according to Charlotte, 'quite irresistibly gracious and good-humoured – I believe that is his "line" when there has occurred anything unpleasant'. The governor congratulated Fitz on the progress of Canterbury and informed him that 'Provincial Govt. will be established among us probably before the end of the year and that all the appointments will be given up to the provinces except the few chief ones'.

'*Entirely* between ourselves,' Fitz wrote to Henry Selfe on the 25th, 'Godley is very anxious that I shall become the Colonial Secretary[1] and if I thought there was a chance of that I would remain here instead of going up to a sheep station. I think I have a good chance as I am almost the only person here who has had an official education.'

A few days later, he took his family to join the Godleys at Riccarton, a

---

1   Equivalent to prime minister of the colony

journey of twelve miles. With Fanny on horseback, the baby in her arms, they climbed the Bridle Path, clambered down the other side, and crossed the river on the ferry punt. A road had been completed from Heathcote to Christchurch ('with houses, gardens and cultivation in sight all the way along'); another road took them from Christchurch to Riccarton.

Fitz had visited the area before; he had painted two small wooden shacks, 'the residence of J Deans Esq'. Now he and Fanny found the Godleys established in 'a wooden house with two rooms … a hired tent, which is servants' hall and kitchen, with a fire out of doors, and a single tent … which is our storeroom and pantry … as rustic as anything you can imagine'. There was a garden with fruit trees, and fields planted with potatoes and corn. In front of the hut was the Avon River, 'deep, clear and cold', with ducks and geese. At the back was an area of native bush 'full of birds singing all day, *tuis* and bell-birds and NZ robins, which are little black and grey birds which light down close to you, like the tamest of English robins in cold weather – and such lovely little green parrots that look so foreign'.

This was the first time Fanny had visited the plains. She was enchanted by the open spaces, the golden tussock 'waving like a sea in the breeze', stretching into the distance as far as the eye could see. On clear nights, the stars shone brightly, the silence punctuated by the hooting of owls. Because of mosquitoes, it was unwise to sit outside after dark although, according to Charlotte, it helped 'to smear yourself perpetually with oil and turpentine, mixed, which is a very dirtying process, even if you don't mind the smell'.

They woke early in the mornings, and went to bed 'almost as soon as it gets dark'. Fanny tended her baby and played with Arthur Godley, and she and Charlotte cooked meals over the campfire. Fitz sketched the hut and the tents, and when Godley returned from work, the two men would sit 'by the fern-fringed stream and talk of the great future to come'.

On Sunday 4 April, they walked to the tiny wooden church of St Michael and All Angels in Christchurch. After the service, the clergyman baptised six babies, including six-week-old Amy FitzGerald, all of them 'crying tremendously' at the font. Next day, Fitz and Fanny returned to Lyttelton.

The Godleys followed in mid-May, in time for the celebrations for Queen Victoria's birthday. There was another regatta (with poignant memories of Edward Ward in his red bandanna), tea parties, dinners, and a 'grand ball' in the evening. Fanny and Charlotte served tea to more than a hundred children, who sang 'God Save the Queen' and 'cheered for us until we were glad to escape'. It was a beautiful sunny day and 'everyone looked so happy walking about in their holiday clothes'.

Three weeks later, Charlotte gave birth to a daughter. 'The little girl is quite funnily like her father,' she wrote. 'Mrs FitzGerald has just been laughing at her.'

…

Fitz was still fretting at his lack of money, still concerned that he might never raise the capital for a sheep station. In February, he had written to Henry Selfe about another plan:

> I am waiting anxiously to know whether you will, together with all those to whom I have written, be able to send me money enough to set up a sheep station. If not I have proposed to Lucius to try and borrow money to buy the *Lyttelton Times* … If I cannot get on to a sheep station I should like to take the newspaper as a piece of property and work it – but I long to be away from all politics and business.

His next temptation was the goldfields in Australia. 'People are leaving the settlement in droves,' he wrote to William Vaux in August. 'I confess if I were not a married man, I would follow the herd and be off to the diggings … Fellows come down here tossing their nuggets about, bidding at auctions for things they don't want, in a filthy state of intoxication, at prices they care not what.'

He had recently lost one of his major roles in the settlement. The Society of Land Purchasers had been dissolved in April, mainly because its members were either too busy or too distant on their stations. As early as July 1851, it was reported to be 'in a state of discord amounting almost to disorganisation'. In May 1852, a member described how 'step by step it grew enfeebled … until, reduced to its Chairman and Secretary meeting merely to look at each other across the table, it finally departed this world one fine afternoon at the Land Office at Christchurch'.

A few weeks later, it was reconstituted as a social club – the Lyttelton Colonists Society – with meetings held once a fortnight 'for the consideration and discussion of matters of social and political interest'. Godley gave a talk on the history of New Zealand, a doctor spoke about scientific matters, and a clergyman lectured on the Reformation. Fitz intended to speak on 'the rise and progress of constitutional government in England', but had to cancel because of an attack of conjunctivitis. 'My eyes have been very troublesome,' he told Henry Selfe in June, 'so that I cannot write at night.'

He had leased another seven acres of land adjacent to the cottage and was fencing it in ('at vast expense'), seeding it with grass, and building a cowshed and stockyard ('operations which have taken all my own funds'). The work was complete by the end of July, by which time it was winter again and icy winds were finding their way through the doors and windows of the cottage. 'The great mistake people make is to imagine that this place is not cold,' he complained. 'Last night was as cold a night as I ever felt. It was bitter.'

On 31 July another immigrant ship, the *Samarang*, dropped anchor in the harbour. It took time to unload the cargo, including the bundles of mail, so letters were not available for collection until several days later. Among them was a letter from Henry Selfe, who had finally succumbed to Fitz's begging letters and agreed to lend him £1600 for a sheep station.

Fitz was now uncertain about the site of the station, as well as the advisability of giving up public office. 'A readjustment of the offices of government will soon be made,' he replied on 9 August:

> and they urge me very strongly not to go up the country but to
> stay here. All seem to wish me to stay. If I do stay and continue
> in some government employment, I will form a small station near
> Christchurch and keep a stockman on it, riding over to see it once
> a fortnight. I shall see my way clearly in another month, by which
> time I earnestly hope I shall have the use of the money you speak of,
> for I know it will make a splendid investment.

Because of the influx of hungry men into the goldfields, sheep from Australia had become more costly and difficult to obtain. He therefore decided to stock cattle instead, 'to sell the milk, getting the calves as fast as possible'. On 23 August, the *Duke of Roxburgh* arrived from Sydney with 63 head of cattle, 'young cows in calf of the finest sort, first-rate heifers of the short-horned Durham breed. They will pay, if not as well, nearly as well as sheep. I am offered the cows at £9 a head; the bull is worth 50gns.'

Fitz bought 50 cows. He also bought the bull, an expensive animal which died shortly after landing. He pastured the cows on a run belonging to Richard Harman and persuaded Harman and his partner (Cyrus Davie) to join him in leasing an adjoining run, 9000 acres of land close to Lake Ellesmere, sixteen miles southwest of Christchurch. The three men would lease the run in partnership – but it was Fitz who would work the land.

As soon as the formalities were completed, he suffered another 'severe attack in the eyes' and became 'more and more anxious to get out of official life which would blind me in a few years'. He also suffered an attack of lumbago, which confined him to the house for more than a week. This gave him the opportunity to write again to Henry Selfe. He had bought cattle instead of sheep, he explained, 'because I could not get sheep … They were first rate cattle … and I thought it better to buy something than to let the money lie idle.'

Also, 'cattle are much the *safest* because they do not get diseased like sheep.'

Selfe had been generous. His loan, worth almost £100,000 in today's values, came entirely from his own pocket. 'The bargain I will make with you is this,' Fitz continued:

> I will keep a regular account debtor and creditor of all I receive *from* you or *for* you, and of all I spend, just as if I were your agent. At the end of the time, you shall divide the profits with me … that is, you shall get back your money with eight per cent interest on it. I will take the remainder … Unless I receive instructions from you to the contrary I shall continue to invest all the profits in fresh stock so as to make the farm as large as possible. Then at any time you like I will begin to transmit the proceeds to you in liquidation of the debt.

He sent Selfe an IOU for £1600, the loan to be repaid four years later. He had, he wrote, 'no doubt but that I shall be able to meet the enclosed bill but [also] to have a good cattle station for myself. And I may be able to persuade you to leave the debt on the station and let me pay an income from it.'

Fitz began work on the station as soon as he recovered from lumbago, often camping overnight on the plains. He hired a stockman and his wife, and with the help of 'five men and a carpenter', he burnt off an area of land and began to build 'a good house of sods, the simple turfs cut from the surface'. He affixed wooden shingles to the roof and inserted iron windows into the walls. He bought two bulls, eleven more cows ('ready to calve in about two months'), dairy equipment and cheese presses.

In Lyttelton, Fanny was 'very tired … very hard worked indeed'. Mary Coster had left the cottage to marry a carpenter in Christchurch and, without a servant to help with the washing and cooking, she felt 'a complete prisoner' in the house. Fitz would soon be without a salary ('a very precarious position') – but nothing could detract from the joy of their marriage.

'Fanny abuses me because I always write about sheep and cattle and not about our beautiful little child,' Fitz wrote to William Vaux. 'It is a very dear little animal, and has got some teeth, by the time this reaches you it will be beginning to walk … We were married two years yesterday – two years I would live over again twenty times if I could and not change a minute of one of them.'

PART III

Fitz becomes a politician

CHAPTER TWELVE

A Boy out of School

1852–1853

I should very much like to be the first Superintendent for Canterbury.

Fitz, October 1852

I would so much rather he were a cow keeper.

Fanny, 22 March 1853

*T*he Canterbury Association had been acting as a sort of absentee landlord, sending long letters of instructions with little knowledge of how matters stood in New Zealand. According to Godley, these letters were 'unreasonable and inconsiderate … inexpressively comic'. According to Fitz, they were 'the most childish and ridiculous compositions possible'.

At the same time, there was 'a growing spirit of discontent', which had begun only a few months after the arrival of the first ships. 'The colonists are beginning to take an active and eager interest in their own affairs,' Fitz wrote to Lord Lyttelton in July 1851. 'But along with this spirit is arising a spirit of hostility to the Association.'

A meeting had been called to debate whether paid officers of the association should be prevented from sitting on the committee. Fitz found this 'deeply humiliating to myself, that I, who worked at the Colonial Reform Society … should find myself in a position of antagonism to my fellow colonists, looked upon with jealousy as the agent for a distant body'.

At the meeting on 28 July, Fitz made a good impression on his fellow colonists, 'speaking with much humour and sometimes with almost poetical eloquence'. Matters failed to improve and, by August 1852, he decided not to continue in what he referred to as 'government employment'. He resigned as immigration agent and continued to feel that he had been treated shabbily. 'The Association here are breaking up the greatest part of their establishment,' he wrote to William Vaux. 'I among others are quitting their service … wholly between ourselves … I do think as a matter of justice and honour, that sent out as I was from England, I was the last person who ought to have been struck off the staff.'

Two months later, he received a letter from Gladstone dated 18 June: 'A Bill … upon the whole a good Bill … passed one House last night and in ten days will probably be law.' This was the New Zealand Constitution Act, drafted by several members of the Society for the Reform of Colonial Government, including Wakefield. It provided for local self-government in New Zealand, as well as for a central parliament.

Under the Act, the six provinces (Auckland, Taranaki, Nelson, Wellington, Canterbury and Otago) would each be governed by an elected provincial council headed by a superintendent. The central parliament (the general assembly) would pass legislation affecting the whole colony. It would consist of a House of Representatives, with members elected on a minimum property franchise, and an upper chamber (the Legislative Council), with members appointed by the governor. The governor also had the right to call and dismiss the assembly.

News of the Act arrived in New Zealand in October 1852 and was greeted in Canterbury with 'universal satisfaction'. News also arrived that the association had resolved to cease operations, prompting Godley to announce his departure for England at the end of the year. According to Fitz, this was 'a public calamity' and, on 10 November, he drafted a petition asking him to change his mind, to stay in Canterbury and stand for election as first superintendent of the province. Godley declined. 'The people here are so anxious for me to stay,' he wrote to a friend in London, 'that it is not without some hesitation and remorse that I refuse … FitzGerald will, I hope, be the successful candidate for the Superintendency.'

The Constitution Act renewed Fitz's enthusiasm for politics and, encouraged by Godley, he changed his mind about abandoning public life. 'I confess that I should very much like to be first Superintendent,' he wrote to Henry Selfe, 'and on the whole, I think I shall have the best chance.' He also decided to stand for the general assembly, explaining on 15 November that he had 'acceded to the request of a large number of the electors of Lyttelton to stand for that place'.

He spent the next three weeks preparing a parting gift for his friend to take home to England. He had already painted several views of Canterbury and, during the final days before Godley's departure, he made a further 22 watercolours, all of which he annotated in detail and bound together in a presentation album.

His first stop was Banks Peninsula. He left Lyttelton on 16 November, travelling by boat around the coast to Pigeon Bay. He stayed overnight with the Sinclair family, then borrowed a horse to ride over the hills to Akaroa, a journey of nine miles through thick bush. He spent two nights in Akaroa, staying with the resident magistrate in his 'snug little cottage half a mile from the beach', and returned to Lyttelton on the 20th.

He left again four days later, this time riding into the foothills of the Alps. He painted the sheep stations that Godley had visited, together with views from the banks of the Waimakariri River. He arrived home in early December and, three days later, was off again, this time to Christchurch, where he painted the Land Office and the bridge over the Avon.

...

On 16 December, the Pilgrims celebrated their second anniversary with horse races, a cricket match, a horticultural show and a ball in the Land Office. Two days later, a farewell breakfast was held in a marquee in Christchurch. One hundred and fifty people attended the banquet and, after a toast to 'Mr and Mrs Godley and may health, happiness, and every blessing attend them', Godley rose to his feet to make his farewell speech to Canterbury:

> For the last five years, ever since the plan of founding a settlement of Church people in New Zealand was first suggested to me, I think I may say almost without exaggeration that the thought of it has hardly been for a moment out of my mind ... No man in this world can go through any enterprise that has greatness in it without being often and sorely disappointed, because nothing great is ever done without enthusiasm, and enthusiasts are often over-sanguine ...
>
> When I first adopted, and made my own, the idea of this colony, it pictured itself to my mind in the colours of a Utopia. Now that I have been a practical coloniser, and have seen how these things are managed in fact, I often smile when I think of the ideal Canterbury of which our imagination dreamed. Yet I see nothing in the dream to regret or be ashamed of, and I am quite sure that without the enthusiasm, the poetry, the unreality (if you will), with which our scheme was overlaid, it would never have been accomplished.

On the morning of 22 December, the Godleys embarked on the *Hashemy*. Fitz and Fanny accompanied them on board. It was, in Godley's words, 'a most painful leave-taking'. Fitz handed over his album of paintings and, two years after they had fallen into each other's arms on the dusty street, the two men embraced once more, this time in farewell.

Fitz was losing a friend as well as a colleague, the one man on whom he could rely for support and encouragement. In January, he gave up his editorial duties at the *Lyttelton Times* and complained to Henry Selfe that 'Godley's going away unfitted me for a time for all occupation whatsoever'. His enthusiasm for the station was diminished and he wrote of 'the disappointments and misadventures, troubles and anxieties of starting a large concern … in the interior which I cannot look after myself except occasionally and where everything, even wood, has to be carted 20 miles'.

The house at the station was almost complete; the dairy equipped with 'large milk trundles, churns, cheese presses, vats and so on'. He had fenced in three acres of land and planted an acre and a half in potatoes, 'which cost a great deal but I was alarmed at the high price of flour and I think I shall save a good deal next year by having the potatoes to fall back on'. He had built a stockyard and cowshed, and bought a dogcart with 'two good mares which go in the cart and are used for riding in the stock and are both in foal by a thoroughbred horse'. 'We are going up to the station the moment the home is sufficiently finished for us,' he wrote on 6 January, 'and shall most likely always live there in future.'

Seventeen days later, he sat alone in the cottage on the hill, writing a letter to Godley 'amid bare walls, all my goods gone or going, my wife and child gone. I am alone for my last night in Lyttelton.' He had tried to persuade Fanny to stay in Lyttelton until the new house was made comfortable, 'but she would not; she would come with me'. Their possessions had been shipped around the coast to Sumner and transferred onto bullock drays for the five-mile journey to Christchurch. Fanny and the baby had travelled with them.

Fitz left the cottage for the last time on the morning of 24 January 1853, riding over the hills to Christchurch to join Fanny, who was staying with friends. He had bought her a pony called Midge ('the most beautiful creature I have seen in the country, as nimble and surefooted as any beast I ever saw'), on which Fanny rode sidesaddle, delighted at last to wear the riding habit with

Fanny on her pony Midge, mounted sidesaddle and wearing the riding habit she had brought with her from London. Fitz referred to Midge as 'the most beautiful creature … as nimble and surefooted as any beast I ever saw'.

Private collection

its long skirts which she had so carefully packed up in London and brought with her on the voyage.

Bullock drays carried the luggage to the station, Fitz drove the dogcart, and Fanny rode alongside on Midge, the first time the pony had 'ever carried a lady'. The Canterbury Plains lay ahead of them, extending to the far horizon, 'as level as the sea, one uniform colour of yellow tussock'. Fitz had marked out a track but, apart from these wooden poles, 'there was nothing between us and the distant horizon to mark the direction in which we had to go, nothing to prevent our straying miles and miles out of our way'.

The Springs station lay 'among the swamps' near Lake Ellesmere, named by Fitz after the springs of 'clear cold water' which bubbled up in the 'slow, deep, sluggish stream' near the house. 'As to the scenery,' he wrote to Lucius:

> you must imagine a dead level plain on one side, of a brownish hue from the long grass lit by the sun, and stretching 40 or 50 miles away to the Snowy Range [the Southern Alps]; on the other, about five miles to the hills of the Banks peninsula, but the bright green of this part shows that it is all swamp. The swamps bound my run on two sides for miles.

The house was still 'a mere sod-walled barrack' and, during the next few weeks, he worked 'like a labourer from morning to night ... my own carpenter, plasterer and upholsterer'. On 20 February, he wrote again to Godley:

> Here we are and both I and my wife are far happier than at Lyttelton ... We are all in a mess but for a station very comfortable. I have a loft for a bedroom, a little room floored and papered for a dressing room, a good kitchen and first-rate dairy. Within a month we shall have a beautiful little parlour with all the household gods set on their pedestals ... My wife and child are quite well, Fanny indeed much better than at Lyttelton which seemed to disagree with her more and more. The little one leads a life which is one continual ecstasy at the dogs, cows, pigs and cats.

'I am blest with one of the rarest companions God ever gave a man for a wife,' he wrote to Henry Selfe five days later:

> A settler's wife must not *bear* or *put up* with difficulties and deprivations. To be perfect she must be blind to them or enjoy them. My wife has no servant nor anywhere to lodge one if she had. We have a first rate farm couple – the old woman a treasure in the dairy – but the dairy and cooking occupies all her time. Fanny has therefore to

be her own servant and nurse her child and even make all its clothes. And her trouble repaid by the cleanest, merriest, healthiest child you ever saw – one year old yesterday.

Fanny, now pregnant with their second child, was enjoying life at the station:

It is very jolly indeed up here far away from everybody and we are all very happy indeed. Amy flourishes most wonderfully and is very fat … We are in a great muddle, the house being quite unfinished; we are drenched in wet weather of which we have had plenty.

Pigs were a new enthusiasm. Fitz had twelve, which he allowed to forage in the swamps around the station ('by giving them a little whey and buttermilk morning and evening, they come back to the house and are quite tame'). He hoped to keep several hundred, 'so as to make great quantities of salt pork and bacon … the swamps affording food for an infinite number of pigs and also being the resort of wild pigs on which we partly depend for food'. These wild pigs, descended from animals brought to New Zealand by Captain Cook, were hunted with dogs. Fanny thought the flesh tasted 'more like goose than pork'.

Fitz was fully occupied on the station: 'What with thatching, plastering, papering, carpentering, making cheese, and looking after the stock, I am having a busy time of it from morning to night.' Once a week he left the station before dawn, the dogcart loaded with butter and cheese for the market in Christchurch. He suffered a bout of rheumatism in February which caused 'much anguish', and during a spell of wet weather in March, he was 'laid up

The Springs station in 1857. 'It is very jolly indeed up here,' Fanny wrote in 1852, 'far away from everybody and we are all very happy.' As for Fitz, 'I was *never* so happy in my life … I am like a boy out of school.'

Private collection

with rheumatism and boils on his hands so bad that he cannot write'. He also lost his entire potato crop, 'a great loss. I suppose the potatoes were put in too late and the ground was too raw.'

But nothing could destroy his high spirits during these early months at the station. 'I cannot tell you how happy I am to have escaped offices and office life altogether,' he wrote to Lucius on 21 March. 'If I did not owe Selfe money, I should regard myself a

A wider view of the Springs station in 1857 (from a damaged ambrotype).

Private collection

rich man.' Two days later, he wrote to Godley: 'I was *never* so happy in my life. Since 1844 I have been tied to the desk – now I am like a boy out of school.'

. . .

Another reason Fitz was happy to be on his station was the arrival of Edward Gibbon Wakefield. He and Wakefield had parted on bad terms in 1850; and they had recently conducted an acrimonious correspondence in the pages of the *Wellington Spectator*.

Wakefield had fired the opening shots. His letter, published on 5 January, referred to Fitz's idea for colonial self-government as 'so palpably a trick that it might almost pass for a joke'. He accused him of being 'insanely jealous' of the association and wrote that 'such total unreason' in a man 'of such ability … confounds me with astonishment'. Fitz replied a few days later, complaining that publication of Wakefield's letter was 'a gross breach of trust'. He then published both letters in the *Lyttelton Times*, leaving 'the public to judge' whether he 'acted rightly'.

Wakefield, who came to live in the colony he had helped to create, arrived in Lyttelton on 2 February, accompanied by the lawyer Henry Sewell, whose mission was to wind up the affairs of the association in Canterbury and transfer its assets and liabilities to the newly created province. Fitz, who loathed his old mentor, had an equally low opinion of Sewell ('a mere country attorney … not fit to tie Godley's shoestrings') – a compliment repaid by Sewell, who referred to Fitz as 'wild and harum-scarum … as unstable as water'.

Using the excuse of a boil on his nether regions which made it painful to ride a horse, Fitz avoided the two men for almost three weeks. When he could prevaricate no longer, he rode into Lyttelton on the morning of

22 February. The meeting in the Mitre Hotel was outwardly friendly ('we met very cordially') but Fitz was uncomfortable and, when Wakefield offered to help Canterbury make peace with the governor, he handled the offer – according to Sewell – 'like a hotplate, afraid to burn his fingers'. He returned to the station, complaining that Wakefield was 'desperate and profligate' and Sewell 'a man of singularly limited abilities'.

Six days later, Wakefield and Sewell left for Wellington. During the next three months, Fitz was again embroiled in correspondence, this time with Henry Sewell; the letters were published in the *Lyttelton Times*. Fitz was 'highly indignant' that Wakefield was making abusive comments about Godley's performance in Canterbury. Sewell took exception to what he called the 'hostile tone' of Fitz's letters, and his 'exaggerated and inappropriate language'.

...

Fitz's rheumatism continued through the autumn and early winter as the province geared up for the election of its first superintendent. He was already showing signs of the ambivalence that would blight his political career. 'It is a great sacrifice to give up public life for which I am most fitted,' he wrote to Godley, 'but my maxim has always been that a pauper ought not to be a politician. I much regret having stood for the Superintendency.' He also wrote to Lord Lyttelton, a letter that misrepresented the facts:

> It would give me the greatest pleasure to lose the election. I was very anxious not to stand and only did so in compliance with the most earnest applications. It will be a great loss to me to leave my business here and devote myself to politics. With my cows and pigs and buildings and gardens, I am happier than I have been for years … Besides, until I effect an independence, I cannot afford it. In a few years I shall be independent, if not rich, and then I can take to public work.

He concluded with a perceptive comment, a brief – and rare – moment of self-knowledge. It had been his duty to stand for the superintendency, he wrote, 'and I am not, of course, without ambition'. However, 'I am violating a principle of which I am convinced, that no man can successfully or usefully engage in a political career who is not independent in his circumstances. It is a great conflict of opposite courses.'

In London, Fitz had played on the fringes of politics. Now he had a chance to become a politician himself, to lead the province that had absorbed his attention for almost three years. It was an ambition that, despite his lack of money, he was unable to resist. Fanny – who understood her husband – had misgivings. 'I fear more than ever that James will be chosen Superintendent,' she wrote. 'I would so much rather he were a cow keeper.'

By June, Fitz had forgotten his doubts, 'my anxiety to be returned as the first Superintendent getting stronger every day'. But he remained out of public sight, as did his rival candidate, Henry Tancred. 'I did not canvas,' Fitz explained (not entirely truthfully) to Godley:

> My absence at the station left me almost in ignorance at what was going on. Tancred ... was equally indifferent. In fact we thought that the people were willing to elect one of us for our personal merits and the settlement would be equally well served in either case ... neither of us was very anxious for the honour.

It was not until 16 July, two days before nomination day, that Fitz finally made the journey to Christchurch. Hustings were set up outside the Land Office and a large crowd assembled at midday on the 18th. Proceedings began at one o'clock. Fitz was proposed first, then Tancred, and finally Colonel Campbell, a 70-year-old veteran of the Napoleonic Wars. Campbell, who had based himself

'Christchurch election for the first Superintendent'. Nomination day, 18 July 1853. Drawing by Dr Alfred Barker, sketched from an upstairs window in his house.

Canterbury Museum (Dr A.C. Barker Collection)

in Akaroa, had been appointed by Sir George Grey to act as commissioner of crown lands in the province (land outside the Canterbury block). He was, according to the *Lyttelton Times*, 'a most surprisingly incapable man'.

Land prices were the main bone of contention. Fitz and Tancred were in favour of Wakefield's 'sufficient price' for land in the Canterbury block, believing the high price of £3 an acre to be necessary, not only to pay for infrastructure and immigration, but also to prevent working-class immigrants buying their own land too quickly and depleting the labour supply. Campbell supported the governor's policy of cheap land – Grey had set a price of ten shillings an acre for crown lands.

The candidates gave their speeches in order of nomination. Fitz spoke for almost an hour. 'The office which you are about to confer,' he began:

> is one which it will never fall to your lot to bestow upon any future occasion. Many a candidate will stand before you on this spot, many a time will you exercise the high privilege you have recently acquired, but never again will you elect the first Superintendent of Canterbury.

Next to speak was Sir Thomas Tancred, who spoke for his brother Henry but did him 'infinite harm' and was 'groaned down by the crowd of working men'. He was followed by Campbell, who 'maundered on in an irrational manner for some ten minutes about having been ill and having tumbled into the Akaroa brook and caught cold'.

Fitz easily won the show of hands and, the following day, he and his friends 'roused themselves and canvassed actively'. When votes were cast on the 20th, he topped the poll with a significant majority. That evening, his supporters gathered in the Mitre Hotel in Lyttelton and, 'over some detestable punch and some very good wine', showed their delight at his success 'with plenty of toasting and speechifying'.

'You would have been very much amused at our miniature election,' wrote young Charles Bowen, who had travelled to Canterbury on the *Charlotte Jane*. 'The utmost good humour prevailed. Shops were shut up. It was a general holiday and there was not a single police case. Lyttelton was however a little inebriated.' Fitz gave a more detailed account, telling Henry Selfe that his supporters in the town were 'drunk for three days, drinking 76 bottles of Madeira in one night at the Mitre'.

Fitz was elected for a term of four years at an annual salary of £500. 'Much as I have to give up and little as I shall gain,' he wrote, 'I confess it is a matter of considerable pride and pleasure that I find myself the first Superintendent of Canterbury.'

He now turned his attention to the general assembly, the first New Zealand parliament. The governor was based in Auckland and it was assumed that the assembly would meet there. 'He might as well call it at London,' Fitz complained to Lord Lyttelton. 'It will cost me and my wife and servant £80 to go there and back, besides living at Auckland for four or five months. Your Lordship can have no idea of the hardship of a Canterbury … settler having to go to Auckland.'

The ballot in Lyttelton took place on 15 August. Large crowds gathered in the town and, with 'two men on horseback, a procession of small boys, a few tattered flags, a big drum, a tin kettle and a fife, you have a small imitation of an English election'. Fitz gave a rousing speech, heckled by a butcher who had imported a sausage machine and was rumoured to add dog-meat to the mix. The audience soon tired of his interruptions.

'Go back to your sausage machine!' yelled a voice from the crowd.

'Yah!' shouted the butcher. 'If I had that Tory in my sausage machine, I'd soon make mincemeat of *him*.'

Fitz rose to the occasion, quoting the Bible to roars of laughter: 'Is thy servant a *dog* that thou shouldst do this thing?'[1]

He won the ballot with another significant majority. And once again, he celebrated in the Mitre Hotel, drinking and singing until four o'clock in the morning. Not only was he the first superintendent of Canterbury, he was also a member of the first New Zealand parliament – and he wrote to Gerald in England asking for £200 to cover his election expenses, 'which elder brothers sometimes pay'.

---

1   Quotation from 2 Kings 8:13

Dignity and Decorum

1853–1854

Oh! don't you remember the chamber, my boy,
Our first parliamentary shop,
With the skylight above, and the four bare walls,
And the rain pouring in from the top?

Crosbie Ward, Lyttelton Times, *January 1858*

Fanny's brother William had not settled at the Easedale Nook station; he was unhappy there, and in August 1852 Fitz suggested that he return to Lyttelton 'to come and doctor in port as there is a very good opening for him'. William declined, sending 'a most melancholy letter, showing that he is in a very morbid state of mind. Poor William! We cannot allow him to leave this colony on any account as he seems to wish, for he would be miserable elsewhere.'

Two months later, William dissolved his partnership with Jackson and returned to Purau Bay where he took employment on a sheep station run by the Rhodes brothers. In early 1853, he accompanied Robert Rhodes to a run in South Canterbury – a journey that involved crossing several rivers. These could be dangerous, particularly when in flood; riders were advised to keep their horses pointing upstream and, to avoid giddiness, to stay immobile in the saddle, fixing their eyes on the opposite bank.

Rhodes and William set out on the return journey in April. There had been days of heavy rain and the Rangitata was flowing high. Rhodes entered the water first. He negotiated the river and waited on the far bank for William to cross. He saw William's horse turn broadside to the current and could only watch as 'man and horse were carried away and sunk'. The horse swam downstream and reached the bank, leaving William stranded on an island of shingle. Rhodes shouted across the sound of rushing water that he would get help from a Maori settlement fifteen miles away. William should stay where he was and wait for rescue.

By the time Rhodes returned with the Maori, William had disappeared. They searched the area for nearly three weeks, before Rhodes returned to Purau Bay. It was assumed that William had drowned, 'perhaps carried out to sea which is about ten miles distant from the spot', but on 15 May, news arrived in Christchurch that his body had been found on the plains, 30 miles from the river.

'The weather was foggy,' explained Henry Sewell, 'and without compass or marks to steer by, the plains are like the open sea. So in all likelihood, he wandered round and round till he sank from fatigue and exhaustion. His boots were found a little distance from him, probably taken off to relieve himself from pain.'

Fanny's favourite brother, Dr William Draper, painted in 1850 shortly before he sailed for New Zealand as surgeon superintendent on the *Duke of Brontë*.

Private collection

William's body was thrown over a packhorse, taken to Lyttelton, and buried on 'a miserable day, the funeral procession dragging up the hill through mud and wet'. Fitz walked behind the coffin as chief mourner. 'Mrs FitzGerald bears it very well,' wrote Charles Bowen. 'Indeed it is fortunate that Amy now occupies her attention so much … FitzGerald has let her suppose that he was drowned – very wisely I think.'

...

Two months after the funeral, Fitz left the station to take part in the elections. And when he was elected superintendent, his friends persuaded him to move to Christchurch ('he will be a cripple from rheumatism if he stays much longer at his station during the winter, short of firewood and every comfort'). Despite writing seven months earlier that he would 'most likely always live' at the station, he hired a stockman to take charge of the Springs and rented a small house 'on the Papanui side of the river'.

On 10 August, he moved his family to Christchurch. The following day he wrote to Lord Lyttelton:

When I left my farm on the plains yesterday morning, a lovely spring morning, I felt as if nothing could repay me for the loss of the comfort of my own home and the delights of independence and these, to me, lovely plains. Since 1844, when I first had my nose put to the desk in a public office, I have never been my own master till last February and I felt very sad at returning again to a drudgery I hoped I had escaped.

Christchurch was 'a straggling place, small wooden buildings dotted about with little pretension to regularity', and both Fitz and Fanny were unhappy in their new home. 'My wife is as uncomfortable as I am in a small white pine box called a house,' Fitz complained to Godley, 'instead of our own comfortable home at the Springs.'

He found an empty building close to the river and, 'in a wonderfully short space of time', had it converted into a council chamber. The walls were papered, the floors carpeted, galleries added for the public and the press, and seats provided for 20 ladies. He bought red-cushioned chairs and built a dais for the Speaker, on which stood 'a respectable dignified chair such as one sees in Masonic halls'. In front of the dais was 'a plain table covered with papers, with the English statutes ranged impressively in front so as to give a legislative look to the place'.

Fitz described his council chamber as 'a most elegant apartment'. Henry Sewell disagreed: the interior, he wrote, had been 'disguised neatly enough but in a flimsy way', the seats were 'of iron hardness', and the building itself was 'shabby in the extreme. A low desolate-looking wooden tenement, all by itself in a potato garden, a quarter of a mile from the inhabited part of town, approached over an open trackless common covered with fern and tussock grass, barely passable in dry weather and miserable in wet.'

As superintendent, Fitz would not be present at council meetings. With the exception of opening formalities and special occasions, he would communicate with members only through correspondence and at meetings of an executive council. He insisted that proceedings be conducted with 'extreme dignity and decorum', that meetings of council should follow the protocol of the House of Commons in London – a policy which led to confusion among council members with limited knowledge of parliamentary protocol.

Elections for the council took place on 10 September. Twelve members were elected, and the first meeting took place on the 27th. It was, according to Fitz, 'a day never to be forgotten in the annals of Canterbury. We went to church in the morning and received the sacraments, the clergy receiving us at the door. I thought it right to establish the precedent in accordance with the custom of corporations in England.'

Members then walked in solemn procession to the council chamber, where the gallery was 'thronged with the leading men and women of the settlement'. Everyone rose to their feet as Fitz entered the room, made his way to the Speaker's chair, and bowed to the audience. He made his opening address 'with emphatic directness':

> There is a certain solemnity about every event which can occur but once in the life of an individual, or the history of a people: of such a character is the act which it falls to my lot to perform, in addressing, from this chair, the first legislative assembly of the Province of Canterbury. You will feel with me, that the language of ordinary congratulation falls far short of the dignity of the occasion.

God, he said, had restored to the people of Canterbury 'a semblance of the revered and tried institutions of our native land ... uniting us by fresh ties to the great empire of which we form a part'. He continued with an outline of the legislation he planned to put before council and concluded with the hope that he would 'govern this Province, so far as it is committed to my charge, to the glory of God, to the honour of Her Majesty the Queen, and to the safety, welfare, and happiness of all classes of her subjects in this portion of her dominions'.

Four days later, he wrote to Godley, enclosing a copy of his opening address and writing enthusiastically about his council ('we shall work well together I have no doubt'). He was sitting at his desk long into the night, drafting legislation by candlelight 'without legal assistance'. As a result, 'my eyes, after six months of perfect relief at the station, are fast breaking down before hard work'.

He wrote again on 23 October, informing Godley that his councillors 'require very cautious driving. They are new to ... public matters.' Together they were 'passing laws as fast as we can which is slow enough for some things but fast enough for accuracy and consideration'. He ended his letter with further complaints – made just four months after his election:

> I have little to tell you but to grumble bitterly at you for inducing me to take part in this government. My health won't stand it. And if this work goes on, it will take many a year out of my eyesight in the decline of life. The fact is my health is too bad for any hard work. Now I look back on the six months at the station as a sort of happy dream.

He had employed Henry Sewell as legal adviser to the council ('we get on well enough,' wrote Sewell in his diary, 'he in his heart disliking me, I thinking meanly of him'). The appointment was intended to provide assistance in drafting legislation, but Sewell spent many weeks in Wellington during this first session of council. 'I am pressed for time,' Fitz wrote on 18 November:

> pressed for eyesight – pressed for ability to write more than I can avoid. I not only do all the work of government with a single lad for private secretary, but, Sewell having been away ... I have had to draft all the Bills and work up all the laws – this in a mere box of a house with babies squalling and all the appliances of a nursery around me is *work*.

Fanny had given birth to their second child on 12 October, a boy named William after her unfortunate brother, so the executive council was forced to 'adjourn now and then to the verandah to make room for baby washing in the sitting room'.

...

While Fitz showed off his newborn son and heir, his brother Robert was on a P&O steamer, thousands of miles away in the Bay of Biscay.

'I do not think my health will stand much longer in this country,' Robert had written from the northwest frontier of India in April 1852. 'The province of Scinde has killed more men by sickness than any part of Her Majesty's dominions'. He described a climate 'unrivalled for its intense heat, for a wind that flames like the blast from the mouth of a furnace, a sun whose rays seem to burn, blight and wither'.

A few years earlier, Robert had suffered what he referred to as 'a serious nervous attack proceeding from a *very* hot climate and *very* free living and excess in women, all of which assailed me and I think the last most'. The doctors applied 'a universal blister, an unpleasantly powerful remedy', and he recovered for a while. The condition returned in late 1852, increasing in severity until he was invalided home in August 1853.

He embarked at Bombay for Suez, then travelled overland to Alexandria, where he boarded the P&O steamer. On 8 October, a letter to Lucius was posted from Malta: 'I expect to be in Southampton on 20 October and particularly wish you to meet me there. I am still so weak that I have been unable to get through this letter, a friend finishing for me.' Twelve days later, after the ship docked at Southampton, the captain wrote to Lucius:

> When Captain FitzGerald joined the ship at Alexandria, I naturally as a brother officer ... felt much interest and anxiety for him. Poor man, he looked like the picture of death when he came on

board and, while in my cabin daily deposing himself on my couch, described his sufferings from illness on his passage from Bombay to Suez … So great had they been that they deprived him of consciousness for some days … As we neared England, Captain FitzGerald's strength gradually declined, his symptoms grew worse and his sufferings from pain so great that his head began again to wander. He was never left for a moment alone and his cabin in the upper saloon deck was kept airy, but nature became exhausted … and he breathed his last almost without pain insensible.

Fitz was 'greatly cut up' when the news reached Christchurch. He spent an evening rereading the letters his brother – whom he had not seen for seventeen years – had written from India. 'You and Lucius are the same to me as you ever were,' he read. 'And though our paths at present lie far apart, yet we may still spend the evening of our days together.'

…

According to Charles Bowen – one of his greatest admirers – Fitz had 'unparalleled talents, with a Don Quixote disregard of self-interest and a hard working zeal which nothing ever daunts'. This disregard for self-interest included his family. Fitz boasted to Henry Selfe that he employed seven servants, but these were all at the station, looking after the livestock and making cheese. There was no one in Christchurch to help Fanny with the cooking, the housework, entertaining Fitz's political visitors, looking after two small children, and coping with a husband who, as Bowen put it, 'is not the most punctual of men'.

By late October, Fanny was 'very jolly and trotting about her garden again, rather disconcerted in advocating former theories about boys, having now got one of her own'. A few weeks later, she began to suffer again from migraines. She remained cheerful ('in good spirits although not strong'), but complained bitterly that Godley had encouraged Fitz to stand for the superintendency, 'as if *men* were not ready enough without inducement to neglect their families and business for politics and wickedness'. She referred to politicians as 'great apes'.

In early December – a few days after the end of the first session of Fitz's provincial council – she was delighted to return to the Springs for the summer. She began planting a garden while Fitz continued his work as superintendent:

I ride into the office, 16 miles almost every day and 16 miles back. And one day a week to Lyttelton, 25 miles, but not back the same day. This is a very hard life but it does my eyes good rather than harm and I get one or two days of quiet to compose the Bills for the next session of the Provincial Council.

Fanny was 'very well except headaches'; his daughter 'a brilliant little girl, talks at a great rate, nothing delights her as much as books'; the baby 'glorious for a three-month-old *kindchen*'. And having suffered from lumbago for many months, 'the rheumatism has given way to lovely warm weather and a course of bottled porter'. There were now 350 head of cattle at the Springs, half a ton of cheese in the loft, and he had begun to breed horses. He had also sold the cottage in Lyttelton. 'What more can I wish for?' he wrote, 'what more to be thankful for?'

At Christmas, his conjunctivitis returned and, by 5 January, his eyes were 'nearly bunged up with inflamed lids … all swelled up and looking like radishes'. The lumbago also returned and by the end of the month, he was confined to bed, sending Fanny's brother George into Christchurch on errands.

George, a truculent teenager, had moved in with them after William's death. Enrolled in the school (held in a room attached to St Michael's parsonage) when the family moved to Christchurch, he was taken out again a few months later, for reasons which, according to Fanny, were 'painful and disgraceful'. 'Do not think me wanting in natural affection when I say I hope he will go home,' she wrote to William Vaux:

> He is so unimpressionable, so selfish and seems to have no feelings whatever of honour or integrity. He is … very slow at learning and in improving his manners. He is dreadfully fond of low company and I have been told uses very bad language out of our presence. James has been most kind to him … but I do not think George cares one button if he (James) were dead or alive … If he stays I shall do my duty by him, but it is not at all a pleasant or loveable task, and I cannot tell you how much I admire James's conduct in burdening himself with him when he has no duty towards him … What a difference between William and George!

In February the family returned to Christchurch, where the second session of the provincial council opened on the 15th. Sewell was back in Canterbury and, instead of complaining about his absence, Fitz now complained of 'his real incompetence to do any practical business. I take refuge in this belief to avoid thinking him thoroughly dishonest.'

Sewell, on his part, complained of Fitz's 'rashness and that rushing at things without thought or care merely for the indulgence of impulses. One of these is a great notion he has of his talent for a fussy kind of industry. He will meddle with everything.'

Charles Bowen found this trait refreshing. 'As to FitzGerald,' he wrote to Godley, 'he is in his glory – the Prov. Council being too small he does everything. They are giving him great powers and he pockets everything he can get – quite conscientiously, honestly thinking that no one else could possibly do things as well as himself, at least in this settlement … if we had not got a go-ahead man here nothing would be done.'

And there was much to do. Detailed policy had to be approved on everything required to build and administer a new province – land regulations, financial and legal matters, labour supply and immigration, education, roads, bridges, scab in sheep – all of which had to be framed in the form of bills and ordinances. According to Bowen, Fitz conducted this second session 'without a single breeze between him and his council. He is almost universally popular.'

CHAPTER FOURTEEN

A Restless Husband

1854

We were like spectators at a theatre before the curtain rises.
Henry Sewell, 7 June 1854

It was as gross and flagrant a piece of treachery as was ever perpetrated.
Fitz, 23 April 1855

*P*rovincial government was up and running but, by late 1853, Sir George Grey had still not called the first session of the general assembly. His governorship was coming to an end; he had no wish to be involved with an elected parliament. Fitz referred to him as 'a dreadful pestilence in the shape of a wicked and mischievous Governor … without an assembly, he has as much power as he pleases and is responsible to nobody'. He complained of Grey's 'immeasurable contempt for law, for Parliament, for the colonists'; and carried away by his pen, asked in what respect the political condition of a New Zealand colonist differed from that of a Russian serf.

Grey left New Zealand on the last day of the year. Three weeks later, his temporary replacement, Colonel Wynyard (the most senior military officer in the colony) summoned parliament to meet in Auckland on 24 May 1854. Fitz decided to take his family with him; at the end of March, it was reported that 'Mrs FitzGerald is preparing to carry her two young children to Auckland – making pretty speeches on the subject of politics and restless husbands.'

The government brig carrying the elected members from Otago arrived in Lyttelton on 2 April. Because the Canterbury members planned to join them, the ship was ordered to remain in harbour for ten days to give Fitz time to adjourn the provincial council. But the brig left on the 8th (according to Sewell, Fitz had 'somehow or other upset the plans and the brig was off in a pet three days before her time'), so they waited for the steamer, the *Nelson*, which had entered service in the colony a few months earlier. This was good fortune, for the government brig was 'a byword for discomfort', and the members from Otago spent almost nine weeks on board as she beat her way north against strong headwinds. The steamer reduced the sailing time considerably, although the journey still involved, as Sewell put it, 'six distinct voyages … to and from the General Assembly'.

The *Nelson* was expected in Lyttelton on 5 May but did not arrive until five days later. Fitz embarked on the 11th, with his family and a nurse. According to Bowen, Fanny was 'very well and quite prepared for the journey', her children (Amy and William – known as Willy) 'fine and sturdy and kept in capital order'. Fitz was tired, 'looking very ill', his eyes 'quite knocked up with work'. Also on board was Henry Sewell, the elected member for Christchurch.

The steamer left harbour in the late afternoon, with 'an agreeable fresh breeze … Smooth water.' The passengers were in high spirits that evening but, after they retired to their cabins, there 'began sounds of rushing waters, creakings, rollings and pitchings. A sou'wester had sprung up off the Kaikouras and was driving us along furiously.' Next morning, they emerged to find the ship 'rolling in the trough of a prodigious sea, and spinning along at the rate of 13 or 14 knots an hour'.

All the passengers were sick during the voyage to Wellington, which lasted nineteen hours. Fitz and his family moved into Alzdorf's Hotel, a large two-storey building on the waterfront. The owner (Baron von Alzdorf, 'a stout Germanic-looking personage') had recently suffered a stroke and the housekeeping 'was at sixes and sevens, the place was dirty, the attendance as bad as possible, altogether miserable'. Fitz and Fanny 'were obliged to pig it in an apartment made to serve the triple purpose of sitting room, bedroom and nursery'. They were, as Fitz wrote on the 14th, 'dreadfully uncomfortable'.

It was blowing a gale when they re-embarked at noon the next day. The anchor fouled, the fore-topmast broke in two, and the gale continued for the rest of the afternoon. The steamer finally left harbour at ten o'clock that night, in 'a fresh breeze from the south-east … an awfully bad one for getting out of Wellington Harbour, throwing up a tremendous sea between the heads'.

Next morning, the ship was 'running fast' across Cook Strait under 'a gloomy sky – heavy rain – thick mists over the land, and a considerable sea'. The weather brightened as she approached Nelson in the evening, and the passengers emerged on deck 'looking crushed and soiled'. They waited four hours for the tide to rise before the ship could enter the narrow channel and steam into harbour past a long boulder bank.

After two days in Nelson, they re-embarked on the 19th. The steamer then grounded on the boulder bank, so they disembarked and trudged 'back again in high dudgeon to our respective abodes'. That night, the members gathered in the Wakatu Hotel. 'The tone [was] rather that of despair,' wrote Sewell (the assembly was due to open four days later), but the evening 'ended in a convivium of cigars etc', and Fitz led 'some capital singing'.

The steamer was freed from the boulder bank in the morning, the passengers came on board in the afternoon, and at five o'clock they set off for Taranaki. At midnight, the wind veered, 'with a high sea and a great deal of rolling', and they spent the early hours of the morning feeling 'sick and miserable'. In the evening, the ship stopped for the Taranaki members to embark, then left again shortly before midnight.

The last leg of the voyage, up the west coast to the harbour at Manukau (a few miles across the isthmus from Auckland), took almost two days. The harbour entrance was dangerous, and this was the first time a steamer would attempt to cross the bar. Fitz was apprehensive. 'It will be a regular fifth of November,' he wrote, 'if they lost the steamer with all of us, nearly 50 members of both Houses.'

After a day of 'heavy seas and a threatening sky', the morning of the 22nd dawned bright and sunny. 'We were off the coast which stretched away on our right,' wrote Sewell. 'We expected the Pilot to be on the look out for us according to specific instructions but none made an appearance.' By early evening, the ship was close to the heads, 'bold headlands with a channel opening into a wide basin, but all about were formidable reefs and bars over which the sea broke alarmingly … One could well account for the terrors of the place.'

No pilot appeared, not even when the captain 'fired guns and burnt blue lights' to attract attention. 'We grow savage,' wrote Sewell. 'The Captain will not venture to take her in himself with the light failing … we must lay all night off and on.'

In the morning, 'a thick bank of fog was rolling out of the mouth of the harbour, obscuring everything and obliterating all the points necessary for marking the course'. It was not until ten o'clock that the fog cleared, 'and then in we went, through an open channel about a mile wide between frightful reefs over which the sea broke'. Having negotiated the bar, the steamer entered a vast expanse of water ('half harbour, half lagoon') and followed the channel to Onehunga. And as they steamed along, 'the tide ran out … and left a swamp-like flat over which was a canopy of grey English looking sky'.

There was no jetty at Onehunga; the tide was falling and the ship dropped anchor 'a mile or so from the village'. To the passengers' dismay, 'no sign of boats or the smallest assistance was visible. Nothing but the ship's boats to land us.' Fitz and Sewell set off in the first boat, 'but the water shallowed, we dodged about here and there for a landing place, and at last managed to get the boat within 20 yards of the shore. There was no help for it but to put off shoes and stockings and wade to land.'

Time was short – the assembly was due to open the following afternoon – so it was decided that 'the ladies, nursery maids and children' should stay at 'a sort of roadside public house' in Onehunga, while the men moved on to Auckland to find accommodation. During the afternoon, the women and children were carried ashore by sailors, and were settled in to the public house. The members then 'streamed along the shore with carpet bags in hand' to a point where vehicles had arrived to take them across the isthmus.

Fitz stayed behind, spending the night with Fanny and the children. Next morning, with 'the weather threatening and rain coming down', the luggage was disembarked from the steamer and Fitz set out for Auckland 'in an omnibus with three horses'. It was a journey of almost six miles; the road over the ridge was metalled in places but the first three miles were 'piteous; a cross between a ploughed field and a quagmire'. Rain was still falling when he arrived in Auckland at midday, 'just in time to be sworn in and afterwards to attend the levee [formal reception] without any change of clothes'.

No accommodation had been provided for the southern members and the town was full ('houses or lodgings not to be had for love or money'). During the afternoon, Fitz and David Munro (member for Waimea near Nelson) 'hunted about for lodgings without success'. They thought of walking back to Onehunga, 'but it poured in the afternoon so we gave it up'. Instead, they attended 'a grand ball' in the military barracks and 'had a shakedown' with a friend.

At Onehunga, it was cold and damp in the public house; the landlady was about to give birth, and there was an outbreak of measles in the house. Sewell's wife spent the night 'in misery' on the public sofa and, when her husband arrived during the afternoon of the 24th, he found 'the unhappy females in a state of unprotected dreariness, most dismal to behold'.

Fitz collected Fanny the following morning, walking to Onehunga in time for breakfast. An omnibus pulled by four horses arrived at midday to carry the women and children through the quagmire. For the next two days, they camped out with friends in Auckland. On the morning of the 27th, Fitz, Monro and four other members arranged to rent Sir George Grey's former house, St Kevin's on Karangahape Road; they paid £150 for three months.

The house was furnished and occupied a beautiful position, with views over the harbour and subtropical vegetation flowering freely in the hedges. Fitz was elated. 'Fancy our actually living in Sir George Grey's very house,' he crowed, 'as if by retributive spite!'

...

Three days earlier (in 'piteous weather – thick heavy rain, and an atmosphere like the lid of a boiling tea-kettle'), the first New Zealand parliament had begun at noon with a 21-gun salute, after which a rather muddy Fitz swore his allegiance to the crown. In the afternoon, Colonel Wynyard gave a formal reception in the building erected to house the new parliament, 'a great wooden barn-shaped affair' nicknamed 'the Shedifice'. The roof leaked, the wind whistled through the walls, and the building lacked even the most basic facilities.

The House of Representatives occupied the upper floor of the building, a long narrow room equipped with seating and a public gallery. Few of the members knew each other, although Fitz was well acquainted with his old enemy, Edward Gibbon Wakefield, who had been elected member for the Hutt, near Wellington.

Until the Constitution Act came into force, Sir George Grey had governed the colony with an executive council of three crown-appointed officials. Members now assumed that power would be transferred to the general assembly, to elected ministers responsible to parliament. Fitz was sanguine about this: 'from all appearances, Wynyard will do his duty in a fair and liberal manner ... and if responsible government be called for, the present holders of office will resign and the government will be conducted by a ministry.'

The reality was more chaotic. 'Nobody guides anybody or follows anybody,' wrote Sewell on 24 May, 'except that Wakefield's powerful mind goes about like a stockman driving in wild cattle.' Fitz was horrified to learn that no preparations had been made for the assembly. 'The government had nothing ready,' he wrote, 'not a bill was prepared, no estimates, no nothing.' Wynyard and the officials 'had no idea what would happen. They thought that bills would ... pass through the House by a sort of natural process ... I have never seen a set of public men so politically ignorant in my life.'

A Speaker was elected and parliament opened officially on 27 May. Fitz, who had spent the morning making arrangements to rent St Kevin's, arrived at the Shedifice 'just in time' for the opening ceremony, which began at two o'clock. A guard of honour presented arms, a military band played 'God Save the Queen', and Wynyard 'marched in, in an upright soldierly way, as if going to give the word of command'.

A military officer with little experience in politics, Wynyard had stepped into the role of acting governor with trepidation. Now, entrusted with the task of inaugurating a parliament, he gave a long and rather nervous speech. He was 'holding office but temporarily', he said, and felt 'bound not to embark on any measure which may embarrass the policy or affect the duties of the Governor'.

He described the assembly as 'an experiment in constitutional government' and explained that his responsibility was to the crown. He suggested that individual members should introduce bills and, if passed by the House, they would be referred to his executive council for consideration.

This was not what members had expected to hear. The Constitution Act had provided for ministerial responsibility, for a degree of self-government free from interference by the Colonial Office in London. During the next four days, Wakefield encouraged members to present a united front. He and Fitz were rivals for the leadership of the House, but Wakefield was distrusted ('a most unprincipled scoundrel') while Fitz, the only provincial superintendent in the House, had left Canterbury 'with great expectations of his doings in the General Assembly'. Several members 'begged' him to take the lead.

It was Fitz who moved the address in reply on 1 June. 'It is not, I hope, presumptuous,' he began, 'to remind the House that there never was an assembly whose proceedings were watched with more anxious attention or more ardent hope than those in which we are about to engage.' Members saw no obstacle to ministers being responsible solely to the House; additional legislation was not required to bring responsible government into being; and Wynyard's suggestion that 'crude and hasty' bills be introduced 'by members under no responsibility' would 'result in disastrous consequences'. It would be better, he said, 'to do nothing at all' because the three men on the executive council 'understand nothing of constitutional government'.

Sewell was impressed. It was, he wrote, 'an admirable speech, very gentlemanly, discreet and temperate; very well delivered and which produced a great effect'.

Next day, Wakefield took centre stage. In a speech lasting three hours, he proposed that, 'among the objects which the House desires to see accomplished without delay, the most important is the establishment of ministerial responsibility'. This resolution was passed three days later by a majority of 29 to 1.

Meanwhile, rumours abounded. Would the old officials resign gracefully or fight to retain their positions? Who would be called upon to lead the government? 'Everyone became jealous, suspicious and irritable,' wrote Sewell, 'and men passed each other glowering.'

Fitz, who had moved the address in reply, had a headstart and, on the morning of 7 June, 'perhaps the most auspicious day that has ever dawned in New Zealand', he and David Monro were called to Government House. Wynyard asked them to lead the government, indicating that 'the officials who formed the old executive should continue for the present to fill their posts and carry on the routine work till their retiring pensions were agreed upon'.

Later that morning, Fitz and Monro – looking 'stately and nervous' – made their way to the Shedifice, where Fitz announced that Wynyard was 'prepared to carry out immediately the principle asserted by the House with respect to responsible government, as far as he is advised that it is in his power to do so'. He asked for a week's adjournment to consider his plans. 'All this was intensely exciting,' gasped Sewell. 'We were like the spectators at a theatre before the curtain rises.'

Next morning, Fitz and Monro failed to agree on policy; Monro resigned and Fitz – in his own words – 'was left as the first Prime Minister of New Zealand'. He replaced Monro with two men: Sewell, with whom he had partially buried the hatchet on the voyage north, and Frederick Weld, 'a real English gentleman'. On 9 June, it was agreed that Fitz, Sewell and Weld should form the cabinet, with Fitz as premier and Sewell as solicitor-general. 'It was a queer affair our walking into the Government Offices,' wrote Sewell. 'They turned some clerks out of a Survey Office, and put us into its desks ... and we three sat down together to make a government.'

During the next two days, they were 'hard at work all day', drawing up plans for government. Because the House was adjourned, there was 'a great deal of gossiping going on, and some intriguing, but it is all tending to give us the support of the best men ... we walk about in a cloud of wonder'.

On 10 June, they worked 'from ten in the morning till twelve at night, concocting bills and sending for information'. On the same day, Fitz had a meeting with Wynyard, who informed him that he was not in a position to devolve responsible government. So he and Fitz worked out a compromise. Fitz and his two colleagues would join the three officials on the executive council, thereby forming a 'mixed ministry' of old officials and elected representatives (the three officials responsible to the crown; Fitz and his colleagues responsible to the House). Fitz was convinced that this was a temporary arrangement until such time as pensions for the retiring officials had been authorised by the assembly.

Elated by his achievement, and inexperienced in politics, he agreed to this ambiguous arrangement – but failed to consult Wakefield about the details. This was a mistake. Wakefield was the architect of colonial self-government and, by 13 June, he was 'fretful, dissatisfied and brewing a storm. He is affronted at being left out of active participation in the government work ... He regards Responsible Government as his own child and must pet and nurse it into being.'

Fitz worked at full stretch during the adjournment, 'such a week of real hard work, night and day, to review all the difficult questions of policy and government'. Obtaining information from the officials was difficult; and Grey had left the colonial accounts in a muddle. As Fitz put it, 'the land department, the outstanding unsettled land claims, the public debt, the issue of scrip, all shows such a mass of confusion, incompetence and illegality as perfectly appalled us'. He accused the officials of 'gross mismanagement'.

The House was packed when parliament reassembled on 15 June and Fitz gave his first speech as premier. He spoke for almost two hours:

> I propose to conduct the business of government in this House as an unofficial member of the Executive Council. If the House be of opinion that it is not desirable that I should continue in that capacity, I will at once willingly and cheerfully retire … I am authorised to say that there will be no difficulty on the part of the present servants of the Crown retiring from office, so as to admit the full introduction of the principle of responsible government, should the House see fit to make a reasonable and decent provision for them, in the event of their resignation of their permanent offices.

The speech was, wrote Sewell, 'very clear, gentlemanly, and agreeably delivered. A little falling off towards the end, but on the whole extremely effective and good.'

The first meeting of the mixed council took place on 20 June and, when Fitz returned to the House, Wakefield took to his feet, 'fretful and dangerous; keenly sensitive about his importance and position … not being sufficiently recognised, and with old grudges against FitzGerald, ready to burst out but kept under restraint'. He gave a long speech, 'full of all sorts of objections to this, that, and the other', but the main thrust was that, 'instead of one homogenous government, we now have two governments in one, the old and new systems bound together in an unnatural alliance'.

Fitz remained sanguine about his ministry, having 'taken office on the clear and distinct understanding that, as soon as the public service required it, and as soon as the Bill was passed granting pensions to the retiring officials, they were to resign and a permanent government was to be formed on the responsible principle'. The newspapers reported that he was showing 'extraordinary ability', and he hoped 'to return to Canterbury having settled the government on a firm and satisfactory basis'.

But the mixed ministry was in trouble. Wakefield was being difficult in the House; Wynyard insisted on keeping the old officials in office; and the officials themselves were obstructive. 'A hundred dangers are ahead,' wrote Sewell on 9 July. 'There is a bar to be crossed over which the surf is breaking … Responsible Government is a very frail bark in imminent peril of being wrecked.'

The ambiguity of the mixed ministry and the 'total confusion' of the treasury accounts led Fitz to call on Wynyard several times during the second half of July. He told him of 'the difficulties that would arise in conducting the business of the country unless a permanent government was formed', and referred to the 'enormous discrepancy between the real expenditure of the government' and that set out by Wynyard in his opening speech. He asked him to dismiss the officials on the executive council – or at least to promise to do so before the end of the session.

But Wynyard was under the influence of the officials; he believed he had no power to devolve responsible government. He told Fitz that the Constitution Act made no specific provision for this, or for the removal of the officials, and that he had received no instructions from the Colonial Office to do so. He was therefore 'forbidden by honour and duty' to accede to Fitz's demands. Instead, he had written to the Colonial Office, and neither he nor the officials had any intention of relinquishing power until they had received permission from London – which would take almost a year to arrive. Fitz was incandescent:

> Then we found and not till then the *treachery* which had been
> practised on us. They never intended to resign until Col. Wynyard
> had received instructions from England. Of Col. Wynyard person-
> ally I only think that he is weak to imbecility … I am quite sure the
> officials intended to resign at the time our bargain was made … It
> was as gross and flagrant a piece of treachery as was ever perpetrated.

On 2 August, Sewell and Weld resigned from the executive council. For a few hours, Fitz was tempted to hang on; he informed Wynyard that 'I myself would continue so long as I could be of the least service or had any hopes of a satisfactory settlement of the question at issue.' He soon realised that Wynyard's 'mind was made up', as he put it, '*upon new grounds*'. So he too resigned.

That evening, Fitz announced the resignations to a silent House, and moved an adjournment until the following day. 'We have been made dupes,' Sewell wrote bitterly. 'We ought to have known better and to have recorded in writing and in express terms, what has been left to vague understandings and oral pledges … we were too credulous.'

The following day, Fitz addressed the House in 'a capital speech which had great effect', after which Wakefield explained that he had been summoned by Wynyard and was now acting as his sole – unofficial – adviser. This was, according to Fitz, 'a great blunder' on Wynyard's behalf, 'a most silly proceeding', and Wakefield's explanation 'the most deeply and keenly insulting speech I ever heard'. He went further:

I have known the Honourable Member for many years and I will not shrink from stating the opinion I have formed of him. I believe that no man, or body of men, has ever been connected for any length of time with him in public life without being thoroughly damaged in reputation, in personal character, and even in pocket. This I say deliberately: I wish the expression to be placed on record.

On 5 August, Wynyard sent a communication to the House promising support for a bill proposing responsible government, to be reserved for approval by the Colonial Office. He also explained that Fitz had known from the start that he would wait for permission from London. Fitz denied this angrily and Wakefield accused him of trying to force Wynyard's hand: it was not the duty of the House, he said, 'to sustain the late ministers in their difference with the Governor'. Fitz then accused Wakefield of intrigue.

The session descended into infighting, 'the excitement intense, and the debates in the House violent to an indescribable degree … no business doing, all the Bills at a standstill, and the future blank'. On 17 August, Wynyard suspended parliament for two weeks to allow tempers to cool. This led to chaos in the House, with members behaving 'like a pack of schoolboys'. Sewell lost his temper and punched one of Wakefield's supporters, who fended him off with his umbrella.

Parliament resumed on the 31st ('Guard of honour, band and Governor, all as usual'), with four of Wakefield's men sitting on the executive council in another mixed ministry. On 1 September, Wakefield made a speech, 'taunting and irritating FitzGerald who turned on him savagely, and attacked him … with too much personality though very ably'. The new ministry lost a vote of no confidence and resigned on the evening of the 2nd.

During the next two weeks – the final weeks of the parliament – members applied themselves to legislation, 'sitting up till midnight, and sometimes till one or two in the morning, hurrying through bills in a hasty and slovenly way, half asleep'. Sewell now led the assembly, for Fitz's mood had become alarmingly high and his colleagues found him 'quite unmanageable'. He was constantly changing his mind in conversation, putting forward one contradictory idea after another at dazzling speed.

'He talked a good deal to this effect after we left office,' wrote Sewell, 'and utterly destroyed his political influence … he is altogether a riddle … he has so much ability that it is grievous to see him destroying himself in this way.' Weld described how Fitz 'went wild. He no longer worked with Sewell and myself, but proposed the wildest plans in the rashest manner and lost amongst his friends and supporters [a] great part of the prestige he had gained.'

…

Meanwhile, in St Kevin's, the residents had formed 'a most agreeable party', with 'much merriment and social life'. Frederick Weld found it delightful. 'Our great relief in all our troubles in office,' he wrote:

> has been the grand national institution of St Kevin's where the FitzGeralds, the Ludlams, the Monros … form a kind of club whenever an evening can be spared from the House … You have no idea what a jolly place it has been and were it not for the jokes and fun of St Kevin's, I don't know what we should have done without it.

There were 20 people in the house and only three wives, so the women acted as housekeeper 'turn and turn-about', with Fanny – who had more experience in such matters – helping the other two. St Kevin's was 'some distance from town', the road was 'a great part of the way execrable', and it was difficult to find servants. 'How they managed I do not know,' wrote Sewell, 'poor Mrs FitzGerald … looked fagged to death.'

On 7 July, when it was her turn to do the housekeeping and both her children had caught measles from the public house in Onehunga, she wrote a short letter to William Vaux:

'Auckland from the verandah at St Kevin's', painted a few months after Fitz and Fanny stayed here in 1854. The house was 'the scene of much merriment and social life' during the first parliament. Painting by John Kinder, 1855, umber wash on paper.

Hocken Collections, Uare Taoka o Hakena, University of Otago

I only have time to say we are here. James is Prime Minister – awfully busy. He has been ill. Amy has had the measles. Willy is ill. I am worked to death (nearly) ... We have been here since 26 May – but I have had housekeeping and everything to do in this private club of Southern Members ... I shall write as soon as I can. Pray forgive this.

She wrote again on 20 August, pouring out her heart at midnight: 'I am not well, from overwork, for besides the children and my private affairs I do all the housekeeping for this establishment consisting of twenty souls.' Fitz was 'in a very excited state', his eyes 'very weak'. She hated Auckland, 'a horrid snobbish place'. As she reached the end of the page, her distress burst from her pen: 'These politics absorb James's attention so much I long for some "England" friends, somebody who knows my bygones. Sometimes I do feel very homesick. These politics I detest most extremely ... I could write lots more but am very tired.'

Fanny's distress is tangible. Her husband was obsessed, highly excitable and difficult to live with. There were days when he was too unwell to attend the House, when he stayed in St Kevin's suffering from malaise and exhaustion ('the work of office was far too much for my health'). He took little part in the final two weeks of the parliament. 'For the labours of the last session I can take little credit,' he explained, 'as my health absolutely forbade me taking so prominent a part as others, while sitting from eleven in the morning till two or three the next morning was a severe trial.'

On 16 September, parliament was prorogued until July the following year. Next morning, Fitz read a letter from Wakefield in the columns of the *New Zealander*. This was an attack on his ministry; and while Fanny packed up for departure, he drafted a reply for publication in the *Daily Southern Cross*. Wakefield was, he wrote, 'a man incapable of speaking the truth when he has an object in view', and he referred to his letter as 'another of the many acts of his life, in which truth and honour have been disregarded'.

He also wrote to Henry Selfe, complaining that he arrived in Auckland 'hoping for rest and quiet ... [but] was compelled by circumstances to form the first administration'. He had found the work 'quite overpowering ... This session has knocked me up very much – made my cheeks thin and my hair grey. I look very old after it.'

CHAPTER FIFTEEN

A Beast with a Bill

1854–1855

His passion for legislating and drawing bills amounts to a mania.
Charles Bowen, 31 March 1855

I am so very sick of politics.
Fanny, 22 April 1855

The southern members set out for Onehunga after breakfast on 18 September, the men walking, the women and children travelling in 'sundry vehicles'. The tide was out when they reached the harbour, there were no boats, and the steamer – instead of sailing at one o'clock as planned – had been delayed until the following morning. So it was back to the public house for a midday meal. 'We were all sick and disgusted,' wrote Sewell. 'The want of care and thoughtfulness about us, and the total absence of all preparation for the comfort of ladies and children, even to the neglect of providing boats to take us off to the steamer made us savage.'

The steamer was moored a mile and a half down the harbour. During the afternoon, boats managed to 'get within a stone's throw of the shore, but it rained cats and dogs'. Sailors carried the women and children to the boats, 'where they sat huddled together soaking in the rain'. The men remained in the public house where they ate a makeshift dinner before the boats returned to collect them.

After weighing anchor at daybreak next morning, the ship made a difficult crossing of the Manukau bar. 'Fearful rollers' were 'breaking right across' and the steamer 'tossed her head up in the air, and pitched down again, almost perpendicularly – then rose again like a duck, and so on, for about a quarter of a mile'.

It was a long and stormy voyage to Nelson, 'huge waves rolling about us'. Everyone felt 'as miserable and cheerless as possible' and all the FitzGeralds were sick. After a few days in Nelson, they re-embarked for Wellington. The steamer reached the harbour entrance after darkness had fallen and, to the fury of the passengers, the captain ('Abominable man! we all vow vengeance against him') decided to wait until first light before entering the heads. So the ship 'hoved to at midnight in the middle of the Strait, where we lay rolling from side to side for several hours in perfect misery'.

The final leg of the journey, through a freshening headwind and rising seas, took two days and was another uncomfortable voyage. 'Everybody sick and miserable,' wrote Sewell. 'We managed to get off the Kaikouras by daybreak. They are always a grand sight; but who can appreciate the picturesque with a horrible nausea of stomach?'

Fitz arrived home (looking 'rather grey') on 5 October, to be fêted as a returning hero. He had attended dinners in Nelson and Wellington, giving 'long explanatory speeches' about events at the general assembly, and as one of the newspapers put it, 'the reception of the ex-ministry in the southern settlements has been most gratifying. Their progress, as the steamer took them from province to province, has been one career of triumph.'

Next day, Fitz gave his honorarium of £116 (intended to cover his expenses in Auckland) to the Lyttelton Colonists Society, 'placing it at the disposal of my constituents for the service of Lyttelton'. He would be pleased, he said, 'if the money were devoted to some permanent work … such as founding a library'. The sum was worth over £7500 in today's money and (although Fanny might have disagreed) he 'did not think it right to draw it when I was at the same time drawing salary from the Superintendency'.

On 9 October, he held a meeting of the electors in Lyttelton; he made 'an effective speech' on the first parliament, which was received with 'great cheering'. 'I ask you not to despair at the comparative failure of the General Assembly,' he said. 'Although we have done but little work, we have shown that Responsible Government is practicable … The introduction of a new Constitution must necessarily be attended with the throes of a new birth.'

Meanwhile, Wakefield was still on the warpath. In a vitriolic letter to the *New Zealander* (in response to Fitz's reply in the *Daily Southern Cross*), he described Fitz as:

> inordinately vain … a self-esteem so swollen and sensitive, as to be frenzied by disappointments which men fit for political life bear with decorum … We meet in open combat; and though I must needs give blow for blow in self-defence, yet will I endeavour to repel his attack with temper and decency.

He set out his own version of events in Auckland, and ended his letter – with little temper or decency – with a list of adjectives. Fitz was, he wrote:

> thoroughly heartless … his ambition is beyond measure … boastful, overbearing, supercilious, and blind to danger … fretful, impatient, very spiteful … either low-spirited and helpless, or reckless as the maniac … readily inflated, and as easily depressed; without magnanimity, fortitude, caution, or patience, but envious, jealous, treacherous, and vindictive; such is the broken-down hero of the first meeting of the New Zealand Parliament.

A few weeks later, Wakefield arranged a series of public meetings in Wellington to drum up support for a political campaign. After a meeting in the Hutt in December – where he spoke for five hours, taking credit for all significant events at the assembly and attributing all the failures to Fitz – he 'drove home in an open chaise, nine miles in the teeth of a cold south-easterly gale at two o'clock in the morning'. He soon fell ill with rheumatic fever; and although he lingered on for another seven years, he would play no more part in politics.

…

Fitz's reference to 'the throes of a new birth' had personal implications too: their third child had been conceived during their final days in Auckland. Fanny, tired from the long voyage home, was 'in a very unsettled state' when they moved into a new house in Cashel Street (which Fitz had rented for £100 a year). It was, he wrote, 'the first time since leaving England that I have got into a comfortable house, with my books and pianoforte around me. It has ten rooms and I am absolutely compelled to have the government offices in the two best rooms.'

Fanny soon settled in to her new surroundings. 'We are getting quite comfortable in our house now,' she wrote to William Vaux in November, 'and are very regular in our hours. We breakfast at eight, dine at one, and drink tea at six. I practise my playing nearly every day for two hours.' Her mother had decided that George should remain in Christchurch, so her brother was working as a supernumerary clerk in Fitz's office 'and this week will begin to go every evening to old Mr Thompson to learn what can be dinned into him. I do not think his moral or intellectual character improves in the least.'

The third session of Fitz's provincial council had opened on 10 October and promptly voted to double its size. The bill to enlarge the council was read for a third time on 13 October, after which – perceiving the vote as 'expressing a want of confidence' – Fitz's executive council resigned.

In an address delivered on the 31st, Fitz promised to reorganise the electorates and commission the building of a new council chamber. He formed a new executive council led by John Hall, a runholder described as 'very energetic but rather fond of quibbling on detail and being amusingly bumptious'. Fitz bullied him unmercifully, treating 'the poor fellow altogether too rudely', and Fanny followed her husband's lead. 'James's present Executive Council doesn't please me at all,' she told William Vaux. 'Mr John Hall who is at the head of it is the greatest bore and nuisance alive and of course constantly coming here.'

Fitz had calmed down since returning from Auckland, but he was still firing on all cylinders ('in the most wonderful spirits and power of work'). On 17 November, because he was 'wholly unable to attend to it', he let the station to his head stockman for a year. This was a disappointment to Fanny, who had hoped to spend the summer recess on the plains. Instead, she had to endure the 'hot and oppressive' weather in Christchurch, with blasts of wind 'blowing like whirlwinds out of a furnace' and raising the dust in the streets.

On 20 February 1855, Fitz took his family to the station to collect 'a great many things'. They set off in the dogcart early in the morning with their servant Emma and Fanny's brother George. As usual, Fitz drove with two horses in the traces, but this time they had been harnessed in tandem, one horse in front of the other. 'The horses had never been in together before,' Fanny told William Vaux on the 23rd:

> James had never driven tandem before, nor had he a tandem whip,
> so here was a pretty turn out. I fully made up my mind we should
> be killed for the leader kept turning round kicking over the traces
> etc etc. However, by the time we had gone through various perils in
> our progress through Christchurch from bridges, rivers, ditches, etc,
> James got the horses '*en train*' ... Over the gullies James went down
> and up at full speed, we could only shut our eyes and hold on like
> grim death. James does not allow 'nerves', you know.

She found the station 'in first rate order ... everything beautifully fresh and clean. The air so delightful – all so peaceful, and no John Halls and Executive Councils nor nasty visitors. It was most delightful.' It made her weep to think that they could be living here, enjoying the plains and – perhaps – making the fortune which Fitz had dreamed about for so long. 'Even James said it almost made him cry to be up there.'

It was a warm, sunny day and Fanny spent hours 'routing at my boxes', the children squealing in delight at the pigs and calves and foals. They stayed overnight and set out on the return journey early next morning. According to Fanny, they looked:

most ridiculous. James was mounted on a wooden stool fixed on a box very high in the air. There were carpet bags and a bath in front, Emma and Willy, then Amy and I, and behind us a large blue bale and a box of ironmongery at the top of which were some eggs, some of which went flying out at the first gully. George sat upon the shafts. We went down quickly to Christchurch, though with the same trouble again with the leader. You may imagine we were all dreadfully stiff yesterday, the driver especially, but it was great fun.

Fitz spent the summer recess 'drafting bills for the next session'. 'The care of the Province completely monopolises my time,' he told Godley. 'The life is one of most severe labour.' Charles Bowen complained that he was becoming obsessed:

Legislation is … his hobby … No music in his house now – no sketching – no nothing. When you go in you stumble over some snob or other whom FitzGerald has picked up for a few days under the impression that he is a 'first-rate man – I tell you – most useful man'. One comfort is that there is variety – for one of them won't last him long.

Fanny worried about this hyperactive behaviour. 'His eyes are looking very bad indeed in consequence of his persisting in sitting up until two o'clock every morning writing horrid ordinances,' she told William Vaux:

I cannot imagine that his eyes … will last at all long under such ill usage, for they are hard worked all day. I do really get more and more disgusted with the Superintendency and politics every day. James gets poorer and more involved every year and saves nothing for the children; everything is spent for public purposes or in entertaining company, while he is at the same time injuring his health. If we had gone on living at the station, our expenses would have been very small and we should have been getting rich, instead of which I can see no escape from this maze of politics. However, it is of no use grumbling and it is selfish in me to trouble you with my grievances.

Fitz had grown insensitive to those around him. He was neglecting everything in his obsession with politics, including his wife and children. In his youth, he had learnt to ignore his father's strictures on religion and duty. Now he was ignoring Fanny's fatigue and distress. Instead of making money, he was losing it, so Fanny – deprived of help in the house – was forced to work too hard. As a result, she was suffering from constant headaches.

This was not what Fitz had promised her in London when he talked of the pioneer life, of farming on the Canterbury Plains, of 'making corn rather than constitutions'. Far from being 'completely of one mind in everything', as Fitz had boasted, she now loathed everything to do with politics. And while Fitz complained to Godley of 'alternate hard work and the depression which follows it', Fanny set out her own complaints in a letter to Charlotte Godley which, in Charlotte's words, 'did not draw a very inviting picture'.

…

In England, Fitz's two closest friends were enjoying each other's company. ('Selfe is very flourishing,' wrote Godley. 'I absolutely delight in him. If he was not so terribly ugly, he would be perfect.') Both men were annoyed by the tone of Fitz's letters. In September, Godley wrote to Selfe that Fitz was 'incorrigible' about money. 'That he would ever be "well off" I look upon as hopeless.' In October, he was 'very angry' at Fitz's criticisms of Henry Sewell ('absolute imbecility in matters of business … no weight, strength or stability of character … he vapours and schemes but does nothing … he is an ass'). Godley, no fan of Sewell himself, admitted that these comments 'frightened' him. He worried that Fitz 'might go wrong when under no control', that power would 'bring out the bad parts of his character'. Fitz was 'so changeable and talks so much from impulse'; his ideas about practical matters were '*childish* … the tone is that of a man who feels himself absolutely unapproachable in wisdom and sagacity'.

Henry Selfe felt the same way. He wrote to Godley that Fitz's tone in a recent letter was 'bumptious'. A few days later, he received a reply:

> I have rather a startling request to make of you; it is nothing less
> than to let me send your *last letter* to FitzGerald himself! I will
> tell you why – his letter deserves comment of a plain-spoken kind.
> For his own sake he should know the impression that sort of talk
> produces on those who have a warm and sincere affection for him,
> and yet it would be very difficult indeed to address such language
> to him directly without appearing to take an unwarrantable liberty.
> On the other hand, a letter written like this, from one friend of his
> to another, evidently without the slightest idea that he should see
> it, and therefore free from all suspicion of impertinence or over-
> freedom, *would* I really think, do him good.

Selfe agreed, the letters were sent, and when they arrived in Christchurch in early March 1855, Fitz was 'too much vexed' to reply immediately. He would wait, he wrote, until he could 'review it rationally'. He eventually replied to Godley on 2 April, choosing his words carefully:

I have no doubt Selfe was right and I am deeply obliged to you for sending me his letter. But it leaves and will always leave one painful impression, namely the utter hopelessness of carrying on a correspondence so many miles apart. I took no copy of my offensive letter. I do not know what I said in it. If it were 'bumptious' it certainly did not convey the ruling conviction of my mind, which is that I never was and never shall be fit for leading in public matters … I have a fatal vice in uncontrollable momentary impetuosity which doesn't do. I am more fitted to aid than to lead, and more fit (and earnestly wish that I were fated) to drive bullocks and grow potatoes than to rule.

He wrote to Selfe three weeks later. He was, he told him, 'very much hurt' by his letter to Godley:

But he was quite right to send it. And it was kind of you to allow it to be sent for that was an act of real friendship. I could not answer it at the time but I thought much over it and I am sure I deserved what you said. Egotism and vanity are weeds to which the soil of *small* public things is very favourable. And I shall be glad if you will always tell me if I make an ass of myself. I have much to remind me that I am an ass. I have not good health. I am put to great expense and can save nothing. I am working hard but not providing for my family and this makes me sometimes very anxious. Nothing will induce me to remain much longer in this life.

Fitz wrote this letter a few hours after completing a long report to Godley on the 1854 parliament ('a volume in the shape of a letter', according to Godley). It had taken him six months. 'I could not find the time,' he explained, 'and since, that sort of lassitude which follows on over work and over excitement has rendered it very difficult to do more than I was absolutely compelled to do.'

By the end of April, when she was almost eight months pregnant, Fanny was in despair. Fitz was demanding care and attention, and the house in Cashel Street was always full of visitors. 'I do not know whether it shocks you or not that I always write my letters on Sundays,' she wrote to William Vaux, 'but if you were here you would make allowances for me, for it is really the only day that I can expect to be quiet and even on Sundays people will come. I am interrupted of course.'

The first visitor in April was David Monro, who arrived in Christchurch on the 4th. 'We had a little singing,' he wrote in his diary, 'and after Mrs F was gone to bed, lots of smoking and brandy.'

Next to arrive was the judge of the Supreme Court, whose visit provided Fanny with some light relief:

> One morning when he was at breakfast, Amy stood for some time contemplating his bald head and then walked off to one of the armchairs and picking out some horse hair from the cushion brought it to him telling him to put it on his head! The old Judge took it very good naturedly but I was obliged to rush off to have an enormous laughing fit.

Then Frederick Weld arrived on the 23rd. 'I am quite worn out and done up with constant visitors and people staying with us,' Fanny wrote that evening:

> what with the children and housemaid's work to do, it is quite undermining my strength ... At this minute I am suffering so much from my head that I hardly know what I am writing about ... I am so very very sick of politics and do not at all like the life in Christchurch where there are all the plagues of a town life and none of the conveniences or comforts. Believe me with best love and great faith in your powers of forgiveness for this very very stupid letter.

…

Elections for the enlarged provincial council had been held in March and the fourth session opened on 11 April. Fitz was living in his office chair – 'smoking, brewing bills, and talking politics all day' – and continued to over-legislate. 'His passion for work was really alarming,' wrote one of his councillors. 'Throw out a hint as to the necessity of an amendment in an existing Act, and he would sit up half the night framing a bill putting into shape his views of the form and extent that such amendment should take.' He was 'a parliamentary platypus ... a beast with a bill'.

Charles Bowen (now the provincial treasurer) was alarmed. 'His passion for legislating and drawing bills amounts to a mania,' he wrote to Godley:

> I often tell him that his overdoing it will disgust sober people – but you can guess what use my talking is ... where I think he errs is in over energy – and too great a confidence in [his] enormous abilities. If we had less legislation and a little more practical looking after, we should do much better. There is too much pomp and circumstance in the management of a little province.

Fitz's hyperactive state was leading to 'chaos' in provincial politics ('more ludicrous than dignified'), with personal feuds and political infighting. He was 'not getting on at all well' with his council and members complained of his 'flightiness' and constant changes of mind. One member wrote a frustrated letter to Godley, referring to:

> FG's peculiar changeableness and hastiness, and his great tendency to set up the theoretical above the simply practical ... I speak the opinion of all who have had to work with him ... They complain of his impracticality and the irritating way he has of refusing to listen to or trying to tear down every plan or argument opposed to his own – and then, days and weeks perhaps after he has been yielded to and action ... decided upon, he comes up suddenly to propose as if quite new the very plan that was offered him. This is ... great waste of time.

Even Fitz's most fervent supporters were unhappy about his bullying and abrupt manner to members of council – although to his friends he remained 'as jolly and good humoured as ever'. He was putting on weight, becoming 'so fat that he cannot button his old coats'. And with his mind fully occupied by legislation, he was neglecting the station and his debt to Henry Selfe. 'I have again and again to apologise to you for not writing more about private affairs,' he wrote to Selfe on 24 April:

> But I will promise you that as soon as this present session of the Council is over I will write fully. It is very melancholy to me to feel that your kindness in lending me so much money has done me very little good. Politics are utterly incompatible with private affairs. And I over and over again wish that I had never dealt in them ... If I had continued to live quietly at the station I should be in the way of doing very well by this time.

CHAPTER SIXTEEN

Spasms of the Heart

1855–1856

I suppose there are dark patches in all lives. I have been passing through
one of my darkest.

Fitz, 11 June 1856

James has neglected everything for public affairs and now we are worse off
than ever.

Fanny, 15 June 1856

*F*itz's difficulties with his provincial council led him to talk of giving
up the superintendency. He was also 'daily trembling in fear of a
summons to Auckland, which I dread much. It is an awful expense.' He wrote
this on 23 May 1855, 'within five weeks of the day to which the Assembly
was prorogued and we have had no notice whether we are to meet up again
or not. I actually do not know whether I am to go up by the next steamer or
not.' His friends were concerned by his state of mind; one of them expressed
'a kind of lurking fear of what he may do at the next session of the Assembly
by mere headlong rashness'.

Fanny, expecting her confinement in early June, was in 'daily fear' too; her
first two deliveries had been difficult because of her small frame. 'She says she
looks forward with great dread to this next fortnight,' one of her friends wrote
to Charlotte Godley on 15 May. 'She has not been *really* well for some time
but I fancy that, when this is all over and she can be quiet and have someone
to help her to look after the children, she will get all right. I don't know what
she will do with *three* if she cannot get somebody besides Emma.'

Fanny gave birth safely on 7 June to a son, named Robert after Fitz's soldier
brother. The baby cried constantly, particularly at night. 'I am so overworked
for lack of servants and overabundance of children,' she wrote to William Vaux
on 25 July, 'that I cannot possibly write letters, so do not think me unkind.
We are all very well, except myself. I have a troublesome cough and my chest
is very weak. Baby will be seven weeks old tomorrow.'

Willy was 'a fine large child and very good. Everyone says he is exactly like James, but James says that he was never so ugly.' And according to Charles Bowen, Amy had grown into 'the prettiest, most graceful, lively little thing I ever saw ... her father has taught the little wretch to make puns'.

To provide additional help in the house, Fitz employed an Irish servant (who 'came as a cook but could not even boil potatoes'). He described her peculiarities to William Vaux:

> On going into our bedroom one day she remarked, 'That's a very big bed: how many people sleep in it'!!! She did not respect my person much for after being with us for three days she found out by accident who I was and remarked 'That's the master! That's her husband, Gad, I thought he was a lodger.' The delicate compliments to my appearance and my wife's trade as a lodging-house keeper were duly appreciated.

...

In July, the provincial council approved the final arrangements for winding up the Canterbury Association and the transfer of its assets and liabilities to the province. The liabilities amounted to £30,000 (almost £1.5 million in today's values) – money that was owed to the association's benefactors. The council voted to repay these debts in full and with interest at five per cent, a vast sum for a colony just four years old.

Members of the association were delighted when the news reached London. 'You cannot exaggerate,' wrote Lord Lyttelton, 'the pleasure and the *sensation* it has caused among the members of the poor old Association here. I do not believe that Selfe and Godley and myself have had such pleasure since we heard of the landing of the first body of colonists.'

Fitz put his signature to the Canterbury Association Ordinance on 10 July, after which he suspended the council to wait for the governor's assent. That night, he was guest of honour at a dinner, 'a capital one with very good wine'. During the evening, he talked of taking the ordinance to Auckland personally; two weeks later, he changed his mind. 'The General Assembly is called ... but I cannot go,' he told Henry Selfe. 'And if I could I would not – we are told in the Summons that the only business to be brought before the House is a bill to provide pensions and a pro forma appropriation bill ... Think of taking me for months away from home to do that.'

Colonel Wynyard had received 'quite a snubbing despatch' from the Colonial Office in London, making it clear that no additional legislation was required to introduce responsible government. As Frederick Weld put it, he was ordered 'to do exactly the thing we had recommended him to do'. Wynyard called the assembly to meet on 8 August, limiting it to a short session and restricting it to a few necessary formalities. Sewell travelled to Auckland, having previously agreed with Fitz not to go ('the man is like an eel'); other Canterbury members stayed away.

Sewell was appointed de facto leader of this brief session. A new governor, Colonel Thomas Gore Browne, arrived on 6 September and prorogued parliament nine days later, having decided that a general election was required. This would be held in December and the next session of parliament would meet four months later.

Fanny was still very tired, still sitting up every night with the baby, but Fitz – blind to her exhaustion and headaches – dismissed the Irish servant in August. He wrote to Godley, Lord Lyttelton and William Vaux, explaining that he wanted to give up politics and return to his station. It was the old story:

> No man should enter political life without private means. I get
> poorer and poorer when I ought to be providing for my family … I
> have quite made up my mind to quit political life altogether and go
> to my farm … I can truly say that I have given myself wholly and
> entirely up to the office, to the neglect of all private, personal and
> friendly matters. I shall therefore resign the Superintendency … I
> long to get back to my cows and my pigs.

'A wife and three children make one look to the future,' he told Godley. 'Amy is becoming infinitely absurd, Willy is a ball of fat, and the new child a sleepless bore. We are all well but me. I am getting fat and my head has been dizzy lately.'

Towards the end of September, a wound on his right hand swelled up with 'a violent inflammation which kept me in bed for some days and incapacitated me from holding a pen for weeks'. He was still laid up when the provincial council reopened on 9 October. He was back on his feet by early November, but was unable to sign his name until the middle of the month when (despite his wish to return to the station) he renewed the stockman's lease for another year.

At the same time, he was preparing for the general election in December. Having declared publicly in August that he would 'never again join in general government affairs', he now announced that he was willing to stand again for Lyttelton. 'If I am wanted,' he wrote on 5 December, 'I have told the electors that they must return me quite untrammelled to act as I please.'

On 18 December, 'a very hot and dusty day', Fitz gave a long speech to his supporters in Lyttelton. On the 21st, he was elected without opposition, 'so much to my disgust, I am again a member and have to make the journey to Auckland'. Ten days later, the new governor arrived for his first official visit to Canterbury. He was accompanied by his wife and daughter, his private secretary, a colonial official, an aide-de-camp, two military attendants and a journalist.

Fitz was in Lyttelton when the party arrived in the harbour on 31 December. He boarded the steamer as soon as the captain dropped anchor and, as he accompanied Colonel Gore Brown ashore, 'the town was all animation and excitement; flags flying from every public building and His Excellency welcomed with continued and heavy cheering'.

Next day, in pouring rain, Fitz and the governor ('a hale and florid-looking gentleman') rode together along the uncompleted road to Sumner. On 2 January, they rode over the Bridle Path to Christchurch, where the whole town was 'in a tremendous state of excitement'. Gore Browne and his entourage were staying with Fitz and Fanny in Cashel Street and, as Sewell put it, 'FitzGerald makes himself very agreeable in his own house and I have no doubt they all enjoyed it.'

Fitz's council had voted him £200 to spend on the governor's reception. On the first evening, he invited 60 guests to a party in the provincial council chamber. On 3 January, Gore Browne held a levee. On the 7th, there was 'a grand ball of nearly 200 persons, a very gay affair'. On the 8th, Fitz held a public dinner in the council chamber. There were 'riding parties – one 40 miles up the country. And levees … with the natives. And all the rest of it.'

The governor and his party left Canterbury on 10 January. 'It is a very long time indeed since I have spent so delightful a week,' enthused Fitz. 'The society of an English gentleman fresh from England was particularly refreshing to me … We were quite delighted with their visit.'

Fanny had a more jaundiced view. It was she who did the housekeeping for such high-profile guests and, since the occasion cost almost double the amount voted by his council, Fitz had paid 'about £150' from his own pocket, a sum representing one-third of his annual salary. 'James has neglected everything for public affairs,' she complained to William Vaux, 'and spent ten times more than I think was called for … This is an example of the way we have lived.'

…

Fitz was now writing letters in which he changed his mind almost by the sentence. The topics were – in no particular order – farming, politics, money, and complaints about other people. He wrote as thoughts occurred to him, outpourings free from any editing process. He never read his letters through and soon forgot what he had written. One day, he would not resign as superintendent until the end of his term of office; a few days later, he would do so 'as soon as I can without desertion'. One month, he planned to give up politics altogether; two months later, he was enthused by the prospect of political success. These conflicting messages arrived in letters to Godley and Selfe in London, together with complaints about money and his inability to provide for his family ('I have £550 a year. My house costs me £100, wages £100, horse £50, all above what I want for myself. My fuel costs me £70 to £100. What is there left to live on?')

Eventually, Godley could stand it no longer. 'It is absurd to say he can't live on £550 a year,' he wrote to Selfe:

> It is not true and I shall certainly scold him for saying so. Nor, if he were a decent man of business, would there be any difficulty in keeping his station together with his office. It is not necessary to work as he does … The fuss he makes is really quite absurd … I say decidedly *don't* encourage him, or send him more money, or express sympathy with him, but simply tell him that you think the responsibility of providing for his family lies on him, and that if he can't discharge it, with such excellent cards in his hands, he will be exceedingly culpable.

Two days later, he wrote to Fitz:

> Your account of your private affairs gives your friends here a great deal of uneasiness. It is positively monstrous that you should be spending your private means, instead of living, as every man ought to be able to, out of his salary. If you can't live on what they give you, you should ask for more; but is it certain that you can't live on it? Have you not too grand notions about the duties of expenditure to which a superintendent is liable? … Live within your official income … and don't think it necessary to do everything yourself. Distribute the business of government more fairly. Take it more easily. It is the worst economy in the world (both from your and the public's point of view) to use yourself up … And now my sermon's closed. Forgive it, and ruminate upon it.

But Fitz ruminated on very little. His mind was running ahead to the 1856 parliament, which was due to meet in April. 'I have kept myself open to take office or not as I please,' he wrote to Henry Selfe on 19 January. 'In fact I do not wish to do so but I foresee that there may be strong parties in the House and I will not refuse to form a government and take permanent office should I be required to do so … it is not impossible that you may hear of me in a few months as Colonial Secretary.' His letter ended with uncharacteristic lack of grammar:

> If I have failed to acknowledge anything, will you forgive me. I look to my wife to do that generally but these babies are obstacles. Indeed my dear Selfe, you have little idea what the obstacles to writing are in a country where labour is so scarce and dear and one must do so much for themselves and can get so little done for them.

In early February, during another spell of wet weather, he spent a week at the station. He wanted 'to see all to rights', but his mood was changing. He was losing energy, sinking into another depression. A few weeks earlier he had been full of enthusiasm, hoping to lead a ministry at the general assembly and even talking of riding overland to Nelson. Now he was suffering from pains in his chest, from 'spasmodic attacks in the heart … which occasion me great distress if I overwork'. And one evening in February, the pains 'came on with such violence as to cause great alarm'.

These angina-type pains were probably the result of stress-induced indigestion or a stomach ulcer, as well as from his tendency to hypochondria when his mood was low. The doctor assured him that his heart was not 'organically affected', that he only needed rest, but Fitz convinced himself that he was dying of heart disease and could not possibly attend the 1856 parliament. 'It is with deep regret,' wrote the *Lyttelton Times* on 27 February:

> that we must give up all hope of Mr FitzGerald's being able to attend the ensuing session of the General Assembly at Auckland. The loss of his services will be felt by the colony at large nearly as much as by this Province. But we are sorry to say that in the opinion of the medical men who have been attending him in his illness, it would be madness in him to think of going to Auckland for some time to come … a total rest from business will be necessary to establish his health which has suffered very much from the work which has pressed upon him too heavily for some time past.

The following day, Fitz was too unwell to open the new session of his provincial council. 'FitzGerald has been ill – dangerously so,' Sewell wrote in his diary three days later:

> He had a succession of seizures, less and less violent, but they have weakened him terribly. He is forbidden to think of the General Assembly, and at present cannot attend to business of any kind. This

is a sad disappointment to him, and a great loss to the Province. Besides it throws a gloom over everything.

Fitz stayed home during the next few weeks. On 23 March, he complained to Henry Selfe that he had been 'very ill indeed, not far from death'. In April, he took his family to stay with friends in the Heathcote valley, Isaac and Janetta Cookson, who were shocked by his appearance. 'Mr FitzGerald was ... so weak and so unfit for business or exertion of any kind,' Janetta wrote to Charlotte Godley:

> He still looks very thin and ill, so altered in looks and spirits you would hardly know him ... The children were all here for ten days ... They are such nice jolly children ... never was there a more fond and devoted mother than Mrs FG, and Mr FG is just as fond and proud of them. It would make you melancholy to see him. Still, he is better and if he would but be quiet and get rest and a change of air, perhaps his strength would return before the winter.

Fitz made a gift for Janetta during his stay at Heathcote, 'a beautiful model of a cutter in full sail, sea and all. He modelled the sea in clay, painted and varnished it; the boat in wood and all covered over with a glass case. I assure you it is a striking ornament in my room.'

In May, Fitz took his family to the station, hoping ('after a few weeks of rustication') that he might recover sufficiently to attend parliament which had opened in Auckland on 15 April. He soon suffered another attack of chest pain and returned to Christchurch. 'I suppose there are very dark patches in all lives,' he wrote to Godley:

> I have been passing through one of my darkest. For months I have been wholly incapable of business public or private, slowly recovering if I am recovering from the terrible illness you may have heard of. I am still very weak and any excitement or overwork brings on the attacks in the heart ... All the doctors tell me rest and care will complete my cure but I cannot myself but think that my life is in a very critical state ... I am quite undecided what to do ... an invalid in a colony is a wretched creature ... I am a dead man if I continue the life I tried to lead.

Fanny was wiser, attributing the chest pains to dyspepsia. 'I think it is a sort of almost chronic indigestion,' she told William Vaux:

> A long course of diet regularity etc and rest will, I think, quite

restore him but he is in a very nervous state at present, and wants attention day and night … James has neglected everything for public affairs … Now with James's bad health and three children we are worse off than ever … All I know is that politics have made us very very poor and I expect after the Superintendency to live at the station with three children and no servants at all so that I shall have to work most tremendously. I don't mind work a bit, but truly wish I were stronger.

Bowles. Christs Cole. Gardens. Summer 1838

'Bowls, Christ's College Gardens', watercolour by Fitz, summer 1838. On the reverse, Fitz noted that the painting included 'the mulberry tree in the Fellows' garden, supposed to have been planted by Milton'.

Private collection

'Pennarth Roads from the deck of the
Eirene', painted by Fitz on 1 December
1843 (the *Eirene* was a cutter belonging
to the Bristol Channel Mission). A few
days later, Fitz began to investigate
employment opportunities at the British
Museum.

Private collection

'The *Randolph* bound for Canterbury ...
sketched from the deck of the *Charlotte
Jane* in the English Channel', painted by
Fitz on 6 September 1850 on the voyage
to Plymouth.

Canterbury Museum (1938.238.6)

'The *Charlotte Jane* sketched from a boat
during sunset in the tropics', painted
by Fitz on 30 September 1850. 'Utter
loneliness seemed the characteristic of the
ship, so small did she appear in the middle
of the vast ocean.'

Canterbury Museum (1938.238.9)

'Sketch taken from the bed in my cabin in the *Charlotte Jane* to which I was confined at the time by an accident', painted by Fitz in November 1850 after playing snowballs with Captain Lawrence.

Canterbury Museum (1949.148.307)

Fitz and Fanny's cottage on the hill above
Lyttelton, painted by Fitz on 16 December
1851, 'a hot day with a good deal of dust
and blow'. A first anniversary painting.

Private collection

'House and tents occupied by Mr Godley'
in Riccarton, painted by Fitz when he and
Fanny were staying with the Godleys in
March 1852. Years later, Fitz remembered
sitting with Godley 'by the fern-fringed
stream' and talking 'of the great future to
come'.

Canterbury Museum (1938.238.31)

'The Residence of Mr FitzGerald immediately above Lyttelton', painted by Fitz on 6 December 1852. Seven weeks later, he sat alone in the cottage, 'amid bare walls, all my goods gone or going, my wife and child gone ... alone for my last night in Lyttelton'.

Canterbury Museum (1938.238.32)

CHAPTER SEVENTEEN

A Missed Opportunity

1856–1857

It is not impossible that you may hear of me in a few months as
Colonial Secretary.

Fitz, 19 January 1956

I am a broken down man and am quitting New Zealand politics,
probably for ever.

Fitz, 27 July 1857

On 1 April 1856, Henry Sewell left Christchurch for the general assembly in Auckland. Fitz was 'far from well,' he wrote before leaving, 'and of course liable to a recurrence of the malady at any moment, especially under excitement ... Mrs FitzGerald and the doctors insist on his not moving from Canterbury; he himself I think has a hankering after the fun.' On 14 April, Sewell received a summons to Government House: the governor told him that 'he had sent for me in default of FitzGerald'. As the only member present from Fitz's mixed ministry of 1854, Gore Browne asked him to lead the government. So it was Sewell who became first premier of the first responsible parliament, although, as he wrote on 23 April, 'if FitzGerald had been here, he would no doubt have been the man'.

Sewell was premier for a month. He steered the bill giving pensions to the crown-appointed officials through the House, and approved Gore Browne's proposal that native affairs should remain the responsibility of the British government. But he failed to command a majority in the House, and William Fox took over the premiership on 20 May. Fox lasted for little more than a week and a third ministry, under Edward Stafford, was formed on 2 June, with Sewell as colonial treasurer.

When news of this political instability reached Christchurch, Fitz decided that he was needed in Auckland; that only he could get responsible government on its feet. He wrote of 'the kind letters' he had received from Auckland, 'from the Governor and from men of all parties. There have been constant changes of ministry but they all tell me if I will only go up the government is mine. Had I been well I could not have refused it. But I am a mere wreck. Nothing else. Utterly prostrate with two hours continual conversation.'

He was missed in Auckland ('I wish FitzGerald had been here,' wrote one politician on 28 May; 'I wish indeed FitzGerald were with us,' wrote another two weeks later), and he soon decided to make the journey. As a distraught Fanny wrote to William Vaux on 15 June, 'I write this on the point of starting for Auckland. James must go and he is not fit to go alone, therefore I must accompany him, but I am obliged to leave my poor children behind which I do not at all like. However, there is no remedy; we cannot afford to take them.' She had asked her old servant, Mary Coster (now Mrs Thornton), to move into the house in Cashel Street during their absence and was confident that 'the children will be quite safe with her and Emma'.

On 17 June, she and Fitz boarded the steamer for Auckland. The voyage took eleven days. Fitz suffered further attacks of pain, Fanny had to nurse him 'day and night' in the cabin, and he was in 'a very weak state' when the steamer dropped anchor at Onehunga on the evening of 28 June. The following morning, they arrived at the house that Henry Sewell had rented in Auckland. It was Sunday and Sewell, returning from church, found Fitz looking 'very poorly … We at once made them stay with us and here they are. We are only too glad to do anything to make him more comfortable, for in truth he is very far from well.'

Fitz hated being left out of 'the fun' of the first responsible parliament. This was his second chance to take centre stage and it might have led to genuine political success. Not yet forty years old, he should have been in the prime of life, but extremes of mood continued to destroy his chances. When he attended parliament and tried to make a speech, he was unable to finish and had to sit down again in a fluster. 'Since he has been with us he has had several attacks,' wrote Sewell on 13 July, 'one very bad. He would go to the House, and meddle with business, so of course he got excited and upset. He is better again now, but the doctors say there is organic affection of the heart, and that he must not undertake business of any kind for a year at least.'

The doctors examined him and told him what he expected to hear, that his heart was 'decidedly diseased'. They prescribed 'absolute quiet as the only thing. I am forbidden to return to England which I thought of doing because the lungs are also unsound.' Ordered not to speak in public, he found it 'rather melancholy to wander about the old scenes not being allowed to open my lips. Now I am wholly forbid to enter the House at all.'

Sewell, about to return to England, had hopes that Fitz could succeed him as colonial treasurer. 'I can't do it – it would be suicide,' Fitz wrote on 11 July:

It is a sad thought but I cannot say I am very sanguine about my recovery. I am so weak – but I give all up to my wife and children. What will become of them I do not know. However quiet on the run, and open air and gentle exercise and no politics will or may do very much for me.

'There is no doubt that I have confirmed disease of the heart,' he wrote two weeks later, 'and must lead a very quiet life for the few years that are left to me.'

He now consulted 'a celebrated Homeopathic doctor who has been very successful here'. A few days later, he was 'an entire convert to Homeopathy which has certainly done more for me in a few days than the old system in weeks'. By 11 August, he was feeling 'very much better indeed', well enough to spend time sitting quietly in parliament, although he found it 'a sad thing to be mooning about the House unable to speak a word'.

Soon he felt well enough to 'do a little by advising on bills out of the House and am trying to flatter myself that I am not wholly useless'. But he was aware of the lost opportunity. 'I should very much like to have been the first minister,' he wrote to Henry Selfe, 'and I believe my accession would have satisfied all parties.'

Parliament was prorogued on 16 August, 'amid torrents of rain, and storms of wind', followed by 'the usual hurryings to and fro of people about to take a sudden departure'. The steamer was moored at Onehunga, waiting to leave at daybreak next morning. Most southern members spent the night there, but Fitz and Fanny stayed in Auckland. 'We were all astir before five o'clock,' wrote Sewell on the 17th. 'We got them some breakfast and at six their vehicle appeared and they departed.'

The weather was rough on the voyage south but Fitz bore the journey 'pretty well'. He returned to Christchurch with a case of homeopathic medicines ('which will I hope save me enormous doctor's bills') and believing that 'the only real thing for me is *absolute rest* … so that the spasmodic action of the heart may cease … and I may get well again – in say a year or so'.

Fanny was delighted to be reunited with her children after an absence of two and a half months. Four-year-old Amy was 'sharp and clever'; Willy, 'a charming child, not so sharp as Amy but more loving and not at all deficient in brains'; Robert, 'lovely but a little demon'. And Fitz's chest pains no longer frightened him. 'The attacks in the heart are still frequent,' he wrote on 3 September, 'but they have lost their malignant character and indeed hardly affect me. Six months ago a change like death came over me, even over the face – now they don't hurt me and my health gets so much stronger that they seem dying out … Indeed it is a change from death to life.'

Several weeks later, he published an address to his electors in Lyttelton. 'Had I been sufficiently recovered from my recent illness to undergo the fatigue of a public meeting,' he wrote, 'I should have asked you to meet me on my return from Auckland.' He set out his views on government policy, together with detailed ideas for remodelling and streamlining the general assembly. 'The whole colony is over-governed,' he wrote. 'The machinery of government is too weighty, too cumbersome, too costly.'

...

'My wife is expecting a fourth child in September,' Godley had written in May. 'Are we keeping ahead of you?' They were – but only by ten months. When Fitz opened a new session of his provincial council on 16 October, Fanny was pregnant with their fourth child.

The stockman's lease on the Springs station was due to expire on 17 November and Fitz decided not to renew it ('he drinks so hard I must make some other arrangements'). Two years earlier, he had bought out his sleeping partners, Harman and Davie, and added another 5000 acres to the run. It was a bad time to sell, 'so what can I do? I am not allowed to *ride*. How can I herd cattle?' He thought of taking Fanny's brother into partnership but, although George Draper was 'a good stockman, he is too young and uncertain to manage so I want to get another partner in whom I can trust'.

He had a partner in mind. On the steamer to Auckland, he had made the acquaintance of Percy Cox, a station cadet looking for work. He asked Cox to join him in partnership and suggested they buy the freehold of 3000 acres at the Springs and take the lease of a run in South Canterbury for use as a heifer station ('to separate off the growing heifers from the bulls'). The southern run, Longbeach, was 60 miles southwest of Christchurch, on the coast between the Ashburton and Rangitata rivers. 'Curiously enough,' Fitz told Henry Selfe, 'it is just the spot where poor William Draper was found.'

Cox accepted the offer. Fitz acquired Longbeach on 17 November, and by the end of the year, he had bought the freehold acres at the Springs. He was pleased with his new partner, 'a very fine fellow … a gentleman, an old colonist, and a man I know and can trust. He puts £1000 into the concern.' Cox would be in charge of Longbeach, while Fitz and George Draper would work the Springs ('George must do the riding for me'). This, wrote Fitz, 'is my plan for the future'.

He soon found an alternative to riding. 'You will smile at my present remedy,' he told Lord Lyttelton. 'It is driving tandem. Not being allowed to ride and any other driving being too slow … A good 12 mph trotting mare for wheeler and a thoroughbred leggy colt for leader, I drive across the plains to my station, 16 miles in two hours, comfortably.'

An out-of-focus image of Fitz on board the circulating medium with two horses harnessed in tandem, Springs station, 1857. A friend described being driven by Fitz at full tilt 'through rough and smooth, moist and dry – more especially through the streets of Christchurch when the leader is in a prancing humour. Remonstrance would be vain.'

Private collection

He had designed an eccentric dogcart for his tandem team, described by one man as 'a gigantic dray on springs', by another as 'the delight of small boys and the terror of all horses'. Between two enormous wheels – eight feet high and painted bright red – was fixed 'a long low-slung shallow cart body' in which Fitz drove standing up, whip in hand. With its huge wheels, the cart rode easily over rutted ground – even over ditches three feet wide. It soon became known as 'the circulating medium'.

On 23 December, a new bishop, Henry Harper, arrived in Canterbury to take pastoral charge of the South Island, accompanied by his wife and ten of his fourteen children. Met by Bishop Selwyn in his yacht, the entire party walked over the Port Hills on Christmas Eve. Their bedding and trunks were loaded onto handcarts and dragged up the Bridle Path; sailors from Selwyn's yacht pulled on ropes in front, the two bishops pushed from behind, and the Harper daughters carried 'bundles containing our best bonnets and finery'. The circulating medium was waiting at the ferry, and Fitz drove Harper and his daughters to Christchurch. They found it an uncomfortable journey, 'so rough was the road and so full of holes that the ladies could hardly keep their seats and also take care of the case containing the Bishop's precious letters patent'.

The following morning – Christmas Day – the 'precious letters patent' were read in St Michael's church during Harper's inauguration. The church was festooned with summer flowers and fruit, and the bishop was 'duly enthroned' in front of a large congregation. 'It must be admitted,' wrote one observer, 'that the appearance of the new bishop made less impression upon some of the younger minds than did that of his six daughters as they moved in procession down the aisle.'

Fitz was feeling better, but he was still 'very much shaken and in rather a precarious state'. His old partner at the station, Richard Harman, had returned from England in the same ship as Bishop Harper, and on 20 January 1857, during a spell of 'excessively hot' weather, he and Fitz rode over the Port Hills together. Harman had not seen Fitz for over two years and was shocked by the change in his appearance. 'FitzGerald is I think quite unfit for his office now,' he wrote to Godley the following day:

> He is so irritable and obstinate that I should be very sorry to have much business with him and even in private yield to him in all discussion rather than run the chance of irritating him. I believe he has quite made up his mind that, even if he recovers for the present, he will probably be carried off suddenly in the same manner as his brother who was in India.

Harman had been acting as emigration agent in London, sent by Fitz in 1854 to despatch further ships to Canterbury. Immigration had dried up after the demise of the association and many of the early settlers were lost to the goldfields in Australia. As a result, little progress could be made on public works and infrastructure. In late 1853, Fitz reduced the land price to £2 an acre, which led to an increase in land sales; and in March 1854 he persuaded the council to pledge £10,000 for immigration.

In 1855, the general assembly claimed a proportion of Canterbury's land fund, reducing the money available for immigration, so Harman made plans to return to New Zealand. The following year, parliament returned full control of the fund to Canterbury. There was a surge in land sales, which bolstered the provincial coffers and opened the door for further immigration. The colony was in need of labour ('to till the land, to sheer the flocks, to make the roads') and, because Harman had no wish to return to London, there was a vacancy to fill.

On 10 February 1857, Fitz wrote to Henry Selfe, again complaining about his health:

> I vary so much, one day quite well, the next in bed half the day with such awful depression from the inaction of the heart that I am not fit for much … Many people are urging me to go to England for medical advice … But I believe the quiet of the station would do more for me … Talking and writing are the two things that weary me most.

A few days later, he announced that he would not stand for re-election when his term as superintendent came to an end. He was thinking of returning to England to obtain the best medical advice.

On 3 March, he received an address from his council members who hoped his departure 'will not wholly deprive us of your services, but that you may be induced to undertake the important office of Emigration Agent for this Province'. They offered him a two-year term of office in London at an annual salary of £400, plus expenses of £780 for the voyage and relocation costs.

On 2 April, Fitz opened the last session of his provincial council. Five weeks later, he wrote again to Henry Selfe:

> I believe I shall go though I really do not wish it personally. I am very happy here, the expense will be very great and I shall be worked in England I well know harder than here. But I have always been drawn into these things and suppose I shall be compelled to return … As to my health, it has been so much better the last month that I really feel like myself but if I do the least imprudent thing, even to eat anything that disagrees with me, I have an attack in the heart instantly. Driving tandem has cured me, giving me air and exercise and *nerve*. I consider myself rather a whip now.

Fitz at the Springs station, 1857. This is the last photograph to show him clean-shaven.

Canterbury Museum (Dr A.C. Barker Collection, 19XX.2.25)

The station would be in good hands during his absence. He considered Percy Cox to be 'a thoroughly trustworthy fellow … the more I see of him, the more I like him … George Draper goes on pretty well too.' Cox had built a house at Longbeach and prepared the run for stock, and in mid-May, he and Draper drove the first batch of heifers south from the Springs.

In anticipation of his departure, Fitz found a tenant for his house in Christchurch. But on 20 June, after council members voted to reduce the money available for immigration, he changed his mind. The future prosperity of the province relied on immigration, he told the council:

> I confess I am greatly mortified to see the opportunity lost by a
> want of comprehension … and to be incapacitated by my own feeble
> health from averting the danger of this timidity and over-prudence.
> All my hopes are destroyed by these unfortunate Resolutions … I
> cannot become the agent of a policy so opposed to my own views …
> I feel that what little health and strength I may be able to devote to
> the public service will be best employed in the Province, in endeav-
> ouring to upset this miserable and timid policy.

For the next nine days, he made plans to remain in Canterbury. He arranged
to extend the house at the station ('it is not large enough for my family, as well
as Cox and George Draper'), and he wrote to the premier, Edward Stafford. 'I
did think of going to England,' he explained, 'but have now given up the idea
and am going down to the station in a month.'

The council gave in on 29 June, voting £20,000 for immigration over three
years, so Fitz changed his mind again:

> I certainly did not think that it would be worthwhile sending home
> an Agent at so great a cost merely to spend the small sums specified
> in your Resolutions; but if the government of this Province be about
> to undertake the work of real colonisation for the next three or four
> years, I shall be glad to resume again the labours which I underwent
> in 1850, as one of the most active agents in the colonisation of this
> country, and, I earnestly hope, with similar success.

All this uncertainty was difficult for Fanny, who gave birth to their fourth
child (a son named Gerald) on 26 June. And while she lay in bed recovering
from childbirth, Fitz too was confined to bed, suffering from 'lumbago and
boils' and feeling 'very seedy indeed'. He was too ill to attend the dissolution of
his provincial council on 30 June; instead he composed 'a valedictory address'
which the Speaker read on his behalf. That evening, he wrote to Henry Selfe:

> The Provincial Council is dissolved today. So my work is done. I
> regret to leave it. They will never find another man who loved his
> work and the Province as well … I sail by the first opportunity … I
> go to get better medical advice well knowing it will do me no good.
> I would ten times rather stay here than go to England but for one's
> wife and children's sake, one must do everything – perhaps change of
> scene and rest on the voyage may do me some good.

In July, he resigned from the general assembly. On the 24th, he took part
in a formal procession to 'a wild-looking spot covered with *toi toi*, fern and

yellow tussock', where Bishop Harper laid the foundation stone of the school, which Fitz had named Christ's College after his alma mater in Cambridge. On the 27th, a cold day with flurries of snow, he wrote two letters. The first was an official letter to London about his role as emigration agent; the second a twelve-page letter to Edward Stafford:

> I am just off for England by the first ship. I am a broken down man and am quitting New Zealand politics, probably for ever. Return, if I live, I certainly shall but not as a politician, so what I say may be of little interest to you. But ... I will say it, and I will say with all the solemnity due to my dying speech on New Zealand politics.

There followed many paragraphs about political matters ('your finance scheme has failed ... if ever I saw my way through a problem in life, and I did sometimes at Cambridge, I see my way through the New Zealand finances'). He wrote about provincial politics and native affairs, about the Supreme Court and the need for more judges, and he ended with a hint that he should like his views made public: 'I should not be sorry if you were to allow this letter to leak out into the southern press; at all events show it ... to your colleagues, and to His Excellency if he would care to read it.'

…

Despite his ill health, Fitz planned to leave Canterbury in style. His four years as superintendent had been characterised, at different times, by shortage of labour and lack of funds. As a result, the major difficulty faced by the people of Christchurch – the hills separating the town from the port – remained unresolved. All goods, imports and exports, had to be carried over the hills, or risk shipwreck on the Sumner bar.

Six years earlier, Fitz had been appointed to a committee set up to examine 'the best means of improving communication between the port and the plains'. After three months' deliberation, the committee recommended that the road to Sumner be completed over Evans Pass (the lowest pass on the hills). The work was estimated to take two years and cost £32,000, of which £5000 was already in hand (£3000 from the Canterbury Association, £2000 offered by Sir George Grey from colonial funds); the balance was to be obtained by way of a loan.

This proposal was approved in January 1852, but the loan never materialised and the £5000 was diverted to other purposes. In 1854, the provincial council set up another committee and, once again, Fitz busied himself with the problem ('his head has been full of every impossible means of communication between the port and the plains'). A year later, after the council voted funds to complete the Sumner Road, he was reported to be 'almost living on the road; he is most energetic about it'.

He then had another idea, 'a scheme about which he is at present mad'. This, as he explained to Godley in August 1855, was 'a tramway along the Sumner Road – a railway for horses – from Lyttelton to the ferry first, and afterwards to Christchurch. The whole settlement is agog with the idea.'

Work on the road stopped again when the general assembly claimed a proportion of Canterbury's land fund, but resumed in 1856 using prison labour. To reduce the amount of rock cutting, the road skirted the cliff at a gentle gradient, after which a 'temporary track' would climb steeply up towards Evans Pass – under which Fitz hoped to build a short tunnel – in a perilous zigzag.

Fitz pushed ahead with the work in the hope that this link between port and plains would form a popular climax to his superintendency. In July 1857, workers were still cutting into the rock. By the end of the month (when he was complaining that, 'when I have done my public business of the day and taken my walk or drive, I just lie down on the sofa and read a novel. I *can't* do anything else'), he was making plans to open the road in a blaze of publicity. 'I am about to drive round it in … the first wheeled vehicle to traverse the line,' he wrote on the 27th, 'and I confidently hope that next year will see the completion of the road by the construction of the tunnel.'

The 'temporary track' over Evans Pass was still unfinished; it was narrow in places and the zigzag was insufficiently surfaced. Fitz was undaunted. On the morning of 24 August, he set out from Christchurch in the circulating medium, with two horses rigged tandem and three members of his council on board. 'My experience of tandem driving,' wrote one of the spectators, 'is that the leader is given to turning round and staring one in the face … decidedly dangerous on the Sumner Road.'

Fitz's dogcart was followed by large numbers of men on horseback, pedestrians carrying banners, and a cartload of musicians playing airs from Handel. They crossed the Heathcote River in relays on the ferry punt, passed under a triumphal arch at Sumner, and arrived at the inn, where Fitz and his passengers enjoyed a hearty meal before setting out for the summit.

Standing up in the cart, flourishing his whip above his head, Fitz encouraged the horses up the hill. When he reached the top of Evans Pass, he looked down at the pale green waters of Lyttelton harbour, 650 feet below, an almost vertical drop as the road 'fell away in a series of zigzags, not by any means inviting'. At this point, his passengers took to their feet, while Fitz edged his horses into the descent.

If a horse had stumbled, if the dogcart had lurched, the whole ensemble might have tumbled over the edge. Men hung onto the horses' heads to steady them, others pulled on the back of the cart to slow it down. Three and a half hours after leaving Christchurch, Fitz drove into Lyttelton under an arch of banners and paraded through the streets, waving his whip triumphantly to cheering crowds.

Although a road this dangerous hardly improved the transport link between port and town (it would never be suitable for commercial traffic), Fitz's drive over Evans Pass was a resounding finale to his term of office. That evening, he chaired a public dinner in the Universal Hotel in Lyttelton. A toast was proposed 'to the health of his Honour the Superintendent' and, when Fitz rose to reply, he was 'received with a perfect tumult of cheers'. He told his audience that roads were a measure of civilisation; that the road he had driven that day was 'a mere beginning' for Canterbury. He then spoke of his imminent departure:

> Canterbury and its interests are very dear to me ... For eight years
> of my life all my thoughts and actions have been bound up in
> Canterbury ... My sole object for visiting England is the restoration
> of my health, and I would not think of leaving the province did I not
> trust that I shall shortly return to it with re-established vigour.

He resumed his seat to 'loud and prolonged cheering'. And when a toast was proposed to 'the health of Mrs FitzGerald and family', he rose again to respond. Fanny, he said:

> had hoped to accompany my journey today and to have paid a
> parting visit to Lyttelton. I beg to assure you that the reason why she
> has not come is not fear of the road, nor want of confidence in my
> skill in driving [laughter]; but the domestic duties that of necessity
> crowd upon her in consequence of our departure for England.

Fanny spent the next five weeks preparing for the voyage, and Fitz booked cabins on the schooner *James Gibson* bound for Sydney, the first leg of the long journey home. According to Richard Harman, both he and Fanny were 'suffering terribly from boils, but I hardly think Mrs FG would allow even such a bothersome affliction as this to prevent her being ready at her husband's call. She is certainly a woman of a great deal of spirit.'

PART IV

Fitz starts a newspaper

CHAPTER EIGHTEEN

An Influential Colonist

1857–1860

Oh! don't you remember FitzGerald, my boy,
FitzGerald who used to so tease;
Who soaped us all down when we ventured to frown,
And frown'd when we most wish'd to please?
The wind blows fresh on FitzGerald, my boy,
As he ploughs through the salt sea foam;
Oh! I'd like to ship for the same sort of trip,
And be paid, my old boy, to go home!

Crosbie Ward, Lyttelton Times, *January 1858*

The *James Gibson* sailed from Lyttelton on 30 September 1857. 'There were no other passengers,' remembered Amy in her memoirs, 'no stewardess, just one black steward. We had awful weather and were three weeks in reaching Sydney.' Fitz was 'very ill' during the voyage, so Fanny was kept busy caring for her husband as well as her children.

When they arrived in Sydney, they took rooms in the Exchange Hotel. Fitz wrote again to Edward Stafford: 'I sent you a parting shot from Canterbury because I knew you couldn't answer me … I hope you have given up that beastly red tapeism.'

On 27 October, still feeling unwell ('my health does not improve, rather the contrary; I can't say how I shall bear the voyage home'), they embarked on a small sailing ship, the *Speedy*, and became reacquainted with shipboard life: meals in the cuddy, long hours on the poop deck, the cold of the Southern Ocean, the heat of the tropics.

The *Speedy* did not live up to its name: the voyage to London took almost four months. The final weeks were cold, with a strong northerly wind. Fitz suffered from a 'bronchial cough'; the children with colds and chills. Finally, the grey shores of England swam into view and, as the ship was towed upriver to Gravesend, Fitz and Fanny stood on deck watching the flat landscape of Kent slide by under a dark and dismal sky.

Godley was in the throes of moving house when news of the *Speedy*'s arrival reached him on 19 February. From his new home in Gloucester Place, he sent

Willy, sketched by Fitz to celebrate his fourth birthday, 12 October 1857. The drawing was made on board the *James Gibson* bound for Sydney.

Private collection

a note to the docks: 'If you and Mrs FitzGerald will make excuses for our want of proper preparations, and will consent to sleep in a room uncarpeted and half full of boxes, we shall be very glad to have you under our roof till you can provide for yourselves elsewhere.'

Reunited in Gloucester Place, Fanny and Charlotte inspected the new additions to the families. Fitz and Godley (now working as assistant under-secretary in the War Office) talked about politics, and Fitz learnt that William Moorhouse – a member of his provincial council, a man he described as 'an unmitigated blackguard' – had been elected superintendent in his place.

The cold winds continued to blow, and three weeks after his arrival, Fitz suffered another 'serious attack on the chest'. A specialist assured him that there was nothing wrong with his heart, that his complaint was neither 'organic nor dangerous', but Fitz would not be persuaded. 'I have no doubt that there is organic mischief, of which the symptoms are unmistakeable,' he wrote. 'And though I may live to 70 in a state of quietude, any strong or prolonged excitement would shake me up in a very short time.'

In April, he rented a house (described by Henry Selfe as 'of very modest and unpretending character') in Grosvenor Villas, Upper Holloway. His salary as emigration agent was low by London standards ('he will hardly make ends meet on £400 a year,' Richard Harman wrote from Christchurch, 'if he could not live here on £550'), so the provincial council agreed to pay his salary from the date of departure from Canterbury – an additional £166.

Fitz and Fanny enjoyed meeting family and friends again, although Fanny was dreading her first encounter with her father, who had not written her a single word since her marriage. His business with Russia had been ruined by the Crimean War, and in November 1857 his company filed for bankruptcy; the newspapers reported 'great regret at the stoppage of the well-known and respected firm of Draper & Co, with liabilities estimated at £350,000'.

Fitz's half-brother Gerald (funded by the family estates in Ireland) was enjoying a wealthy lifestyle in a large house in Berkshire. Richard was rector of Winslade in Hampshire; Lucius was recently married; and their stepmother had fled abroad to escape her debts (a situation described by Robert in India as 'that cursed swindling business of Mrs FG ... [she] can never show her face again in England to any friends of the family').

William Vaux was still at the British Museum, still living in Gate Street; and Fitz saw Henry Selfe every day, for they shared an office at 32 Charing Cross. Selfe had joined the committee of the Canterbury Association in September 1850; as legal adviser to Lord Lyttelton, it was he who wound up its affairs in London. Now he was acting as agent for the province. He and Fitz relished each other's company. They enjoyed jokes and puns, and there was always laughter in the office. But Fitz had to explain why he had so often thought of selling the station ('at £3000; your share £2000, mine £1000') and had never done so, and why he had so rarely sent his friend the promised dividend.

On 24 September, he was guest of honour at a dinner in the London Tavern, at which he gave 'an eloquent and glowing speech' about New Zealand. He compared the colony, 'where the position of the labouring man is what it ought to be, that of independence and plenty, where I have never seen an hour's real want under the most trying circumstances', to England, 'where I now behold a poverty which I have not seen for the last eight years'. New Zealand, he said, 'had grown from nothing into English confidence' and was 'the very best field for English colonisation'.

Two months later he was once more in pride of place, this time at the annual Canterbury dinner. Lord Lyttelton was in the chair and Godley proposed the toast to Fitz's health: 'Mr FitzGerald was the first who landed in Canterbury after the settlement was founded and I shall never forget the emotion with which I threw myself into his arms. Both of us, I am sure, will look back on that moment as one of the most affecting and memorable of our lives.'

Godley also referred to the energy that Fitz 'brings to bear upon everything in which he engages'. Henry Selfe agreed. 'It is impossible,' he wrote to the new superintendent, 'for me to bear too strong testimony to the energy and ability with which he is conducting the emigration service.'

Fitz advertised for emigrants in national and local newspapers, offering assisted passage to 'agricultural labourers, shepherds, carpenters, other country mechanics, and domestic servants'. With the help of one clerk and a messenger boy, he negotiated shipping contracts, ensured reasonable living conditions on board, employed matrons and schoolmasters, and visited every vessel before departure, 'taking a final survey of the ship and shaking hands with this, that, and the other of the cabin passengers'.

Richard Harman had prepared the ground well, publicising the province with leaflets, posters and visits to major towns. Fitz had instructions to send a ship every month. As a result of Harman's efforts, the work was easier than in 1850. He travelled the country, interviewing every applicant and insisting that each emigrant contribute to the cost of the voyage. 'I am quite persuaded,' he informed the provincial council, 'that *cash payment* is what makes the great distinguishing feature between the Canterbury emigration and any other. Give up that and you will get a lower class of men altogether.' This sometimes led to a lack of flexibility. One evening, when Fitz was in Kidderminster:

> a poor widow called on me at the inn. I took a great fancy to her but what can I do? She has *five* children. She seemed a thoroughly good hardworking woman. I said I would take her for half the fare, £34. Where she will get it, I don't know. The poor rates pay her five shillings a week.

He travelled to Deal in Kent to address a meeting of boatmen whose livelihoods (guiding ships under sail through the treacherous Goodwin Sands) had been lost with the advent of steamships. When emigration was put forward as a solution, Fitz suggested the establishment of deep-water fisheries at Timaru, a new settlement in South Canterbury. He agreed to relax the requirement for cash payment but insisted on accepting only married men. 'If young men want to go out under my auspices,' he told them, 'they must get wives. Married men with large families, and grown-up daughters in particular, are our greatest treasures.'

He despatched orphan girls from institutions to train as domestic servants, 'sent out at the expense of benevolent ladies in London'. Single women were in short supply in the province and Fitz believed the benefits would be 'incalculable'. The first consignment of nine orphans, aged between fourteen and sixteen, sailed with the Deal boatmen in December 1858.

In early April 1859, Edward Stafford arrived in London to investigate the possibility of a steam mail service to New Zealand. Fitz was looking better, he wrote on the 11th, 'but still ill'. He was invited to dinner with Fitz and Fanny on 12 May. Fanny's confinement was imminent, he wrote in his diary that night, and the children were 'grown much and looking very well indeed'.

Fanny gave birth to their fifth child, a boy, on 1 June. Three weeks later, Fitz wrote to Lord Lyttelton: 'I want to ask you to be Godfather to my young son. And I want to call him after you to connect one member of my family by name, not only with you but with the great work in which we have been associated. My wife joins with me, both in the request and the motive.'

Lyttelton attended the christening on 4 July, standing by the font as the baby was baptised with his name. And during a conversation in Grosvenor Villas later that afternoon, he spoke of Fitz's intention, as he put it, 'to desert Canterbury'.

...

Legend has it that Fitz was offered two colonial governorships during his time in London, both of which he declined because of ill health. The truth is somewhat different.

In Christchurch, he had read a speech by Gladstone complaining of 'the difficulty in getting men to take the office of governor to a colony'. This fired him up and he wrote letters to Godley, Selfe, Lord Lyttelton, William Vaux, and John Ball, who had recently been appointed under-secretary of state in the Colonial Office. The letters contained strong hints of his suitability for the role of governor ('I think they might find worse governors than one who has studied the subject as long as I have'), leavened by expressions of modesty and reluctance ('but I don't want this, I had rather return to the cows and the plough').

The first available governorship was in British Columbia, an area of Canada (including Vancouver Island) which had converted to a crown colony in August 1858. Fitz would have enjoyed the poetic justice if he had become governor of the old Hudson Bay territory. Instead, the post went to Sir James Douglas (who had previously managed the company) – a man with an in-depth knowledge of the region.

The second governorship was in Moreton Bay (Queensland), which became a crown colony in 1859 when it separated from New South Wales. In April that year, Fitz approached Lord Carnarvon, who had replaced John Ball as under-secretary in the Colonial Office. 'I said if they wanted a man to *work*, they may send me,' he told Lord Lyttelton. 'I am not at all anxious for it but I should, I confess, like the offer.' On 14 May, he received a letter from Carnarvon:

I ought long since to have written to you in reference to our recent conversation upon the Governorship of Moreton Bay, which was then vacant, but I have been so severely pressed by other business that I have been unable to do so from the want of time. Indeed, now that Sir G Bowen's appointment, of which I was not aware at the time of our conversation, is public, I have little to explain or to add except to mention that, although I wrote to [the Colonial Secretary] on the same day that I saw you, the arrangement with Sir George was already concluded.

Fitz put a brave face on the disappointment. 'It is only recently,' he replied on 19 May:

that my health has been sufficiently re-established to enable me to contemplate again taking any public office. I am not at all desirous of doing so … But having spent many years in the constant study of colonial questions and had somewhat peculiar opportunities for watching them working, I hoped you would not think me presumptuous in offering to place my services at the disposal of the government.

Now, after the christening of his fourth son, he had to explain himself to the boy's godfather. 'I wish to say a word as to a remark which fell from you at my house,' he wrote to Lord Lyttelton:

You seemed to think that because I entertained the idea of taking the governorship of another colony, I intended to desert Canterbury. I assure you, I never thought of doing so. My wish is to live and die there, but it is idle to conceal from myself the fact that I shall be of no use there publicly except in the assemblies, and that I am forbidden to join them, both by my health and pocket.

'Every man wishes to rise in his profession,' he continued (with a distortion of the truth):

and, having been left by my father most unfortunately without one, I made one for myself, a colonial politician. I confess a wish to rise in it. I should greatly like to be a governor of an English colony and I think I should make a very much better governor than some to whom I know governorship has been offered in my time … But if I went to such a place for a few years, I should return to Canterbury as to my home … Pardon my saying so much about myself, but I don't like you to think me a deserter.

Fitz had now become 'enormously fat'. His friends believed him to be in a 'remarkably strong' state of health, but despite assurances from the doctors, he continued to believe that he was suffering from heart disease, and that his life span would be short. 'My health,' he wrote, 'is as good as it *ever* will be again.'

In addition to his emigration duties, he was raising subscriptions to buy books for the library of Christ's College, organising an appeal for funds to build a cathedral (for which he commissioned the architect, George Gilbert Scott, to prepare the plans), and obtaining copies of British parliamentary papers for the library of the New Zealand parliament.

He bought an iron clock tower and despatched it to Christchurch. He involved himself in the creation of deep-water moorings at Timaru, writing letters about anchors and mooring chains. And with a vote of £1500 from the provincial council, he organised the despatch of equipment to install a telegraph line over the Bridle Path between Lyttelton and Christchurch: 20 miles of wire, batteries, insulators and 250 iron poles.

'I suppose the government hates me for sending so many despatches,' he wrote in March 1859. 'I am by this mail sending tenders for bridges and proposals for importing salmon and various little matters.' He recommended the export of frozen spawn for a salmon fishery, 'by which not only the province and colony might be supplied, but even Australia which has a climate not suited to the fish'.

His most cherished plan was the horse tramway to Sumner. He had made a clay model of the Port Hills ('for railway purposes – I think it will make a sensation') and he obtained an estimate of £70,000 from 'one of the largest railway contractors in the world' to lay the track and build a tunnel under Evans Pass. He assumed that, when the province could afford it, the tramway would be replaced by a railway following the same route.

His plan was opposed by the new superintendent, William Moorhouse, who came up with an even more adventurous scheme of his own. Instead of a line of steep gradients and sharp curves following the Sumner Road, the Moorhouse plan was daring and simple. He proposed a direct route, a straight line between Lyttelton and Christchurch: a tunnel under the Port Hills.

The Pilgrims had talked of a tunnel almost as soon as they arrived in Canterbury but Fitz had rejected the idea as too expensive. He had not changed his mind. 'It would not be wise to penetrate the hill by a tunnel,' he wrote to Moorhouse. The cost would be 'far beyond the means of the Province for years to come'. And he wrote to John Hall, who also opposed the tunnel: 'Some will say I am prejudiced in favour of the Sumner Road – I look on it as a triumph of my own engineering opinion.'

The provincial council set up a committee to consider the two proposals. Fitz and Henry Selfe were appointed commissioners in London and they referred the matter to the railway engineer, George Stephenson. Fitz tried to persuade Stephenson of the advantages of his horse tramway, but in August 1859 Stephenson 'negatived' the idea, deciding in favour of the Moorhouse scheme.

The tunnel through the Port Hills (at 3000 yards one of the longest tunnels in the world at the time) was estimated to cost £200,000, with another £50,000 for the six-mile railway to Christchurch. This was to be funded by a loan of £300,000, an enormous sum for a province less than ten years old. 'Nothing has ever occasioned me more anxiety than the railway,' Fitz wrote at the end of August. 'It is a great experiment which will put us at the pinnacle of greatness or ruin us.'

...

The supply of emigrants slowed in early 1859, mainly because of increased prosperity in England, and Fitz began to feel nostalgic for Canterbury. 'Emigration has fallen off,' he wrote to John Hall on 17 March. 'I have written for my discharge. I want to get back to the colony.'

Six months later, he received a reply from Christchurch asking him to remain in London for several months beyond the term of his contract. 'We hope he will stay,' wrote Charles Bowen. 'Mrs FitzGerald evidently wishes to stay and she has more sense for his interests than he has himself.'

'I am entirely at the disposal of the government if they require my services at the termination of my present agreement,' Fitz wrote to Moorhouse on 17 September:

> It was my wish on private grounds to return to the colony ... But the steps I have been led to take in respect to the railway are such that I feel that the government may wish me to remain to complete the arrangements for getting that work under weigh ... My private wishes remain unchanged, but I am induced to submit ... by the contractors having expressed a wish that I should remain till the arrangements were completed.

By this time, Fitz and Selfe had raised an initial loan of £70,000 from the Union Bank of Australia and signed a contract with a firm of engineers. There was much to arrange; but Fitz's thoughts had returned to the colony. 'I can't tell you how I long to be back in Canterbury,' he wrote to a friend in Christchurch, 'but when we shall get back I really don't know. This abominable railway which *sits* on me night and day will I suppose keep me in England some time longer.' He continued with news of the children:

Gerald is a demon …He has the brains of all the family and uses them to touch, worry, fidget, fiddle, meddle, bother and bore from morning till night … Robert cries all day long and Willy is … the pleasantest company. The new baby Lyttelton lies in bed cooing and is a most perfect angel, but as Gerald was exactly the same up to two years old, we know what we've got to expect.

To Lord Lyttelton, he gave news of his godson: 'I am hourly assured on the highest authority that it is an angel in disguise. To me, it presents itself as one vast *lung* which far surpasses Big Ben in sonorous effect, especially in the solemn hours of the night.'

The symptoms of heart disease had disappeared; instead Fitz was dividing his time 'between rheumatism and coughs'. His cough, exacerbated by smoking, became worse during the winter months and, believing that his lungs were 'shaky', he began to worry about tuberculosis.

In January 1860, he chaired an anniversary dinner celebrating the foundation of the Australian colonies. In February, he attended a service in St Paul's Cathedral at which a memorial pulpit ('erected by his personal friends and brother officers') was dedicated to the memory of Robert, his soldier brother. The next few weeks brought snow and hail to the streets of London, a prolonged cold spell which led to a bout of bronchitis. 'I am seedy,' he wrote on 13 April, 'obliged to be very careful with lungs.'

'Confined to the home' for the rest of the month, he wrote letters about Moorhouse and the railway ('I am sick to death of the whole thing'). And as warmer weather arrived in May, he made plans to return to New Zealand and settle down to life as a farmer. 'I lost a great deal too much money, not to say health, to have anything to do [with politics] again,' he told Lord Lyttelton. 'I have quite made up my mind never to touch public affairs again unless they should make me a governor which is very unlikely. I have others beside myself to look after and I have done enough for Canterbury. Besides I am getting *old*.'

…

Fitz changed his mind a few weeks later, having opened his morning paper to read that 'a Bill has been brought into the House of Lords for altering the constitution of New Zealand'. He met with other New Zealand colonists and, 'although acting in the dark, we felt that the Bill ought to be opposed at once'. The colonial secretary was out of the country, so they arranged a meeting with the leader of the opposition, who agreed to delay the bill for three weeks, 'a great step gained so late in the session'. At the same time, Fitz wrote a paper to be presented to parliament, 'simply praying that the Bill might be delayed until the colony has time to petition on the subject'.

The New Zealand Bill ('for the better government of the native inhabitants of New Zealand and for facilitating the purchase of native lands') concerned responsibility for Maori affairs. When Gore Brown devolved responsible government to the New Zealand parliament in 1856, he had retained power over native affairs. The general assembly had recently challenged this situation, asking Gore Brown to hand over responsibility. This he refused to do. Instead, he wrote to the Colonial Office proposing that the British government should establish a council to decide on Maori policy.

Fitz published his paper on 5 July. The bill, he wrote, was 'superfluous, dangerous, unnecessary, and irresponsible'. Great difficulties had arisen because control over native affairs had been retained by the crown. The assembly had acquiesced in the arrangement ('though not willingly or hopefully') because members considered it to be a temporary measure. The bill would make this unsatisfactory situation permanent:

> As one who has taken a share in the government of the colony for some years, I most earnestly protest against the passing of this Bill, *without the knowledge of the colonists*. Their lives and fortunes are involved in this measure. They are totally ignorant that any such measure was about to be proposed, and they ought to be allowed time to petition Parliament on the subject … I dread beyond expression the consequences of placing the two races in a position of antagonism at a very moment when sound policy would suggest the merging of their interests in a common government.

He sent copies of the paper to all politicians with an interest in colonial affairs. On 11 July, he chaired a meeting of New Zealand colonists, speaking 'at some length' about the evils of the bill. On the 30th, he published a second paper, explaining his fears of racial tension in more detail. 'The policy of this Bill,' he wrote, 'is a policy of separating the races … of sowing in the minds of the Maori a jealousy and mistrust of the government of the settlers. The passing of this Bill will be the death warrant of the Maori race.'

Two days later, he was in the gallery of the House of Lords when the bill was presented for its third reading. He had letters of support from a number of peers but Lord Lyttelton, in one of his periodic fits of depression, made a lacklustre speech. The bill passed without a division, 'with an indifference', as Fitz put it, 'which was little short of contempt'. He made his views clear to a member of the House:

> When I recollect the long, earnest, well-informed, and intelligent debates I have heard in the Houses of Legislature in New Zealand

... and then turn to the miserable exhibition of listlessness, and
boredness, and ignorance ... in your Lordship's house, I ask myself,
in the name of common sense, which body is most likely to come to
a sound and right conclusion?

Having passed through the Lords, the bill was sent to the Commons and
Fitz was put to 'a great deal of extra trouble to get up an opposition when I
want all my time to prepare for going away'. After several postponements, the
second reading was scheduled for 20 August. Fitz led a deputation to meet
the prime minister and did his best to lobby members of parliament, many
of whom had left London for the summer season. On 17 August, he wrote a
letter to *The Times*:

The Bill is opposed by ... all the Tory party who have paid any
attention to it. It is opposed by many of the Whigs; it is opposed
by men of every section of the Radical party; it is opposed by
some of the Irish members, and it is well-known that it is disliked
by many members of the government itself. I ask, as a matter of
common fairness and honesty, will the few members still in town
allow a measure to pass which I fully believe would be thrown
out by a majority of three to one in a full House and after fair
discussion?

The bill was withdrawn on 21 August, a defeat attributed by one minister
to 'an obstinate opposition on behalf of certain influential colonists'. As Fitz
wrote to a friend in New Zealand, 'no labour, time or money has been spared
but ... on the eve of sailing to the colony, it has been a very severe tax upon
my time and attention'.

...

Fitz had fulfilled his quota of emigrants for the year, despite the slowing of
supply. 'I must resign at once,' he told Henry Selfe in July:

that is as soon as the August ship goes, and I may as well go in her.
There can be no further ships till the vote for 60/61 shows how
much money they will vote [for emigration]. We could not hear of
this vote till January or February. It would then take two months or
more to fill a ship ... Nothing would justify me in staying here doing
nothing all that time.

The 'August ship' was the *Matoaka*, due to sail from Bristol on 4 September.
Fitz wrote his resignation and booked three cabins. During his last weeks in
London, he 'had no time to *think* at all. The ship, packing, parting, the New

Zealand Bill at which I worked incessantly, have all kept me so busy that I can realise nothing but the necessity of *working against time.*'

During recent weeks, he had been in regular correspondence with Godley, whose health was in decline and who was spending the summer in Malvern. 'The doctors assure me I have no disease,' Godley informed him, 'and that what I suffer from is overwork and over-thought acting on a nervous, excitable temperament. I fancy there is much analogy between your case and mine in that respect.'

The doctors were wrong. Tuberculosis had spread to the lymph nodes in Godley's throat, causing 'acute pain, especially in swallowing'. In July, he and Charlotte moved to Filey on the Yorkshire coast, where the doctors ordered him not to talk. 'We have been thinking of, and deploring, the impossibility of seeing you before you sail,' he wrote to Fitz on 30 July:

> We don't know how to reconcile ourselves to it at all. But there is, alas! no help for it. Perhaps, as regards myself, it is *more wholesome* that I should not see you; for as to seeing you without talking, such an idea of course is visionary in the extreme ... My wife joins in sincere sorrow and much love.

'The very sad state of poor Godley's health throws a great gloom over the gloomy enough period of parting from you all,' Fitz wrote to Henry Selfe six days later:

> There may be many whom one will never see again but in his case it is a certainty ... It is very sad to feel that I have seen the last of so dear and true a friend. And I cannot disguise from myself that this exodus is on the whole a much sadder thing than the last. One is different at 30 and at 40. Different with no children and with five. Different in the strange excitement of enterprise and in the sober execution of duty.

'Canterbury is my home,' he continued. 'And though it is on many accounts distasteful to me to sacrifice politics and public affairs for the lower occupations of trade and farming, yet with my growing family, that is plainly what I have to do.'

There was a farewell banquet in his honour ('a pleasant little dinner') and, on 28 August, Fitz and his family travelled by train to Bristol. The *Matoaka* lay at anchor in the King's Roads where the River Severn broadens into the Bristol Channel, an area where Fitz had 'often walked about as a lad'.

He supervised the loading of their luggage (29 trunks, another pure-bred

Durham cow, and eight kegs of rennet for making cheese). The family embarked during the afternoon of 3 September. That night, Fitz sat in the cabin reading a letter of farewell from Godley, written in Filey on 26 August:

> I write one line only, to bid you sadly farewell, and to say how thoroughly our hearts go with you and your dear wife … it is a great and grievous loss to us, especially as I cannot but feel the improbability of our ever meeting again on this side of the grave … So we must look to meeting, my dear friend, in a better country, where I hope and trust the remembrance of the work we have done together may be a possession for ever … Don't answer this – it is useless and only too sad.

Fitz ignored this final sentence, putting pen to paper to write a farewell letter of his own:

> I could not leave England without answering your last letter …
> Nothing can be sadder than this parting – very different from
> the last. It is all without the buoyancy of youth and of the former
> delightful uncertainty and expectation. It is connected with the
> certainty of having separated for ever from many dear friends.

It was 'a still lovely moonlit night', the quiet of the cabin 'very delicious after all the trouble and weariness of the last month'. 'My dear Godley,' he wrote as he reached the end of the page:

> You are my last thought in England. To you I owe everything for
> having directed the wavering inclinations of a life hitherto useless.
> The *work* we have been engaged in is not so much the work which I
> have made as the work which has made me … In the hope and great
> longing to meet again even in this world, your faithful friend, James
> Edward FitzGerald.

CHAPTER NINETEEN

Without Fear or Favour

1860–1861

I shall be curious to see what safety valve your political energy will take.
John Godley, 25 March 1861

I am very quiet now, but fear I shall break out some day.
Fitz, 4 March 1861

The *Matoaka* was a clipper ship, built for speed to carry tea from China and wool from Australasia. With a tall mast, large sail area and narrow hull, the clipper moved fast through the water – so this second voyage to New Zealand should have been much shorter than the first. However, because of lack of wind ('calm the whole way beyond all belief and very tedious as we were so frequently becalmed'), they were at sea for 88 days.

Luckily for Fanny, who was pregnant again and feeling queasy, there was only one day of high seas. Fitz too felt 'seedy' at the start of the voyage, but perked up after the first week and soon became 'wonderfully well'. The ship was 'very comfortable' and Fitz's cow produced 'an abundance of milk, plenty for our children, a great luxury'. But according to Fanny, the singing by the cabin passengers was 'detestable – I shall never again go in a ship which has a piano'.

Robert learned to 'shin up a single rope, hand-over-hand into the mizzen top, a wonderful thing for a boy of five'; Gerald ('desperately wicked') became 'the special pet of the second mate'; and Amy enjoyed watching the other ships encountered at sea. 'One of the most lovely things you can see on the ocean,' she wrote in her memoirs, 'is a three- or four-masted vessel going before the wind with all her sails set – she looks like a great bird.'

Towards the end of the voyage, when the *Matoaka* was making her way through the Southern Ocean, the children began to suffer from 'awful chilblains' and Fitz from mouth ulcers and bleeding gums, 'an attack of low fever and scurvy which pulled me down greatly and was a horrid bore at landing'.

As the ship approached Lyttelton on the morning of 2 December, Fanny gathered her children on deck, remembering her first view of these volcanic hills as the *Charlotte Jane* sailed up the harbour almost exactly ten years before.

She had given her pony Midge to Anne Gresson, wife of the lawyer Henry Gresson. When Anne heard news of the *Matoaka*'s arrival, she saddled the pony and rode over the hills with 'a loaf of baker's bread and some fresh butter', food which the children consumed with delight. Invited to stay with the Cooksons in the Heathcote valley, Fitz and Fanny (together with 'bag and baggage, animate and inanimate') travelled by cart over the Sumner Road, which was still 'a dangerous narrow ledge, half-finished, running along the face of a precipice and climbing the steep ascent of the hill by a most perilous zigzag'.

A letter from London (which had arrived on a faster vessel) was awaiting their arrival. Fanny's father had died from a stroke just seven days after the *Matoaka* sailed from Bristol. This was, according to Fitz, 'a happy result for all'.

After six days in the Heathcote valley ('compelled to rest and recover strength'), Fitz moved his family to the Gressons' house in Christchurch. He found the town 'immensely altered for the better'. Three years earlier, it was described as 'a little patch of scattered houses, a mere nothing in the vastness of the plain'. Now it was bristling with property, 'an entirely new town'.

On 26 December, Fitz loaded his family into the dogcart, flourished his whip and set off for the Springs station. For the first part of the journey, they drove along a road between fields of grass and grain, then followed the old track through miles of tussock country. And when they reached the station, Fitz discovered that Percy Cox had 'neglected to get me a home ready'. The house was no larger than it was in 1853; now they had to share it with Cox, his wife and baby daughter.

While Fanny settled five children into one small room, Fitz returned to Christchurch. He hired a bullock team, piled up a dray with luggage, and left for the Springs early next morning. By late afternoon, there was no sign of him, so Fanny sent out a stockman, who found him sitting quietly on a bank, smoking his pipe, the bullocks all 'tangled up in a knot at the bottom of a gully'.

During the next few days, Fitz spent all his 'time and attention getting homed and carting up my goods'. On 2 January, Fanny wrote that 'we are very uncomfortable here and are building two bedrooms'. The following day, Fitz complained that 'we are pigging it here, with hardly a box opened yet'.

During his absence, Cox and George Draper had been 'running some 80 milch cows, besides several hundred cattle; we made about six tons of cheese in the summer and one or two hundredweight of butter per week in the winter'.

From time to time, they drove calves and young heifers down to Longbeach ('splendid fattening country') and returned with the fattened stock.

After correspondence with Fitz in London, Cox had taken another station owner, Charles Hunter Brown, into partnership. Renamed Brown, Cox & Co, the partnership was divided into 20 shares: Fitz (9), Hunter Brown (6), Cox (3), and George Draper (2). Fitz had understood that Hunter Brown's money would be invested in a separate run; instead, he and Cox had bought up small parcels of land around the station, increasing its size to almost 30,000 acres.

Cox soon left for an extended visit to England and Fitz began to 'wade through the accounts'. He found himself:

> most bitterly disappointed … the expenses have been really eating
> up all the profits and most mysterious investments have been made.
> [Cox] had no right to take Hunter Brown's money and invest it in
> land on this run. H Brown was to become a partner solely to procure *a
> new run*. If this could not be done, he ought to have left. We are now
> driven into a position I never contemplated and am disgusted with.

He complained that Cox had 'a most pig-headed obstinacy in his own opinion and … a great want of common sense'. George Draper, on the other hand, 'has gone on capitally'. He had recently been joined at the Springs by his brother Edmund, who also made a good impression ('I like Edmund very much').

Now Fitz was in charge again, he employed a married couple and six stockmen. He constructed a mile of fencing, 'which will cut us off from the plains altogether', built a cottage for the men, and sowed five acres of land in wheat and 20 acres in oats. Other farmers were ploughing their land and reseeding it with English grass (which fed more animals per acre than the native tussock) and Fitz could 'see no return for our money but to lay it down in English grass, a long and costly work'. This would, he explained to Henry Selfe, 'eat up our profits for a long time. The return will be in the great increase of capital. I hate the work but really don't see how it can be avoided.'

He was in high spirits during these first weeks at the station, bubbling with energy and fun ('I can ride 30 or 40 miles without being more than very tired and have been all day in water, draining land with the plough'). The children were happy too, although Amy disgraced herself by 'dashing wildly and joyfully into a large field of alfalfa which was ready for cutting – this did not go down well in the eyes of my father'.

George Draper taught the older children to ride, and Amy accompanied him on long days in the saddle. 'If you fall off,' he told her, 'I won't take you out again.' 'And if you don't sit straight in the saddle,' her father added, 'you shall not ride at all.' As a result, she grew up to ride like a stockman, despite using a sidesaddle. Eight-year-old Willy became a good horseman, too, 'a most perfect centaur' according to his father. 'He got a fling on his back coming home with me the other night. I got pitched off a few minutes after and we lay there and laughed at each other.'

In late March, news arrived from London that one of Fanny's sisters, who had married a merchant in Russia, had died in childbirth, far from home in Taganrog on the Black Sea. 'Mrs FitzGerald has lately lost a father and a sister,' wrote one of her friends. 'She is very poorly.'

Almost nine months pregnant, the news led Fanny to be more fearful than usual of the coming ordeal. She gave birth safely on 8 April (to a boy named Maurice), but Fitz was in an insensitive mood. 'I have another son,' he told Henry Selfe. 'These incidents have lost their novelty and cease to be amusing. As I can't be worse off now, I wish for the pleasure of being the father of twenty children, and it seems likely my wish may be granted. We are all well.'

But Fanny was not well. She was exhausted and remained out of sight when William Richmond (a member of Stafford's ministry) spent a night at the station in early May. According to Richmond, Fitz was 'quite himself again, and as wicked', while four-year-old Gerald was 'a splendid little creature – as naughty as can be – and to see him and his father together is worth a journey – anything more amusing I never did'.

Next morning, Fitz drove Richmond into Christchurch in the circulating medium, 'his patent cart with wheels eight feet high', driving the horses at full tilt 'through rough and smooth, moist and dry – more especially through the streets of Christchurch when the leader is in a prancing humour. Remonstrance would be vain.'

…

Fitz had returned to Canterbury determined to remain a cattle farmer ('my boys will be stockmen'). He refused to stand for the superintendency in the election to be held in July, although several friends encouraged him and even Fanny thought it was a good idea. 'For the sake of the Province,' she wrote, 'Mr FG ought to take it and it is now at the advanced salary of £1000 per annum, much better, worth having.'

He also refused to stand at the general election in January, despite his successful opposition to the New Zealand Bill, which was 'much appreciated by the colony'. Parliament was due to meet in April, when it was expected that Stafford's government would fall. 'So my going to Auckland would be equivalent to taking office,' he told Henry Selfe, 'which I am not prepared to do at present.'

'I am very quiet now,' he wrote on 4 March, 'but fear I shall break out some day.' During the next five weeks, he remained out of sight, 'writing away very quietly at his station'. His resentment of the railway and the tunnel, his fears for the financial future of the province, spilled into a long letter published in the *Lyttelton Times* on 10 April.

During his own term as superintendent, he had raised loans of just £30,000 to fund immigration. Now, with a proposed loan of ten times that amount, 'the public must decide whether the government is to be conducted upon a system of honourable and creditable finance or upon schemes of wild speculation, which too often are the prelude to public dishonesty and ruin'. It was time, he continued, to 'take the public purse out of the hands of time-serving, log-rolling,[1] speculating, popularity hunting – and events compel me to add, utterly unprincipled – Superintendents'.

Moorhouse was in Australia when this letter was published. The London contractors had pulled out of the tunnel project in November after finding seams of hard basalt rock, so Moorhouse sailed for Melbourne at the end of January. He obtained a loan of £300,000 from the Union Bank of Australia, and engaged a firm of Australian railway engineers. He returned to Christchurch on 29 April, greeted by a victory procession and a band playing 'See, the Conquering Hero Comes!'

Moorhouse was another big man, a lawyer who had worked as a builder and was skilful with his fists. He also had the common touch, a quality which Fitz confused with vulgarity. Fitz was dismissive of Moorhouse – and Moorhouse was exasperated by Fitz. 'FitzGerald,' he wrote on 6 May:

> has written and published a most ill-timed document and injudi-
> cious letter. Indeed he has done all in his power to annoy me
> and discount my administration ever since his return. I don't care
> much about myself – but I cannot respect his want of prudence in
> attacking the credit of the Province ... Mutual friends ... are of the
> opinion that I may (under the circumstances) take credit for having
> exercised some self-denial.

The feud between the two men led to a parody ('a bucolic – after Virgil') published in the *Lyttelton Times*:

> FitzGerald! Once again we meet!
> Thee warmly doth the country greet!
> If thou to me assistance lend,
> Then I will be thy dearest friend.

---

1   Log-rolling: trading favours

Oh, Moorhouse! Fortune's favoured son!
Thou hast her every gift but one.
If to my counsels thou'll attend,
I'll make thee great and be thy friend.

Nay, Fitz, I fear thou hast forgot
That I'm in power and thou art not;
My plans are formed, take that for granted,
And keep advice till 'tis wanted.

Oh! Moorhouse, Moorhouse, half an ounce
Of sense is worth a pound of bounce;
Be wise: thy reckless schemes resign,
And wholly trust to me and mine.

Now hearken! Rather, I declare,
Than give our fortunes to thy care –
Rather than trust thy plans or thee –
I'd sink the country in the sea.

Fitz's friends in England were watching developments with interest. 'I shall be curious to see what safety valve your political energy will take,' wrote Godley:

> if you neither go to the Assembly nor stand for the Superintendency.
> It is ridiculous to suppose that you will be satisfied with helping
> heifers to calve and pulling bullocks out of the swamp. Moorhouse
> must be feeling rather nervous, I guess, at the feeling that you are
> watching him and have nothing else to do.

Godley understood his friend. Fitz was indeed building up steam and would soon find his safety valve. 'Among other ideas which have passed through my mind,' he had written to Gladstone in October 1849, 'is that of connecting myself with a New Zealand newspaper. It is not an unworthy object to direct the developing energies of a colony through the agency of an honest press.'

Now, on 6 May 1861, he attended a dinner with a group of men who shared his opinion of the tunnel. After the meal, he threw an idea into the conversation:

> I said I saw no hope for a better state of public feeling here unless
> there was a new newspaper started which would tell the truth
> without fear or favour. In five minutes talk the thing was settled. If
> I would undertake the management of it, it was to be started and
> £500 was put down on the spot.

Thus was the *Press* founded, a newspaper which began life to oppose the *Lyttelton Times*, which Fitz accused of 'gross partiality' towards Moorhouse and the tunnel. It was also 'the sneaking wish of my life and I believe would suit me more than anything'. The contributors included Richard Harman and John Raven (a wealthy clergyman), and Fitz agreed to 'write and exercise a general superintendence over the matter'.

A few days later he was kicked by a horse, 'a very nasty kick in the thigh from a young colt I was breaking in'. Unable to walk, he left Fanny at the Springs and was driven to Christchurch to stay with Mary Thornton in her house on Papanui Road.

On 14 May, John Raven wrote to George Watson, a printer in Lyttelton, asking him to 'come over to Christchurch tomorrow morning by the early cart'. Watson duly arrived at the Thornton house, where he agreed to work for the newspaper, and to sell his plant and equipment to the *Press*. A few hours later, Fitz employed a young editor (George Sale, fresh from Trinity College, Cambridge). The same evening, he wrote to the headmaster of Christ's College:

> I want your regular assistance for my new paper ... to appear imme-
> diately. You must give me an article weekly on some pleasing literary
> topic. Review of books, education and schools, inspection of schools
> ... We mean, please God, to have the first paper in the colony and to
> elevate and vindicate the press. I want *all the talents*. And I give you
> no choice, you *must* help, regularly and vigorously ... The state of the
> colony demands help *from all*.

Richard Harman had recently resigned his seat on the provincial council (representing Akaroa), giving Fitz the opportunity to stand in his place. 'The present crisis is one of vast moment,' he wrote to the electors:

> If the railway be made with proper security and in a businesslike
> manner, it will probably be a great step in the progress of Canterbury
> ... If, on the contrary, the work is badly managed, it will be a terrible
> burden to all of us for many years to come. The conduct of the
> present Government in this matter has been such as to afford little
> confidence in any arrangements it may make, and to call for utmost
> watchfulness on the part of the Council.

Fitz won the by-election on 16 May. On the same day, the provincial council approved the bank loan for the tunnel, after which it was promptly suspended by Moorhouse.

George Watson moved his plant and equipment to a three-room cottage

The first home of the *Press* in 1861, John Raven's cottage in a paddock on Montreal Street, Christchurch. The Press Office is in the cottage on the left; the figure standing in the doorway is George Watson, the printer.

Fairfax Media

on Montreal Street, which had been lent to the newspaper by John Raven. On 18 May, Fitz left the Thorntons and moved to the Gressons' house, where he spent the next five days hobbling about with a stick and writing articles for the first issue.

The paper was to be published weekly on Saturdays, a six-page tabloid selling for sixpence. On Friday 24 May, Fitz and Watson worked at the printing press 'from two o'clock until eight a.m. the next morning ... to get the first number out in time'. Fitz had written a poem to introduce the paper:

> Ye Editors, where'er ye be,
> Welcome to your fraternity
> A younger brother, born today
> To share your just and rightful sway –
> To spread the Truth – to scorn the shams,
> To scare the fox, to spare the lambs,
> We come. Our aim and object bless,
> And give three cheers for this our Press.

He had also written most of the first issue ('you will see all my mind in this paper') and mentioned his own name a great deal. The first article was a justification:

> We make no apology for the publication of a new newspaper. We
> are under the impression such a paper is wanted ... If we did not feel

this ourselves – if we had not heard it on all sides for months past ...
THE PRESS would never have been published ... We hereby respond
to a call which has become general from all classes of the community
and ask for the support of the public for 'THE PRESS'.

He then attacked Moorhouse and the tunnel:

We look over the estimates and calculations made by the government to justify their belief that the Railway would pay, and we are
at a loss to determine whether those figures are the result of *folly* or
of *fraud* ... We shall return to this matter week by week, for we are
satisfied that the public have been thoroughly humbugged from
the start.

And he set out his belief that Moorhouse had suspended the provincial
council as soon as his election was announced in order to prevent him taking
his seat:

Why was the Session of Council ... cut short? ... We all know!
Because there was one man who had made these matters the subject
of enquiry – who had talked with engineers and capitalists in
London on these very subjects ...When Mr FitzGerald stood for
Akaroa it became necessary to hurry matters in the Council. When
the writ was returned the game was up ... The Superintendent ...
shrank from the contest ... [and] turned tail when he found himself
pitted against the newly elected member for Akaroa.

This was a dramatic conceit, for Moorhouse had received news of the
election result after (not before) he suspended the council. Fitz published a
retraction on 1 June, but he still put the boot in. 'The fact remains,' he wrote,
'that the Session of Council was ... most discourteously concluded.'

...

Ten days after the first edition was published, Fitz wrote to Lord Lyttelton:

I have no apology to make for not writing to you before, except that
driving bullocks, and digging, draining and all the other occupations
of an enterprising agriculturalist are not favourable to letter writing.
And now I write to beg that you will pay the sum of £1.6.0. to
Stanford, Charing Cross, for which sum the *Press* newspaper will be
forwarded to your address every mail. The *Press* is generally understood to be established for the purpose of presenting to the world

the principles of FitzGeraldology – according to my view, however,
it is to present the true faith to a stiff-necked generation.

The 'editor' of the paper, as George Sale himself put it, was 'a newcomer with no knowledge either of the colony or the province and with no experience whatever of newspaper work'. His editorship was 'only nominal'. It was Fitz who directed policy, Fitz who wrote the articles about Moorhouse and the tunnel. As a result, he became increasingly unpopular in Canterbury. He was accused of 'violent writing'; the *New Zealand Chronicle* distilled the general opinion into one sentence: 'There is no honest man but FitzGerald and the *Press* is his prophet.'

Fitz was proud of his notoriety. 'There is hardly a more unpopular man in the country than I am just now,' he crowed. 'The *Press* is an object of intense hatred to the people who abuse it, but buy it and read it.' He admitted that his articles were 'a little strong, but my duty is to write down Moorhouse and all his mob'.

Wiser heads disagreed. 'I am very sorry to say,' wrote one of his supporters, 'that FitzGerald's sudden onslaught on Moorhouse and general tilt at everyone has damaged our power of putting him forward for the next Superintendent with *any chance of success* … It is very aggravating.'

During June and July, the *Press* continued to fulminate against the tunnel. It was a wet winter ('rain, rain, rain, the roads almost impassable with mud and slush') and on 17 July, 'one of the wettest July days we have known in Canterbury', large crowds gathered to watch the superintendent's wife 'turn the first sod' on the railway.

After the formalities, the official party gathered in a marquee for 'a well-furnished repast on a most extensive scale'. And while the notables of Christchurch enjoyed the banquet, crowds of drenched onlookers tried to storm the tent. The noise of the rain and the crowds almost overwhelmed the speeches. Moorhouse, shouting at the top of his voice, referred to 'the dawning of a great future for Canterbury'. Another speaker – looking pointedly at Fitz – yelled that 'the sod which has been turned today covers the grave of thick-headed prejudice'.

At this point, the onlookers surged into the marquee and mayhem ensued.

CHAPTER TWENTY

No Common Man

1861–1862

I have quite made up my mind never to touch public affairs again.

Fitz, 19 April 1860

He will, of course, take to politics again. He is fit for nothing else.

John Godley, 3 September 1860

*F*itz spent his days working on the station, his evenings writing articles for the *Press*. He delivered his copy to Montreal Street on Thursdays when he drove into Christchurch to deliver his butter to market, using the journey to break in young horses to harness. 'When I tie a colt alongside a steady old leader, he can't do much harm,' he explained, 'and the journey on these roads takes it out of him pretty well.' Soon Fitz and his dogcart became 'one of the sights of Christchurch, driving out and coming in from the Springs', standing on his feet, 'long whip in hand with a tandem team'.

'The FGs are living at the Springs with their six healthy strong children,' wrote Janetta Cookson. 'William and Amy and Robert all ride and scramble about and lead very healthy outdoor lives, most expert and fearless riders already.' According to Fitz, five-year-old Gerald was 'at war with mankind' and two-year-old Lyttelton 'too fat to comprehend anything at all. He eats perpetually and digests like a sausage machine. I am tempted to sell him for veal.'

Selfe's son Jim (aged 19) was a regular visitor. He had arrived in Canterbury in 1860, on Fitz's persuasion. He was proving unsatisfactory, drinking too much and mixing in 'low company'. 'Jim can't bear stations where there are ladies,' Fitz complained to Henry Selfe. 'He does not treat them with proper respect.' Fanny scolded him for coming in from the run and stretching out on the sofa with muddy boots. 'And this,' wrote Fitz, 'in a country where there are no servants to clean up is aggravating to the female kind. Fanny goes at him about such things.'

Household manners were one thing, sartorial elegance another. Fitz had lost weight since returning from London. He had grown a beard, he wore his hair long, and his clothes 'always hung loosely about him'. 'I saw FitzGerald today,' wrote one of his friends, adding a sketch of a face obliterated by a long beard and large hat. 'About the head an old straw hat [with] black crepe ribbon. Rest of the man to correspond ... Hat very old and tattered – crepe very shabby – under it all *our FitzGerald* of old, not changed, and as amusing and clever as ever.' Charles Bowen was more graphic:

Sketch of Fitz in a letter from J.W. Hamilton to J.R. Godley, Christchurch, 19 February 1861. 'I saw FitzGerald today. Here is an attempt at his portrait. About the head an old straw hat [with] black crepe ribbon. Rest of the man to correspond.'

Canterbury Museum (John Robert Godley manuscript collection, 131/39, item 244)

He drives the 'circulating medium' about everywhere with two queer looking brutes in it rigged tandem. He himself has the sort of coat on that you see on a cabby, and if it is cold he completes the resemblance by tying two or three dirty loose wrappers around his neck. A few weeks ago he insisted on playing Johnny Gresson at backgammon for his hat (a very low crowned beaver child's hat) and won it. He seized it, put it on and drove off out of the town hurrahing – and has worn it ever since night and day I believe.

Fitz's clothes were those of a station hand. In September 1861, he wrote that he was hard at work digging up the tussock and sowing English grass. And 'spade in hand', he was 'ditching and banking for two days in the rain to keep the cows out of the crops, all other hands being busy sowing oats'.

Having come round to Percy Cox's opinion that land surrounding the Springs should be purchased when it came up for sale (to avoid it falling 'into the hands of small settlers which would completely spoil our place and lower its value'), Fitz sold his 20 acres near the Heathcote River for £750 and used the proceeds to buy 300 acres bordering the station. At the same time, he was failing to pay interest on Henry Selfe's investment. 'I did not declare a dividend,' he wrote on 6 September, 'because there were so many small debts to be collected and very heavy payments coming due in the current half year. I cannot see my way to any income at all out of this place at present … It is not my fault so much money has been sunk in *land*. I have gone on buying only with a view to save the spoiling of what we had.'

…

Moorhouse was re-elected superintendent on 30 August. His nomination was unopposed. 'I could not bring myself to stand just after writing the *Press*,' Fitz told Selfe. 'It would have been a great sacrifice of character had I turned round and opened myself to the charge of having written it solely to get power.' But he was re-elected to the provincial council on 13 September, despite failing to attend the nomination in Akaroa the previous day. 'At this time of year,' he explained, 'the business of a farm cannot be neglected without a considerable sacrifice.'

Seventeen days later, there was 'a fearful tragedy' at the station. Fitz had imported several pedigree shorthorn bulls from England, one of which, Regicide ('a strikingly handsome creature'), was known to be 'savage'. Every morning, he was taken out of his stall and allowed to roam free with the cows. In the afternoon, after the cattle had been driven back to the yard, the head dairyman, John Strange ('our best man'), would manoeuvre the bull back into his stall.

On the afternoon of 29 September, Strange had been drinking brandy and was, as Fitz put it, 'a little fresh'. When the cattle arrived at the yard gate:

> the Bull walked back towards the run and Strange like a madman walked after him and tried to turn him on foot on the open plain. As the Bull would not turn he struck him on the head and the Bull rushed him and threw him. He then got up and set the dogs on the Bull which as they did not pin him only made him worse. The Bull tore him all to pieces.

Fitz was walking in the fields with the Draper brothers, 'when we saw the girl with the children screaming and waving her hands'. George and Edmund:

> ran across the fields and jumped over the fence and though most gallantly going close up to the beast they could not get him off. At last the boy rode up, having seen them from the distance jumping over the fence, but he could not get the mare up to the enraged animal who was all this time goring and tossing the man. George Draper then jumped on the mare which by the way had no girths and having spurs got up to the Bull's head and a few strokes of the stockwhip drove him off.

Regicide, photographed at the Springs station. The bull was sold during the farm sale on 19 October 1862. Three days later, he won first prize at the Christchurch Agricultural Show. A journalist attending the show was unimpressed: 'The bull Regicide was in miserable condition; and the blinkers on his eyes, necessitated by his bad temper, did not improve his beauty.'
Private collection

Edmund set off at a gallop to find the doctor in Christchurch (travelling 'sixteen miles in an hour'), while Fitz and George carried Strange into the house and Fanny tried to staunch the flow of blood and guts. 'He lived 24 hours suffering most horribly,' wrote Fitz. 'Indeed I never passed so dreadful a night. His cries were most piteous. He poor man was very fond of us ... His moans have been ringing in my ears ever since. "Oh master dear master what pain I do endure."'

Strange died the following afternoon. At the inquest on 2 October, 'the jury returned a verdict of accidental death and expressed a desire that Mr FitzGerald should be requested to confine the bull in proper enclosures'. As Fitz wrote to Henry Selfe: 'It is a very nervous thing to have such an awful brute about the place ... it has so shaken my nerves that I have been almost unable to ride a horse since.'

...

On 17 October, Fitz and Fanny attended a ball at the Christchurch Club. Two days later, they set out for Longbeach in the circulating medium, taking six-month-old Maurice with them. The southern station was running short of supplies and the dogcart was loaded with 'about a ton of cargo'.

After several hours, they reached the banks of the Rakaia ('the worst of our rivers … half river, half mountain torrent, the whole space of the river bed up to a mile in width'). Fitz edged the horses into the water, trusting in the stability of the dogcart with its enormous wheels. Fanny clung on to the side. They had almost reached the far bank when there was a sudden lurch as one of the wheels hit a boulder, out of sight beneath the swirling waters. The horses came to a halt and, peering over the side of the cart, Fanny told Fitz that the wheel had come off. 'And down we came, fortunately in a sand hill.'

The axle had broken, 'shorn off close to the wheel', but the cart remained upright. According to Fitz, this proved 'the peculiar value of my cart for it does not upset or even go down much, even with the wheel off.' It was, however, 'an expensive accident as I had to hire a trap to get home, as well as a bullock dray to carry the load on to the southern station'.

He advertised for the dray on 24 October, two days after Moorhouse opened the new session of the provincial council. Sitting in the elegant timber-built council building that he had commissioned before leaving for London, Fitz threw himself into the work with his usual obsession – and his usual complaints. 'I am really unfit for the wear and tear of public life,' he wrote on 4 November. 'I am now in the Provincial Council and in one week feel the work a great deal too much for me. If it went on long I should knock up altogether.' Much of this was self-inflicted. 'I well remember,' wrote another member of council, 'what a serious expenditure of stationery there was, what a strain was put on the waste-paper basket, and what a bulky volume of Provincial Ordinances resulted from his love of work.'

It was now six months since the founding of his newspaper and Fitz reviewed its progress. It was, he wrote, 'triumphant', its articles reprinted throughout New Zealand. But his mood had begun to sink almost as soon as the first issue was published ('that night at the press cut me up and I have been very shaky since'). 'I ought not to have been led into such an undertaking,' he complained to Henry Selfe. 'It was too much for me … a constant call upon one's brains and an anxiety which an old hand like myself ought to have avoided.' But, he continued, loyalty to Godley still strong in his mind:

> what I want is to change the mind of the whole community to withstand the jobbing speculating reckless spirit of the day … And fully admitting, my dearest friend, that I can't afford it and on many grounds ought not to do it, yet I can't regret that I have begun for all works in this life open to me it seems to me the noblest. To protect so long as I have any strength left the edifice we helped to rear together. That is my defence.

In December, he received a letter from Godley, who had read the first two editions of the *Press* with disquiet. He thought the articles 'injudiciously violent in tone, and to say the truth, by no means equal to your usual standard in style and matter'. He agreed that a second newspaper was needed in Canterbury, 'but the object aimed at would have been more effectually attained by a moderate and judicial tone, which would also have been more consonant with your own position, as a leader in the Province'.

Henry Selfe shared this opinion. 'Men of calm temper and judicial fairness seem by late accounts to be sadly wanting in Canterbury,' he wrote to John Hall:

> I can't express to you with how much regret I, for one, have read
> the newspapers since the *Press* was started … There was room for
> righteous indignation … But what had to be said might have been
> said as forcibly and far more effectively had it not been mixed up
> with wild inaccurate calculation, scurrilous personalities, and too
> frequent reference to FitzGerald's crochets [foibles] … I am sorry on
> every account the *Press* was started.

Fitz tried to justify himself. He accused Selfe of having 'no idea of the degradation of public sentiment in this place … the sort of men who are creeping into public favour. Men with vulgar manners, low aims and bad principles.' And while admitting to Godley that his tone 'was rather strong at first, and is still so sometimes', his letter continued with an attack on Moorhouse, referring to the superintendent as 'the miserable character who has got into power and keeps himself in it by the most unscrupulous means'.

Fitz now spent most of his days in Christchurch, either in the newspaper office or in the council chamber. He stayed with friends in town, driving down to the Springs 'about twice a week', while Fanny was 'almost always alone … looking thin and rather fagged and is very much overworked'. When Selfe suggested that Fitz employ more cadets to help at the station, she sent a weary reply: 'When there is so much difficulty in procuring servants at any wages, I rather dread increasing the household work, which already falls rather heavily on me.'

The family celebrated Christmas at the station and Fitz returned to Christchurch in early January, shortly after the *Lyttelton Times* published an article written by a Moorhouse supporter. It began with a description of Fitz at a council meeting:

> Looking at him as he sits at the table with a heavy listless air,
> dabbing a screw of paper into the inkstand and transferring
> the black fluid to the sheet of paper before him, you will at first
> recognise nothing particular in him. But when he raises up his pale

and prematurely-aged-looking face, strokes his whitened beard, and casts his icy pale-grey eyes around the Council Chamber, you see at once there sits no common man ... He reminds you rather of the Sphinx gazing with strong eyes straight through time to the confines of eternity, shunning all sympathy with what is human. Watch him closely, however, and hear him speak (and he gives you plenty of opportunities of doing so), and you may penetrate even the umbrous depths of James Edward FitzGerald ...

To a mind well-stored with facts he adds a powerful imagination and a caustic wit [and] extraordinary powers of both analysis and synthesis. When he speaks it is with fluency and power. His emphases are good, his articulation clear, and his tone rich and sonorous; but he is merciless in his opposition and his ego is repulsive. Therein lies his weakness as a leader of a party, for however much his hangers-on (of which there are several in the Council) may be dazzled by his brilliancy as an orator, few could abnegate themselves sufficiently to do all his bidding, and fewer still can love him.

These were strong words – although relatively mild compared to the tone of his own attacks – but Fitz had little time to feel aggrieved. He was busy moving his newspaper from the cottage in Montreal Street to larger premises, a former butcher shop in Cashel Street, which the proprietors had leased for £475.

The first issue printed in Cashel Street was published on 11 January 1862. A few days later, a black-edged letter arrived from London with news that John Godley had died in November. This came as 'a great shock' to Fitz, 'a severe blow'; and his grief was exacerbated by the knowledge of his own neglect. Since his return to Canterbury, he had written frequently to Henry Selfe to keep him informed of progress at the station, but despite constant requests from Godley, he had written to him only three times.

Godley's first request was made in November 1860. 'I suspect,' he wrote three months after Fitz embarked on the *Matoaka*, 'that my constitution, always a feeble one, is pretty well used up ... I long earnestly, more and more so I think as the future becomes cloudy and uncertain, to see New Zealand again. In the meantime, I live on news of it. Take pity on me and write to me.'

Fitz did write, in January 1861 and again in June. 'I was very glad to hear from you at last,' Godley replied in September, 'having been seriously hurt by your silence. No man can have much real regard or affection for another, if he won't take the trouble, when specially asked, to write (say) three or four letters, occupying three or four hours, to him, in the year.'

Fitz received this letter in December. He replied promptly but with little grace (words written when Godley was already in his grave):

> I protest against my friendship being measured by the length or frequency of my letters. It is not the time which letter writing takes, that is nothing. It is all a matter of *habit*, and for many years I have had a repugnance to taking a pen in my hand except on business ... Pray don't doubt my most affectionate remembrance, even if I don't write. But as I know you feel it, you shall not complain again.

Fitz prepared a memoir of his 'very dear friend', which he published on 29 January in a four-page supplement to the *Press*. 'It is a real blow,' he wrote seven days later to Henry Selfe. 'I did not expect it. He lasted so long amidst symptoms which were at first thought alarming that I hoped he would finally overcome the danger ... Godley's loss has made a blank in my life which nothing can ever fill ... He was my one hero.'

...

On 12 February, when temperatures soared to 105 degrees, the *Matoaka* returned to Lyttelton with a young man on board who carried an introduction to Fitz in his pocket. Nineteen years old, Edward Chudleigh walked the 30 miles from Lyttelton to the Springs station to ask for work. Edmund Draper had recently returned to England, so Fitz employed Chudleigh in his place.

Fitz was angry at the time, having received a letter from Percy Cox. Before sailing for England, Cox had 'reluctantly and doubtfully acquiesced' to Fitz's idea of ploughing up the native tussock and replacing it with English grass. Distance had given him perspective and he now 'doubted the financial results of such a scheme'.

It was not only the grass. As Cox wrote in his memoirs, 'Mr FitzGerald was a charming individual; refined and cultured; the most beautiful speaker I have ever heard; in one word – a *genius*. But, like many another genius, he was erratic, and I do not think his most enthusiastic admirers ... would credit him with being a practical man of business.'

Believing that Cox was merely 'in dudgeon with my not agreeing with his management', Fitz decided to break up the partnership. At the same time, Henry Selfe asked him to give £1000 to his son Jim. Unable to find the money, Fitz hoped to persuade Jim to become his partner in place of Percy Cox, to leave the £1000 invested in the station.

Jim arrived at the Springs to discuss the matter towards the end of February. 'I had a long talk with him,' Fitz told his father:

I told him why I should break up partnership with Cox. And that it was a great object with me not to sell this place at a loss. The population is coming round here so fast, that there will soon be a town here … I propose to establish a village, get a public house and store. The railway going south will come close by. It is then a mere folly to sell an estate now which will realise five times the sum five years hence.

I told Jim that there was no income to be made now. Every farthing must go to lay the land down in English grass, but then it will be worth £30 an acre … I have got 30 acres of beautiful grass in on fresh broken land and have already ploughed 60 or 70 for next year … If we could get rid of the cattle and put sheep on the English grass there is no farm in the country to surpass this for richness.

But Jim wanted an income; he rejected the offer in April. 'Well,' wrote Fitz, 'if I am to pay Jim £1000 I shall sell the whole most likely … I do not think from Jim's letter that there is any use trying to induce him to alter his mind. So you may assume that he will have his money, and then the place will be sold or mortgaged by next August.'

Fitz had only himself to blame. He had published an article in March, titled 'Cadets', in which he railed against young men of good family sent out to gain experience on rural stations in Canterbury – of which Jim Selfe was one. The article filled the entire front page of the *Press* and, according to Fitz, 'made such a sensation that copies were bought up by the dozen to send to England'.

It began in the style of a self-important zookeeper ('the Hippopotamus … is a hamphibious hanimal, as can't live on land and always dies in the water') and continued with an attack on the character of cadets:

> There is a class of human beings in this country of whom this description forcibly reminds us – men who can't get on in their own land and are always ruined in a colony … not a ship arrives that does not bring some one or more young men, brought up in the social rank of gentlemen, but without money, intellect, cultivation, learning, capacity for labour, good behaviour, or any feature of mind or body which can enable them to retain in England the position in life their fathers filled. These men are not only useless in a colony, they become the pests of its society.

Cadets were often the black sheep of their families, the parents trying 'to get rid of the boy altogether'. Fitz complained of their letters of introduction, 'the coolness with which scapegraces are consigned to colonial families in the assumption that they will be welcome guests'. He complained about their behaviour, 'lazying about doing little work; abandoning the ordinary wages of labour in consideration of being esteemed gentlemen'.

He qualified his words at the end of the article, explaining that he did not 'speak indiscriminately. A young man who has a small capital, or will have a small capital at some future time, has a distinct career before him.' But Jim Selfe may not have read this far. Fitz had described him in similar terms ('his talk is all about dogs and horses and bullocks and sheep ... his manners are more of a groom than a gentleman ... he has no real work in him at all'), and he perceived the article as a personal attack. He declined to enter into partnership with Fitz and sent a copy to his father in London – who referred to it as 'unnecessarily savage'.

Pain may have strengthened Fitz's tone: the article was written while he was suffering an attack of lumbago. 'For the past week I have been almost wholly in bed with severe rheumatism,' he complained on 6 March (two days before the article was published). 'I was obliged to send for a doctor yesterday but am now getting better. Still, writing from bed when you sit up with difficulty is not favourable to correspondence.'

A month later, he was suffering 'incessant attacks of lumbago ... a positive torture in the back', and was in two minds about the future. 'If I sell out,' he wrote on 8 April, 'I am not at all sure I shall not go to Christchurch and devote myself to the *Press*, or perhaps go into the general government ... I am quite certain to be in office should I go ... I am refusing to stand for any place till Cox comes out and I get rid of this disastrous partnership.'

Fanny was alarmed. 'James talks of going to Christchurch to live over the Press Office,' she wrote to Selfe. 'I hope this will not be the case. He has already done himself in once or twice by sitting up late writing. It was a dreadful tax in the winter and as he got no remuneration for it, it is all work and expense and no profit.'

In a final effort to make money from the station, Fitz sent 170 head of cattle south to Dunedin. Gold had been discovered in Otago in May 1861, since when the population of the province had almost doubled. Cattle were selling for high prices (£30 a head) and Fitz hoped to make 'a good deal of money' by driving fat stock south to the diggings.

On 10 April, George Draper and Edward Chudleigh set out with the cattle, including 90 'big bullocks' which Fitz had bought from a neighbouring run, 'outlaws [which] had never been inside a yard for years; directly they came within sight of one they would charge anything and everything and clear away'. According to Percy Cox, 'such a "put-together" mob of wild cattle required

Fitz and Fanny at the Springs station, photographed by Dr Alfred Barker on 15 May 1862. Fitz had returned from Dunedin a few days earlier. He was 'miserably ill with rheumatism' – although this did not prevent Fanny conceiving another child at about this time.

Private collection

at least six to eight experienced stockmen, and it would have taken them all their time – driving all day and watching all night – to get them safely down.'

The drive to Otago should have taken between two and three weeks; in the event, it took more than two months and the cattle 'often got back by night further than they had been driven by day'. It became progressively colder and the two men lay back-to-back at night on the frozen ground, each with a dog in their arms for warmth. Sixty bullocks were lost on the way ('many of them were never heard of again') and the rest were so emaciated on arrival that they sold for only £16 a head.

As the animals headed south, Fitz boarded the steamer for Dunedin with a large quantity of cheese, which he hoped would sell for a higher price than in Christchurch. He was away for a fortnight, arriving home in early May, still 'miserably ill with rheumatism'.

Two weeks later, Percy Cox returned from England. When he arrived at the Springs, he found station affairs to be 'in such an extraordinary mess' that he 'did not know which way to turn to set them right'. Fitz now understood Cox's reason for buying land, but this made little difference to his animosity. 'Cox has come back and I confess I like him less than ever,' he wrote unkindly on 12 June. 'If you can understand a very, very narrow, ill-educated mind ... and not quite a gentleman ... you have the sort of man. Besides he has grown quite ugly which is inexcusable.'

Settlers had been arriving in the area in increasing numbers, obtaining land by making a 'challenge' for leasehold acreage, in which case the leaseholder had either to buy the freehold or lose it. The Springs was therefore shrinking in size, the leasehold acreage whittled away by the sale of freehold rights. According to Fitz, the station 'is not tenable any longer for cattle, it is bought up all over and what remains is so surrounded by fences that it is not fit for fattening'. The fencing was inadequate too, 'tempting our cattle to jump into neighbouring crops'. In February, his cattle had destroyed 80 acres of oats sown by an adjacent freeholder, resulting in a lawsuit and the payment of compensation.

The final straw was the loss of Longbeach at the end of May. The boundaries of the southern runs were inadequately surveyed and disputes were common. Eighteen months earlier, the owner of an adjoining run ('a mean, hard-hearted man') had claimed a significant proportion of Longbeach. He lost the case but then tried a different tack: 'He gave us notice that, if we did not abandon our claim, he would buy 5000 acres all along the best part of the run so as to make it untenable.'

Unable to buy the freehold of 5000 acres, Fitz and Cox had no choice but to sell the lease of the entire run for £500, 'a most blackguard transaction'. The loss of Longbeach, Fitz told Selfe on 12 June, 'is very serious. It wholly frustrates my plan of supplying the Otago market. Indeed it frustrates our whole concern. We shall sell the whole of our cattle and divide the freehold land and rest of the goods.'

He raised a loan of £924 from the Union Bank of Australia to buy 300 acres of freehold land at the Springs. He laid out 44 acres in sections for a new town to service the growing rural population. He planned the roads and named them after his family: James and Edward streets; William, Robert, Gerald, Lyttelton and Maurice streets; Kildare Terrace; FitzGerald Place. And on 20 June, it was announced in the *Press* that sections for the new town of Lincoln would be auctioned 'at an early date' at a reserve price of £12.

CHAPTER TWENTY-ONE

The Grand Demonstration

1862

We are here this evening standing on the threshold of the future, holding
the issues of peace and war, of life and death, in our hands.

Fitz, 6 August 1862

I told Stanford to send a copy of my speech to Mr Gladstone. I should
like to know if he thought me visionary.

Fitz, 13 January 1863

As the election for superintendent approached in July 1861, Fitz
had – briefly – changed his mind and given thought to standing
against Moorhouse, before changing it again on the grounds of 'sacrifice
of character'. 'Nothing would induce me,' he wrote (referring to provincial
superintendents in general), 'to hold an office which is held by … swindlers,
illiterate carpenters and drunken printers.'

He was equally changeable about parliament. Twelve months after writing
'I am as determined as ever not to enter general politics again', he was elected
to the general assembly, standing unopposed (as 'the best politician in the
province') at a by-election in Ellesmere on 10 June 1862. His failure to make
an appearance on election day was considered 'rather lukewarm' by the electors,
but it was bitterly cold and he was still suffering from lumbago.

'I have been sorely vexed with constant and violent rheumatism day after
day,' he told Henry Selfe on 12 June:

> and have to stay helplessly in bed and cannot attend to anything.
> The constant pain at every movement for week after week is really
> wearing me out. And yet I grow fat, I suppose from lying in bed.
> The last time I went to Christchurch, I was a week in bed simply
> from driving up … I do not at this moment know how I am to live.
> I can't work. I am quite helpless … I must however do something for
> a living.

Three weeks earlier, news had arrived of the death of Edward Gibbon Wakefield. Fitz could hardly mourn his loss but, from his bed at the Springs, he wrote an even-handed obituary, referring to 'that sad eccentricity' in Wakefield's 'moral sense, which seemed to hang like a heavy chain around the neck of his genius'. This was published on 21 June – by which time Fitz had found a way of making a living.

'The proprietors of the *Press* have resolved to give me up the paper if I will take it,' he wrote excitedly on the 22nd:

> I have accepted the offer … The affair is solvent, that is the liabilities are less than the assets, and it is paying about £25 a month … The property consists of a leasehold, 20 years to run, of a first rate section in Cashel Street with first rate buildings. I shall add to them at a cost of about £500 which will give me a capital home over and around the presses. In fine, I shall sit on my own dunghill and crow.

'It is the only thing I see out of which to make a living,' he concluded. 'I intend to make it the best paper in the Southern Hemisphere.'

Draper and Chudleigh returned from Dunedin on the 27th, exhausted after so many weeks in the saddle ('we were neither of us sorry,' wrote Chudleigh, 'to get into our beds again and live in other ways like Christians'). The following day, the proprietors of the *Press* issued a notice dissolving their partnership 'by mutual consent' and explaining that 'the business will in future be conducted by James Edward FitzGerald, by whom all credits will be received and all debts will be paid'.

On 29 June, Fitz boarded the steamer for the 1862 parliament, held that year in Wellington because of complaints about the length and hardship of the voyage to Auckland. Fanny had not wanted him to go ('I do hope he may not be induced to go') and Fitz himself had been undecided until almost the last moment. 'He solemnly declared a few days before he went that he would not go at all,' wrote Charles Bowen. 'Mrs FG did not think he was going two days before. He is getting wilder in his movements every day.' When he finally made up his mind, he said he was going for a 'change of air', to 'enable me to get rid of the rheumatism'.

…

Fitz arrived in Wellington on 1 July, a day after the assembly was due to begin. Only eight members had made an appearance, so parliament was prorogued for want of a quorum.

The Stafford ministry had fallen the previous year, replaced by William Fox as premier, with Henry Sewell (now back in New Zealand) as attorney-general.

Together with the northern members and government officials, Fox and Sewell had left Auckland on the *White Swan* on 28 June. The following day, the steamer hit a rock south of Napier, forcing the captain to drive the vessel aground. The passengers landed safely ('a most wonderful escape') and eventually arrived in Wellington. But the governor, who had left Auckland on 1 July in the *Harrier*, was still absent.

The missing governor was Sir George Grey, who had returned to New Zealand in 1861 to replace Colonel Gore Browne, who – in Fitz's words – had made 'a fearful mistake' in purchasing 600 acres of native land in Taranaki ('the Waitara purchase') against the protests of the Maori chief. This led to the outbreak of war in Taranaki in March 1860, which was described by Fitz as 'unnecessary and unpolitic', and which 'might have been and ought to have been avoided'.

Grey was appointed for a second term because of his greater experience in native affairs. Despite referring to him during his first term as 'a dreadful pestilence in the shape of a wicked and mischievous Governor', Fitz welcomed his return: 'If he will perceive that *the* work to be done is to amalgamate the Maori into the constitution, not to keep them distinct, he will do great work ... I am sorry for Gore Browne but it was really necessary to recall him. He had not a *ghost* of right on his side.'

The governor's failure to arrive in Wellington and the south-easterly gales that battered the coast were causing hearts to flutter. 'The non-arrival of the *Harrier*,' Fitz wrote anxiously, 'is making us all nervous. Good God if Grey is lost.' While waiting for the governor, members passed their time 'in idleness, seeing and talking to people, with a small admixture of business'. There were dinners to attend and Fitz renewed his acquaintance with Henry Sewell. 'I think I can perceive a change come over him,' Sewell wrote in his diary, 'the change from the boy to the man. He has lost a good deal of his animal spirits. Still he is entertaining.'

Fitz sent articles to his newspaper, headed 'from our Wellington correspondent', and joined other members in Bellamy's (the parliamentary refreshment rooms), 'singing and joking and drinking whisky toddy'. He sang Irish songs but, according to James Richmond, a member from Taranaki, he had 'lost his voice – no wonder if he always burns the candle at both ends as he does now. I never heard of a man in bad health taxing mind and body as he does but I suppose he can't help it.'

Richmond was entranced by Fitz. 'FitzGerald is my delight,' he wrote. 'His manner is quite free from assumption or anything that repels, he is as full of antics as if he were a young thing and full of health ... All he writes is written off hand and it is difficult to imagine that he is ever venomous in heart. But he is brilliant and bold and gives his fancies the rein.'

Grey finally arrived in Wellington on 11 July, the *Harrier* having been blown off course towards the Chatham Islands. Three days later, he opened the assembly in the provincial council chamber which, in Sewell's opinion, was 'an improvement on Auckland but bitterly cold'. Native affairs were high on the agenda.

The war in Taranaki had lasted a year and imperial troops had been sent to quell the rebellion. A ceasefire was declared in March 1861 but unrest continued. Hostilities were threatening to break out in the Waikato and the politicians were fractious: 'everybody is quarrelling with everything. It is a Babel of voices and opinions.' According to Sewell, the cost of the war ('little short of half a million') had been 'wasted by the colony in this miserable squabble with the natives. Is it not lamentable to think of?'

On 25 July, Fitz made a speech against the Fox ministry in a debate on responsibility for native affairs. The vote, taken on the evening of the 28th, was tied. The Speaker cast his vote against the government, Fox resigned, and the following morning (after Stafford declined the offer) Fitz received a letter: 'The Governor presents his compliments to Mr FitzGerald, and would feel much obliged to him if he would call upon him, in order that the Governor may consult with Mr FitzGerald regarding the formation of a new ministry.'

Fitz also declined the premiership, 'for reasons with which the House has nothing to do and which therefore I need not mention'. He would have liked to lead the government but the timing – with the imminent loss of the Springs and recent developments at the *Press* – made it impossible. As he told Selfe after he returned to Christchurch, 'Sir G Grey pressed me very warmly to take office. I would have done so but for the mess our things are in here.'

Instead, he agreed to act as kingmaker, 'to do what he could to bring about a combination of parties … all day long trying various expedients'. On the 30th, he was 'trying to patch up a government' headed by Alfred Domett. His negotiations were successful and Domett became premier on 6 August.

…

Meanwhile, Fitz had been preparing a political statement. 'FitzGerald is going to make a grand demonstration about native affairs,' Sewell wrote on 18 July. 'I am afraid it will be rather in the nature of an Extravaganza.'

When he arrived in New Zealand, Fitz shared the prejudices of most nineteenth-century colonists. Indigenous peoples were seen at best as a nuisance to be pacified; at worst as savages to be dispossessed of their lands, allowed to 'die out' as Anthony Trollope put it ('the people are dying out, – and thus and thus only, will the Maori difficulty be solved').

When a Canterbury tribe contested a land sale in 1856, Fitz told the governor that 'raising the expectations of the natives will induce them to expect more hereafter', thereby creating 'a great evil'. Five days later, he complained to the secretary for native affairs about a plan to add Maori chiefs to the electoral roll. This would, he wrote, 'convoke the greatest alarm … The very idea of the Governor influencing the Assembly through the agency of the native race would awake a flame throughout the colony and place it in a most dangerous position.' The following year, he wrote in similar vein to Stafford: 'One thing is clear, the natives are about to take a part in politics. If they enrol as voters, there will be a civil war. The English populations … will not submit to the rule of Maoris. They will draw the sword and, to my mind, it will be a sacred cause.'

His opinions had matured since then and he now held the opposite view. 'The Natives are not represented in the Assembly,' he wrote in July 1860. 'I am sorry for it … there is no doubt they will gradually become so … That is the great end to be desired.' He identified Maori with Irish Catholics and compared government policy in New Zealand to the repression used by the British in Ireland.

He had boasted to Henry Selfe that 'all the oldest, wisest, ablest and best informed colonists in the North Island agree with the policy put forward in the *Press*.' Politicians disagreed, accusing him of 'knowing nothing about the Maori question' – which was true enough. In 1858, Maori represented just six per cent of the population of the South Island (a percentage which shrank during the next four years as immigration swelled the numbers of European settlers) and there was little native unrest. It was easy for Fitz to take the moral high ground.

The three main resolutions that he planned to put to the House in the debate on native affairs, scheduled for 30 July, were remarkable for their time:

1. That in the adoption of any policy or the passing of any laws affecting the Native race this House will keep before it as its highest object, the entire amalgamation of all Her Majesty's subjects in New Zealand into one united people.

2. That this House will assent to no laws which do not recognise the right of all Her Majesty's subjects of whatever race within this Colony, to a full and equal enjoyment of civil and political privileges.

3. That a recognition of the foregoing principle will necessitate the personal aid of one or more Native Chiefs in the administration of the Government of the Colony; the presence of members of the Maori Nobility in the Legislative Council, and a fair

representation in this House of a race which constitutes one-third of the population of the Colony.

Because of the change of ministry, the debate was postponed for a week. On the evening of 6 August, Fitz rose to his feet to propose his resolutions. The House was agog, eager to listen to 'the most eloquent of our public men, one who possesses the happy gift of discoursing beautifully upon every subject – sensibly sometimes, beautifully always'.

It was a rule of the House that speakers should not read from notes, so Fitz had prepared his speech well. Based on the power and rhythms of William Pitt's great speech on the abolition of slavery (which Fitz referred to as 'by far the finest piece of oratory of any we possess'), he had committed his speech to memory and he spoke it 'almost word for word as originally planned, without hesitation or faltering'.

'Mr Speaker,' he began. 'If I were to say that I rise with a feeling of great diffidence to move the resolutions standing on the paper this evening, I should very feebly express the sense of weight which oppresses me when I contemplate the task I have undertaken.'

He described the background to the war in Taranaki and told the house that he would 'say a few words … upon the future prospect of the Maori race':

> I ask my honourable friends to look this steadily in the face. What
> is the present aspect of the Natives toward you? I say they distrust
> you. They do not believe in the peaceful professions either of the
> Government or of the Governor. They think … that you are only
> waiting for an opportunity to pounce on their lands, and to supplant
> them for ever in the homes of their fathers … Should we not think
> exactly the same in their place? … Sir, I solemnly believe there
> are only two possible futures before the Maori people. You must
> be prepared to win their confidence, or you must be prepared to
> destroy them. If you do not win their entire confidence, you will be
> compelled to destroy them.

He ended with a stirring piece of oratory:

> I solemnly believe that this is the last chance for the Maori. The
> present state of things cannot last. The condition of the colony is not
> one of peace; it is a state of armed and suspicious neutrality … Once
> light up again the torch of war in these islands, and these feeble and
> artificial institutions you are now building up will be swept away
> like houses of paper in the flames. Tribe after tribe will be drawn

into the struggle, and you will make it a war of races. Of course you will conquer; but it will be the conquest of the tomb … You will be compelled, as other nations have been compelled before, to hunt the miserable native from haunt to haunt till he is destroyed like the beast of the forest.

I am here tonight to appeal against so miserable, so inhuman a consummation. We are here, Sir, this evening standing on the threshold of the future, holding the issues of peace and war – of life and death in our hands … I appeal tonight to the House, to inaugurate a policy of courageous and munificent justice. I have a right to appeal to you as citizens of that nation, which, deaf to the predictions of the sordid and the timid, dared to give liberty to her slaves – I appeal to you tonight in your sphere to perform an act of kindred greatness.

Fitz resumed his seat aware – perhaps – that he had given the most significant speech of his life, a speech remembered in years to come as the most moving oration ever heard in the New Zealand parliament. It was, wrote one of the members, 'a marvellous effort of eloquence. On he went, giving utterance to an unbroken flow of polished sentences, full of meaning, full of grace and eloquence, thrilling some, fixing the attention of others, and convincing all that, physically and mentally, nature had made him for an orator.'

Henry Sewell disagreed, referring to the speech as 'FitzGerald's grand demonstration … a very brilliant and eloquent speech, such as he alone can make … but after all it was mere declamation, without substance'.

Fitz's resolutions were debated for the next two days. The first two passed without a division; the third (Maori representation in parliament) was defeated by three votes. Considering it 'mere humbug' to pass two resolutions without the third, Fitz withdrew them all, 'with a view to bringing them forward again in the next session'.

On 11 August, he relived moments of past glory when he chaired a dinner for 'the old members of the session of 1854, the Patriarchs of the Constitution'. Fifteen members of the 1854 parliament dined at Bellamy's. It was, according to Sewell, 'a very pleasant dinner party, plenty of singing, champagne and punch … FitzGerald was as usual the life of the party … His vivacity is tremendous and his wit and animal spirits are amazing.'

But the temper of the House was deteriorating, caused at least partly by Fitz's arrogance and constant changes of mind. 'He is certainly a very brilliant man,' wrote Sewell, 'but then it is a kind of firework, it blazes and dies out.'

Even James Richmond was exasperated, referring to Fitz as 'a great donkey with all his Irish genius'. Politics were descending into a 'sort of wild-beast kind of life … people on one side say sharp and bitter things against people on the other. Nobody has a particle of charity or forbearance.'

Fitz gave two major speeches in late August, one on ministerial responsibility, the other on a Native Lands Bill. He also arranged for his speech on native affairs to be printed in Wellington and sent to Stanford in London, for onward transmission to his friends in England. 'You will say it was wild and theoretical,' he wrote to Lord Lyttelton, but:

> the oldest hands and best native scholars tell me it would solve the native difficulty at once. If the present government breaks down … I shall try and go in for office to carry my native policy into effect … I told Stanford to send a copy of my speech to Mr Gladstone. I should like to know if he thought me visionary.

…

At home in Canterbury, Fitz's two-month absence from the Springs might have made life easier for Fanny (one less mouth to feed) – if Willy had not fallen off a horse and broken his collarbone; if it had not been the coldest winter the settlers had so far experienced; if she had not been expecting another baby. Charles Bowen was lost in admiration. 'Mrs FG is wonderful,' he wrote. 'She manages all those children, and sometimes the station, and yet is always jolly and still looks wonderfully young. She is a regular brick.'

'Mrs FG and the little FGs and I are keeping house together,' wrote Edward Chudleigh. 'They have been so kind to me.' On 2 July, Fanny 'played and sang all the evening' to an assembled company of stockmen, 'airs of all nations and in as many languages, so we are not always in a savage state'. She repeated the performance on 11 July when George Sale (who had given up the *Press* to try his luck in the Otago goldfields) was visiting the station, by which time the frost had hardened on the ground and there had been several days of heavy snow.

Chudleigh kept a diary during his time at the station, much of it charmingly misspelt. The 14th, he wrote, was a day of 'very harde froaste', and Amy and Willy were 'out on the run all day collecting the cattle'. At daybreak next morning, he and Draper left for Longbeach, driving the heifers which Fitz had sold to the new owner of the southern run.

During the next ten days, the ground remained frozen, the ice in the swamps and puddles more than six inches deep. Fanny – almost four months pregnant – found it hard to keep warm. When Draper and Chudleigh returned on the 26th, they found her complaining of sickness and stomach pains.

On the 28th, Chudleigh cleaned his 'saddle and bridal which wanted it very much', and 'helped the children catch and clip their fowls, mend the yard, and make nests in the hen house'. Fanny remained in bed with abdominal cramps and vomiting. Her condition deteriorated during the night ('she is realy very ill'). Early the next morning, Chudleigh drove into Christchurch with a note for Alfred Barker.

Barker had retired from medical practice but, as a friend of the family, he set out immediately for the station. He soon realised that Fanny was at risk of a miscarriage, and ordered her to stay in bed. A few hours later, Chudleigh returned with Anne Gresson, who would stay at the Springs until Fanny was well enough to move to Christchurch.

The weather continued cold and damp. It rained continuously and Fanny was kept in bed with blankets and hotwater bottles. On 1 August, she came downstairs in the afternoon. Four days later, Anne Gresson made arrangements to take her to Christchurch. They left the station in the circulating medium on the morning of 6 August (the day Fitz gave his great speech in the general assembly), with Amy and Willy riding alongside. 'The track is almost impassable,' wrote Chudleigh that night:

> I was fully employed thrashing on the leaders to keep them from being stuck altogether. We met the judge half way down coming to look for his wife. He took off his hat to the ladies and would have passed on had I not spoken to him. He has the worst seat on a horse I ever saw.

The jolting of the dogcart was dangerous in Fanny's condition; she was put to bed as soon as they reached the Gressons' house. Ten-year-old Amy stayed with her mother, and Willy and Chudleigh returned to the station, leaving after sunset and driving through darkness in 'the densest fog I have seen out here'.

During the next two weeks, Fanny remained 'dangerously ill' in Christchurch, while Chudleigh and Willy worked on the run, often spending twelve hours in the saddle ('a long time for a boy of nine years'). On 22 August, Chudleigh noted that Fanny was still 'very unwell. Dr Barker and Mrs Gresson will not let her move yet on any account.'

...

News of Fanny's illness might explain Fitz's erratic behaviour during the later stages of the 1862 parliament. Struggling with conflicting loyalties – aware that he should return home to his wife; desperate to stay in Wellington to influence Domett's fledgling government – the politician prevailed. In mid-August,

Fanny received a letter explaining that, although he would leave the session early, he could not return to Christchurch until the end of the month.

He finally arrived in Lyttelton on 1 September, and was met by Chudleigh and Draper with a spare horse. After breakfasting at the Mitre Hotel, they set off along the Sumner Road. As they climbed the zigzag to Evans Pass and rode down the hill to Sumner, Fitz entertained them with (in Chudleigh's inimitable spelling) 'very amusing stories of the Mourays'. When they arrived at the Gressons' house, he found Fanny looking pale and wan. 'If Mrs Gresson had not brought her to Christchurch,' he told Henry Selfe, 'perhaps I would have lost her.'

There was much for Fitz to do now he was home. There were public meetings to address about recent events in parliament, arrangements to make for closing down the station, and accommodation to provide for his family. Cox had left the Springs on 28 August and, as Fitz put it, 'all the matters which ought to have been entirely settled are still left for me to do ... I shall never see him again if I can help it.'

He moved Fanny to the house of Dr James Turnbull in Madras Street. A kindly man with a strong Scottish accent and a wooden leg, the doctor gave orders that she was to remain very still; under no circumstances should she return to the station. On 4 September, she was well enough to write a note to Chudleigh, 'full of household instructions'. Next day, she was looking 'much better' and, on the morning of the 6th, Fitz and Amy set out for the station to pack up the house. That night, Fitz played his guitar and 'sang some beautiful old English and Scotch songs and told us the most amusing stories of the Members at Wellington. He approves of ammalgammateing the Mourays with the Europeans.'

Two days later, Fitz loaded up the circulating medium with 'six children and the nurse with their iron beds and bedding, two boxes about three hundredweight each, two baths and perambulator, and innumerable other things amounting to over a ton'. He drove into Christchurch ('without a mishap of any sort'), deposited the children and the nurse at Mary Thornton's house, and returned to Fanny in Madras Street.

On the 14th, he wrote a disingenuous letter to Henry Selfe, who had written several times to complain about the article on cadets and his failure to repay his debt:

> I am greatly pained by the tone of [your] correspondence ... You
> write about the article in the *Press* about cadets as if it was a personal

attack on you … If I had the least idea that any remarks would apply to you and yours, I would rather have left a public duty unperformed than have penned a line which would incidentally wound your feelings …

As to my money … you know that at any time it only required the slightest hint from you to induce me to sell up and refund the capital. *It has hardly repaid me one farthing up to the present time.* I say this in order that you may know I have not been taking advantage of your kindness and not paying interest merely because I was spending it … Jim will be paid the whole of the debt as soon as the estate is sold.

Fanny was still 'very weak, lying on the sofa' in Dr Turnbull's house, and builders were at work on the Press Office in Cashel Street, extending upwards with a new first floor and constructing a family house alongside. In the meantime, the family was scattered:

I have not had a place to lay my head since my return and have only today got a room and a table and chair. My letters and books I cannot get at … My home will not be complete for a month and I shall be put to a pretty expense living the children in one place and myself in another. I have never been so miserable or unsettled since I have been in the colony.

And his days as a farmer were over: 'I nearly died of rheumatism last winter. It is all folly trying to lead an outdoor life.'

He returned to the Springs on 15 September to discuss the farm sale with the auctioneer. The list of stock included Regicide and 40 'well-bred milch cows'; 40 horses 'consisting of harness and saddle horses, several magnificent carthorses, and some very excellent young stock'; 25 pigs; 'fowls and turkeys'. There were 'drays, harness, ploughs, harrows, rollers, a great variety of tools', and equipment in the dairy ('long reputed as one of the most complete in the province'). Everything was to be sold 'without the slightest reserve'.

On 13 October, Fitz made another journey to the Springs to pack up the furniture. Two days later, he and the auctioneer arrived at the station. 'Tomorrow and the Springs will be no more,' wrote Chudleigh in his diary that night. 'The eventful 16th has at last come and all the pet horses and fence destroying old cows are to go to the highest bidder.'

At half-past nine in the morning, a number of carts set out from Christchurch. Two hours later, lunch was served at the station and the sale commenced at noon. The bull and cows were sold first, 'then the horses, then the agriculturall implements'. Chudleigh spent the day 'going about on horseback and in the yards like a steam engine … Lots of fellows got drunk and we had a regular Tiperairy riot. They stuck to the rule where ever you see a head, hit it. We soused them with buckets of cold water.'

The pigs, fowls and dairy equipment, 'with innumerable other things', were auctioned on the second day of the sale, bringing the total proceeds to £2500. And by the evening of the 17th, as Chudleigh put it, 'we have now got rid of all things alive and dead'.

CHAPTER TWENTY-TWO

Friend Whititera

1862–1863

FitzGerald … is an architect of the most perfect theories: he builds them
up, tires of them, topples them over and builds others in their place.

Colonel Gore Browne, 15 June 1858

Mr FitzGerald sometimes allows his pen to get the better of his judgement and lays about him in very gladiatorial style.

Fitz, 25 May 1861

'I am in such dreadful confusion,' Fitz wrote on 12 November. 'My
papers, letters and goods have been scattered here and there. In fine,
such confusion and discomforts I never suffered. However, I get into our new
home on Monday when we shall soon all get square.' He moved his family
into their new home on the 17th. It was 'a plain, comfortable house' where they
lived 'literally over my types and presses'. It was a hot November, the streets 'a
cloud of dust, most trying to the eyes'.

Fanny disliked living in town. The children, too, were unhappy; they missed
the fresh air and open spaces of the plains. 'We hated town life after our free
one on the station,' Amy wrote in her memoirs. 'I missed my riding more than
anything else.' Even Fitz was nostalgic: 'the loss of the Springs greatly affects
me. It was like the paternal estates to me.'

On 6 December, they spent an evening with William Richmond who was
making another visit to Christchurch. 'They sang together and separately,'
Richmond told his wife. 'FitzGerald was very hoarse and did not sing well.
Mrs FitzGerald did.' A week later, after 'an awful day, a hot wind with blinding
dust blowing furiously', Fitz wrote a friendly letter to Henry Selfe. He was, he
wrote, 'comfortably settled' in his new house:

> and am steadily at work on my paper. It seems to me that, if please
> God I keep my health for a year or two, I shall have a noble estate in
> this paper to dispose of, but it is a great pull on the brains, a constant

The second home of the *Press* in Cashel Street. The original (single-storey) butcher shop is on the right. The first floor and family home alongside were built in late 1862.

Fairfax Media

> drain on the brain to produce material … Fanny is, thank God, well again but very near her confinement. The children are very well but not as jolly as at the station.

It was about this time that the future novelist Samuel Butler arrived at the *Press* with the first of three philosophical articles written under the pseudonym 'Cellarius'. Butler, who met Fitz in London, had arrived in Canterbury in 1860 with a reference to Percy Cox in his pocket. He took an up-country sheep run and renewed his acquaintance with Fitz, visiting him in Cashel Street whenever he came to Christchurch.

The article, a review of Darwin's *On the Origin of Species* in the form of a dialogue, was based on a conversation between Fitz ('F') and Butler ('C').[1] Published in the *Press* on 20 December, it 'excited a great deal of discussion in the colony', including 'a contemptuous rejoinder from the bishop'. Butler sent a copy to Darwin in England, who replied that it was 'remarkable for its spirit and for giving so clear and accurate a view of Mr D's theory. It is, also, remarkable for being published in a colony exactly 12 years old.'

---

1   The article was later used in Butler's novel *Erewhon*

Fitz was proud to have published the article ('I believe in Christianity and I believe in Darwin'). He was equally proud on New Year's Day 1863 when he tried his hand at typesetting. 'Sweet Maid Marian,' read his first lines of type, addressed to John Raven's young daughter. 'Your commands are law to me. They are printed on the tablets of my heart, as this, my first attempt at type setting, is printed on this paper. I will wait on you at your Christmas tree, to receive your thanks for this first proof of my affection.'

On 14 January, George Draper boarded ship to return to England. Fitz and Chudleigh accompanied him over the Port Hills, and they opened a bottle of 'champaign' to speed him on his way. That evening, Fitz wrote to Lord Lyttelton with news of his godson, who was 'blooming and fat beyond description. He is slow and stolid but presents considerable argumentative powers, the wicked one above him retaining his pre-eminence in crime and eccentricity.'

'The government here is rather sad,' he continued. 'Borrow and waste, borrow and waste, that is the motto. Moorhouse has depraved the public mind in matters of money more than can be believed … I have left the Provincial Council for I look on it [that] nothing but a public calamity will bring men to their senses.'

Fitz had resigned from the council on 18 December. Four weeks later, Moorhouse resigned as superintendent and Fitz was asked to stand in his place. He agreed to put himself forward as a candidate but soon withdrew his name, having decided that he was not prepared to 'struggle' for office. Canvassing, he explained in the *Press*, 'is a task revolting to the self-respect of a right-minded man'. That was his excuse. The more common view (expressed by a member of council) was that 'FitzGerald would have no chance in the contest for the Superintendency. He has so thrown away his influence and position and made so many enemies by his very unsparing use of his pen.'

The second candidate, Samuel Bealey, was elected unopposed on 5 March 1863. He was described by Fitz as 'a shopkeeper in mind and manners', and even more rudely by Charles Bowen as 'a mild platitude-grinding nobody'. Bealey owed his election, Bowen explained, 'to the mistrust of FitzGerald which has become so general … even his friends had no heart for the fight for they did not know what trick he might play them … His ability will always make him a marked man and often a useful one, but he will never be trusted again as he has been trusted – never.'

Fitz now decided that Moorhouse would have been the better superin-tendent. 'I really liked Moorhouse much better,' he told an astonished Lord Lyttelton. 'Moorhouse was a character, now we have descended to a *nobody*.'

…

The child Fanny so nearly miscarried was born three weeks before the election, a second daughter named Evangeline (Eva). And Fitz, full of contradictions, his mood once more in overdrive, had become alarmingly overwrought. 'I do sometimes look on him as mad,' wrote Bowen on 13 March:

> He is a fellow of most infinite resource that I should not pity him much if he stood alone, but I tremble for his wife and family. He has just given notice that he intends to bring out the *Press* as a daily paper! Against the advice of every single friend in the Province to whom he ever spoke … It is certainly a wild, rash step.

The *Press* became the first daily paper in Canterbury on 17 March 1863, an eight-page paper selling for 3d. The first issue complained about the weather ('Christchurch was visited by one of the most violent north-west blasts we have ever experienced') and included a series of puns ('why must the present government of Canterbury be feebler than the last? Because it has been de-Bealey-tated').

The *Lyttelton Times* declined to follow suit. 'We have no present intention of coming out daily,' wrote the editor on 20 March. 'In the opinion of the proprietors, the time has not arrived for taking such an extreme step.' Fitz was dismissive of such caution, although a daily paper took more of his time and he often worked late into the night ('as usual, here I am at one o'clock in the morning trying to write in the midst of proof sheets etc and the mail closing at six').

The strain soon began to tell. 'I am now so unwell that I can't write except briefly,' he told Henry Selfe on 13 May. 'I have been fighting against a bad chest attack and yesterday the exertion of getting out "the summary" was too much and I have been in bed all day … I wonder if any man is so often ill as I am. The half of my life is illness.' Publishing a daily newspaper was, he continued, 'a real hard life and a great speculation. The expenses are appalling.' He remained sanguine about his prospects: 'I am sadly in want of money because it is difficult to get in money as fast as it goes out, but on my books I am making from £2000 to £3000 a year, and in a year more I shall be I suppose in full receipt of that income.'

The Springs station had been put up for auction four times but, according to Chudleigh, Fitz had talked it up too much. As a result, 'there was not a bidder; everyone was afraid to bid as the place was expected to go so high'. In Fitz's opinion, this was the fault of Percy Cox and Hunter Brown: 'Thanks to *partners*, I am sick of the whole thing … We have been unable to sell the Springs estate at any sacrifice and, of course, get nothing from it at all. I really think if I had not got into the *Press*, I should have left Canterbury.'

The fourth auction in April 1863 was listed as 'absolutely without reserve', but even this failed to find a buyer. During the next eighteen months, the run was sold in small increments, 'bit by bit', until it was 'all gone to strangers … the sacrifice of a noble estate'. It was a great pity, Fitz complained to Selfe, that Jim had refused to enter into partnership ('the property will be worth £50,000 one day'). Instead it sold for £5 an acre, most of it on three-year credit.

'The Springs property sold very badly,' wrote Percy Cox, 'under some misunderstanding as to reserve … Altogether the most tremendous mess was made of the whole transaction.' Fitz's excuse was that he had been too busy with the *Press*. 'Could we have sold it all off at once,' he wrote in November 1864, 'there would have been no trouble but I could not attend to it. I was obliged to turn to something so I took on the paper and it took my whole time.'

Fitz had estimated his 45 per cent share of the partnership at between £4000 and £5000. In the event, total receipts from the liquidation amounted to £5856. When the accounts were drawn up and his liabilities deducted, Fitz's share was calculated at £2467, most of which he did not receive until the partnership was dissolved in September 1865.

…

The *Press* published a second article by Samuel Butler ('Darwin among the Machines') on 13 June 1863, a time when Christchurch was working itself into 'an ecstasy of excitement' for the marriage of the Prince of Wales in London on 9 July. The city was decorated for the occasion, a grand procession was planned, and Fanny was asked to plant one of two commemoration oaks. The rain fell in torrents on 8 July, filling the streets with mud, but the sun broke through next morning and the celebrations took place on a bright sunny day.

Two thousand people took part in the procession. A guard of honour came first, with an open carriage pulled by four horses; inside were Fanny and Rose Bealey (the superintendent's wife), 'the ladies who had consented to plant the commemoration trees'. They were followed by a large number of children, the three elder FitzGeralds dressed in their Sunday best, 'trudging through liquid mud over their boots'.

Then came the fire brigade with two engines, a plough on a decorated dray, the millers and bakers, and 50 butchers on horseback with a banner reading ROAST BEEF OF OLD ENGLAND. The city banner was followed by members of the provincial council, Henry Gresson in his legal robes, Bishop Harper in his full regalia, and members of the general assembly – including Fitz – looking formal in top hat and tails.

The staff of the *Press* and the *Lyttelton Times* had joined forces. Their drays carried a working printing press and banners with the mottos: WE PRINTERS

Share the Universal Joy; Tyranny Trembles at the Creaking of the Printing Press; and – in a rare display of amity – The United Press of Canterbury.

In Cashel Street, the house and the Press Office spilled into each other. Compositors were dragged into the parlour to practise with the glee singers; the children set up a theatre among the boxes and packing cases in the printing office yard; and the family sitting room doubled as Fitz's study. One of his paintings, a seascape, hung over the fireplace and the room was filled with books. Here, puffing at his pipe, he wrote his leading articles, interviewed agents and held forth on politics.

Believing his newspaper to be a powerful political force, he wrote in startlingly strong terms about Canterbury matters, denigrating almost everyone in public life. 'Nothing to me is more remarkable in New Zealand history,' he explained, 'than the importance of the press over Superintendents and its power in the Provincial Councils.' Journalism, he continued, 'is certainly by far the pleasantest mode of interfering in politics because one is uncontrolled in any way and I see gradually but surely what a powerful effect is to be produced on the public mood, even on one's foes, by the continual dripping of a daily paper.'

He arranged for his articles on native affairs to be translated into Maori and distributed in native villages, consolidating his reputation as a friend. Maori referred to him as 'Whititera', a transliteration of FitzGerald (which also translates as 'the sun shines'), a name of which he was inordinately proud.

Some of his articles on Maori affairs were ill informed, particularly those relating to the Waitara purchase which occurred during his absence in London. 'He was quite ignorant of the whole facts,' wrote Frederick Weld in 1861, 'but quite decided in opinion … He is reported to have said it would only puzzle him to read both sides.'

On 2 May 1863, Fitz wrote that fear of renewed hostilities was 'a panic-stricken fiction of diseased minds'. Two days later, skirmishes broke out again in Taranaki, and in mid-July – on the governor's sole authority – imperial troops marched into the Waikato. Fitz now redoubled his efforts.

'Our attention has been called to an article on the Waitara question … from the Canterbury *Press*,' wrote the editor of the *Taranaki Herald* on 8 August:

> We should say 'another article,' for it is but one of many on the same subject which have appeared in that journal. We confess that to us the *Press* on Native affairs is no longer entertaining or instructive. Its crude theories and half understood and misreported facts make very dull reading in this northern part of New Zealand.

Four days later, the editor sent a copy of the offending article to William Richmond who, in Stafford's absence, had been acting premier at the time of the Waitara purchase: 'Will you look through this and say whether you think an action for libel … would lie with reasonable chance of success … I am afraid FitzGerald loves his own side better than truth.'

Fitz may have got his facts wrong – he rarely checked details before putting pen to paper – but his instincts were remarkably astute for their time. As he wrote to a member of parliament in London:

> The present suspicious and sulky attitude of the great bulk of the native race has its origin, partly, at all events, in a multitude of petty grievances arising out of unfulfilled promises. Instead of letting them alone, and giving them what they ask for when it is a matter of indifference [to us], we have treated them like children and acted as if we knew much better what was good for them than they do themselves. Their conclusion has been that in all this manipulation we were looking to our own object and interests, and not to theirs; and I cannot tell them that this is altogether a mistake.

Fitz had been enthusiastic about Sir George Grey's return to New Zealand; now he was disappointed for a second time. He deplored Grey's belligerent approach to native affairs. At a public meeting in Christchurch on 10 August, he gave a speech about Grey's invasion of the Waikato ('this wicked act'), which had not been sanctioned by the general assembly. He moved that parliament should be called as soon as possible, but the meeting was, as he put it, 'in an excited and martial spirit'. His motion was defeated, while an amendment supporting the governor was passed unanimously.

He had greater success on 7 September when he addressed the electors of Ellesmere at a meeting in the Lyttelton town hall. Avoiding the subject of the Waikato, he read out the resolutions he had put to the 1862 assembly. He would, he said, 'move [them] again and again, so long as I shall be a Member of the House, until I obtain their recognition'. The electors of Ellesmere might view these resolutions as 'an impracticable dream' but he hoped to prove them wrong:

> Do you think I am so foolish as to suppose that giving a Native a vote will solve every difficulty in … government? Are you the better for having votes? Is there any mysterious power in going up to the hustings and giving a vote for a candidate which makes you better men? No; but it is the feeling of all that the power of voting implies.
>
> The vote is the symbol of the great truth that you are each of you a part of the government under which you live, that you are not

living under laws imposed on you from without, and maintained by external force, but under laws to which you have given your free consent and therefore cheerfully obey … If you could once get the Natives to feel that they were a part and parcel of yourselves, to feel that they were making laws as well as you, to acquire an interest and confidence in your government, you would find every difficulty in the way of carrying the law into force vanish away.

Fitz's motion was carried by 70 votes to 4, although the *Lyttelton Times* made the snide comment that 'out of the 51 persons qualified to vote for the Ellesmere district, not more than five or six were present'.

…

The 1863 parliament had been summoned to meet in Auckland on 19 October. Disappointed at having declined the premiership in 1862, Fitz hoped that he would be 'called to office – I can't help it … I feel it coming on me'. He boarded the steamer on 10 October, sailing up the east coast of the North Island and breaking his journey in Napier to meet with 'some of the leading Chiefs of those parts'. He arrived in Auckland on the 19th to find 'everyone talking about the war. The streets bristled with bayonets and resounded with the tramp of soldiers and militia men.'

The ministry which Fitz 'patched up' the previous year had proved to be 'very weak', with Alfred Domett 'quite unfit to be the head of a government'. Matters came to a head on 27 October when ministers 'came to the conclusion that they must have a more efficient head'. Domett 'kicked at this proposal and positively declined it. His colleagues thereupon resigned and he perforce was obliged to go with them, so out they all went.'

Fitz 'very much wanted' to replace Domett. He was disappointed when the governor called instead for William Fox – and horrified when the new ministry[1] endorsed Grey's approach to the war and enshrined his hard-line policies in legislation. The government imposed martial law, suspended habeas corpus, and passed the New Zealand Settlements Act, which allowed for the creation of military settlements and the confiscation of almost three million acres of Maori land. It authorised a loan of £3 million from England to cover the costs of the war, 'in addition to the three and a half millions which we owe already … reckless extravagance which must bring the colony to bankruptcy'.

During a short parliamentary session, Fitz raised his voice in protest against these 'insane' policies, against 'a machine for tyranny and oppression borrowed

1 The Whitaker-Fox ministry, with William Fox as colonial secretary and Whitaker (who sat in the Legislative Council) as premier.

from the worst days of Irish history'. Such policies, he said, would drive Maori to desperation, extend the areas of rebellion, and provide the government with opportunities for further confiscations. The Settlements Bill, he told the House on 5 November, was an:

> enormous crime … to be committed against a race to whom we
> have refused the right of representation in this House, and who are
> not able to appear at the bar of justice to plead their own cause … I
> know it is of very little use addressing the House on this subject; as I
> know the mind of the House is made up as to what it will do … All
> I can do is to enter a solitary protest.

On 17 November, during the second reading of the Loan Bill, he deplored the saddling of a young colony with a massive debt. And he spoke again for Maori: 'I do appeal to the House on behalf of the native race … they are worthy of a better policy.'

The southern members now decided to put forward a motion that the seat of parliament be moved from Auckland. Fitz had already booked a cabin on the steamer leaving on the 24th, but was persuaded to delay his departure. He had long argued that 'the whole colony is made to suffer because the government has chosen to set itself down in a remote corner of the islands', and despite believing that change was 'nothing short of an impossibility', he agreed to propose the motion in the House.

On the evening of the 25th, he delivered 'a long, able and conciliatory speech'. The debate lasted well into the night; the division bell rang at two o'clock in the morning. As the members streamed into the lobbies, Fitz's motion was passed by 24 votes to 17. The result was announced at quarter past two 'and was received with great cheering'.

CHAPTER TWENTY-THREE

A Prophet in the Desert

1863–1865

I attribute my success to a close and constant attention to the business
part of the paper.

Fitz, 24 May 1864

If I could get rid of debt to men who, having got you in their hands,
squeeze you like a lemon, I should be a rich man in five years.

Fitz, 15 January 1865

Heartened by his success in moving the seat of parliament, Fitz remained in Auckland until the end of the 1863 parliament. He embarked for Lyttelton on 8 December and arrived home on the 14th, two weeks after the opening of the railway from Christchurch to Heathcote – the first stage of the direct link to Lyttelton, the first railway in New Zealand.

The train made its inaugural journey on 1 December. A public holiday had been declared, the station was garlanded with flowers and flags, and a brass band played military music. The small 50-horsepower engine, 'The Pilgrim', had been shipped out from England and it stood on the tracks, freshly painted and oiled, its polished brass gleaming.

It was a windy day, raising the usual clouds of dust. Samuel Bealey and members of the provincial council climbed aboard the wooden carriages, while a triumphant Moorhouse stood on the engine plate and raised his hat to the crowds. At two o'clock, the engine blew its whistle and puffed out of the station. It arrived at Heathcote ten minutes later. For the next six hours it ran backwards and forwards, its carriages filled with the people of Christchurch.

The city was growing; thirteen years after the arrival of the first ships, it was beginning to look like a modern town. 'Poor Godley would not know it at all,' wrote Fitz after returning from Auckland:

> Miles of straight streets are formed and metalled, with houses
> gradually filling them up and every trace of the old country

The 'Big School' at Christ's College, Christchurch, designed by Fitz and built in 1863. The headmaster described the design as 'rather sublime than beautiful ... the roof ... of an extraordinary span and of very massive timber'. Photograph taken in 1867 when Willy and Robert were pupils at the school.

Alexander Turnbull Library, Wellington (PAColl-8850)

disappeared. Large stone banks and houses two or three storeys high. Cabs on stands and water-carts watering the streets, and all without gold or troops or foreign aid. A nice little theatre with Shakespeare plays. A new town hall building which will hold 700 or 800 people ... It is all like a dream to me.

He was particularly proud of his own contribution: a stone-built schoolroom for Christ's College. He had volunteered to design the building when it was commissioned in 1862, congratulating himself that he would then 'have done something of every art'. He 'took a great deal of trouble, not being an architect, to calculate the pressures, wind included'. He intended his design to convey 'massive strength, stability and simplicity of character', and the finished building was, in the words of the headmaster, 'rather sublime than beautiful ... the roof ... of extraordinary span and of very massive timber'. It was used for the first time for the annual examination on 15 December (the day after Fitz returned from Auckland); the boys were asked to 'give three cheers for Mr FitzGerald' before opening their papers.

Meanwhile, Fanny was singing again in public, performing soprano solos in musical society concerts. Fitz was proud of her success: 'Fanny continues the prima donna in all the oratorios. I assure you I have heard a great many much worse professional singers.' Edward Chudleigh attended one of her concerts, and wrote in his diary that 'Mrs FG was accounted the best musitian in the room'.

At home, Fanny was working as hard as ever. Domestic servants were in short supply and many of the available women had never worked in a home or a kitchen. As a newcomer to Christchurch explained:

> The great complaint, the never-ending subject of comparison and lamentation among ladies, is the utter ignorance and inefficiency of their female servants ... An English lady, with even an extremely moderate income, would look upon her colonial sister as very hard-worked indeed. The children cannot be entrusted entirely to the care of an ignorant girl, and the poor mother has them with her all day long; if she goes out to pay visits ... she has to take the elder children with her ... [and] there is not much rest at night ... with the inevitable baby.

Fourteen-year-old Amy helped Fanny with the housework and the children. She was growing into an attractive young woman and was often photographed by Alfred Barker (a keen amateur photographer), sitting in his garden or leaning against his mantelpiece. She still missed the freedom to gallop across the plains, but 'several gentlemen were most wonderfully kind in lending me horses and taking me out riding'.

...

'Fifteen months ago, the *Press* was a miserable little paper once a week,' Fitz wrote to Henry Selfe in January 1864:

> Now it is a firmly established daily journal, advertisements worth £120 to £150 a week and steadily increasing. Expenses it is true are enormous but when all the plant is paid for and I am not called to put my hand in my pocket every month for more, the income will be very large. At present, I am poorer than ever with very large profits on the books.

And he was building again, 'raising my whole office to get more room and shall then have 140 feet of office room, 15 feet wide on two floors'. Competition with his rival newspaper (nicknamed 'The Little Tin Times') was a powerful motivation. The two papers disagreed about most things, 'taking opposite views on every conceivable question under the sun'.

For almost three years, Fitz had done his best to attract circulation and advertising away from the *Lyttelton Times*, and now he obtained the contract for provincial government printing, which had been 'the monopoly of the *Lyttelton Times* for the last seven or eight years'. He achieved this by undercutting his rival, more concerned to score a point than to make a profit.

This competition was proving expensive. The *Press* had become a daily paper in March 1863. Five months later, Fitz moved to a larger format ('as large as possible in the present circumstances of the settlement'). He increased the number of pages and upgraded to better quality paper. These developments – all intended to take readers and advertisers away from the *Lyttelton Times* – required a staff of 45 men (full and part-time), as well as new plant and equipment from England.

In 1863, he had given himself a salary of £846. The following year, he increased his drawings to £1268. All other profits were channelled into the business to pay expenses and buy new machinery. He kept a careful eye on the pennies: 'I attribute my success to a close and constant attention to the business part of the paper. For example, I keep the daily cash book myself, and every farthing down to the threepenny sale of the paper over the counter passes through my hands every evening.'

At the same time, he was ignoring the bigger picture. Because he was so busy with politics, he had entrusted the financial aspects of the business to a firm of land agents and financiers that specialised in the affairs of absentee owners. This was a partnership between Richard Harman and a young land agent, Edward Stevens ('one of the most clear-headed and least sanguine accountants I ever met').

Harman & Stevens began dealing with affairs of the *Press* in late 1862. At first, Fitz found them 'very satisfactory' and, on 9 October 1863, he signed a power of attorney giving the firm authority to handle 'the management or disposition of my property, whether real or personal'. He was also building up an overdraft with the firm; he described this as 'large advances at times to make me meet my engagements which they have made from a full knowledge of the soundness of my business'. The charges were high (5 per cent commission, 10 per cent interest) and, as the months passed, as Fitz spent the profits on new plant and machinery, he failed to service the debt. Instead of making quarterly repayments as agreed, the commission and interest were merely added to the capital advanced by the firm. And as compound interest began to bite, the amount outstanding increased at an alarming rate.

On 10 April, while Christchurch was enjoying a spell of fine autumn weather, he retired to bed with bronchitis and remained there for several days, complaining that his life was 'one escalating grind. A daily paper is an awful thing and no mistake.' A few weeks later, when the cold weather had arrived and the Port Hills were covered with snow, he received a letter from Henry Selfe expressing fears about his 'financial speculations' and complaining gently that his loan had not been fully repaid. Fitz's reply was written impulsively, within an hour of receiving the letter:

> I reply at once to your fears ... I know well that many persons thought I should be ruined by the *Press* ... but I assure you I have never taken a step without the best advice and most careful consideration of all contingencies ... I advise to you I am very hard up for money and can't get much for myself because a large business can't be made in a day.

Fitz's editorials were written as impulsively as his private letters. 'It is really incredible the shovelfuls of dirt which a man will consume when once he has taken to nasty habits,' he wrote of William Fox; and he blamed Sir George Grey for invading the Waikato, for exacerbating 'this sorry and disgraceful war'. The governor was 'cold, impassioned, watchful, and truthless', his 'great and mysterious reputation' built, 'not on the honest labours of his own genius, but, like the churchyard ghoul, on the burned remains of the blunders of those around him'.

In April 1864, he wrote a stirring editorial about the battle of Orakau, at which 300 Maori held out against a force of 2000 soldiers:

> No human situation can be conceived more desperate or more hopeless – their lands gone, their race melting away like snow before the sun, and now their own time come at last ... There will be men in after times whose pens will narrate the causes and outcomings of this contest, and who will seek, in the objects of the war, the key to its disasters. They will say it was not a war for safety or for law, or for truth or liberty, but it was a war dictated by avarice and prosecuted for spoliation. It was a war ... to destroy a race that we might dwell in their tents ...
>
> But if there be anything in the whole miserable story to excite the admiration of a generous mind, it is the sad spectacle of those grim and tawny figures, gaunt with the watching and weariness, the wounds and nakedness of a long campaign in the bush, staring over their ragged palisades on the hosts of their conquerors from whom escape was impossible, and wailing out their last chant of death and defiance – *ake, ake, ake* – for ever! for ever! for ever!

He found it deplorable that 'one race should meet in Parliament and make laws for another race without having the slightest knowledge of its feelings, wishes or grievances'. He wanted the imperial troops (now standing at almost 10,000 men) to be sent home; for the colony to take responsibility for its own defence. Why, he asked, should British taxes 'be used to destroy a brave and noble race?' Referring to himself as 'the prophet in the desert', he warned that, 'if this cruel, wicked, vile war lasts six months longer, I will come overland to England and get up public meetings all over the country to proclaim against the iniquity of the proceedings'.

...

A few weeks before Fitz wrote these words, his brother Gerard, now editor of the *Invercargill Times*, was 'burnt out and lost everything'; after which Fitz 'put on £1250 more of insurance ... on my place. I now have £4000 insured and nearly £4000 on the books altogether, so that I should have enough to start again. Fire is an awful thing in the colonies.'

Three months later, the *Press* nearly suffered the same fate. On the evening of 11 June, Fitz was playing a game of chess 'when the servant ran in and said there was a great fire close to the back of the office. I went up to the window on the stairs and there was a house in flames close to us.' He told Fanny 'to get all the children up and dress them', and sent an employee to call the foreman:

> The men all soon came and we cleared out the whole office, every type and part into the garden, ready to bury it with earth if necessary. My premises being all enclosed, I thought it better than carrying it through the streets. If the fire had not stopped, I should have got all the machinery out as well. Fanny, with the assistance of some friends, emptied the whole house so, if we had been burned out, we should have saved everything.

The fire, which destroyed an entire block, was 'a great fright to all of us', and Fitz was soon 'laid up with a bad cough which I can't shake off'. He was still in bed when he received a disturbing letter from Henry Selfe:

> You are not using me well and I must tell you so plainly. Another mail and not a line from you about our money matters. I have not deserved this at your hands and you know it. It is hard that you should force me to say it. I bitterly regret that, in the vain hope of being of service to you and yours, I even had any business relation with you. I must now request that those relations may be finally closed ... I have never received a line of account from you since you left [London] three and a half years ago. I don't think the fact of my

true and hearty affection for you is any reason why this should have been the case. If you feel, as I suppose you will, vexation at receiving this letter, I can only say that your vexation cannot exceed mine in having to write it.

Fitz had repaid £1000 of the debt from proceeds of the farm sale. The sum of £950 remained outstanding and, as Selfe pointed out, he was 'absolutely without security'.

Fitz's first reaction was to put the lease of the Press buildings up for sale (advertised as 'extensive premises in Cashel street, now occupied by the *Press* ... including a first-class dwelling-house ... The whole can be readily converted into a first-class hotel'), although he soon regretted this hasty decision and withdrew the property from the market.

He wrote to his friend ten days later. He had read his letter 'with great pain, not however so great as my surprise ... I will say that your addressing such a letter to me ... was an act not only unnecessary but for which I cannot consider there was any excuse.' He informed him – disingenuously – that he had never intended to send statements of account ('it is for you to say what I owe you. It is for me to pay it'). The money would, however, be raised at once ('I have been greatly pressed with work and have not been well, but if I have to throw all I am worth into the market, at a tithe of its value, it shall be done'). However:

> You know how I got into the *Press*. It was no premeditated design of mine. I drifted into it but ... it grew so rapidly under my hand, such a great business growing up, that I was compelled – say tempted – to order fresh plant, build fresh buildings and so on, merely to meet the work that homed in. And if I had stopped, it would ... be simply throwing away the chance of a fortune. Harman & Stevens have very literally aided me in meeting my engagements and know all my concerns to a farthing. I have been compelled to get advances, but the time is coming when I shall be free.

In September, he again reneged on his promise: 'My property is leasehold so I can't borrow on it ... I thought after much consideration you would not wish me to break up a magnificent business by a forced sale. Times are very bad here indeed.'

Godley had left him a legacy of £1000, payable after the death of his father. Godley senior had died the previous year, but there were legal complications and the legacy remained unpaid. So Fitz sent Selfe a power of attorney: 'I wish you to take the legacy ... the speediest way of discharging your debt.'

During the next few weeks, he was distracted by ill health (another 'sharp attack on the chest' which put him 'all behindhand'), as well as by financial worries. Not only did he owe money to Selfe, he was also falling increasingly in debt to Harman & Stevens. Harman could see what was happening ('if only FitzGerald would put on the drag[1] he would do well enough'), but Fitz still believed that the *Press* would be 'a noble estate one day', that he would be 'comfortably off' at last, that he would finally make his fortune.

In early November, he met with Stevens to complain that he was 'paying a very high rate' for his overdraft. If he had known his credit would cost so much, he told him, he would not have consented to engage in the business at all. This was rebutted by Stevens, who replied that had the firm been aware of the size of the loan required, 'we should have felt it necessary to steer clear of such a transaction'.

Fitz's overdraft now amounted to £4000 (£210,000 in today's values). Stevens was only too happy to convert this into a loan secured on the Cashel Street premises, together with its plant and goodwill. The terms of the loan were interest at the prevailing bank rate, plus 5 per cent commission. 'We may say,' wrote Harman when he confirmed the details on 14 November, 'that it is an arrangement which we should wish terminated as soon as your convenience would allow.'

…

The Whitaker–Fox government had resigned in October after 'bitter and unseemly quarrels' with the governor and a lengthy exchange of letters which, according to Fitz, was 'utterly – I am not afraid to use so strong an expression – utterly disgraceful to the colony'.

Although it had been agreed that the next parliament would meet in Wellington in March 1865, Grey called a short session in late 1864 to appoint a new ministry – to the fury of southern members, who had to travel to Auckland in the height of summer. 'I can't stand it,' wrote Fitz, 'and as soon as I come back, I shall resign and leave politics … Fanny I am sorry to say is about to present me with number 8 … I hope I shall be back from Auckland before her confinement … if I don't get my head broken by the mob which is on the cards.'

On 14 November, he wrote to Charles Adderley in London (a colleague in the Canterbury Association, now a member of parliament). Adderley passed his letter to *The Times*, which published it as written by 'a gentleman of great authority and influence in the colony'. In what the newspaper called 'highly-coloured statements', Fitz described the conduct of the New Zealand parliament during the previous three years. He reserved his greatest scorn for

---

1   Brake used on horse-drawn carriages

the governor: 'I, together with others, denounce Sir G. Grey as the sole cause of the renewal of the Native war, and as having pursued a course of conduct which has destroyed the last shred of trust and confidence which the hostile tribes entertained in our faith and honour.'

Fitz left for Auckland two days after writing this letter, embarking on the *Phoebe* ('a very good steamer'). It was a crowded voyage: the steamer brought members from Otago and 'picked up all the southern members on our way, from Wellington, Picton, Nelson and Taranaki'. After five days at sea ('a wonderfully fine passage'), the *Phoebe* arrived in Auckland on 21 November in the morning.

A few hours later, Grey called for Frederick Weld ('the man most likely to get the support of the Assembly'), and Weld spent the next day forming a government. Now it was his turn to ask Fitz to join a ministry ('Weld was very anxious for me to join the government'), but Fitz declined. His latest opinion was that he could 'do more good out of government' through the columns of his newspaper.

The Colonial Office in London had recently offered to relinquish control over native affairs, and Weld – who shared Fitz's political views – had accepted the offer. However, the governor, as commander-in-chief, would remain in charge of imperial troops in the colony. This division of authority – the course of the war determined by the governor; the purse strings controlled by parliament – together with the high cost of the troops and their poor performance in bush country, led Fitz and Weld to believe that parliament should assume full control of the war. Their policy, which became known as the 'self-reliant' policy, called for the removal of imperial troops and for the war to be concluded using local militia.

When parliament opened on 24 November, Fitz informed the House that Weld was 'a man of tried courage', that the colony was 'safe in his hands'. On 7 December, he made another significant speech, this time on military defences, in which he accused the Whitaker–Fox government of having 'sacrificed every principle of responsible government'; it had behaved 'disgracefully'; and its actions had caused 'irretrievable mischief'. The progress of the war had proved that 'it takes ten Englishmen to kill one Maori'. He referred to the imperial troops as 'mercenaries' and commented that their presence was 'making cowards of us all'. 'The real truth,' he concluded:

> is that at present there is an utter want of confidence between the
> two races. We do not believe what the Natives say, and they don't
> believe us ... We have our views of them; they have their views of us:

both probably wide of the mark … It seems as if all that is wanting
is someone … who could interpret the one race to the other.

Fitz was unpopular in Auckland, partly because of his attitude to the war,
partly because he had proposed the motion to move the seat of parliament
('we trust,' wrote the *New Zealand Herald*, 'that … our citizens will neither
pelt Mr FitzGerald with rotten eggs, nor fling him into the muddy "intake"'[1]).
And towards the end of the short, nineteen-day session, he found himself in
trouble with the military.

On 9 December, an advertisement was published in the morning paper,
the *Daily Southern Cross*: 'The soldiers, having heard of Mr FitzGerald having
called them cowards, are all over the town making inquiries what sort of a man
he is. It is to be hoped no one will point him out, but that the poor fellow
will get away quietly.' Fitz had planned to leave Auckland the following day
but, having read the paper, he sent a public letter to the commanding officer:

> conveying to you, and to the officers and men under your command,
> a distinct contradiction of the charge it contains: that I ever, directly
> or by implication, accused her Majesty's troops of cowardice. There
> is no pretence for such a statement. I had taken my passage in the
> *Airedale* tomorrow morning, but shall postpone my departure to
> afford the opportunity of offering any further explanation which
> may be desired, and to take the necessary steps for prosecuting the
> authors of the libel.

Parliament was prorogued four days later, after which 'members rushed
away to get ready their portmanteaus and pay their bills'. Fitz embarked on
the *Queen*, which left the quayside that afternoon. The following day, there
was 'a grand public demonstration in the shape of an open-air meeting … in
which Auckland … hissed and groaned Mr FitzGerald to its heart's content'.

…

Four weeks after he returned to Christchurch, Fanny gave birth for the eighth
time. While Alfred Barker attended her in the bedroom, Fitz wrote another
letter to Henry Selfe. They had partially made up their quarrel ('don't let this
business cause any coolness between us. I value your friendship too much
… one cannot afford to lose an old friend of twenty years'), and Fitz was in
complaining mode.

First, he grumbled about his newspaper ('to write up an article every day,
read up the current political events in the colony, and manage the business, and

---

1   The intake for Auckland's water supply

be called off to attend a session at Auckland, and make up arrears on returning, is a very hard life indeed'). Then he grumbled about Harman & Stevens:

> Harman & Stevens took my business when I was in difficulties, arising solely from the difficulty of finishing the Brown Cox affairs. They agreed to maintain my credits but upon conditions, the effect of which I did not perceive at the time, but which amounted to an interest of huge dimensions. I am overdrawn to them now about £4000. I have got them to modify their terms but, even now, I am paying them interest and commissions at the rate of 32% … £300 for the last quarter alone. And yet where to raise money to get rid of them? I do not know in these times.
>
> They know as well as I do that my business is a magnificent one … My whole expenditure last year was £800 with a large family in the most expensive town in the whole world … I have not a horse or a carriage. I dine with my children at one o'clock … No one can call me extravagant. If I could get rid of debt to men who, having got you in their hands, squeeze you like a lemon, I should be a rich man in five years. And I have laboured like a horse to achieve this position.

He broke off briefly at this point: 'Dr Barker has just called to me as I write to inform me that I am presented with another boy, number 8.' Next morning, he added a postscript: 'Fanny is well and the baby a boomah.'

PART V

Fitz goes to Wellington

CHAPTER TWENTY-FOUR

The Road to Hokitika

1865

Make the road, Johnny, my dear Johnny!
Make the road, Johnny, my little man!
Anywhere, anyhow, over the mountains;
Do it as quickly, my boy, as you can.

Punch in Canterbury, *1865*

*I*n the New Year of 1865, Canterbury was experiencing a depression, a downturn that began a few months earlier and would soon turn into a slump. Advertising revenue was in decline, but despite complaining that times were bad, Fitz enlarged the *Press* to six pages. 'I put it in larger type to save expense,' he wrote. 'Well, of course, it costs more and my advertisements fell off in the very week I started it.'

For at least a month after the birth, Fanny remained 'very weak after her confinement and in need of care'. Fitz, too, was in need of care, having suffered a 'very severe accident' on 19 January. He was returning from the races in Riccarton, travelling in the Christchurch Club dray. The driver had been drinking, the horses ('going at too free a pace') swerved into a fence and the dray capsized. Fitz dislocated his shoulder, cut his elbow and bruised his face. He was, he told Henry Selfe, 'terribly shaken'.

During the next few weeks, while Fanny recovered from childbirth and Fitz recovered from the accident, Christchurch became a gold town.

...

The yellow metal had been discovered in Canterbury, on the west coast of the province, on the far side of the Southern Alps.[1] Large numbers of gold diggers were making their way overland from Christchurch, travelling on almost

---

1   The West Coast was still part of the province of Canterbury; it became the County of Westland in 1868 and formed a new province (Westland) in 1873

impassable tracks across the mountains, or landing from ships at the mouth of the Hokitika River. On 20 January, the *Press* reported that 'the exodus to the west coast is already assuming determined appearance'. And by 15 March, as Fitz told Selfe, 'Canterbury is now a gold country and no mistake.'

The provincial government required large amounts of printed matter and Fitz, instead of opting out of his contract, felt 'compelled to build a fresh engine and machine room and get fresh machinery'. During the first week in March, he printed 50,000 forms in three days, 'a great achievement for this small office' – although the new machinery was proving difficult to handle:

> One cannot get men who understand machinery and I actually had to go to work at the machine myself, and study its movements, when they could not get the fine adjustments right. However, I got it right at last. Now it is all driven by an engine of six horsepower and I have all the costly machinery in a fire-proof building so that I am less nervous about being burned out as I could remove the type in a fire but never the machines.

He was 'paying shamefully' for his overdraft with Harman & Stevens; but despite the economic depression, despite the high cost of his loan, he saw only a rosy future. Dunedin had grown rich on the Otago goldfields – during the previous four years, gold to the value of £7 million had passed through the town – and he prophesied a similar future for Christchurch:

> If the diggings go on as all the old miners expect, the *Press* will be an enormous affair by this time next year and it would be insanity in me to let the leading business slip out of my hands … If I have got on as I have in this famine, I can hardly fail to do well in the coming time. But at the moment to lay my hands on £1000 would be very hard indeed.

He believed that a direct link with the goldfields would lead inexorably to a 'great burst of trade'. There were no harbours on the west coast, only rivers with hazardous bars, so if the gold was carried over the Southern Alps (instead of going by sea to Australia or Nelson), it would all flow into Christchurch. At a public meeting on 2 March, the provincial council was urged to build a dray road over the mountains. The economy would receive a much needed boost if the bullion was brought into Christchurch under escort, if diggers passed through the town on their way to and from the west coast, and if the goldfields were supplied with goods and provisions by road. The problem was to find the easiest route over the mountains.

The diggers were using a rough and dangerous path over the Hurunui Saddle in North Canterbury, but this was hardly practicable for horses, let alone for wheeled traffic. A better route up the Waimakariri and Bealey valleys had been discovered by Arthur Dobson (son of Edward Dobson, the provincial engineer) in 1864, although this was extremely steep on the western side.

John Hall, now in charge of public works in the province, wrote to Edward Dobson on 14 March, instructing him to provide, 'as speedily as possible, the report of an engineer upon the practicability and cost' of building a road over the Southern Alps. Dobson left Christchurch the following day and spent six weeks in the mountains, investigating Arthur's Pass, as well as other potential routes to the west coast.

On 29 March, fired by the need to kickstart the economy, attract more advertising and sell more newspapers, Fitz wrote to the superintendent, Samuel Bealey: 'It is clear that the right pass has not been found. If the government would assist with expenses, I am prepared to start with a party. We shall be six in all and we shall explore the head branch of the Waimakariri, the old Maori pass to the Arahura.'

The provincial government offered £100 and, on 31 March, Fitz confirmed that he would take two of 'Cobb's coaches' to 'the farthest point possible' on the Waimakariri and survey the passes at the head of the river. He added a postscript: 'We start at nine o'clock tomorrow morning. As the expenses will considerably exceed the grant, we take no servants.'

Fitz's expedition – nicknamed the 'picnic party' – set off on 1 April. The leader writer of the *Lyttelton Times* had his tongue in his cheek as he wished them well:

> We do not attach much importance to amateur exploration in a case of this kind; but there are with this party some gentlemen professionally as well as naturally adapted to the work. Even if the main part of the expedition go no further than Cobb's light coaches will carry them, the supplies they take will be a most valuable aid to the hill parties now at work. Therefore we wish and hope for a successful result to their labours, although they do start on the First of April.

Cobb & Co's American-style coaches had been introduced to Canterbury the previous year. They were 'a kind of roofed van, open at the sides and suspended front and back on thick leather bands which allow it to swing freely in every direction'. The coaches could 'bend and twist about, ford rivers, and go over the roughest ground'. They had a 'swinging, rocking motion ... creaking and rolling like a ship at sea', and even on level stretches, 'the shaking and the bumping were something to be remembered'. As well as suffering from motion sickness, passengers finished their journeys with bruises and aching joints.

The first night of Fitz's expedition was spent in 'White's accommodation house' on the banks of the Waimakariri River; the second night at a station near the base of the foothills. Next morning, the coaches were pulled up Porters Pass and onto a high plateau of rolling tussock grassland. The third night was spent at the Craigieburn Station. On the morning of 4 April, the coaches travelled 'over a very good road' to Cora Lynn, a sheep run on the Cass River, the most isolated and distant of Canterbury's pastoral stations.

No wheeled traffic had travelled further than Cora Lynn but Fitz pressed on, the men walking, the coaches 'labouring over the boulders' along the river bed of the Upper Waimakariri, 'the roughest travelling which has ever been performed by coach'. After crossing the Bealey River in the late afternoon, the party stopped for the night. It was an uncomfortable spot, densely covered with spiny speargrass:

> Darkness was on the earth before arrangements for the night were
> well commenced; and as if the spear-grass was not a sufficient
> aggravation of the natural horrors of the wilderness, it was found
> necessary to pitch the camp on one side of a creek, and to leave the
> coaches on the other side. The coaches being larder, store-room, and
> everything, a great many wet-footed trips across the creek were the
> consequence of the arrangement.

It rained during the evening, and the men lifted their spirits by drinking hot whisky toddy. Next morning 'broke misty and thick' and much colder. At nine o'clock, the coaches set out again, labouring over larger boulders as they approached the headwaters. By mid-afternoon they had reached a point beyond the Crow River junction, 'where the increasing roughness of the river bed and the presence of an admirable camping ground with good feed for the horses counselled the formation of a permanent camp'.

Earlier in the day, the party had encountered three men who were working with Edward Dobson. Fitz left a note with them, explaining that his party would 'examine the headwaters of the Waimakariri' in the hope of finding a pass between the Waimakariri and the Arahura, a river that flows into the sea five miles north of Hokitika.

He was too late. Not only had Dobson explored the area ('I had previously examined the western sources of the Waimakariri and taken a set of levels which showed the impracticality of getting a road in that direction'), he had also decided on Arthur's Pass for the road over the mountains. As he wrote to John Hall on 5 April (a few hours before Fitz arrived at his campsite), 'the most practicable pass from the Waimakariri to the Taramakau is that by the Bealey and Otira gorges. I am now setting out the line of the road.'

On the afternoon of 6 April, the 'picnic party' walked four miles upriver to the junction with the White River, at which point Fitz returned to camp while his companions set out to explore the headwaters on foot. And for the next three days (according to the *Lyttelton Times*), he had 'nothing to do but sketch and shoot ducks and return to camp for dinner'.

One of the explorers was injured on 8 April. He dislodged a rock while climbing a steep slope, 'letting down a whole stream of boulders from the mountainside above him'. When the camp was alerted next morning, Fitz walked upriver to join the rescue party and helped to carry the injured man back to the campsite during an afternoon of heavy rain.

This was the end of the expedition. The coaches set out for Christchurch on 10 April, the injured man lying in a hammock. The first night of the journey was spent at Cora Lynn (where the weather was 'very threatening'); the next at Craigieburn (where the weather turned 'frightfully violent'). The coaches descended Porters Pass on the 12th and, after another night in White's accommodation house, the weary travellers arrived in Christchurch the following evening.

Fitz was happy to be home with his wife and children and a comfortable bed. The following day, he wrote a report on his findings which was published in the *Press* on 15 April. He had failed to find a pass to the Arahura, but he paid tribute to Cobb & Co's coaches:

> The last few miles of the river bed, especially the last ford of the river where the boulders were the size of parlour chairs, would have seemed impassable had we not seen these capital horses and light American wagons take them without shirking and without accident … The journey was accomplished without the slightest injury to the wagons.

And he wrote to Henry Selfe:

> For an old codger like me who cannot bathe in cold water because it gives me the rheumatism, a fortnight's excursion into the middle of the mountains and the neighbourhood of the glaciers, which I saw for the first time, was very energetic. Fancy my wading all day long up to the middle in glacial waters without catching cold or rheumatism!

...

Four days after Fitz returned from the mountains, Fanny performed in a concert in the town hall, singing a duet by Donizetti and a solo, 'The Maid of Judah', which she sang 'perfectly, giving the most perfect expression both to the words and the music'.

On 28 April, the General Synod opened in Christchurch, attended by five bishops and a large number of clergy. On 13 May, Fitz and Fanny entertained the bishops in Cashel Street. 'It was like a select London dinner,' Fitz told Selfe, 'every man distinguished in some way. I can't tell you how we enjoyed it.' And during the evening, he asked Bishop Selwyn to baptise his four-month-old son.

Three days later, he made a speech in synod ('moving a resolution about the unity of the church'), after which Selwyn baptised the baby in St Michael's church. The boy was named Selwyn in honour of the bishop but, as Fitz told Selfe, 'the children all call him "The Primate". He goes by no other name.'

On the 18th, Fitz gave a lecture to 'the working men' of Christchurch on wage levels, economic theory and free trade. Six days later, he and Fanny watched Rose Bealey turn the first sod of the southern railway, which would soon pass close to the Springs station. After the ceremony, Fitz spoke on behalf of the general parliament, referring to its 'occasional eccentricities'. He also mentioned his opposition to the railway: 'I would have had far less pleasure in replying to this toast at any time during the last two or three years because I felt you were pursuing a policy detrimental to the interests of this Province.' Now that gold had been discovered on the west coast, he had changed his mind. Canterbury, he said, should 'take advantage to the utmost of its resources and credit for the future'.

The provincial council had now commissioned the longed-for road over the mountains. Dobson took charge of the work and the road from Christchurch to Hokitika, 156 miles long and wide enough for four-horse coaches, was completed in as little as fifteen months. But even this was too slow for Fitz. Less than two months after the work began, he was bullying the council for being 'most stupidly slow in getting the road through'. He wrote an article in the *Press*, anticipating the arrival of the first gold transport from Hokitika:

> Many of our readers must have observed careering along the streets
> the team of splendid greys that is to draw the treasure cart on
> its triumphal entry, and in the prospect of the magnificent scene
> when, decorated with flags and surrounded by its victorious guard,
> the wagon shall roll along with its precious freight, the centre of a
> jubilant procession.

His mood reached another high while the road was under construction, while he waited for the 'great burst of trade' that would result from the gold transport. 'It is quite on the cards that Christchurch will be another Dunedin or even Melbourne,' he crowed to Henry Selfe. 'And if I can get £20,000 for my paper, I shall sell out.'

At the same time, he was involving himself in engineering matters – on which he considered himself an authority. In July, he wrote a memorandum about the shape of steamships, which, he explained, had been designed to look like sailing ships 'but are *different*'. He used diagrams to prove his point and suggested that models be made to test his theory, which should enable steamships to move faster through the water. He would, he wrote, 'be glad to work with some few others in undertaking these experiments'.

Railways, too, attracted his attention. 'I have lost all faith in him,' he wrote of George Stephenson, who was advising on the construction of the tunnel. 'He is not at all esteemed as an engineer and, but for his name and family connections, would be nobody ... The tunnel here is as badly laid out as it could possibly be ... and the placing of it on an incline was one of the stupidest blunders ever made.'

Spoil from the tunnel was being used to reclaim the foreshore in Lyttelton, providing solid ground for building railway yards and warehouses. The Harbour Commission recommended that the spoil should also be used to construct two breakwaters. Fitz, who had a plan of his own to improve the harbour, considered this idea 'most useless ... They said my plan was bad because it did not give room enough, when it gave *more dock room* than the whole of London docks put together.'

With comments like these, it is hardly surprising that people had a jaundiced view of his opinions. 'FitzGerald considers himself a man of genius,' wrote one perceptive journalist. 'His main article of faith is that nothing can possibly succeed in which he does not take a leading part; whilst the fact is that nothing does succeed which is left mainly to his guidance.'

...

Fitz had spent the last few months wondering whether he had been right to turn down a ministerial role in the 1864 parliament. 'At one time I was on the point of doing it,' he mused in February, 'but the temptation is passed away for the present.' Three months later, he decided to stay out of government. 'I have been asked to join every ministry which has been formed since New Zealand was a colony,' he wrote to Selfe on 15 May:

but I never will unless I am forced. I am far more influential out of a ministry than in it. I am living now, daily seeing the work of the last few years coming home. The natives are beginning to trust me and I have been deeply gratified by what the Bishop of Waiapu and others from the north have told me, that the natives all look to Whititera … I look to the coming session of the Assembly to make some great step in Maori policy.

On 15 June he wrote again to Selfe, returning to the subject of money. Godley's estate was now in the Court of Chancery, so payment of his legacy was further delayed: 'If you will accept the power of attorney to receive the £1000 under the legacy and the interest at 10% in the meantime, you will do me a great favour and I am sure will not lose yourself.'

'We have very bad times here now,' he continued, 'worse than I have ever known, but I have scraped through and the tide must turn as it always does in these colonies. We shall have a great burst of prosperity next year when we shall make up for lost time … The road to the goldfields is progressing and we shall reap the benefit next summer.'

The *Lyttelton Times*, a broadsheet, had recently announced that it would follow Fitz's example and become a daily paper. As a result, Fitz had determined to 'enlarge my paper to the same size':

> It required but little extra plant to do so. And I did it … I now for the first time stand on nearly the same footing as the *Times* and if, with so many disadvantages and the competition of so beastly a journal, I have managed to work the *Press* up to its present position, I have little doubt that I shall now steal ahead of them with considerable rapidity.

All this had cost money, 'such large demands for fresh plant and buildings, to maintain the position of the paper, that all the earnings have been eaten up'. He had done nothing to reduce his overdraft, which continued to increase, but he remained optimistic: 'I have not the faintest doubt as to success … you will see a great alteration in my affairs next year.'

CHAPTER TWENTY-FIVE

An Ordinary Rooster

1865–1866

I hope I may be allowed the chance of showing whether I am only a theorist
and article writer.
Fitz, 11 September 1865

He knows that digging is done by spades although it is his fancy to call
them reaping hooks.
James Richmond, 18 August 1865

*O*n 22 July, Fitz left Christchurch for the 1865 parliament, which was
due to open four days later. Wellington had been chosen as the new
seat of government and builders had been at work in the provincial council
chamber, adapting it for use by the House of Representatives. Fitz was
anticipating great things as he made preparations for departure:

> I believe good times are coming ... The old war party has broken
> up ... My party now stands in great power [and] I look on Weld as
> having joined my party. We have it all our own way and the next
> session will see such legislation as my heart delights in ... In my
> opinion, next session will be the turning point in the history of New
> Zealand.

With Frederick Weld as premier, the self-reliant policy would finally be
put into action. As Fitz wrote to Gladstone in February:

> For three years I have preached that most unpopular doctrine in
> colonies, that we must defend ourselves. The tide is at last turning
> and views which were not listened to formerly are now accepted.
> You will be asked to remove the troops by our Ministry.

His morale had been boosted by Gladstone's reply, which he received at
the end of June:

I know no person with whose ideas of Colonial policy ... I have more cordially concurred with than yours. If this has been the case before, I certainly have no cause to alter now ... It is, so far as my memory serves, the first occasion on which the true doctrine, in pure and undiluted condition, has come to us from across the water.

Fitz arrived in Wellington on 23 July to learn that the minister for native affairs had resigned. Weld hoped to appoint Fitz in his place but he declined, clinging to the belief that he was 'more influential out of a ministry than in it'. But Weld was persistent; he persevered for almost three weeks until Fitz changed his mind ('in the present critical state of affairs, I felt that I ought not to refuse').

To everyone's surprise, the governor accepted his appointment with good grace. 'Widely as I have differed from Sir George Grey,' Fitz explained to Gladstone, 'and sincerely as I have criticised his conduct, His Excellency has received me as a minister with great kindness.'

Henry Sewell (attorney-general in the Weld government) was delighted. 'FitzGerald has joined the government,' he wrote on 13 August. 'This was arranged yesterday (Saturday) and I expect a great disturbance in the House on Tuesday in consequence thereof. He is a great strength and help to us in many ways but especially at this moment. He has a prestige with the natives which it is our duty to turn to good account.'

James Richmond, another member of the ministry – who had fallen out with Fitz since admiring him so much in 1862 – had mixed feelings. In agreeing to the appointment, he wrote, 'I eat a little dirt. Great as his abilities are, his rash judgement has been yet more prominent for the last four years and has done us no little harm ... I hope he will lose something of his overbearing manner towards those who differ from him.'

The press also made its opinions known. According to the *Wellington Independent*, the appointment was 'an experiment, the result of which we will watch with some anxiety ... we think the experiment ... is a very bold one under any circumstances'. The *Lyttelton Times* was equally surprised. 'It is as if a notorious poacher had been induced to turn gamekeeper,' it explained, before commenting that Fitz was 'popularly conceived to be wildly theoretical, and no more to be restrained by common sense than a squib in a drawing-room'.

Fanny, too, was amazed. 'Last week, he swore by all his gods he would not [accept office],' wrote Charles Bowen on 14 August. 'Poor Mrs FG is terribly alarmed as he has left the *Press* to take care of itself and does not even mention it in his letter.'

Fitz set to work with his usual energy, believing that he was the only man with the ability (as he put it in November) 'to interpret the one race to the other'. During his first six days as minister, with the help of William Rolleston, under-secretary in the native department, he drafted three bills to present to the House.

His first ministerial speech was delivered on 18 August to a full House and a crowded public gallery. He spoke for an hour, outlining his policy and presenting his bills, and was more circumspect than usual. He ended by reminding the House that 'it is not the duty of a minister to be a political partisan alone'. While in opposition, he 'may have expressed strong opinions', but he was 'mindful of the heavy responsibility' which had fallen on him since taking office. 'If I am permitted to remain a member of this ministry,' he concluded, 'I do confidently hope that in spite of all the difficulties by which we are surrounded, we shall be able to bring this country out of its present disastrous conditions.'

Fitz as minister for native affairs, 1865. 'I believe good times are coming ... We have it all our own way and the next session will see such legislation as my heart delights in.'
Private collection

The speech took the House 'by storm' and Fitz sat down 'amidst loud and prolonged cheering'. As the *Lyttelton Times* was forced to admit, he had risen to the occasion: 'No flights of oratory, no impossible theories disguised by a cloud of words, but – believe it who may – an approach to the intensely real and practical. Office has certainly sealed his lips, and transformed the would be bird of Jove into an ordinary rooster.'

Richmond was more cautious. 'There is a very natural and healthy mistrust of FitzGerald,' he wrote a few hours after Fitz had given his speech:

His talk and writing has had an excessive unreality about it and I think clever, well-informed and brilliant debater as he is that he very often loses the plain thread of reason in his views … I think he calls things by the wrong names … he knows that digging is done by spades although it is his fancy to call them reaping hooks.

During the next seven weeks, Fitz ordered the publication of a Maori newspaper and proceeded with his legislation. The Native Rights Act ('the best thing we did') was passed on 26 September; this gave Maori full status as citizens of the colony, natural-born subjects of the crown with the same rights and privileges as other British subjects, 'entitled to all the privileges and protection of British law'.

The Native Commission Act was introduced to help Maori achieve the right of political representation, the birthright of natural-born citizens. Voting rights were based on property, so the Native Lands Act established a land court to convert communal Maori tenure into franchise-friendly ownership. In the meantime, Fitz authorised a commission to investigate 'the most expedient mode of defining an electoral franchise to be conferred temporarily'.

'I have sacrificed a great deal to take office,' he wrote on 11 September, 'but having done so, I confess I hope I may be allowed the chance of showing whether I am only a theorist and article writer.' On the 13th, he wrote to Gladstone, enclosing a copy of his first ministerial speech. The following day – with an eye on a long ministerial career – he changed gear again, deciding to move his family to Wellington.

'The paper will be relieved of my going,' he explained to Henry Selfe, 'as I shall bring my family up here and let the home in Cashel Street for offices. This will really earn the business cash and help to clear the concern. There will be a great burst of trade in Canterbury this summer and the *Press* will be left a fine property.'

Before leaving Christchurch, he had suggested that Fanny should spend a month with him in Wellington, 'for a change of air in the course of the session'. When she arrived, it was not for 'a change of air' but to find a house in the city, grand enough for a minister to entertain his colleagues, large enough to accommodate his growing family, and cheap enough for Fitz's financial situation – an impossible task, as even Fitz had to concede.

…

His ministerial career had started well but, to his colleagues' dismay, he soon began to return to his old ways. 'I like FitzGerald exceedingly,' wrote the chief adviser on native affairs, 'but I was amazed at his self-confidence and harshness.'

On 29 August, when asked to speak against time in a thinly attended House, he let his restraint slip, referring to Auckland and Dunedin as cities 'of mushroom growth, their commerce a bubble, their population a retinue of camp followers and gold diggers'.

Next day, the House was in an uproar, with members from Auckland and Otago 'vowing vengeance'. According to the correspondent of the *Lyttelton Times*, 'the members of the Government hung their heads, and declined to adopt or justify, by a single word, the obnoxious expressions of their colleague'. Nine days later, Edward Stafford, as leader of the opposition, appealed to Weld 'to guide and moderate' the behaviour of his minister, to prevent Fitz using 'language calculated to irritate'.

The Weld ministry was in 'troubled waters'. There were financial problems (treasury accounts in confusion, a high and rising national debt), the government was close to bankruptcy, and Sir George Grey was being obstructive about troop withdrawals. 'We sit up night after night,' wrote Sewell on 24 September, 'till one or two o'clock, fierce fighting about everything, in the midst of which business and government move on slowly.'

Frederick Weld was close to a nervous breakdown; by early October he was suffering such bad headaches that he was 'unable to do any work'. Matters came to a head on the 10th, when ministers called a meeting of their supporters to explain that 'certain things were necessary to maintain the credit of the colony, and if these were not given, we could not undertake to carry on the government'.

These 'certain things' included a bill to increase stamp duties. Taxation was an essential element of the self-reliant policy. Funds were required to cover the costs of the militia and native auxiliaries, which would replace the imperial troops and bring the war to an end. Although this policy had been agreed during the 1864 parliament, ministers had not spelt out the financial implications ('we are silent about that for the present'). It was, as Sewell put it, 'one of our cardinal points – indispensable for enabling us to meet our increased expenditure. To fail in it would be fatal to our policy.'

The meeting on 10 October was, according to Sewell, 'fully attended showing an absolute majority but there were indications of but faint-hearted support – this man quarrelled with us on this point, and another on that. Altogether it was clear that we could not rely on very earnest support for our financial policy. The truth is men don't like taxation.'

When the bill to increase stamp duties came before the House the following evening, a member from Otago, Julius Vogel, proposed a hostile amendment 'which if carried would have the effect of deranging our whole plan … It was clearly a case of battle.' A division was called; the votes were tied. The Speaker cast his vote for the government but, as Sewell explained, this was still 'a defeat ... indicating that it was hopeless for us to carry our measures through'.

Weld was absent from the House ('he remains very ill'), so Fitz 'went away to confer with him'. On hearing the news, Weld decided to resign. He and Fitz drove to Government House, where Sir George Grey 'begged us to take time to reconsider'. So the ministers returned to the House, 'we moved the adjournment and separated to take counsel with our pillows'.

Early next morning, they gathered in Weld's house. He was still determined to resign, on the grounds that the House would not give him 'that full and cordial support (in imposing additional taxes) which was necessary to carry out our policy of self-reliance'. A few hours later, he 'went to the Governor with our resignations' and recommended that Grey should send for Stafford.

On 13 October, Weld raised the strength to make a short statement in the House, after which parliament was adjourned to give Stafford time to form a ministry. The next few days were filled with 'gossip, rumour and speculation as to what Stafford would or could, or wouldn't or couldn't do'. Fitz was 'laid up with gout' and spent the time writing letters.

'We have done our duty trying to persuade the country to undertake its duties,' he wrote to Henry Selfe on the 15th, 'and must wait the result ... As to the native question, I frankly say I am very sorry to have lost the opportunity so soon of carrying out my measures ... I am glad however we were defeated on *finance* not on native policy.'

The House reconvened at midday on the 17th. 'It was curious,' wrote the *Lyttelton Times*, 'to watch the faces of the ex-ministers as, with portentous solemnity, they seated themselves on the front row of what are known as the opposition benches ... they appeared scarcely able to realise the fact that they are out of office.'

Stafford told the House that he did not intend to form a ministry until after the general election a few months later. He cancelled the commission to confer a temporary franchise on the Maori population, and although (as Fitz put it) 'he did not propose to alter the self-reliant policy, he chose for his defence minister a man who had never concealed his contempt for the whole idea'.

Sewell added a bitter note to his diary: 'The whole affair is a burlesque and would not make a bad comedy if the interests involved were not so serious ... We are politically dead. Weld and his friends are bitter and indignant ... FitzGerald gives up in disgust.'

...

Fitz left Wellington on 20 October before the end of the session, and arrived in Christchurch two days later. On 2 November, he addressed a meeting in the Christchurch town hall to explain recent events in parliament. He should have called this meeting in his constituency in Ellesmere, but he preferred to appear on a wider stage. The hall was 'crowded with one of the largest and most enthusiastic assemblages we have ever have seen'; he rose to his feet to the sound of 'loud and prolonged cheering'. He spoke for more than two hours:

> The question which will be put by every one of you this evening ... is why did Mr Weld's ministry resign? That is the question I have had over and over again put to me in the streets of Christchurch since I returned from Wellington, and it is principally to answer that question that I am here tonight to meet you ... We did not resign in a mere pet. It was a matter of long deliberation and consultation ... The actual question on which we resigned was a matter of no special importance. It was not because of one division ... not [because] the opposition beat us ... but because our own supporters, in the face of a general election, would not come up and vote for those additional sources of revenue which we believed to be necessary for conducting the affairs of the colony.

He continued with an attack on Stafford – whose provisional government was 'utterly deplorable, a violation of the constitutional rights of the country' – and concluded with a résumé of his career:

> I have been for a long time in the public service of New Zealand. I have taken a large part in affairs here and at home ... I gave the best part of a life to the foundation of Canterbury [loud cheers] ... I have been once at the head of the general government ... But there is no period of my life to which I shall look back with such satisfaction as those two months during which I was able to give some little assistance to carrying out the policy of my respected and highly-valued friend, Mr Weld.

Fitz resumed his seat 'amidst loud and long-continued applause'. As he wrote to William Rolleston on 10 November, 'We are having such public meetings here. Fancy my being a popular character once more! I think I like the other thing better.'

The following day, he sprained his knee ('a displacement of the cartilage') and was confined to bed for several days, brooding on his financial position. 'My paper was never doing so badly as now,' he told Selfe. 'The state of trade is so dull at present that it does not pay to advertise at all. Of course this cannot last but in the meantime it is very serious.' The road over the mountains was still unfinished but he remained 'perfectly confident that, when the burst of trade comes … I shall come out with a good property'.

During the next few months, he continued to attack Stafford in letters and in the columns of his newspaper. He described him as 'a man of no real ability at all. A perfect humbug who has lived on the brains of others all his political life … dishonourable in the last degree in private life, scandalously dishonest as a public man.' And Stafford's ministry was 'selfish, vulgar and unscrupulous beyond all expression, the feeblest ministry which has ever guided the destinies of any country'.

At the general election on 12 February 1866, Fitz was returned unopposed as member for the larger constituency of Christchurch. Provincial elections were due to be held in May and he now began a long and hard-fought campaign to oppose the re-election of Moorhouse as superintendent. He was not prepared to stand himself ('I should have to make such a fight of it as I am not inclined to do; it would be utterly disgusting'). Instead, he acted as agent for James Lance, a wealthy army officer. He raised money for the campaign and, by April, was 'working the elections with a method and an energy that the other side does not even understand'.

In mid-May he held a public meeting that was so disrupted by Moorhouse supporters that Lance had to flee out the back door. Fitz fled too, to the delight of the *Lyttelton Times*:

> To think of Mr FitzGerald – that big man, with the big words, and
> the big voice, and the big stick, descendant of a hundred fighting
> forefathers, and the greatest orator in New Zealand – being scared
> from the platform of a public meeting! Advising a retirement
> for strategic reasons, sloping, absconding, vamoosing, hooking it,
> skedaddling, running away!

Fitz's pride had taken a beating (Moorhouse, he complained, was 'just the man for a mob'). He was further discomfited on 30 May when Moorhouse was re-elected with a resounding majority.

CHAPTER TWENTY-SIX

A Painful Parting

1866–1867

It is a sad thing to lose FitzGerald in politics, but for the sake of his family
we cannot but rejoice.

Charles Bowen, 4 February 1867

What have I to be disappointed with? No public man in the colony can
look back to a career which yielded greater satisfaction.

Fitz, 4 April 1867

On 28 June, Fitz embarked on the steamer for the 1866 parliament
in Wellington. He had spent the previous eight months hankering
after a role in government, his ministerial experience having renewed his
enthusiasm for political power. 'I think it possible I shall be in the general
government again,' he had written in November. 'I do not think the country
will stand Stafford.' He was more forthright on 25 December (after a convivial
Christmas dinner):

> If he is not driven out of the government the first week of the
> session, I shall retire from politics. If the people generally have no
> sense of constitutional rights and will stand such conduct as his, they
> are really not worth fighting for. And I shall spend the few remain-
> ing years I live in making money.

But Stafford was made of sterner stuff. After the opening ceremony on 3
July, he plunged the House into work, introducing seventeen bills in ten days,
as well as 'a mass of papers on finance, statistics, and information of every
conceivable kind'.

The 'Weldite' opposition argued in vain about who should lead them. Weld
had not stood for re-election; Sewell had returned to England; and although
Fitz wanted to lead the opposition, 'a good many people think he has not
sufficient tact to head a party'.

Four weeks into the session, Fitz held a meeting ('a council of war with champagne') with members of the opposition, one of whom, Arthur Atkinson, was new to parliament. 'FitzGerald is bloodthirsty,' Atkinson wrote in his diary that night, 'and proposes to tear Stafford limb from limb by a vote of no confidence.'

On 8 August, the Stafford ministry announced a reduction in the share of general government revenue given to the provinces. This had 'a startling effect upon the House' and members adjourned to Bellamy's 'where a tremendous hubbub ensued'. It was soon agreed that 'the assault on Stafford' should take place on 14 August. Fitz was asked to propose the motion of no confidence, raising his hopes that, if Stafford fell, he might form a government of his own.

On the afternoon of the 14th, he rose to his feet in the House and spoke for almost two hours. 'Mr FitzGerald made a good speech,' wrote the correspondent of the *Lyttelton Times*:

> but not one of his best. Where he dealt with pure politics, with the
> character of the Premier and his colleagues, or with the history of
> past sessions, he was strong, because he was at home. But his subject
> led him into figures ... His friends remarked that he did not make
> the best of his case; his opponents said that he was entirely mistaken
> from beginning to end.

With little time to prepare for a speech that involved financial details, and forced to speak extempore without reference to written notes, Fitz made heavy weather of the statistics. In reply (according to Atkinson), Stafford 'made an ass of himself by losing his temper and speaking of FitzGerald with vulgar abuse'. The House was in an uproar by the time Stafford finished speaking, and was adjourned 'to give members time to think matters over'.

Fitz was furious at what he referred to as Stafford's 'utterly injudicious speech', complaining – another instance of the pot calling the kettle black – that the premier had been 'personally rude', as well as *silly* to an insane extent'.

On the afternoon of the 15th, 'a more simple amendment' was moved, 'that the ministry as at present constituted does not possess the confidence of the House'. This was a motion of no confidence in Stafford's ministers (as opposed to Fitz's motion against Stafford personally) and, when it came to the voting, Fitz's motion was lost 'on the voices'. The amendment went to a division and was carried by 47 votes to 14.

Stafford resigned on the 16th, after which the House was adjourned for five days. The following morning, angry that his motion had been defeated and 'feeling that he had been made a tool of by his friends', Fitz gave up again 'in disgust'. He packed his bags and embarked on the steamer for Lyttelton.

He was in Christchurch when parliament reassembled on 24 August and Stafford informed the House that he had formed a new ministry – and sitting on the ministerial benches were several members of the former opposition. Stafford remained in power and Fitz's colleagues had, as he put it, 'consented to forgo their feud with Mr Stafford and sit down in loving companionship with the man they had so eagerly and so wrathfully denounced'.

Four days later, Fitz sent an official request for leave of absence for the remainder of the session. But on 6 September, after news arrived in Christchurch of a bill to impose stamp duties, he re-embarked for Wellington. As a newspaper correspondent put it:

> Mr FitzGerald, who had retired in a sulk … re-appeared upon the stage prepared to vote with the opposition against the imposition of stamp duties, notwithstanding he had been a member of Mr Weld's ministry which proposed this identical system of taxation last year … It would have made a fine picture to portray the expression of sovereign contempt with which he surveyed the new ministers, all his old colleagues, reposing contentedly on Mr Stafford's bosom, whilst he alone was cast out.

Fitz attended the House for the next two weeks, but spoke 'in a style much less animated than usual'. On the evening of 24 September, he again abandoned parliament, 'withdrawing', as the *Lyttelton Times* put it, 'in a fit of irritation'. Thirteen days later, Fanny gave birth to their ninth child, a daughter named Katherine.

…

Fitz had been under a great deal of stress during these last few weeks. His hopes of leading the government had been thwarted; he was 'extremely disappointed' that his political allies had joined a Stafford ministry; he was concerned about Fanny's imminent confinement; and he was in trouble with Harman & Stevens.

His debt had now increased to £8836, an enormous sum worth almost half a million in today's money. Less than a quarter of the debt was secured and, according to Harman in a letter written on 21 August (three days after Fitz returned to Christchurch after the fall of the Stafford ministry), the firm was suffering 'great inconvenience and anxiety'. The letter ended with the words: 'we cannot afford to continue, as at present, seeing nothing at all from the *Press*.'

In a reply written on 28 August, Fitz complained about the high rates of interest and commission charged by the firm and suggested that 'the present agreement be terminated'. Harman agreed, writing on 7 September that the firm would no longer carry out the business of the *Press*. A new agreement would be made under which the firm would become a preference creditor.

Three weeks later, Harman & Stevens formally terminated the contract. 'I wish I could believe that we shall either of us come well out of it,' Harman wrote on 29 September:

> I will not, however, conceal from you the fact that I feel *great* anxiety about our position in reference to you, and that however much we may feel inclined to give time and meet your convenience generally, we are not quite our own masters in the almost absolute impossibility which exists at present of getting our money.

A warrant of attorney, giving full security for the unsecured portion of the debt, was drawn up in October. Fitz also agreed to make repayments every quarter; Harman informed him that £250 (more than £11,000 today) was the minimum sum the firm would accept for the first payment due in January 1867.

Fitz had enlarged his newspaper, in both size and number of pages, in anticipation of 'the great burst of trade' that would result from the road to Hokitika. Each change of format required additional plant and machinery, the cost of which had eaten into the profits and further increased his debt. The road was completed in July 1866 but it was not until 5 December that the gold transport set out on its first journey over the mountains. The scarlet bulletproof wagon, drawn by a team of four grey horses with an escort of six armed outriders, made a splendid sight as the cortège assembled for departure outside the provincial government buildings.

All Fitz's hopes were pinned on the transport, but when the wagon left Hokitika on the return journey, it took with it (according to the *West Coast Times*) 'the following quantity of gold: 000,000 ounces'. A telegraph service linking Christchurch and Hokitika had opened earlier in the year; and on 14 December, the escort sent a telegram from a staging post in the mountains: 'GOLD ESCORT ARRIVED HERE AT TEN THIRTY THIS MORNING FROM WEST COAST WITHOUT ANY GOLD AND LEFT FOR CHRISTCHURCH AT ONE TWENTY-FOUR.'

Despite the lack of a harbour on the west coast – ships were often wrecked on the shifting bar of the Hokitika River – the easiest method of transport was by sea. The banks, gold buyers, merchants and diggers saw no reason to change their habits. They declined to send gold by the overland transport, and continued to import supplies from Australia and despatch gold to Nelson or Melbourne, 'preferring to run the risk of bars and storms and sea-misadventures than risk the roads, even under the care of an escort'.

Fitz's dreams of a gold-fuelled boom were over. The scarlet wagon would make no second journey over the mountains. No new readers of newspapers would come flocking into Christchurch. The downturn in trade would continue, the economic depression would deepen, advertising revenue would continue to fall.

There was another lost opportunity to rub salt into the wound. The first part of the southern railway (to Rolleston, a few miles from the Springs station) had opened in October. The second part of the line (to Selwyn on Lake Ellesmere, even closer to the Springs) would open a year later. The coming of the railway had raised the value of land but, in 1864, Harman & Stevens had forced Fitz to sell his remaining freehold acreage to reduce his overdraft.

. . .

One of Fitz's preoccupations was to find a method of regulating the expenditure of the general government. As early as 1856, he wrote that 'the House of Representatives is a body not fit to be entrusted with the expenditure of the public revenues'. Eight years later, he set out his ideas in the *Press*, describing the methods used in England and explaining how they could be adapted to colonial government. He recommended the appointment of an independent auditor and comptroller of finance, a man whose brief would be to investigate the legality of every item of government spending.

He returned to the subject in early 1866, interweaving it with further attacks on the government. Stafford's scheme to impose an income tax was 'one of the most ridiculous proposals which ever emanated from a public man'; his failure to appoint a comptroller-general of finance showed 'contempt for the constitution'. Relations between the two men deteriorated further during the 1866 parliament, after which Fitz continued to attack Stafford in the columns of his newspaper.

Fitz's ideas about public accountability first appeared in the *Press* in 1864 and Stafford – a reader of the newspaper – had taken notice. He was aware that the government was in need of a comptroller-general. He also knew that Fitz was better suited for the job than any other man. Fitz had made a mess of his personal finances, both at the station and at the *Press*, but he understood British constitutional and legal history and had a good grasp of public finance. He also had an eye for detail and – when he was in the right mood – could muster huge amounts of energy and enthusiasm.

He had, however, been excessively rude about Stafford, and the two men were hardly on speaking terms. Fearing that a direct approach would have 'very bitter consequences', Stafford asked his secretary, Edward Wakefield (Edward Gibbon's nephew), for advice. Edward Wakefield was one of Fanny's admirers – referring to her as 'the best of women and very clear-headed' – and towards the end of the year, he 'conveyed to her what was in Mr Stafford's mind, leaving it to her to act on it as she thought most prudent'. And what Fanny thought most prudent was that Fitz should accept the job of comptroller-general.

On 30 December, twelve days after the telegram from the gold escort had dashed his hopes – a time when he was 'so unwell and out of spirits' – Fitz stood by the font as his third daughter was baptised in St Michael's church. As he played his part in the ceremony, he grieved for his newspaper. 'There would be nobody to look after the *Press*' if he moved to Wellington; the editor 'would never be content to write without proper and consistent instructions and these he would never get … if I gave up that part of the business'.

But with the first repayment of his debt due in January, he had little choice. Later that day, he wrote to Stafford accepting the 'permanent and non-political office of comptroller of the public revenues' at a salary of £800 a year ('inclusive of clerical assistance' – he had to employ and pay his own clerk). Three days later, he wrote to his electors in Christchurch:

> By the last mail I forwarded to the Speaker my resignation of my
> seat in the General Assembly. It has been evident for some time that
> my health would compel my retirement from political life … I retire
> from political life, and especially from the representation of your city,
> with great regret … I beg to return you my most cordial thanks for
> the kindness and confidence with which you have honoured me.

This letter was published the following morning in the *Lyttelton Times* and the *Press*; the announcement 'occasioned much surprise'. On 6 January 1867, Fitz took the steamer to Wellington for discussions with Stafford. It was a chilly meeting but both men were on their best behaviour. According to Edward Wakefield, 'Mr FitzGerald walked into the office, shook hands with Mr Stafford, and they sat down in friendly consultation.'

Fitz returned to Christchurch on 14 January, travelling with Sir George Grey, who was making his first visit to Canterbury in fifteen years. Grey was received with enthusiasm and, during the next eight days, Fitz attended a number of official functions as Moorhouse entertained the governor with 'balls and levees', and accompanied him into the railway tunnel in a 'truck trimmed with scarlet cloth'.

Grey left on the 22nd to travel over the mountains to Hokitika. Six days later, Fitz embarked on the *Phoebe* to return to Wellington. And while Fanny packed up the house in Cashel Street and made preparations for departure, he spent the next two months setting up the comptroller's office and finding a home for his family. 'It is a sad thing to lose FitzGerald in New Zealand politics,' wrote Charles Bowen on 4 February:

Fitz playing the fool for Dr Alfred Barker's camera, c.1865. On the left: 'At a Temperance Meeting'. On the right: 'After a Temperance Meeting'.

Private collection

> But for the sake of his family we cannot but rejoice ... I wish he had an independent fortune ... what a saviour of society he would be. FitzGerald is quite grey-haired now and looks old. But he is young as ever in fun and chaff. He is still the jolliest, most amusing and sociable fellow in the world. I do not think there are many like him in that respect.

Newspapers throughout the colony published fulsome tributes on Fitz's retirement from politics. The *Lyttelton Times*, so long an enemy, gave him a generous send-off – in words that read almost like an obituary:

> No man connected with Canterbury, we might say with New Zealand, has been more prominently before the public eye, or exercised a wider influence on public affairs. And assuredly no one has maintained a higher character for all that is upright, honourable and chivalrous than Mr FitzGerald. He has sometimes stood alone in his opinions and has perhaps more frequently stood on the side of the minority than of the majority in political strife. But his speeches were always listened to with interest, both from the weight of his authority, and the brilliancy of his eloquence ... We have often had occasion to oppose him both in matters of provincial and colonial

politics … but we can join with our fellow-colonists in saying 'We are all proud of him.'

Even Moorhouse was inclined to be generous. 'FitzGerald and I have shaken hands … and are now on speaking terms,' he wrote to Henry Selfe. 'At some distant day, we may even be cordial friends. I trust we have already ceased to be enemies. Had he not wantonly, and I may say perversely, ill-used me at every turn during these many years past, we might have jointly performed great things … I am ready to try and forget everything.'

On 27 February, Fanny organised a farewell concert in aid of the Women's Refuge, a concert acclaimed as 'the most decided success which has yet been obtained for a benefit'. The concert ended with 'sustained applause' and, as the *Lyttelton Times* put it, 'the only drawback to the evening was the approaching departure of Mrs FitzGerald from Canterbury, a loss our musical society cannot afford'.

Fitz's farewell ceremonies came later, after he returned to Christchurch on 25 March to help Fanny with 'the turmoil of removing a large family from one part of the colony to another'. The staff of the *Press* hosted a 'complimentary dinner' on the 30th, with toasts, speeches and singing. Five days later, the province gave him a farewell dinner in the town hall. Eighty men attended the occasion (although Moorhouse was conveniently absent on the west coast). One of the speakers 'deeply regretted' that Fitz's oratory would no longer be heard in parliament, 'oratory that nightly filled the gallery with ladies [laughter] and the damage done to crinolines was something terrible [roars of laughter]'.

Charles Bowen proposed the toast to Fitz's health, paying tribute to his 'talent and energy', and referring to his sometimes unpopular opinions: 'If anyone does good to a community whose interests he has truly at heart, if at the risk of losing a passing popularity, he perseveres in the course which he honestly thinks is the best, let all honour be done to him. And this was precisely the case with Mr FitzGerald.'

As Fitz rose to reply, he was 'received with very great applause which lasted for some time'. He thanked the province for the honour of the occasion and said that his reasons for leaving Canterbury were 'altogether private and related partly to my means, and partly to my health'. He went on to make one point very clear:

> It has been said that I am retiring from public life under a feeling
> of anger and disappointment – anger because the policy which I
> advocated has not been successful and disappointment because my
> talents have not achieved that recognition to which I believe them

entitled. This has been said in some public print but I do not care very much for that; everyone knows the value of those little amenities in which journalists sometimes indulge [laughter and cheers], and I ought to be the very last man in the world to object to them [renewed laughter].

It was not pleasant to receive such a tremendous thrashing as I and my friends received in the late contest for the Superintendency [laughter]. Some people might suppose that this has something to do with my retirement, and others might attribute it to the defeat which my party sustained in the General Assembly. I beg to assure you that this is not the case. All public men must expect to meet with defeat; and it is only natural that they should feel some disappointment, not on their own personal account, but on account of the measures they had advocated. But the feeling of disappointment did not last long [hear, hear] …

What have I to be disappointed with? No public man in the colony can look back to a career which yielded greater satisfaction. I have at all times received every recognition which I could possibly expect, and ten times more than I have ever deserved … I can say that from the time at which the colony acquired representative institutions up to 1865, no ministry has been formed in which I have not either held or been urged to hold a prominent position [cheers]. If after that there can be found anyone to say that I look back on my career with dissatisfaction, or that I am retiring from public life in disgust, I have nothing whatever to say to him [cheers].

As he came to the end of his speech, as his final words of farewell approached, he struggled to retain his composure:

I cannot deny that I find this parting exceedingly painful and I would rather not trust myself to dwell upon it. I have received such an unusual amount of personal kindness and goodwill, even when I was most unpopular, that I cannot say all that I wish. Although I am about to leave the Province, I hope I might often visit Canterbury. My heart and soul will be with you.

CHAPTER TWENTY-SEVEN

Chesney Wold

1867–1868

A great old rambling house, planted lonesomely in the midst of huge
gardens, orchards and paddocks.
Katherine Mansfield, 'About Pat', 1905

Karori was a cold, bleak place and I found it very dull.
Amy Levin (née FitzGerald)

On 9 April 1867, Fitz and Fanny embarked on the *Taranaki* with their
seven younger children (the two elder boys were at school in Christ's
College and would live with Alfred Barker until the end of the Easter term).
It was a poignant half hour as the *Taranaki* steamed out of the harbour. Fitz
was not only leaving the province for which he had worked for seventeen
years, he was also leaving the *Press* (his 'splendid property') in the hands of its
principal creditors.

As Fanny discovered when searching for a house in 1865, rents were high
in Wellington and land was expensive to buy. With debt repayments making
inroads into his salary, Fitz had been forced to look elsewhere for a home.
His problem was solved when he met a quarry owner who had recently built
a house in Karori, a tiny settlement in the hills six miles west of Wellington.
The owner was intending to use it himself, but he melted under pressure and
agreed to let the house to the new comptroller-general, together with fourteen
acres of land bordering the Karori Stream.

Fitz moved his family into a hotel in Wellington until their furniture and
possessions arrived from Christchurch. In the meantime, he hired a dogcart
and took Fanny and the children to see their new home. They drove along a
narrow, twisting road that wound its way through steep bush-covered hills and
over a rickety bridge, a journey described as 'up steep, steep hills, down into
bushy valleys, through wide shallow rivers, further and further'.

'Chesney Wold' (the house on the left) in Karori, photographed in 1870. Amy hated Karori, describing it as 'a very small village arrived at by a very bad road among the hills. It was a cold, bleak place and I found it very dull.'

Private collection

The sparse settlement of Karori, with just 70 inhabitants, lay in a secluded valley surrounded by hills. The house (named 'Chesney Wold' after the stately home in Dickens' *Bleak House*) was some distance beyond the settlement, a 'long, low-built house' with twelve rooms and deep verandahs, and just one other building nearby. Twenty years later, it would become the childhood home of the writer Katherine Mansfield, who described it as 'a great old rambling house planted lonesomely in the midst of huge gardens, orchards and paddocks'. In 1867, it was 'planted lonesomely' in a sea of rough grass and scrub.

The family moved into the house towards the end of April. On their first night in Karori, they lay awake listening to the sounds of their new surroundings: the Karori Stream 'running over the brown stones', the sudden cry of an owl. In the morning, the birdsong began, loud and melodic, reminding Fanny of the birdsong at Riccarton.

Part of the Karori valley was cultivated; the rest was still covered in bush – farmers allowed their cows to roam free with bells around their necks. Amy described the settlement as 'a very small village arrived at by a very bad road among the hills. It was a cold, bleak place and I found it very dull.' The boys were more enthusiastic: they enjoyed walks in the hills with 'cow bells ringing all over the place'. And eight-year-old Lyttelton found a vocation. He was, Fitz explained to his godfather, 'a rather peculiar boy, very slow and stolid with a remarkable affection for plants and flowers. I have made him head gardener.'

…

The 1867 parliament opened in Wellington on 9 July. It was a poignant occasion for Fitz who, after five consecutive years in the House, could take no further part in proceedings. Stafford still led the government and – to Fitz's chagrin – it was he who achieved Maori representation in parliament.

During his farewell dinner in Christchurch, Fitz had spoken of his confidence that a measure for Maori representation 'will be passed at no very distant day'. A few months later, he helped the minister for native affairs draft the Native Representation Bill, under which four Maori members would sit in the House of Representatives. The bill passed its second reading on 14 August and became law in October.

This was a major achievement – the first time an indigenous population in any British dominion had been granted representation in government. Stafford was premier at the time but it was Fitz who raised the idea, Fitz who cast the first seeds upon the soil. As Stafford put it – in words which Fitz himself might have written – 'it was only a fair measure of justice in a country where one law ruled all Her Majesty's subjects of both races'.

Another excitement of the 1867 parliament was the news, which arrived on 22 August, of Sir George Grey's dismissal by a Colonial Office exasperated by his high-handed attitude to the war. The assembly put on a show of loyalty, but Fitz was delighted. Grey had disappointed him in both his terms as governor, and he shared James Richmond's assessment of him as a man whose 'manner is gentle and amiable to a marvellous degree but one remembers the claws under the velvet'.

Richmond was perceptive about Fitz, too. He referred to him as a man of great ability but rash judgement, 'for ever insisting on applying constitutional maxims and asserting constitutional rights when they don't apply … a species of formalism very astonishing in a man of FitzGerald's calibre'. This side of his character made Fitz a better bureaucrat than politician; it enabled him to work his way through legislation, reading every clause of every bill and writing long letters about points of detail.

He drafted bills on financial matters – and sometimes found it difficult to control his pen. On one occasion, he wrote to the colonial treasurer 'recording my earnest protest and remonstrance' against a bill he was drafting. 'So serious … does it appear to me that I can only hope some fortunate accident may defeat the whole measure and leave matters as they are until the colony has become more alive to its true interests.'

As comptroller-general, he not only controlled the issue of public money, he also checked every single item of government expenditure. He had to certify that all payments were legal, that they had been authorised by parliament, that funds had been set aside for the purpose, and that 'all the money voted by parliament for a certain purpose was used for that purpose and for no other'. According to Amy:

> This led to the most amusing war between my father and the ministers in power. From time to time, ministers wanted to divert money to other things according to *their* discretion, but they always came up against a brick wall when they tried to extract any money from my father except for the exact purpose for which the House had voted it, and who sometimes – to their supreme disgust – replied to their appeals in verse.

Fitz was now a civil servant, forbidden to hold political office or to engage in political affairs. He could no longer make eloquent speeches on policy; he could no longer write strongly worded articles on government affairs. Frustrated by the need to curb his enthusiasms – and less than seven months after moving to Wellington – he cooked up another scheme of colonisation.

...

Sir George Grey had told him of land around Lake Taupo that provided rich opportunities, and that was 'as well grassed as his own lawn'. A lull in hostilities with Maori had lasted a year now and Fitz – his mood rising again – was full of confidence. 'I want your best attention,' he wrote to Donald McLean, minister for native affairs, on 29 November:

> First for myself, I want to exchange the repose of the Comptroller's office for more kindred pursuits. 2. I want to see my way to open a career for half a score of lusty sons and daughters and it may be more in long array hereafter. 3. Above all, I want to devote myself to the work of my life – the colonisation of this country. 4. I want to do some practical work in the native question.

His idea was to buy 'some 300,000 or 400,000 acres' from Maori. 'But I don't want to deal with this like a solitary squatter. I want to make a *great settlement* there.' He would be joined by 'good practical colonists' and would persuade 'the best of the young chiefs' to join the enterprise:

> You may say that there is not much work left in me for such a task.

> True, I am now transferring bodily work to my sons but, in very few
> years, I shall have more of muscle and sinew to dispose of in my own
> family than falls to the lot of most men … I do not know whether
> my name is known up there. I have been told that it is, and the
> natives might like me to come and live amongst them … I want to
> deal with the native question … and to leave behind me some more
> work worth a man's doing before I die.

'You may smile at this letter as that of an enthusiast,' he concluded. 'Only
remember what I have seen done at Canterbury … These things surpass any
dreams I formed when I was engaged in helping to found Canterbury. One
sees how difficulties vanish before work and pluck.'

In December, he met with McLean to discuss the scheme and on 16
January, his mind running at high speed, he set out his plans in another letter.
The acreage had now grown to 'as much as 30 miles square, even 50 miles
square, say from a million to a million and a half acres', sufficient for '500,000
sheep and several thousand head of cattle and horses'. He planned to 'establish
manufactures for … blankets and woollen articles for clothing … thus saving
vast expense in the transit of the wool to the manufacturers in England and
back in the shape of goods for use'.

Excited by his idea, he asked McLean to open negotiations with Maori
'without loss of time. If it is thought desirable, I shall probably be able to meet
the natives in April or May.'

…

Fanny felt isolated in Karori. She missed the musical society, she missed the
glee singers. Her only musical outlet was to improve the singing in the newly
built church in the settlement. Some distance from Chesney Wold, the little
church of St Mary's would not acquire a harmonium for several years; hymns
were sung to the sound of a tuning fork. Fitz bought a hymnbook with pages
of blank staves, Fanny filled in the music, and Amy (who had inherited her
mother's singing voice) rode her pony from house to house to teach the people
of Karori to sing.

The wooden church was unstable in high winds and Fitz, who had designed
the schoolroom at Christ's College, was asked to provide for its 'immediate
protection'. He made a model with his planned additions, two transepts and an
ornate wooden tower, and the work was carried out during the early months
of 1868. To help raise funds, he organised a 'sacred concert' in the church on 8
January and persuaded the élite of Wellington (including Edward Stafford and
the bishop) to make the journey to Karori. 'The concert may be said to have

been a success,' wrote the *Evening Post*, although 'a quartetto was somewhat flat and feeble, and the choruses not quite up to the mark'.

Seven days after the concert, Henry Selfe and Lord Lyttelton arrived in Wellington. Selfe was taking an extended holiday, partly for health reasons and partly to visit his son Jim. He was accompanied by Lord Lyttelton, who came to visit the province he had done so much to create.

The steamship dropped anchor 'on a lovely afternoon'. Fitz went aboard to greet his friends, but there was little time for conversation as they sailed the same evening for Canterbury. Ten days later, he and Fanny followed them south, disembarking in Lyttelton on 5 February 1868. The railway tunnel had opened three months earlier and it took just six and a half minutes to travel through the hills, and another ten minutes to Christchurch.

They arrived in the city to find it submerged under several feet of water. For two days, the Canterbury Plains had been deluged with rain, 'such cataracts of water, that in many parts of the open plain the water was soon rushing along like a wave'. The water surged down rivers and creeks from the foothills of the Southern Alps, turning much of the plains into one vast lake. The Waimakariri burst its banks north of Christchurch and poured into the Avon, which flowed through the city.

The river had begun to rise on the morning of the 4th; bridges were submerged and boats were out on the streets. 'My pretty garden ... is several feet under water,' wrote Alfred Barker at half past ten that night. 'The flood is closing round my house, having long ago filled the kitchen and put out the fire. It is now rising at the rate of four or five inches per hour up the steps ... It is strange that this should have occurred just as Lord Lyttelton came out to visit us.'

William Moorhouse had arranged a number of celebrations to welcome the visitors. The official banquet was held on 5 February. The floods had begun to abate during the night but water still filled the streets and it was a rather sodden crowd of notables who assembled in the town hall. Fitz was absent because of 'indisposition', having been seasick on the voyage, but also – perhaps – because he had little desire to hear his friends eulogise the tunnel.

Moorhouse had been lucky with the economic climate. The early 1860s were prosperous years, with high prices for wool and a boom in land sales, which filled the provincial coffers. Construction of the tunnel was well underway by the time of the economic depression; and now that it was open for traffic, goods and people were transported with ease from the port to the plains. During his speech at the banquet, Lord Lyttelton said he was 'astonished' there had been 'any absence of unanimity' about the project.

Fitz on the morning of the 'welcome breakfast' in Christchurch, 6 February 1868. 'FitzGerald is quite grey-haired now and looks old. But he is young as ever in fun and chaff ... still the jolliest, most amusing and sociable fellow in the world.' Photograph by Dr Alfred Barker.

Private collection

Fitz came into his own the next day when 'early settlers of all classes', the original Canterbury Pilgrims, held a welcome breakfast for the visitors. Many of those invited were marooned on their stations but, as Barker put it, 'we had a very pleasant meeting of as many as the flooded state of the country would allow to attend. The large Town Hall was filled and it was good to meet again with many an old face one had known long ago.'

In the morning, Fitz sat for Alfred Barker's camera, wearing frockcoat and waistcoat, his top hat on his knee, his grey hair brushed long over his ears. At midday, he took his seat in the town hall, in pride of place at the top table, Lord Lyttelton on one side, Henry Selfe on the other. His speech of welcome – more stirring oratory – reduced several members of his audience to tears. After referring to the official banquet the previous day, he spoke of this gathering of early settlers as having 'a more special character':

> It is a sort of return match – a breakfast given by those who partook
> of the hospitality of his Lordship and the Canterbury Association
> ... at Gravesend on the eve of our departure from England. If ever
> there was a moment in which one might be forgiven a feeling of
> deepfelt and unaffected emotion, that moment is the present. There
> are times in every man's life when he is compelled by circumstances
> to look back upon the past, and ask himself what is the result of his

labours, what are the fruits of the years that have passed over his head. Such a time is the present for you, my Lord, and for many of us who are here today.

For my own part, when I see beside me in this far-off corner of the world, old familiar faces which I never expected to see again in this life, scenes come rushing back upon my memory of those days in the long past, when we laboured together in a spirit of ardent hope and earnest enthusiasm for that object of which we are here today to commemorate the greatest achievement. Dreamers and visionaries we were then called, as men will ever be called who set before themselves higher objects, and indulge in nobler aspirations than the working world around consents to deem practicable.

He talked of the Pilgrims who had 'passed that wider and deeper ocean on whose brink we are all standing, and have entered upon the rest and the reward of their labours'. He spoke of the Ward brothers, drowned so soon after arriving in Canterbury; and of John Godley, whose memory 'seems to me to loom ever larger and larger through the mists of time'. The younger men at the tables, those with 'bright eyes and beardless chins', had filled 'our broken ranks with fresh recruits', and at home in the nursery, 'a large infant army in long and bright array [is] rising up to carry on the work which their fathers commenced'.

'We were sent out,' he continued – in a remark which led to roars of laughter – 'not only to subdue the earth but to people it; and I cannot but think that in whatever else we may have fallen short, we have not been unmindful of our duty in this respect.'

CHAPTER TWENTY-EIGHT

A Rigid System of Economy

1868–1870

I am afraid it will utterly undo me. I am too old to be hurt
and I can but die.

Fanny, 13 May 1868

Your poor wife, who I fear is much *jaded* by incessant work.

Lord Lyttelton to Fitz, 3 April 1872

*F*itz and Fanny stayed in Christchurch for the next ten days. Fanny gave a concert in aid of the Female Servants Home, to a packed house; they attended a ball in honour of Lord Lyttelton, and admired a statue of Godley that had recently been erected near the site of the proposed cathedral. Fitz had been asked to give a speech at the unveiling of the statue ('principally because Godley and FitzGerald were great friends and no man could do the oration in more excellent taste') but he declined the honour 'on grounds of illness'. He was, he admitted privately, 'afraid of doing it badly or breaking down'.

Now, as he gazed at the familiar figure of his old friend standing high on his pedestal, he remembered 'the days when the Godleys lived in the garden cottage at Riccarton and we sat by the fern-fringed stream and talked of the great future to come'. Those days were, he wrote nostalgically, 'like the days of first love. They come back upon me with a fascination I cannot describe.'

On 20 February, three days after returning home, he wrote to a politician in New Plymouth, enclosing a prospectus for the Taupo scheme and asking him to raise support in Taranaki. On 4 March, he celebrated his 50th birthday. He continued to work on the Taupo scheme but his spirits were sinking, and renewed fighting in Taranaki in May put an end to his plans. Now he had no choice but to settle down to his job as comptroller-general.

Every morning, he harnessed his bay horse and set off in the pony carriage, driving through the hills to his office in the parliament buildings. During

Fanny in Dr Barker's garden in February 1868, when she and Fitz were in Christchurch for the 'welcome breakfast' to Lord Lyttelton and Henry Selfe. Photograph by Dr Alfred Barker.

Private collection

the evenings and weekends, he and his sons worked on the land at Chesney Wold. They fenced paddocks and sowed them with English grass; they planted orchards and made a garden. And the house was always full of laughter as the children played pranks on each other and on their parents.

Willy and Robert had enrolled in the newly founded Wellington College; the younger children were attending the local school in Karori, a 'very inferior school' according to Fanny. After he gave up the Taupo scheme, Fitz decided to take the boys out of school with the intention of teaching them himself. 'I should do all in my power to prevent [it] were they doing any good there,' wrote Fanny, 'but I really think, if Mr FG perseveres in teaching them, they will do better with him.' So Fitz spent his days in the office in Wellington and his evenings teaching his sons at home. 'I am working harder than ever,' he wrote, 'reading up all the classics and mathematics again to teach the boys is a terrible grind.'

A significant proportion of his salary was set aside every month to fund the quarterly repayments to Harman & Stevens, and the money available for housekeeping was limited. 'We are obliged to institute a rigid system of economy,' Fanny wrote to a friend on 13 May 1868 (when she was five months pregnant with her tenth child), 'but I fear the giving up of one of my nurses will prove a false step. For as it is, I feel I do all I can and I am afraid it will utterly undo me the amount of extra exertion which will fall upon me when I feel each day more unequal for work.'

Three days later (the letter having 'been in Mr FG's pocket for two or three days'), she added a postscript:

> Since the beginning of this letter, Mr FG has further developed his plans. After the boys leave school, all domestics are to be discarded. Mr FG thinks it won't be *much more* for me to do. I mildly suggested my inability to do the family washing etc, but he thinks we might do *without washing* … What will be the end of all this, I don't know. If it happens, I shall be sorry for Amy. As for me, it is no great matter. I am too old to be hurt and I can but die … Mr FG thinks one year of this will free us but what shall we be at the end? Of course I tell you this in perfect confidence, but it is such a relief to unburden to a woman.

Washing and ironing for a family of eleven was no small task – struggling with hot copper, washboard and mangle, and heating irons on the stove – particularly as the youngest daughter was still in nappies. And this in addition to providing food for the family, looking after the children and helping with their education. Sixteen-year-old Amy helped in the kitchen – and Fanny remembered how, as a child, her definition of domestic economy had amused their friends in Christchurch: 'something very nasty and very little of it'.

···

In early July, the new governor opened the 1868 parliament, at which four Maori members took their seats in the House of Representatives. Fitz sat proudly in the gallery as Tareha Te Moananui made his maiden speech, speaking in his own language with a translator at his side. Laws, he said, should be made for the benefit of both races; members of parliament should always do 'that which is good'.

Fitz's mood began to sink after his Taupo enthusiasm faded. 'Poor FitzGerald writes in very low spirits,' wrote Charles Bowen in June. 'He takes a gloomy view of everything and writes like Cassandra about the future.' And Fitz wrote to Sir George Grey, complaining that 'the standard of public life is lamentably low', that he looked 'upon matters with extreme gloom', that he was 'daily anticipating some great disaster'.

Grey, who was returning to England, was given a farewell banquet on 8 September but Fitz stayed away. 'I could not reconcile it with honesty, or consistency,' he explained, 'that one who has been so earnest and conscientious an opponent of all the policy of your government, should take part in a demonstration which could not but be regarded more or less as indicating approval of the past.' He then made a reasonably gracious apology: 'Though I never consciously said a thing I did not believe, I may very often have erred through partial or incorrect information; and if I have ever done you a wrong from that cause I beg your forgiveness.' Finally, he enclosed copies of three of his speeches, 'which may amuse you on the voyage'.

Fanny was now 'very seriously ill'. A few weeks after complaining in May that she felt 'each day more unequal for work', she nursed her two elder sons through scarlet fever, after which her health declined as her pregnancy progressed. Remembering her illness at the Springs station before Eva was born, and frightened of giving birth in the isolation of Karori, she retired to bed in Chesney Wold. 'Had it not been for my husband's good nursing,' she wrote three months later:

> I do not think I should be alive now. The doctor attributed it all to
> overwork of years, and anxiety of mind, and orders me '*rest*' – which
> is like ordering paupers to drink port wine. Our life at present is a
> very hard one, for we only have one servant and, with ten children –
> and teaching – working – washing – bread-making etc – myself and
> my eldest daughter have much to do.

Fanny gave birth to their tenth child (Otho, a boy named after one of Fitz's eleventh-century ancestors) on 16 September. While she recovered slowly in Karori, Fitz fumed at the recent publication of letters written by Edward Gibbon Wakefield at the time of the foundation of Canterbury. The list of subscribers included the governor, Lord Lyttelton, Henry Selfe, Bishop Harper, Edward Stafford, Richard Harman, Edward Stevens, the editor of the *Lyttelton Times*, and William Moorhouse, who had the pleasure of ordering 25 copies. With readers such as these, it was discomfiting for Fitz to see himself described as being '*all* imagination and *no* action … singularly feeble and heedless … immensely presumptuous … the most provoking man I have ever had to deal with'.

Meanwhile, his financial position was parlous. Harman & Stevens hoped to receive £250 a quarter, an obligation which Fitz – on a salary of £800 a year – was clearly unable to meet. Despite the lack of servants in Chesney Wold, despite teaching his sons at home, he had managed to repay just £836 during the previous two years.

Fitz in Dr Barker's garden on 4 December 1868, when he was in Christchurch to negotiate with Harman & Stevens about the *Press*. Photograph by Dr Alfred Barker.

Private collection

On 21 November, he embarked on the steamer for Lyttelton. He had a proposal for Harman & Stevens, 'the best which I am able to offer'. He suggested setting up a company for the *Press* with capital of £4000, of which he would take shares to the value of £2000. He would retain his leasehold interest in the Cashel Street premises, renting them to the newspaper for £150 a year. He offered the premises, together with his 50 per cent shareholding, as security for his debt. He also agreed 'to pay over … the proceeds of my share of the sale of an Estate in Ireland, about to be sold under my Father's will', an estate of 734 acres still waiting for the death of an elderly life tenant in County Louth.

He confirmed his proposals on 27 November: 'If you will kindly give me a reply to this letter before three o'clock today I shall be able to proceed with the negotiations for the formation of the Company without embarrassment.' The Press Company was duly formed on 1 December 1868. And that evening, when he met Edward Chudleigh on a visit to Christchurch from his new home in the Chatham Islands, Fitz merely said that he was in town 'looking after the *Press*'.

Alone with her children in Chesney Wold, Fanny wrote a long and rambling letter to Lord Lyttelton. She told him about her illness and her exhaustion. She told him about life in Karori, how the church choir was 'going on satisfactorily', how Fitz had 'composed a very pretty hymn' to a poem by George Herbert. And she described how Lyttelton's nine-year-old godson had a 'new accomplishment which is catching bees and sucking the honey off them and then letting them go again. He always knows which bees to catch and is never stung.'

…

It was not just the *Press* that took Fitz away from home: one of his duties was to inspect the provincial accounts in Auckland, New Plymouth, Nelson, Christchurch and Dunedin. In November 1869, he was again in Christchurch, staying with Alfred Barker and accompanied by fifteen-year-old Willy, who had forged a friendship with Barker's son Francis.

Willy was walking with a stick, the result of an accident in May when he and his brothers were collecting firewood at Chesney Wold. He was using gunpowder to split a tree trunk when, 'something going wrong with the fuse, the charge exploded before he got away'. A shard of wood penetrated his leg. The wound failed to heal and, after arriving in Christchurch, he complained of fever and aching joints. Barker diagnosed rheumatic fever and confined him to bed.

Fitz was not unduly concerned. According to Charles Bowen, he was 'as amusing as ever. His spirits are really extraordinary and it is a real pleasure to see him again ... The other night he kept us laughing all night with stories about the Governor and Stafford but I could not attempt to retell them.' Barker photographed him wearing his trademark tam o'shanter and indulging in a mock argument with William Rolleston, the new superintendent.

On 8 December, Fitz returned to Wellington, leaving Willy in the care of the widowed Barker and his three children. 'Just now we have a sick house,' Barker wrote on the 17th:

> A friend of ours, son of Mr FitzGerald, has been laid up for the last month with rheumatic fever and will, I fear, be confined to his room for some time. In such times of sickness, I sadly miss dear Emma's experience for though Lizzie and Mary do all in their power and Francis has come out strong in the nursing line, yet they make but a poor mess of it.

Barker sent a summons to Karori and, on 27 December, Fanny embarked on the steamer for Lyttelton. She tended her son in Barker's house for almost five weeks; his bed was carried into the garden every day so he could enjoy the summer sunshine. He recovered under his mother's care and, by the end of January, was well enough to return home.

A few weeks later, Fanny received a letter from London with news of her mother's death. Mary Draper's will (written after Fitz's near-bankruptcy at the *Press*) made 'an inalienable provision' for her eldest daughter, leaving the capital in trust for Fanny's children and instructing her executors 'to pay the dividends and income to my daughter, Fanny FitzGerald, during her life for her sole and separate use, independent of her husband and his debts'.

Fanny in Dr Barker's garden on 29 December 1869, the day after arriving in Christchurch to look after Willy, who was in bed with rheumatic fever in Dr Barker's house. Photograph by Dr Alfred Barker.

Private collection

Fitz was delighted. The inheritance was tied up in trust, safe from Harman & Stevens, and at four per cent interest would provide additional income. The economic depression was lifting and he was feeling more cheerful. 'I am happy to say,' he wrote to Lucius, 'that I am now over all my *pressing* difficulties and am in no fear of a bankruptcy.'

CHAPTER TWENTY-NINE

An Island in Sight

1868–1871

This colony is marching on its ruin, with rapid and certain steps.
Fitz, 2 November 1870

Let us go, my friend ... Make an island into a garden.
Fitz, 8 December 1870

As Fitz walked into the parliament buildings one day, he was pointed out as 'the most eloquent man in New Zealand'. He was proud of this reputation and resented his enforced silence on political matters. He began with good intentions ('as to politics, I have ceased to care further as I am paid to keep out of them') but he soon began to make his views known more publicly.

His first effort was a four-column letter in support of the self-reliant policy published in the *Wellington Independent* in December 1868. Six months later, Edward Stafford was defeated in a vote of no confidence. A ministry headed by William Fox took power, with Donald McLean as native and defence minister. In a conversation with Fitz on 26 June 1869, McLean asked him for his 'views on native matters'. Delighted to be involved in politics again, Fitz set out his opinions on fourteen closely written pages:

> My removal from public affairs and party ties may have enabled me to take a somewhat calmer view than those who have been engaged in political struggles ... I beg you to look at the words of my speech in 1862 describing the necessary result of a prolonged war with a race only just emerging from barbarism and very easily hunted back into it. Have not these words *literally come true*? ... ten years more spent as the last have been will result in the abandonment of this island or the extinction of nearly the whole of the native race.

On 15 December, he wrote again:

> I do not believe there will be any permanent peace in the colony
> until we make it worth the while of the natives in every district …
> to keep the peace … I would not venture to have put these thoughts
> down so decidedly if they were new or transient. They are the
> convictions of years of study and I see no reason to alter them.

Eleven days later, he wrote a long letter to Henry Selfe with a detailed explanation of the self-reliant policy. And Selfe, presumably with Fitz's permission, arranged for the letter to be published in London. The pamphlet appeared in early March 1870, just when two commissioners from New Zealand were in London to ask the colonial secretary, Lord Granville, for a treasury guarantee on loans worth £2 million and for imperial troops to return to the colony (the last regiment had left in February).

Fitz opposed the return of imperial troops, so the timing might not have been coincidental. 'It seems an unusual course,' the commissioners complained to William Fox on 15 March:

> for one of the highest civil servants in the colony … [to give] advice
> very contrary to the course we were urging Lord Granville to take,
> and we were told that Lord Granville had expressed grave doubts
> as to the truth of our representations on the ground of their contra-
> diction by letters he had seen from New Zealand … There is really
> no knowing how much mischief … this will do us.

On 1 June, Fitz arrived home 'somewhat beaten' after a four-day voyage from Auckland. Five days later, Fox accused him of trying to influence the Colonial Office. It was his duty as premier, he wrote, to present the correspondence to parliament and he was therefore giving Fitz 'the opportunity of offering to the government any explanation you may wish relative to the complaints made by the commissioners'.

So Fitz was forced to apologise, expressing 'great regret' that his words had been perceived to impede the work of the commissioners in London and recognising 'the principle that any such attempt on my part would be inconsistent with the understanding on which my office is held'. But, he continued (disingenuously):

> I was only speaking as any casual observer reading the public press
> of the colony, the debates in the Assembly, and the published
> accounts of the colony might speak. It did not occur to me that
> such an expression would be deemed to have more significance as

coming from the Comptroller; and I can only express my regret that it should have been taken for more than it was worth.

'I have admitted to the government,' he told Henry Selfe, 'that there is an inconvenience in my engaging in politics in any way ... I have had my say and shall say no more.'

By this time, despite his prophecies of doom, the war was effectively over. Lord Granville refused the request to return imperial troops to the colony. And as Fitz boasted to Henry Selfe, 'the government has been compelled to suspend its active military operations because all the money has gone and there was a Comptroller who would not give a penny more than was voted'.

...

The weather turned cold in early July, with ice and snow on the road to Karori. 'Our roads this winter are nearly impassable,' Fitz wrote on the 4th, 'quite so at night-time, so I see little of anyone. This is my busy time of year mustering up my yearly balance sheet.'

Next day, Julius Vogel, now the colonial treasurer, announced a massive development programme designed to lift the colony from stagnation to prosperity. His plan, known as the public works policy, involved large-scale investment in infrastructure and immigration, funded by loans worth several million pounds raised on the London market. This bold scheme proved popular – both with politicians and the public – but in Fitz's opinion, it was 'too mad a scheme to discuss ... a piece of simple insanity for which the authors should be put in a lunatic asylum'. As he wrote to Lucius:

> Speaking between ourselves, I cannot conceal from myself that
> this colony is marching upon its ruin, with rapid and certain steps.
> The interest on our debt is ... paid by borrowed money and yet the
> present government is borrowing several millions more ... And the
> sort of men at present in power and getting influence is such as to
> disgust one with the whole affair ... Our Treasurer ... formerly kept
> a small tobacconist's shop, I am told, on the diggings ... a man of
> ability and honest enough in business, but a gambler to the bottom
> of his soul.

He was feeling gloomy about his private prospects too: 'We are all going downhill fast enough. For myself, I have little to complain of and much to be thankful for. My only wish is to live till my sons are able to earn their own living and support their mother. The world has denied me the satisfaction of leaving much behind me.'

Amy, a 'coming out' photograph taken in 1870. According to Edward Chudleigh, she was 'the most ellegant lady I know, perfect in drawing room and perfect in her white apron and looped-up dress'.

Private collection

He wrote this letter in Wellington, before hurrying home to babysit his children. Amy was 'coming out' in society that evening, attending her first ball. Fanny was sharing in the pride of the occasion, so Fitz was needed at home. 'We can't leave such a family alone at night,' he explained, 'which I am not sorry for as balls are not in my line.'

Amy, eighteen years old now, was a sought-after young woman. Edward Chudleigh (whose spelling had not improved) was a little in love with her. He visited Wellington from time to time, staying in Chesney Wold. 'Amy has full charge of the house and works very harde,' he wrote in his diary. 'She is the most ellegant young lady I know, perfect in drawing room and perfect in her white apron and looped-up dress. She will be one of those women whose value as a wife is priceless, so good, clever, thrifty and eminantly ellegant.'

As Amy took her place in society, she was helped by the politician Dillon Bell and his wife Margaret, and 'through their kindness' she enjoyed herself during the parliamentary sessions when Wellington was the hub of New Zealand social life. Except for her first ball in July when she was accompanied by her mother, it was Margaret Bell who acted as chaperone, who arranged Amy's hair in elaborate styles, and provided her with 'a lovely ball dress each year; other dresses I had to make, but people were very good in giving me things and I was able to do them up myself'.

...

In August, Fitz received a letter from Buckingham Palace in London. He had been awarded the CMG (Companion of the Order of St Michael and St George) in the Queen's Birthday honours, a medal given for services to British interests in the colonies. He was cheered to receive the honour, despite expressing the opinion that such medals were 'more an appeal to the snobbish than an award for the loyal feelings of colonists'.

On 29 September, he gave a lecture in which he explained how social structures in ancient times evolved into modern systems of government. He also took on the role of examining schoolboys in Latin. 'Fancy my examining the school here in Virgil and Horace,' he crowed to William Rolleston. 'One gets almost as audacious as Moorhouse in one's old age.'

In October, another letter arrived from London, this time with distressing news. Henry Selfe had died on 6 September, a sudden death from 'complications of gout'. Fitz was dismayed. 'The loss creates a blank in my life that nothing can ever fill,' he wrote. 'Godley was a greater man but they had both very big souls.'

Selfe's death led to a period of introspection. Fitz had written many harsh things about political colleagues over the years. At the same time, he had let down the two men to whom he owed so much: Godley by failing to write letters; Selfe by treating his loan in such a cavalier fashion (the loan was finally repaid in 1869 when Godley's legacy was released by the Court of Chancery). It was too late to make amends to his friends, but he now sent an obliquely worded apology to Edward Stafford, the man who had rescued him from bankruptcy:

> My dear Stafford, I told you one day that I was giving up smoking and that I would give you my pipe. I have not given up smoking – at least I took to it again after one week's continence. But I see no reason why [you] should suffer for the fault of my physical infirmity … I was going to get the pipe silver mounted and send it to you when all of a sudden it burnt through in a large hole.
>
> Two events happened coincidentally, one that I have invented a new form of pipe which, if I could bring myself to do anything to make money, I should have patented … The other event was the arrival of some Chatham Island Ake Ake wood … which had been about 50 years in the earth … and was the best wood I ever had for carving.
>
> So I have carved a pipe for you which I hope Mrs Stafford will take from you, for it is really too delicate and I may say without vanity too good as a work of art to be made use of … I had to make the tools to carve it … I beg you will accept this as the offering of one who has spoken many harsh words of you amongst others, but who is getting old and desires to live and die at peace with all men, especially with those who have [done] their share in the colonisation of New Zealand.

Fitz was still angry about the public works policy, as annoyed at Vogel's profligacy as he had been about Moorhouse and the tunnel. And he was still grieving for Henry Selfe when Edward Chudleigh arrived in Karori with the 'Ake Ake wood'. As a result, he rediscovered, 'you have no idea how strongly, the old instinct of getting away from civilisation ... the true opposite of the *maladie du pays*'. He was ripe for a new scheme of colonisation.

Chudleigh was running a sheep station in the Chatham Islands, a remote archipelago 500 miles east of Christchurch. During conversation over dinner in Chesney Wold, he told Fitz that the only white farmer on Pitt Island (the second largest in the archipelago) was thinking of selling up, having made his fortune selling pork and potatoes to whaling ships. The island was wild and mountainous, with no natural harbour – but Fitz was in receptive mood.

On 23 November 1870 (the day before his apology to Stafford), he wrote to William Rolleston, who was embroiled in a constitutional row with his provincial council in Canterbury:

> I have an island in sight which I hope to be able to purchase in a few months. It seems to me to contain all the requirements for the absolutely secluded life which my disappointment at the state of New Zealand induces me to adopt for the remainder of my days. Are you ready to come? ... My wife is very anxious to go and, if you and perhaps one other swell would join, we would make a model republic.

Two weeks later, he wrote again, his romantic ideals spilling onto the page:

> I do long for some partners in the Pacific where one's young men may see visions and one's old men dream dreams ... sheep and cabbages and cows and horses are companions quite as agreeable almost as intellectual and ten times as grateful as men. Let us go, my friend ... Make an island into a garden.

Rolleston did not share his romanticism. 'With regard to taking refuge elsewhere,' he replied, 'I am not prepared to give in now I am in for a fight ... I don't like either encouraging you in isolating yourself. You are exercising your sane influence for good more than you can have any idea of yourself.'

Fitz was not put off. 'It is of no use, my dear friend,' he wrote on 28 December, 'to talk to me of staying in the colony if I can get away. I am doing no good that I know of.' A friend was leaving on a visit to the Chatham Islands, 'and will take our commission to buy at once for anything up to £2000, we cannot go further ... as to myself personally, the *Press* has cleaned me out ... But we shall all go to the island ... and work and make money.'

Fanny was inspired by Fitz's enthusiasm because she felt so isolated in Karori. She was still exhausted by overwork, still wearing herself out with children, babies and housework. Fitz's salary was reduced by payments to Harman & Stevens, they were living with little or no domestic help, and the children 'have appetites which are the wonder of all and the delight of all but their father'. Even a remote island in the Pacific seemed preferable to life in Chesney Wold.

She changed her mind in January when she began to experience the familiar signs of early pregnancy; it was a relief when the owner of Pitt Island decided not to sell. This brought Fitz's final scheme of colonisation to an end, allowing him to concentrate his energies on attacking Julius Vogel and the public works policy.

Having been rebuked for writing publicly about politics, he now used more subtle means to undermine the government. Stafford was leader of the opposition, his policy to 'watch the government to ensure that the finance of the country shall be prudent and economical'. He was against further borrowing and he found an ally in Fitz who, as comptroller-general, had to approve all payments out of the treasury. Vogel saw it as 'his duty to sustain running paper warfare with the Comptroller', but Fitz had friends in the House who supported him against any attempt to weaken his authority.

The battle increased in intensity during August and September 1871 – a time when Fanny, still exhausted, was expecting the arrival of their eleventh child. After her illness in 1868, it was thought unwise for her to give birth in Karori, so she was invited to stay with friends in Wellington where their fourth daughter, Geraldine, was born on 15 September. She returned to Karori after the birth and began making tentative plans to sail for England to spend a few months with her family.

Fitz was oblivious to Fanny's distress. He had no concept of the efforts involved in cooking, washing and ironing; in giving birth and looking after children. While Fanny wore herself out in Chesney Wold, he spent long hours in his office in Wellington and socialised with friends in the evenings. Ten days after Fanny's confinement, he attended 'a very jolly dinner party' where he drank whisky toddy and sang Irish songs till midnight.

Even when he was home in Chesney Wold, he would often shut himself in his study, writing business letters, working on a history of the English exchequer, and drafting a book on political history. He wrote to Gladstone about the possibility of establishing 'a Bank for the Colony of New Zealand on the same footing as that of the Bank of England', and came up with a new idea, 'the taking of the whole Pacific islands under our protectorate'.

He wrote of this plan to Lord Lyttelton, who replied in February 1872 with a gentle reproof: 'I shall be very glad if you will write to me oftener, and tell me of your local affairs, and domestic too. Your wife wrote me a letter some time ago … I thought she might be coming home for a bit. I trust she is better.'

Five weeks later, Lyttelton wrote again, thanking Fitz for his letters, 'which are very pleasant to read for your unfailing energy and hopefulness. I must say they are a contrast in this respect to one I had from your poor wife, who I fear is much *jaded* by incessant work. I much wish she could come home for a bit.'

Fanny did not go home. There was no money to pay for her passage, but at least Fitz had reduced his debt to Harman & Stevens. By the end of 1870, he had repaid 'more than £1000 out of private means'. Five months later, he signed over his half share in the Press Company (reducing the debt by £1504). In June 1872, he handed over the premises in Cashel Street (another £650), after which the outstanding debt was calculated at £3845 – about £167,000 in today's values.

Fitz now regretted leaving the *Press*. 'If I could find any business to afford me a chance of making six or seven hundred a year,' he wrote to William Rolleston, 'I would quit the government service at once. If I had not been compelled to sell the *Press*, I might now have taken it up again and made it pay – soon at all events.'

CHAPTER THIRTY

FitzGerald's Folly

1872–1877

I am again very hard up from having built a house.

Fitz, 4 June 1874

My home as a boy was built on a point overlooking a harbour, one of the most beautiful spots and one of the finest views I have ever seen.

Otho FitzGerald

*I*n May 1872, it rained every day for two weeks in Karori, turning the settlement into a sea of mud. This persuaded Fitz and Fanny to consider a move to Wellington. Six months later (about the time Fanny became pregnant for the twelfth time), they bought seven acres of land at 'a remote and undesirable site', high on a cliff between Clyde Quay and Oriental Bay. Fitz raised a mortgage of £700 and, 'in his original fashion and with his usual enterprise', employed contractors to build 'a house for Mrs Fanny FitzGerald'. Ownership would be in Fanny's name to prevent it falling into the hands of Harman & Stevens.

Fitz designed the house, a similar building to Chesney Wold with its wooden construction, long arcaded verandahs and gabled first floor. Building work was underway in August 1873 when he wrote to his brother in Berkshire, complaining that he was still receiving bills for expenses at the *Press* ('I had one for tea passed only last week'). And with blithe disregard for his debts, he explained that 'these building societies are the most admirable institutions for enabling me to raise money on easy terms and create a property'.

'Fanny has just presented me with a *twelfth* child, a son,' he continued (referring to Edward, born on the 14th). 'I have become hardened and reckless as to these repeated calamities.' His older boys were 'growing up drinking nothing but water and abhorring smoking. They beat me in that respect for I smoke more than ever.'

The eldest boy, Willy, had now left home. After recovering from rheumatic fever, he had been employed as private secretary to Henry Sewell, the newly appointed minister of justice (it was, admitted Fitz, 'kind of Sewell considering how I pitched into him'). When Sewell resigned in October 1871, Willy moved to Auckland to work as secretary to the chief justice, Sir George Arney. And when Arney administered the colony between the departure of one governor in March 1873 and the arrival of another three months later, Willy acted as his aide-de-camp and, according to Fitz, 'lived like a swell at Government House'.

Four years after the accident, Willy's leg had still not healed, despite an operation in early 1873. There was an 'open abscess' where the wood had pierced the flesh; the bone was infected too. 'I confess,' Arney wrote to Fanny nine months after he and Willy returned to Auckland, 'that I have long looked with sorrow upon the traces of suffering which William, in spite of all his amiable self-negation, has manifested … He is looking weak and delicate, is patient and good (as it seems to me) almost beyond patience.'

…

Fifty-five years old now, Fitz was calming down. He no longer complained of heart trouble, lung disease or rheumatism, although his eyes had been troubling him 'for the first time in 20 years'. His efforts to give up smoking had failed and he had 'long since' lost his singing voice. He was still gloomy about the political situation. 'The colony is at present rolling in wealth and borrowed money,' he wrote, 'and the idiots think it is going to last – a thing obviously impossible.'

In April 1874, he and his family moved into their new home, which Fitz named Clyde Cliff. It was, he told Lucius, 'built on a cliff overlooking the harbour and town of Wellington, a most magnificent panoramic view. And if I live a few years longer, I shall have paid off the mortgage on it and shall have a valuable property behind me.' But it had been expensive to build and he was 'again very hard up'.

Clyde Cliff was a large house, with five rooms and a kitchen on the ground floor and seven bedrooms above. It was provided with all modern conveniences: running water in the kitchen and bathroom, gas points in all rooms, and a gas stove in the kitchen. The bathroom had a geyser to heat water for the bathtub, and the separate WC boasted a toilet seat of polished kauri.

There were no neighbours in this remote spot and Fitz was 'thought quite mad to build in such a place'. The house soon became known as 'FitzGerald's folly', not only because of its distance from town, but also because of its exposed position, battered by the high winds for which Wellington was famous. Some of the acreage consisted of the steeply sloping cliff; the rest Fitz laid out in gardens.

A large lawn sloped towards the cliff and a narrow path led downhill to Oriental Bay. Every morning before breakfast, the FitzGerald boys ran down

Amy, photographed shortly before her marriage to W.H. (Willie) Levin in May 1876.

Private collection

Willie Levin, photographed by Webster Bros in London in December 1876. He was described by Amy as 'quite one of the best men who ever lived, good in every way and to everyone'.

Private collection

Otho 'endeavoured to make these meetings as frequent as possible. Unfortunately she became engaged to a prominent merchant so my means of revenue came to an end.'

This prominent merchant was William Hort Levin – Willie Levin – the richest young man in Wellington. His father, Nathaniel Levin, had established the merchant house of Levin & Co and married a daughter of Abraham Hort, the first rabbi in New Zealand. In 1869, Nathaniel was appointed to the Legislative Council (the first Jew to sit in the New Zealand parliament), by which time Willie had taken over the family firm, his wealth increasing 'with phenomenal rapidity'.

Willie and Amy were introduced by his aunt, Margaret Bell (another daughter of Abraham Hort), and their engagement was announced in October 1875. The family in Clyde Cliff had mixed feelings. 'We had a very pleasant visit from Mrs FitzGerald,' wrote a family friend on 26 October:

> and she spoke her feelings very freely. She is satisfied and believes Amy will be happy but she is not at all *elated* nor much pleased at being repeatedly told how charming the match is *because* WL is so

rich! She says Amy's family and connections are rich in things no money can buy and that she can't feel it any honour for a FitzGerald to become a Levin ... Some of the brothers do not at all admire the connection, nor relish having a Jew for a brother-in-law!

In the past, Fitz had used the word as a term of denigration (Edward Stevens was 'a thorough Jew', Julius Vogel 'a clever little Jew') but he and Fanny were soon won over by Willie's intelligence and charm. Amy's brothers took a little longer – until Willie came up with an ideal sweetener for boys whose food was rationed for economy:

> In the town there was a famous pastrycook whose goods were very much sought after. One day our future brother-in-law suggested that we should pay a visit to this pastrycook and consume as much as we could possibly eat, at his expense. We were delighted to be given this opportunity of showing our gastronomic ability and made up our minds to enter into the undertaking thoroughly. A meeting was called, a leader appointed and it was arranged what each one was allowed to eat. Buns and all such things as would have quickly satisfied our appetite was taboo and a careful plan was carried out ... I have not much recollection of what it all cost, but I know we all did full justice to the undertaking.

Fanny gave birth to their thirteenth and last child in February 1876, a

'Pendennis', Tinakori Road, Wellington, the house built by Willie Levin shortly before his marriage.

Private collection

daughter named Mabel. In March, after the death of the life tenant in County Louth, Harman & Stevens filed their claim to Fitz's inheritance. In April, Willie Levin converted to the Anglican Church and, on 20 May, he and Amy were married in St Peter's church in Wellington.

Willie's parents were absent in London but the wedding was still a major occasion, 'reflecting the social standing of both families'. After a ceremony conducted by the bishop, Willie took his bride to his new house in Tinakori Road. A large property with extensive grounds, it had been designed to his specifications, with a circular window on the second floor providing a clear view of his shipping in the harbour.

...

A few days after the wedding, news arrived that Lord Lyttelton (who suffered from chronic depression) had committed suicide by throwing himself over the banisters of his house in London. The news came as a shock; Fitz had been aware of Lyttelton's depressive nature, but had never imagined it would end in tragedy.

First Godley, then Selfe, now Lord Lyttelton; the old guard of the Canterbury Association was slipping away. And it was not just the association. A bill was passed in 1875 to abolish the provinces, including Canterbury which had absorbed so much of Fitz's adult life. With the advent of steamships and railways, with faster transport and communications, there was less need for the provinces to govern themselves and a greater need for centralisation.

Fitz had foreseen this development. 'One thing is quite obvious,' he wrote as early as 1856, 'the colony is over-governed enormously. The general or the provincial governments must go, the question is which.' In 1864, he prophesied that superintendents would soon be consigned to history; three years later, he predicted that the provinces would be abolished 'in a very short time'. In the event, it had taken another nine years; but when the Act came into force on 1 November 1876, superintendents and provincial councils were swept away, replaced by a network of county councils and boroughs.

By mid-November Fitz was in Christchurch, attending a conference to coordinate provincial railways into a general system for the entire colony. On the 22nd, he was guest of honour when William Rolleston, the outgoing superintendent, laid the foundation stone of a new railway station. Fitz gave an entertaining speech, remembering – to much laughter – the years when he was known 'as the one bitter and remorseless enemy of all railway progress'.

He was still in Christchurch when Amy and her husband embarked on a steamship for San Francisco, with plans to travel overland across America and spend several months with Willie's parents in London. As the ship built up steam, 'the vessels at the wharf were gay with bunting and a large number of friends of Mr and Mrs Levin gathered on the wharf to wish the pair a pleasant journey and a safe and speedy return'.

Six months later a telegram from London was delivered to Clyde Cliff. A cable link from New Zealand to Sydney, and thence to London by relay, had opened in February 1876 – a watershed in speed of communication. When Fitz and Fanny first arrived in the colony, it took months for news to arrive from England; now messages could be received in a matter of hours. And joyful news it was too: Amy had given birth to their first grandchild.

Amy and Willie returned home in December with news of the family in England. 'Amy says you suffer from deafness,' Fitz wrote to Lucius. 'We are both getting old now. I was 60 last March. But I can still do a good day's hard work and a bit of digging in the garden to boot.' And Fanny was singing 'as well as ever; she is out tonight at a practising for a concert, to which she trudges through the mud about two miles every night'.

…

In his spare time, Fitz drafted bills for the government, a task for which he was sometimes paid. This came to an end in October 1876 when he was working on a bill for Donald McLean. After 'a long and animated discussion' in the House about the need to reduce expenditure, mention was made of 'the bonus of £250 to Mr FitzGerald for drafting bills'. One member commented that this 'looked much like bribery'; another wanted it reduced to a nominal sum of £5. This was rejected, so Fitz kept the money – but he felt aggrieved. 'I have always been most willing to do such work without pay,' he wrote to McLean, 'so long as I find time to do it … But as exception is taken to the *principle* of my being paid for work outside of my department, I must decline altogether.'

The abolition of the provinces extended the work of the comptroller's office; and in late 1876, the civil service moved into a new building constructed on reclaimed land on the waterfront. It was an enormous structure, built to resemble an Italian palace and intended to symbolise the growing importance of central government. The offices were equipped with cast-iron fireplaces and lined with kauri panelling.

Despite the greater comfort of his new surroundings, Fitz was sad to leave the parliament buildings where he had rubbed shoulders with politicians every day. He was often seen at his old haunt, which was just a short walk from his new office – and where the sparse figure of his old enemy, Sir George Grey, was now in evidence.

Grey had returned to New Zealand in 1871, and had entered the House four years later to fight the abolition of the provinces. As effective leader of the liberal opposition, he had taken a populist approach to politics, prompting Fitz to complain that he was 'a political delusion, stumping the colony making speeches which read to me like those of a child or an idiot'. In October 1877 – much to Fitz's disgust – Grey took the helm as premier of a liberal ministry.

...

On 15 January 1878, Fitz arrived in Christchurch on official business. Ten days later, he boarded the coach for Hokitika. He had visited the West Coast several times to report on the accounts, but this was the first time he made the journey over the mountains.

The coach was drawn by five horses, the design unchanged from the coaches he had taken up the Waimakariri in 1865. Leaving at three in the morning, they set off in darkness towards the Southern Alps. The horses were changed at the foothills and passengers took to their feet as the road climbed upwards. The horses were changed again at Porters Pass, after which the coach travelled across high tussock grasslands to the junction of the Bealey and Waimakariri rivers, where a small hotel had been built for the accommodation of travellers.

Next morning, the coach set off at first light for the most dangerous part of the journey – the crossing of the ice-cold waters of the Waimakariri. The horses were immersed up to their flanks and the wheels of the coach were under water as they lurched and bumped over the boulders on the river bed. The coach then travelled up the Bealey valley, crossing the river several times and climbing through bush with glimpses of mountains and waterfalls. 'No words,' wrote Fitz, 'can describe the grandeur of the scenery.'

The road now became tortuous, carved into the side of a precipice. Again the passengers had to walk as the coach negotiated narrow ledges cut into the solid rock. Having crossed the highest point at Arthur's Pass, the road zigzagged down the Otira Gorge for almost 2000 feet, 'with such sharp turns that at several corners the leaders' feet are within a yard of the edge; they curve round and round like circus horses'.

After descending through a forest 'of dense and lofty trees' to the Tasman Sea, the coach drove along a sandy beach to Hokitika, where Fitz was met by his brother Gerard, who had been working here as resident magistrate since 1865. After thirteen years on the goldfields, Gerard – a popular man in Hokitika – was out of a job, having indulged (as Fitz told Lucius) 'in the old digger's trick of getting drunk for a week at a time … although the gold diggers would rather have his decisions drunk than another man sober'.

PART VI

Fitz grows old

CHAPTER THIRTY-ONE

An Afflicted Family

1878–1884

I've stood beside the bed
Where frail youth lay dying,
And seen hot tears shed,
And heard sad friends sighing.

Fitz, 'The Flower', July 1888

hese were boom years in New Zealand, and Fitz's opposition to the public works policy had faded. 'We still continue in a state of wonderful prosperity,' he wrote four months after his return from Hokitika:

> and shall as long as we can get loans. And really none of the money is wasted, it all goes into railroads, roads, telegraphs, etc … We have over 1000 miles of railways and telegraphs to every smallest village, with English news rarely more than two or three days old. Telephones everywhere.

But as the winter of 1878 arrived in Wellington, and cold winds battered the house on the clifftop, his spirits began to sink. His financial situation was difficult ('an awful trial for me with so many pulling at the purse strings and old debts weighing me down'), and the news from Canterbury was depressing for a man who had owned – and lost – large tracts of land in the province ('I was hearing only yesterday of my old workmen on the station, one worth £15,000, another £20,000, another man £50,000. There are scores of labouring men in Canterbury who have done as well. Land they bought for £3 an acre is worth £30 now').

He and Fanny had been lucky with their children: their brood of thirteen was thriving. Fitz had boasted of their good health, writing before Willy's accident that 'they have never one of them, except Amy, taken a drop of medicine in their lives'. Now his elder sons were 'just going off in the world'.

Willy, Fitz and Fanny's first-born son, a young man of 'singularly sweet temper and genial, pleasant manners'.

Private collection

Robert, 'now in charge of a bank himself', photographed shortly before his accident on the rugby field in 1878.

Private collection

Gerald, the hyperactive toddler who grew into a successful surveyor and engineer – as well as a bit of a dandy.

Private collection

Lyttelton, the 'rather peculiar boy ... with a remarkable affection for plants and flowers', who grew up to exchange the law for the church.

Private collection

Maurice, Fanny's favourite son, described by his sister as 'very handsome; his expression was really beautiful'.

Private collection

Evangeline (Eva), 'a popular girl with many friends', photographed shortly before her marriage in 1885.

Private collection

Selwyn, named after his godfather, Bishop Selwyn, and known to his siblings as 'the Primate'.

Private collection

Otho. 'His innocence and simplicity,' wrote his father, 'are most touching.'

Private collection

Geraldine, born in Wellington in September 1871, photographed as a chubby-faced toddler.

Private collection

Geraldine, Fanny's devoted companion after Fitz's death. She and her mother became a familiar sight in Wellington, 'driving around town in the family gig'.

Private collection

Edward, born in Karori in August 1873, a boy whose 'heart was in horses and boats'.

Private collection

Edward in military uniform, photographed shortly before sailing for South Africa and the Boer War, January 1900.

Private collection

Willy had returned from Auckland and, after qualifying as a lawyer, had made 'a brilliant start', earning 'very nearly £700 in his first year'. Robert worked for the Bank of New Zealand and was in line for early promotion ('now in charge of a bank himself').

A tall young man of 23, Robert had taken to rugby with enthusiasm, playing for the Wellington Club in matches against Dunedin and Wanganui. Rugby was a rough game – one newspaper referred to 'excessive violence'; another to 'packed scrummages, with kicking and punting and mauls in goals, and half-points scored for force-downs'. On 6 July 1878, Robert was injured in the scrum, 'sustaining bad bruises on the chest and other injuries'. Undaunted, he finished the match, after which he 'indulged in a cold bath while greatly heated by his exertions in the game'. As a result, according to the *Evening Post*, 'he caught a violent cold which speedily developed into acute inflammation of both lungs'. On the evening of 15 July, he suffered 'an obstruction of circulation caused by a clot of blood and died painlessly within a few moments'.

Clyde Cliff was a house filled with the sound of children's voices and young men's laughter. Now it fell silent. One day, Robert was a strong, athletic young man enjoying his prowess on the rugby field; eleven days later, his father and brothers stood in the Bolton Street cemetery for the first burial in the FitzGerald family plot. It was not the custom for women and children to attend funerals, so Fanny stayed home with her daughters and younger sons, with the curtains closed to keep out the light.

On 6 September, the family did their best to celebrate Otho's tenth birthday. 'I thought how nice it would be to have a salute fired for the special occasion,' Otho wrote in his memoirs:

> So I wrote to the Colonel [of the armed constabulary] and ... asked
> if he could send a member of the force up to my home with a gun
> to fire a salute in honour of the event. He quite entered into the
> solemnity of the occasion and the soldier arrived and honoured me
> with a salute.

In October, Fitz was appointed auditor-general (in addition to his role as comptroller) at an increased salary of £1000 a year. In November, Amy gave birth to a second child. On the last day of the year, Willy was married in New Plymouth. His bride was Ella Smith, daughter of the commissioner of crown lands in Taranaki. She was suffering from tuberculosis, and Willy brought her home to Clyde Cliff and into Fanny's care.

On 15 March 1879, the four elder boys – all members of the volunteer fire brigade – were called into action when a major fire broke out in the city.

As they helped to battle the flames, the family in Clyde Cliff gathered in the garden. From their vantage point on the clifftop they watched the walls of fire sweep through the streets; as night fell, the embers glowed red in the darkness.

Four months later, Sir George Grey's ministry was defeated. His majority was too small and his ministers had bickered among themselves ('A more disconnected, disunited, ill-assorted party ... never sat within this House before'). A general election was held in September, and there were celebrations in Clyde Cliff when Willie Levin was elected to parliament.

In October, Fanny organised a concert 'in aid of St Mark's Organ Fund'. On 6 December, Amy and Willie's third child was born. And on New Year's Eve, Fitz and Fanny raised their glasses at midnight to toast the start of a new decade.

...

In April 1880, their servant, Mrs Williams, began to feel unwell. She was running a fever, and complained of a sore throat and pain in swallowing. In early May, Eva and Selwyn showed the same symptoms. 'The FitzGeralds have diphtheria in the house,' wrote Edward Chudleigh when he arrived in the city on 14 May. 'Selwyn and Eva are both ill and Mrs Williams is fast coming to an end. What an afflicted family they are.'

Fanny nursed her children for days without sleep, watching them struggle for breath as the leathery membranes formed in their throats. Eva survived the disease, but fifteen-year-old Selwyn suffered a distressing few days – gasping for breath, his neck swollen, his face turning increasingly blue – before he died on 16 May. Two days later, Fitz and his sons returned to the Bolton Street cemetery to bury him alongside his elder brother.

In June, thirteen-year-old Katie complained of fever and a sore throat. For ten days, she suffered the same distressing symptoms as her brother. She died on the 29th, and Fitz stood by the graveside for a third time as his daughter joined her brothers in the earth. 'Poor FitzGeralds,' wrote Chudleigh when he heard the news, 'they are sore afflicted.'

Four weeks later, Fitz and Fanny's youngest child, five-year-old Mabel, began to suffer from headaches and a stiff neck. A rash appeared on her body, and she shrank from the light. The doctor diagnosed meningitis. Once again Fanny sat by the bedside of a sick child; already exhausted by the deaths of two of her children, she stayed up every night for three weeks. And after Mabel died on 21 August, Fitz made a fourth journey to the cemetery.

On 3 September, he received a letter from John Hall (now a successful politician who had succeeded Sir George Grey as premier), asking him, 'with a view to assisting the enquiry by the Public Accounts Committee into the system of keeping and auditing the public accounts of the colony, to proceed to Australia and make a full investigation of the systems in force there and report thereon to the government'.

Four days later, Fitz boarded the steamer for Sydney, taking nineteen-year-old Maurice with him to act as his secretary. He would be away for almost four months. Fanny was left to grieve alone.

…

Fitz and Maurice spent three weeks in Sydney (New South Wales), two weeks in Brisbane (Queensland), four weeks in Melbourne (Victoria), four weeks in Adelaide (South Australia) and eight days in Hobart (Tasmania). They embarked for New Zealand on 15 December. The first stage of the voyage home was spent in the teeth of a southwest gale and the steamer struggled through heavy seas. After stops in Bluff, Dunedin and Lyttelton, they arrived in Wellington on 21 December, in time for a bleak family Christmas at Clyde Cliff.

Fitz prepared his report during the next few months; he described the accounting systems used in the five Australian colonies, explained the practices used in England (obtained from the House of Commons) and other European countries, and compared them with those used in New Zealand. When the report was presented to the general assembly in June 1881, Hall congratulated him 'for the readiness with which you undertook the arduous duty … and for the ability with which you have performed it'. The report would, he wrote, 'be long recognised as one of great value upon a subject which, though necessarily technical, is really of much interest'.

All this hard work had served to keep Fitz busy, to temper his grief at the loss of his children. At the same time, his economic confidence was shattered. The colony had entered a recession in 1879; by 1881 this had turned into a depression that would last for sixteen years. John Hall's government had cut civil service salaries, initially by ten per cent, and the financial outlook was gloomy.

Family news was no better. Maurice – Fanny's favourite child, the best looking of the FitzGerald brood, 'a truly beautiful young man' – was diagnosed with tuberculosis shortly after returning from Australia. Willy's wife Ella died in Clyde Cliff in March 1881. Willy himself was diagnosed with Bright's disease, a chronic condition caused, it was said, by poison from the wound in his leg leaking into his kidneys. The bone was necrotic; the doctors talked of amputation.

As well as running a busy legal practice, Willy edited the New Zealand Law Reports ('recording all the chief decisions of the Supreme Court and Court of Appeal'). He spent his spare time on the water: he was always photographed sitting down with a stick in his hand, but he could still handle boats and canoes. A member of the Star Boating Club, he competed in races and regattas and, on weekends and holidays, 'in his beloved canoe, took many a long and adventurous cruise about the coast and on the rivers and lakes of this island'.

News of the death of William Moorhouse in September led Fitz's mind back to the early years of the *Press*. His attitude to his old enemy had softened over the years ('he has so many good points that one not only likes him but can see why others do so too'), but it still rankled that Moorhouse was fêted for his tunnel while Fitz's contribution to the province of Canterbury – the maintenance of high land prices – had, as he put it, filled the coffers with more than a million pounds. 'One who creates wealth,' he huffed, 'has a little more claim on his country than one who spends it very badly.'

In April 1882, Willy married Frances Featherston. Two months later, when Gerald (now working as a civil engineer on the Blenheim railway), married Esther Budge, Fanny was making plans to take Maurice to a sanatorium in England. 'My hands are more than full,' she wrote, 'and I fear I have to go north with Maurice.'

Fanny and Maurice embarked on the clipper *Lady Jocelyn* on 22 February 1883 – four days after Willy's first child was born. They were travelling with John Hall and his family, as well as the first cargo of frozen produce to be despatched from the North Island ('5704 carcasses of mutton, 352 quarters of beef, 10 fish, 326 ducks, and three tubs of butter'). Hall had resigned as premier in 1882 and, exhausted by two and a half years in office, was returning to England for a rest.

It was not a peaceful voyage; the first leg to Cape Horn was particularly rough. As Hall wrote in his diary on 4 March, 'wretched night, no sleep, ship knocking about dreadfully'. He abandoned his swing bed, having been 'pitched to the ceiling', and tried to sleep on the floor. For twelve days, the ship rolled through the waves, 'labouring heavily, lurching to top of lee bulwarks'. On the 13th, a heavy sea broke over the main deck, sending a 'large body of water down main hatch … never saw such wind and sea, and hope never to see the like again'.

There were other difficulties, too. Water for washing was reduced to two pints a day per passenger, the vegetables in the storeroom began to rot – the stench permeating the ship until they were thrown overboard – and on one memorable evening, Hall killed a rat in his wife's cabin.

Fanny played down these dramas, merely commenting that Maurice 'received little benefit' from the voyage 'because of drawbacks'. According to the London correspondent of a New Zealand newspaper, the tedium of the journey 'was beguiled by dancing, concerts, and similar amusements, a lady named Mrs FitzGerald affording special pleasure by her pianoforte playing'. And the long voyage – 110 days – gave Fanny and Hall plenty of time to forge a friendship.

The ship arrived in the English Channel to a dense fog that lasted for days. 'We could hardly see a couple of ship's lengths,' wrote Hall on 4 June. 'Foghorns going all day.' Four days later, the ship 'had most narrow escape from running down schooner in very thick fog, only distinguishable when almost under bowsprit'.

The *Lady Jocelyn* docked in London on 13 June. Fanny and Maurice spent a few days with her brother John, who made them 'most comfortable' in his house in Notting Hill, before travelling by train to the sanatorium in Bournemouth where the treatment was, according to Fanny, '*very expensive*'.

Maurice soon won over the doctors. 'I can quite understand your great anxiety about your son,' wrote Dr Dobbs:

> He is a young man of quite exceptional charms, even to a stranger.
> I do not think his case hopeless and I do not think you could
> have done better than bring him to England, whatever may be
> the ultimate result. I think the sea voyage *home* will very likely do
> as much for him as anything and after the disease has received its
> appropriate remedial treatment here.

But when he examined the sputum under a microscope, the doctor thought 'worse of Maurice than he did at first'. It was agreed that he should remain in the sanatorium for a month, so Fanny returned to London alone. She attended a party given by Gladstone's wife, and 'greatly enjoyed' a concert conducted by Hans Richter. She visited Charlotte Godley in her house in Gloucester Place, and spent an evening with Fitz's old flame, Rose Paynter, now Lady Graves Sawle.

By 4 July, she was in Winslade, staying with Fitz's brother Richard, who (enriched by the Irish estates) was living in style with a butler, housekeeper, footman and three housemaids. 'There are such lovely paintings in the house,' wrote Fanny, 'it is such a pretty rectory.' At dinner one evening, she was seated next to an admiral who 'gave me a lecture about the National Debt of New Zealand'.

On 13 August, Maurice was considered well enough to join his mother in Weston-super-Mare, after which they stayed with friends in Wiltshire where, in Fanny's words, Maurice 'got rapidly ill … great pain, blood spitting and spasms'. On the 18th, they 'hurried' to John Draper's house in London. 'I can only *trust* as I have always done,' Fanny wrote to John Hall, 'and try to keep up both his spirits and mine.' Although she made an effort to see friends in London ('I am engaged every day this week … and appoint four people per day to call'), not everyone understood her difficulties ('I got quite an *angry* letter from Sir Henry Thring … blaming me for not writing to him at once on arriving, that he might show us due attentions'). Meanwhile, 'appealing letters' arrived every day, 'all begging us to visit them. It is very kind but distracting.'

Fanny could not afford further treatment at the sanatorium, so she booked cabins for the voyage home. On 1 September, Maurice 'quite suddenly' began to cough up blood. 'He has broken a blood vessel,' she told John Hall on the 5th. 'Last night he was very bad and has lost much blood. It is quite inexplicable and uncalled for this attack. It is so unfortunate. We have paid half our passages … and I really don't know if he can go.'

For three days, she never left her son's bedside. The haemorrhage slowed but Maurice was allowed neither to speak nor to cough. 'Dr Bruce says he must not think of moving probably till the end of next week,' she wrote again to John Hall. 'While there is the slightest tinge of colour, it might bring on a heavy attack and kill him very quickly. It is very hard on them in NZ to write such bad news and I get such terribly anxious letters from Mr FG.'

On 11 October, when Maurice was considered well enough to travel, they boarded the iron sailing ship *Oamaru* bound for Lyttelton. It was another long and dramatic voyage. Shortly after leaving Gravesend, the ship encountered heavy winds and put in to Torbay for shelter. Two months later, in 'a fierce gale' that began on 12 December, the main deck was flooded, the upper rigging was torn away and a lifeboat smashed to pieces. Fanny and Maurice celebrated Christmas in the cuddy and arrived in Lyttelton on 12 January 1884.

After two nights with friends in Christchurch, they embarked for Wellington. The steamer encountered 'a strong northerly gale with heavy seas, the ship labouring heavily throughout'. A telegram had notified Fitz of their arrival and, when the steamer docked at midday on the 15th, he was on the wharf to meet them, 'rejoiced' at seeing his wife and son again after an absence of eleven months.

CHAPTER THIRTY-TWO

The Flash of a Meteor

1884–1888

You know what a lovely and loving boy he was … He was so grieved for
me. He only lived for me.
Fanny, 19 July 1886

This is the seventh child the FitzGeralds have buried. How very sad.
Sir John Hall, 4 June 1888

itz had, according to Fanny, been 'very wicked while I was away'.
Sixty-five years old, he had enjoyed himself socially; but he had
also spent time musing on old age and rereading old letters, including some
from Walter Savage Landor. 'I was only a day or two [ago],' he wrote to Alfred
Domett (premier during the 1862 parliament), 'reading a pile of letters from
that delightful old pagan, written 30 or 40 years ago. How alternatively young
and sad they made me feel. His friendship when I was young knit me to the
age then passing away.'

Willy had been invited to stand for parliament during Fanny's absence,
but ('like a boy of sense') had declined. Instead he had been elected to the
Wellington City Council. And Eva ('a popular girl with many friends') was
'walking out' with James Poole Brandon, a dapper, good-looking civil servant
and – it would prove – a rather feckless young man. Their engagement was
announced in April.

Willie Levin resigned from parliament in March, following an attack
of rheumatic fever. Three months later, he and Amy embarked on a luxury
steamship for a voyage to Australia 'for the healing effects of the sea air'. Amy's
brother Lyttelton travelled with them. Having completed his articles in Willy's
legal practice, he was now working as a lawyer in the small town of Bulls near
Wanganui. He disliked his new profession; the voyage gave him time to think
and, in late October, he sailed for Melbourne to train for the priesthood.

Maurice's health had improved after his return to Wellington (Fanny attributed his recovery to 'some (quack) medicine at 30/- a bottle I got from England'). By the end of the year, he was compiling Hansard records of parliamentary debates for the first thirteen years of the New Zealand parliament. An official Hansard was started in 1867, and Fitz suggested that the records be backdated to the first parliament in 1854. He also suggested that Maurice undertake the work, 'not seeking any remuneration, but on the understanding that when he finished the work the government should give him such acknowledgement as they deemed suitable'.

The premier agreed but the press was unhappy. 'We believe we are not wrong in asserting that this young gentleman is a son of the Comptroller-General,' wrote a journalist on the *Evening Post*, 'that he is a mere youth without any literary or political experience, and that his delicate health has for some time precluded any active pursuits. Of course such an appointment is simply a sham.'

The appointment was not a sham; Maurice had learnt much from his father during their four-month visit to Australia. He started work in November 1884, consulting newspaper reports and official journals, and writing to every available member of the House asking for memoirs and notes of speeches. He

View from the garden at Clyde Cliff, overlooking the city of Wellington, late 1880s. Fitz is on the right. His efforts to grow vegetation after the reclamation works have clearly been successful. Photograph by Arthur Thomas Bothamley.

Alexander Turnbull Library, Wellington (F-62586-1/2)

then reconstructed the debates in the form of Hansard – and since these years coincided almost exactly with Fitz's parliamentary career, he was able to enjoy his father's high-flown oratory. He suffered a setback in the summer. 'Maurice is getting *much worse* after getting much better,' Fanny wrote in January. 'I fear he must give up Hansard. If I were rich, I should send him home by direct steamer to Dr Dobbs.' But Maurice persevered with his work, treating the project almost as a race against time.

While Maurice buried himself in parliamentary papers, the house trembled as engineers blasted the rock on which Clyde Cliff was built, steepening the cliff above Oriental Bay. Reclamation works had been underway since 1883 and the engineers had now reached the western side of the harbour. Fitz was paid for the stone removed from his cliff, which was reused for the reclamation. When the work was finished, he threw topsoil and seeds down the newly sculpted rock, encouraging the vegetation to take root and grow.

On 8 February 1885, Eva married James Brandon and moved into his house in Thorndon Quay. She was three months pregnant, and gave birth to a full-term baby on 24 August. A child conceived out of wedlock was a social stigma in these strait-laced times: it was clear that James Brandon was no Willie Levin.

Early the following year, when Fitz's brother Gerard was appointed editor of the *Timaru Herald*, his wife Jane spent several weeks in Clyde Cliff while Gerard found accommodation in Timaru. Fitz thought her bossy, and wrote unkindly that she was 'a plain-looking woman who keeps Gerard in very good order'.

On 11 April 1886, Jane boarded the *Taiaroa* for the voyage south to Timaru. That night, the steamer was wrecked near Kaikoura and most of the passengers drowned; Jane's body was found washed up on a beach a few days later. Gerard was too distressed to make arrangements, so she was brought to the Bolton Street cemetery and buried alongside Fitz and Fanny's children.

A few weeks later, Maurice was told by the doctor that 'the disease has stopped, you may live for years and it is quite *improbable* you can have any great bleeding from the old lung'. Fanny was overjoyed. 'He was so wonderfully well,' she wrote. 'He was taking castor syrup and port wine, both bloodmakers.'

On 21 June, she saw a spot of blood on his pillow. 'You had better not take the syrup and wine,' she said.

'No matter,' he replied.

Next day, there was more bleeding and, at four o'clock in the morning on the 23rd, Maurice coughed up more than a pint of blood. 'He thought it must be the new lung,' wrote Fanny, 'but *no*, and he had six bad bleedings from *old lung* and it choked him up.' For two weeks, she remained at his bedside, refusing to leave his room, refusing to sleep:

> He suffered very much but at last died quietly. I saw his appealing lovely blue eyes before me and heard him saying 'Oh! Mater, it is very hard.' No sleep – panting, coughing – and so grateful, patient, thankful … He was so wise. And on Thursday night, he talked in such a manner, he made even Dr Fell weep.

Fanny's favourite son died on the morning of 10 July. The following afternoon, his father and brothers made the familiar journey to the Bolton Street cemetery. 'The praises of his contemporaries follow him,' wrote one of the newspapers, 'poor young gentleman, to his early grave.'

Maurice had completed his work on Hansard: the first four volumes were published in 1885; the fifth and final volume was finished in March 1886. Eight days after the funeral, Fitz watched from the gallery as one of his friends, Robert Stout, presented the final volume to parliament. 'When he undertook the work,' Stout told the House:

> Mr Maurice FitzGerald … was suffering from the illness which has lately cost him his life … not only did he perform the work ably and well, but he was in fact one of our young colonials who took intense interest in the early history of the colony … the colony has lost in him one of its most promising sons.

Sir George Grey (still in parliament at the age of 74) was not concentrating. 'Do I understand he is dead?' he asked.

'Yes,' replied Stout.

'Then,' said Grey, 'it might be a proper thing to erect a tombstone to his memory, with an inscription showing that this was the last work of his life.'

On the same afternoon, Fanny poured out her heart to a friend: 'You know what a lovely and loving boy he was. He was as firm as a rock and as patient as an angel … He was so grieved for me. He only lived for me … My life is empty now.' And she wrote to John Hall: 'After six years constant attention to him, you can guess *what the blank is.*'

Fitz watched Fanny grieve for her son. He described her distress in his chapter of a romantic novel which he wrote at about this time:

> She had seen the roses fade from the cheek of her lovely boy, her most fondly cherished, and weeks and months as they rolled along still told the fearful truth, that the cold clammy hand of death had sat its seat upon his brow. He lingered long but he died at last … and the

graves where the roses bloom in summer tell how fondly the inmates of these narrow houses were loved on earth. They had all gone, one by one.

...

Meanwhile, Amy was confined to bed in Tinakori Road with suspected tuberculosis. 'Amy is very poorly,' Fanny wrote nine days after Maurice's death. 'I have to go there every day.' And Willy's health was in terminal decline. 'He told me in the best of voices,' wrote Edward Chudleigh when he dined with him in August 1885, 'that he was dying with no possible hope of recovery of Bright's Disease ... This man is a hero ... He makes no long faces but goes through his duty brightly.'

In May 1888, Willy showed 'signs of haemorrhage in the lungs, from which moment his case was regarded as hopeless'. At midday on 2 June, he slipped into a coma. He died six hours later, leaving a widow and three children, the youngest less than two years old.

One obituary recalled the 'cheery smile, the pleasant honest voice of the light-hearted, wise-headed, loyal, straightforward Willy of many friends'; another referred to his 'singularly sweet temper and genial, pleasant manners'. *The Star* (formerly the *Lyttelton Times*) referred to the sense of loss in Clyde Cliff:

> Great sympathy is felt here for his parents. This is by no means the first loss of the kind suffered by Mr and Mrs FitzGerald. Their afflictions have been many and this, the latest, is not only peculiarly keen in itself but comes cruelly soon after the death of Mr Maurice FitzGerald, a bright and promising young man.

Five hundred mourners attended Willy's funeral on 4 June. 'This is the seventh child the FitzGeralds have buried,' John Hall wrote in his diary that night. 'How very sad.'

...

During these years of loss, Fitz channelled his grief into intellectual pursuits. He wrote articles on such disparate subjects as metaphysics (the possibility of a fourth dimension), the disputed authorship of Shakespeare's plays, and a reconciliation of evolutionary theory with the book of Genesis ('to show the harmony between the doctrine of evolution and the scriptural account of the Creation'). He gave lectures on art and architecture, the benefits of physical fitness, and – of course – politics.

From the Tory attitudes of his youth, his political sympathies were moving to the left, towards a kind of socialism. He had read the works of Marx and

Engels, and in a lecture in 1882 on 'the possible future developments of governments in free states', he described the differences between capitalism (which he referred to as 'competition') and communism:

> The doctrine of competition is based on the belief that the main-spring of human action is self-interest; communism, in the faith that it is, or ought to be, the subordination of self-interest to the sense of human brotherhood … The great question for the future is, in what way and to what extent can the State encourage and stimulate the movement by which working men may become shareholders in industrial enterprises, and so become the recipients both of wages and profits.

The answer was a redistribution of wealth:

> These colonies of our own Empire, which have grown up as if by an enchanter's wand on the shores of the Pacific … stand in a position peculiarly fitted for the attempt. Tradition and precedent, and old world forms and prejudices, and a superstitious reverence for private over public rights, have not yet interwoven round us their inextricable web. The memory, though yearly growing fainter, still lingers amongst us, of those early days in these settlements, when a community of toil, and an almost equality of wealth, bound us all, class and class together, in a strong community of feeling and interest.

In 1886, the London Chamber of Commerce offered a prize of £50 for the best essay 'formulating a practical working plan for the federation of the colonies and the mother-country'. The maximum length was 75 pages of foolscap – of which Fitz took full advantage. Using his experience of drafting bills for parliament, he wrote his essay in the form of a statute, 'an Act for the Reform of the Imperial Parliament, and for providing for the Representation of the Colonies therein'. 'It seems to me,' he explained in a letter to Gladstone, 'that the future of the British Empire depends on two things – (1) winning the loyalty of Ireland (2) retaining that of the colonies. The second point is the subject of my essay.'

Fitz was awarded second prize. The five best essays were published in a book, *England and Her Colonies*, a copy of which arrived in Wellington at the same time as another book published in London. *New Zealand Statesmen and Rulers*, written by William Gisborne (a civil servant and politician who had retired to England), comprised a series of perceptive portraits of New Zealand politicians. Gisborne described Fitz as:

No ordinary man. He wrote very well, and his speeches were those of a real orator. He was at the same time a good debater, and he had considerable power of humour and pathos. His mind was imbued with large principles, and was richly stored with information of various kinds. A thorough Irish gentleman, he was, like his countrymen, quick, impulsive, witty, and winning in manner and conversation. There were no rising statesmen of the day in New Zealand of whom greater expectations were formed.

So far, so good. But, Gisborne continued:

The pity of it is that those expectations were not fulfilled. In politics Mr FitzGerald has been a brilliant failure; his parliamentary career has been the flash of a meteor – dazzling for the moment, but leaving no lasting trace behind … He would not give, and he could not command, confidence … He was rash, impetuous, and inattentive to good advice; he had too much faith in himself and too little in others … and, especially, he never possessed in adequate measure that rare attribute of a statesman, the art of playing a losing game. Either too jubilant or too depressed, he never knew that 'golden mean' of temperament which moderates elation in victory and sustains hope in defeat.

Fitz and Fanny were both dismayed by this painfully accurate portrait. Fanny 'brooded over the meteor analogy until the end of her days', and Fitz buried himself in another great project – preparing a series of financial accounts of the colony since 1832. 'Much time and labour have been bestowed upon this compilation,' he explained in July 1888 when he presented the completed work to the governor, 'in the hope that it may be found not without interest or usefulness as a contribution to the history of New Zealand.'

The *Evening Post* was impressed: it referred to 'balance sheets so simple in their construction that we venture to think they would be intelligible and readily understood even by members of Parliament'.

CHAPTER THIRTY-THREE

White Azaleas

1888–1895

I toil on amidst figures, feeling that I am building houses of sand between
high and low water marks.

Fitz, 19 May 1883

There are hundreds in Wellington who have had a helping hand from
Willie Levin.

Evening Post, *18 September 1893*

When Amy was diagnosed with tuberculosis in 1886, she refused to
spend her time shut up indoors, as recommended by the doctors.
Instead, she wanted 'plenty of air', so her husband bought her 'a sweet little place
in the Wairarapa and there I spent the greater part of every summer with the
children, out all day riding or driving and very often sleeping in a hammock
hung in a roofed balcony'.

Amy recovered. Her lungs healed and, on 1 December 1888 (the last night
of the first New Zealand Musical Festival), Willie Levin and her parents sat
proudly in the audience as she sang – 'with suitable power and dignity' – the
soprano solo 'Sing ye to the Lord' from Handel's *Israel in Egypt*.

Fitz's health had been affected by 50 years of almost continuous smoking.
He suffered from chronic bronchitis, and it was rumoured that he would soon
retire from the audit office. In July 1889, the newspapers reported that 'Mr
J.E. FitzGerald, who has been ill for some time, is about to be granted four
months' sick leave, and will take his departure for England by the *Doric* on the
25th inst., returning to New Zealand in November next.'

On 24 July, the Girls Friendly Society gave a musical evening in Fanny's
honour; she and Fitz boarded the steamship *Doric* the following afternoon.
The ship was operated by the White Star Line, one of a new generation of
steamships which reduced the sailing time to 40 days, with refuelling stops
at Rio de Janeiro and Tenerife. It was a comfortable voyage, with few other
passengers in cabin class. Originally bound for London, the ship was diverted

to Plymouth because of a strike in London docks. The *Doric* steamed into Plymouth Sound on 2 September, reminding Fitz and Fanny of the evening, almost forty years before, when the *Charlotte Jane* set sail for her long voyage to Canterbury.

Next morning they boarded the train for London, where they booked into a hotel in Pall Mall and Fitz sent a cable to Wellington. 'The many friends of Mr J.E. FitzGerald,' wrote the *Evening Post* on 5 September, 'will be glad to hear that a private cable message has been received to the effect that the voyage home has benefited his health.'

After four weeks in England renewing acquaintance with family and friends, Fitz and Fanny returned to the *Doric* which left Plymouth on 5 October. 'Letters received by the last mail,' wrote a New Zealand newspaper four weeks later, 'give very favourable accounts of the health of the Comptroller-General … who is described as having improved surprisingly during his trip Home and as being "Wonderfully well" since he reached England.'

They arrived in Wellington on 28 November to learn that Otho (who worked as a bank clerk) had been seriously ill in Clyde Cliff. He had begun to feel unwell a few days after his parents left in July:

> I caught a severe cold, which later developed into double pneumonia. If it had not been for the fact that the woman in charge of us did not know how to put on a mustard poultice, the doctor said I would have probably died … The woman knew that in such cases it was a good thing to apply a mustard poultice to the part affected, but she hadn't any idea of the amount of mustard that she ought to use, and in her anxiety to relieve my suffering she applied about three times the proper quantity, with the natural result that my chest was like raw beef.

Otho recovered – but illness had changed him. He gave up sport, which had previously occupied all his spare time, and buried his head in religious books. In 1890, he decided to follow his brother (ordained as deacon in Melbourne) into the church. Fanny wrote to John Hall for a reference, and Otho left for Melbourne on 5 January 1891, carrying a letter from Hall explaining that he was 'steady, industrious and conscientious'.

Appointed a lay reader, he was put in charge of 'a beautiful little health and tourist resort in the mountains'; but finding everything in Melbourne so 'completely different' from New Zealand, he fled back to the docks and boarded a steamer for home. He changed his mind again when the ship arrived in Tasmania, so he returned to Melbourne to find 'the Bishop … so annoyed at the way in which I had behaved that … he sent me, as a punishment, to the worst place in the diocese'. This was Bendigo, a gold-mining town 100 miles northwest of Melbourne. Otho worked here for several months until he fell ill again, after which he returned home and found work as an assistant curate in Wellington. 'His innocence and simplicity,' wrote his father, 'are most touching.'

…

Fitz's four-month break had given him renewed enthusiasm for work in the audit office. On one occasion he summoned a colleague to see him with a note written in Irish brogue: 'Sorr, I want to collogue wid ye – drop in at me orphice if ye plaze.'

Fitz photographed in 1890, a few months after returning from his brief visit to England.
Private collection

In April 1892, he wrote to congratulate Sir George Grey on his eightieth birthday, referring to their disagreements in the past as 'matters of local and transient interest'. Grey replied with generosity; he recalled how he and Fitz had walked together to the top of the Port Hills on that long-ago afternoon in 1850:

> I had before me a vista of hills dominating level and fertile plains
> and a vast ocean, upon which roamed two young men, one with
> a bad knee which rendered it necessary to rest from time to time.
> They were absorbed in a deeply interesting conversation on found-
> ing nations and creating new governments. I was one of the two and,
> as my companion spoke, I admired his talents, eloquence, and the
> largeness of his conceptions, and thought, if we could act together,
> what hopes of usefulness for each of us, what a change might be
> wrought in the world.

Fitz's nostalgia for the past led him into religious musings, too. His faith had been shaken by the loss of so many of his children, and after Willy's death he poured out his heart in more than a hundred stanzas of religious rumination.

He borrowed the title from a parable for children ('Not lost but gone before') and his poem is filled with longing that his dead children were alive and happy in what he called 'the spirit world':

> ... When I think of those who never more
> Shall brighten our home-circle with their love,
> Whom Death's cruel mandate has sent on before
> The dark hereafter's mystery to prove;
> Think what they were, portray'd by memory,
> I ask what now they are, from earthly garments free.
>
> Those gone forever like the passing year,
> Or like a sunbeam fading from the sight,
> Or like sweet music dying on the ear,
> Or like a fleeting vision of the night;
> The love, the pride, the hope that round them grew,
> Fonder with each year's promise, gone like summer's dew ...
>
> Their various forms upon the mem'ry press,
> Sometimes as infants on their mother's knee,
> Sometimes array'd in childhood's loveliness,
> Sometimes in radiant boyhood's bravery;
> And some best loved as when they left the earth,
> By manhood crown'd with all of truest manhood's worth ...
>
> Not lost, but gone before! Is the dream true?
> Shall I see them again in some hereafter?
> Again our old fond intercourse renew,
> And listen to the music of their laughter,
> And see their forms once more as fresh and bright
> And beautiful as when death stole them from our sight?

The poem was privately printed. Fitz gave copies to his family and friends – including Amy, whose marriage was, in her own words, 'one long happiness, surrounded by love and with no money troubles which weigh so heavily'.

...

Willie Levin also suffered from chronic bronchitis. In early 1891, feeling 'not up to work', he embarked with Amy on a steamship for an extended visit to London. They would be away for more than eighteen months. During his absence, Willie decided to 'withdraw from active management', leaving Levin & Co in the hands of his managers. 'A violent cold and sore throat is trying me much,' he wrote in October 1892, a few days before they embarked on the *Doric* for the return voyage to New Zealand.

In April 1893, Wellington was shocked by the sudden death of the premier, John Ballance, who had been leading a liberal government for the last two years. Because the body was travelling to Wanganui for burial, the funeral proceedings began at half past six in the morning. Fitz was one of the official mourners. He left Clyde Cliff at dawn and made his way to the ministerial residence in Tinakori Road, where large numbers of politicians, councillors, civil servants and 'all the leading citizens' – including Willie Levin – were milling around outside. The coffin was placed on a gun carriage and Fitz took his place in the procession as the cortège, accompanied by a military band, moved through the streets to the railway station.

This was the largest funeral ever held in the city ('never in the history of Wellington was there such an assemblage') – but it soon would be eclipsed by another.

Willie's bronchitis returned in the cold winter weather. He began coughing again in July; his condition worsened during the next few weeks and on 15 September, after a prolonged coughing fit, Amy found him 'very dull, he did not seem to understand what I said to him'. It was a stroke, 'a clot of blood on the brain, and in a few hours he passed away'.

One of the most popular men in Wellington, Willie was a philanthropist, 'the benevolent merchant, beloved by thousands, respected by all'. His funeral on 17 September far surpassed that of John Ballance five months earlier. 'The city mourns,' wrote the *Evening Post* next morning:

> Flags everywhere fluttering at half-mast in the cold breeze, thoroughfares thronged with serious-faced foot-passengers, tramcars overladen till even standing room was difficult to obtain, cabs and carriages hurrying along – such was the scene in Wellington yester-day afternoon. All were converging in one direction – the direction of the late Mr W.H. Levin's residence in Tinakori-road. An air of sorrow pervaded every thing and every one. Large numbers of those hurrying along bore wreaths and crosses, white azaleas being the prevailing bloom, and even little children bore small branches of them.

The coffin, covered in a white silk pall, was carried in relays by the staff of Levin & Co. Fitz, as chief mourner, walked behind the coffin with three of his sons. Huge crowds followed the mourners; thousands more gathered in the streets. 'Never before in the history of Wellington,' read one of the obituaries, 'has there been such general and deep mourning. There are hundreds in Wellington who have had a helping hand from Willie Levin.'

…

The long depression of the 1880s had deepened towards the end of the decade, despite renewed government borrowing. The trade union movement had grown during these years of depression; civil service salaries had been cut; and in 1890, Fitz was instrumental in founding the New Zealand Public Service Association to act as a union for civil servants. He was elected its first president.

A liberal government came to power the following year, bringing with it a marked change in policy. It overthrew the middle-class monopoly of the House and passed a number of measures to alleviate the lot of the working man. The minister of lands, John McKenzie, brought in legislation to benefit small farmers, including an Act which allowed for the compulsory purchase of large pastoral estates and their subdivision into smaller units.

In August 1892, the elderly Gladstone became British prime minister for the fourth time ('who could foresee an octogenarian Prime Minister?') and put all his energies into a bill to allow Home Rule for Ireland. This provided Fitz with an opportunity for a final appearance on the political stage. 'If I were called on to make a speech on the Irish question,' he wrote to Charles Adderley (now Lord Norton) in London:

> I would describe the state of all the colonies as I have known them
> in my lifetime … the press of every Australian colony and of New
> Zealand for so many years teeming with abuse of the English
> government. I could tell of Governors hissed in theatres, and of one
> Governor of New Zealand accused of burning down Government
> House … I would then describe the colonial world around me
> now – the exuberant and sometimes absurd display of loyalty to the
> Queen and mother country, and even the growing desire for closer
> ties by federation … and I would ask my hearers what has been the
> magic spell which has effected this wonderful transformation scene?
> It is all expressed in the words Home Rule.

There had been two experiments in the last 50 years, he continued, one in Ireland ('a miserable failure'), the other in New Zealand ('a miraculous success'). This, he concluded, 'is the whole case in a nutshell'.

Norton sent this letter to Gladstone and, on 15 January 1893, Fitz received a telegram: 'NORTON ALLOWS ME TO ASK YOU WHETHER I MAY IF NEEDFUL MAKE PUBLIC USE OF PART OF YOUR LETTER WHICH DESCRIBES THE CONTRAST IN THE COLONIES BETWEEN NEW SYSTEM AND OLD. GLADSTONE.'

Fitz cabled back: 'CERTAINLY IF IT CAN HELP THE CAUSE.'

On 30 March, during the second reading of the Government of Ireland Bill, Gladstone stood at the despatch box in the House of Commons with Fitz's letter in his hand:

> Will the House forgive me if I read an extract from a letter written by a gentleman whom I had the privilege of knowing 50 years ago? His name was FitzGerald. I do not know whether he was an Irishman [laughter] … Mr FitzGerald went out to New Zealand as a colonist 50 years ago, when I had the honour of calling him my friend. He has been all that time a leading man, a thorough colonist, and a thorough Imperialist.

He quoted Fitz's letter and sat down to 'tremendous cheers'. 'It is admitted on all hands,' wrote the *New Zealand Herald*, 'that the introduction of the extract was the greatest bit in the Premier's speech. It is curious that Mr Gladstone's old friend in New Zealand should thus have afforded him the opportunity of scoring so heavily on one of the most important occasions of his long and eventful public life.'

···

By this time, Fitz was again drafting legislation for parliament ('proving that the old hand has not lost its creative power'). In 1891, he drafted the Local Authorities' Accounts and Audit Bill. The following year, he drafted the Civil Service Bill and a bill to amend the Revenues Act.

In 1893, he was elected president of the Wellington Citizens Institute, a society formed 'to diffuse knowledge of political, social and ethical principles among the community'. He gave the inaugural address on 8 November, his socialist credentials once again on display. In a long and closely argued speech on politics and economics, he informed his audience that 'socialistic philosophy, and a prudent application of its principles, may be the only road by which … civilisation [may] be preserved from destruction and decay'. And he spoke of a less class-conscious future:

> We live in an age in which the tide is running strongly in the direction of obliterating class distinctions. On the one hand, members of the upper class are compelled to engage in a multitude of occupations in which, a generation or two ago, they could not have engaged in without loss of caste; and, on the other, there has been a large and steady advance by the lower classes in education and refinement …
> It will indeed be a happier world when the only title to honour and

the only distinction of class will be found in rectitude of conduct, purity of morals, and gentleness of manners.

Three weeks later, the women of New Zealand voted for the first time in a general election. Female suffrage had been discussed in parliament four times in recent years, and the bill passed on the fifth attempt – but not until a petition, more than 70 yards in length, was presented to parliament.

It was John Hall – who had re-entered politics as a member of the conservative opposition – who presented the bill, and it was he who carried the rolled-up petition into the House. 'I shall require a little assistance here,' he said as the loops of paper 'began to embarrass him'. One of the clerks stepped forward to help 'and soon the solid roll was bowling along the floor to the other end of the chamber, which it reached without appearing at all diminished in size'.

The petition contained almost 32,000 women's signatures – but not that of Fanny FitzGerald. Fitz's socialist credentials did not extend to female suffrage. He disapproved of this 'novel and daring experiment' (New Zealand was the first country in the world to give women the vote), and Fanny followed his lead.

The Electoral Act was passed on 19 September 1893, two days after Willie Levin's funeral. 'Women's suffrage will shortly become law,' wrote Fitz's old friend William Richmond, who lived nearby in Wellington. 'If it is true that man is in obstinacy *a mule* (as *Mrs* FitzGerald says he is), woman (as *Mr* FitzGerald says) is *mulier*.[1] You will want to get a Latin dictionary for this letter.'

John Hall supported female suffrage on the assumption that, given the opportunity, women of all classes would vote for conservative politicians. He was wrong. The liberal government was returned in November with an increased majority and Fitz wrote to congratulate Hall 'on the triumph of the female franchise – exactly what I predicted – the utter destruction of your whole party. As I never believed in your party, I am of course not sorry at the result, but I claim sagacity for foreseeing the result that, as a rule, women will vote with their water.'[2]

...

Fitz's bronchitis ('this killing cough') stayed with him during the winter of 1894. He resigned as president of the Public Service Association, and was too sick to attend the first meeting of the newly formed Incorporated Institute of Accountants of New Zealand, of which he was elected president. In October,

---

1   Latin for 'woman'
2   By instinct

when he was 76 years old, he made a note of the pension he had agreed with the audit office:

> Mr FitzGerald will become entitled to a pension of £500 if he shall resign the office of Comptroller and Auditor-General on or after the 28 day of February next, which pension will be increased by the sum of £16.13.4. for each and every year that he shall remain in office after the above-mentioned date.

Rumours abounded that he would now retire (his resignation was even reported in the Australian newspapers), but he continued to work, travelling every day to the government buildings, still in charge of the audit of the entire colony. His fingers were arthritic, his eyesight was failing, and he could no longer carve wood for relaxation. Left unfinished was a set of wooden chess pieces carved with a penknife, each piece with individual features. His final effort was a frame for his own portrait, carved with an intricate design of leaves, buds and flowers. He attached a few lines to the back:

> This is a portrait of one who was said
> To have been better known by his hat than his head.
> But this frame explains how a story still lingers
> That he used to be known by the work of his fingers.

CHAPTER THIRTY-FOUR

Joining the Majority

1895–1896

If I should die tonight …
The memory of my selfishness and pride,
My hasty words, would all be put aside …
Think gently of me; I am travel worn;
My faltering feet are pierced with many a thorn.

Fitz, printed poem, 1896

O n 28 February 1895 – the day he became entitled to his pension – Fitz wrote a note to his family: 'The old man would be much pleased if his children and grandchildren will come to afternoon tea on Monday 4th March at Clyde Cliff to condole with him on entering his 78th year.'

He was indeed an old man. And as old men sometimes do, he wrote long letters of philosophy and theology, mainly to his friend William Richmond, who had published several papers on the subject. Richmond, who shared Fitz's 'keen sense of humour and pungent wit', was known as 'one of the most scholarly men in the colony'. 'Like you,' he wrote to Fitz on 9 March, 'I place the ultimate seat of authority in matters of Religion in the Human Reason and Conscience. We have to make a choice between that and an Infallible Church or Infallible Bible – in neither of which can any really cultivated layman put his trust.'

Fitz's health worsened during the winter, but he continued to travel to his office every day – a particular trial when it was cold and wet and the wind howled through the streets. In late June, he and William Richmond were both felled by severe attacks of bronchitis. 'Our old man is also in bed,' Fanny wrote to Richmond's wife on 3 July. 'It began on Saturday. The Sunday night I was up nearly all night … Last night he did not cough, so I was only up for medicines.'

Fitz remained in bed throughout July. He was still unwell on 3 August when the newspapers published the proceedings of the previous day in parliament. Under the headline 'The Minister of Lands attacks the Auditor-General', it was reported that 'the Audit Department came under the heel of the Minister of Lands in the House yesterday afternoon, that gentleman making a savage attack on the officers of this important branch of the public service'.

This was John McKenzie, a large man with working-class roots and a broad Scottish accent who was subject to 'violent outbreaks of rage', particularly about bureaucratic procedures with which he had little patience. He began his attack by saying that Fitz was 'a determined partisan'. Then, 'working himself into a white heat, he declared at the top of his voice that the government were surrounded by men in that building whom they could not trust'.

At this point, Fitz's friend Robert Stout waded into the fray. 'It is not right,' he shouted back, 'that Civil servants should have serious charges hurled at them in that manner. The Minister should formulate his charges, and have an investigation held.'

Fitz photographed towards the end of his life. He is replaying his 'ministerial mode' pose from 1865 – although this time he needs a walking stick.

Private collection

McKenzie retorted that he 'would not withdraw one word'. Fitz, he said, had a 'personal "down" on him, and … had written a letter about him which no gentleman should write' and which was 'the drivelling of an old man'. The Speaker demanded that this comment be withdrawn but McKenzie was in full flow, shouting that he could 'show things about the Audit Department that would astonish the House'.

Stout spoke again, his voice choked with feeling. 'When we are all forgotten,' he said, 'the Auditor-General will be written of by the future historians as the greatest man who ever sat in the House of Representatives. Mr FitzGerald is a man of the highest honour in the public service.'

Fitz was gratified that Stout had defended him so 'stoutly' (as he enjoyed phrasing it when he was feeling better), but at the end of the exchange, the premier, Richard Seddon – another big man with working-class roots – delivered the coup de grâce. He had, he said, 'the greatest confidence in the Civil Service, but there are a few exceptions. As for Mr FitzGerald, he is not that high and mighty or noble soul that he has been depicted to be.'

...

The following day, when the house and garden were 'quite overwhelmed with snow', a black-edged envelope was delivered to Clyde Cliff. William Richmond had died 'rather unexpectedly' during the night. Fanny intercepted the letter. At first, she 'did not dare' tell Fitz, but she told him next morning. 'The best man in New Zealand gone,' he said. 'I shall shortly follow him.'

'We don't mean to send any flowers,' Fanny wrote to Richmond's daughter, 'for I think they only add to our misery. When Willie Levin died, they were terrible.'

Fitz wrote the following day, explaining that it was only 'the duty I owe to others' which prevented him 'following to the grave one for whom I entertained the closest feelings of friendship ... There is a void left never to be filled again in this life. It is thus we feel that there *must* be another. Without it, life is an *unfinished tale* – an unsolved problem.'

Fanny continued to nurse Fitz as he coughed his way through the night. 'My husband does not progress at all satisfactorily,' she wrote on 7 August, the day after Richmond's funeral. 'We have very trying nights and I am getting very weary.' Four days later, she wrote that Fitz was 'a little better. He had a more peaceful night.'

On 29 August, he felt well enough to speak in public, an address to the second annual meeting of the Institute of Accountants. Standing on the podium, his white hair showing no sign of baldness, his long white beard resting on his upper chest, he was still an imposing figure. He thanked the members for 'the honour you have done me in making me your first President', but recognised that 'I owe that position to your respect for the office I fill, rather than to any personal claim to distinction as a professional accountant'.

A few days later, he was back at work, managing a staff of 23 audit officers and a budget of more than £8000 a year. It was a heavy responsibility for a man of his age. Fanny had hoped he would retire after the latest bout of illness, but McKenzie's attack – endorsed by the premier – had stung him. Resignation might be perceived as defeat.

...

It was around this time that Amy sent her children's tutor, Henry Large, to

Clyde Cliff with a pair of spectacles she had found in the house. Fitz returned them with a scribbled note:

> The spectacles are not mine. 1) They don't smell like mine, but are scented with feminine odour. 2) I can't see through them at all so there is no temptation to stick to them. 3) Those I have lost are pinch noses, these are ear stickers … I therefore return them and am sorry Mr Large should have had the trouble of coming up … Conundrum: 'Why must Mr Large marry a rich woman? Give it up? Because his wife must become in herself a *Largess*.

Father and daughter wrote many such notes to each other. They shared a love of puns, and Fitz and Fanny were frequent visitors to Amy's house in Tinakori Road. But at the end of the year, they learnt that an ill-judged promise would soon deprive them of their eldest daughter.

It was a promise made on Willie Levin's deathbed. 'A short time before the end,' Amy wrote in her memoirs, 'he seemed to be trying to speak and I said, "do not trouble, you want to tell me to go to England and send the boys to university". And he squeezed my hand in answer and I said I would do so.'

Willie's estate was valued at £246,221 (over £23 million in today's money), an enormous sum for a small colonial town. Gerald was appointed executor and trustee, at an 'annual salary' of £400. It would be difficult to administer the estate from Blenheim, so he resigned from the survey department and returned to Wellington, where he took a partnership in an architectural practice.

Amy was also an executor but, in December 1894, she 'conveyed her interest as executor to the

Amy Levin, photographed after her husband's death in 1893.

Private collection

trustees who discharged her from liability'. She then made plans to fulfil her promise to take the children to England. By the end of the year, she had booked cabins in the *Gothic*, 'the finest passenger steamer which has ever been in New Zealand waters'.

'Rarely has the … wharf presented a more animated appearance,' wrote the *Evening Post* on 8 February 1896:

> than it did between 11 and 12 o'clock today … between the farewel-ling friends of passengers, the ordinary spectators, and the numerous wharf employees working in the vicinity, there was a scene of rare activity. Punctually at noon the warps were cast off, and … the huge vessel, in splendid steaming trim, backed out of her berth, and proceeded out into the fairway … The passengers include Mrs W.H. Levin, who is taking Home her family to be educated.

Fitz and Fanny stood in the garden at Clyde Cliff, watching the *Gothic* steam out of the harbour. And standing on deck with her children, Amy watched the buildings of Wellington grow smaller, her old home standing alone on its clifftop, one of the last buildings to disappear from sight. 'And so,' she wrote, 'I left my home and came to England. Friends advised me not to do so and, on looking back, I think they were right. But a promise is a promise.'

Less than three weeks later, Otho followed his sister to England to complete his training for the priesthood. 'You will never see me again,' said Fitz. And late one night, when the house was quiet and Fanny had gone to bed, he wrote a poem of immense longing and regret:

> If I should die tonight,
> My friends would call to mind, with loving thought,
> Some kindly deed the icy hand had wrought,
> Some gentle word the frozen lips had said,
> Errands on which the willing feet had sped.
> The memory of my selfishness and pride,
> My hasty words, would all be put aside.
> And so I should be loved and mourned tonight …
>
> Oh! Friends, I pray tonight,
> Keep not your kisses for my dead, cold brow –
> The way is lonely, let me feel them now.
> Think gently of me; I am travel worn;
> My faltering feet are pierced with many a thorn.
> Forgive, oh hearts estranged, forgive, I plead!

When dreamless rest is mine I shall not need
The tenderness for which I long tonight.

…

It was now that Fitz began to have problems with his memory. He suffered recurring dreams about insanity and early one morning, after he had drifted back to sleep:

> I dreamt … that I was *Mad*. It was a dream of singular vividness, reality, and horror … I dreamed that I was on a visit in some great man's house, where there was a good deal of company … I was intensely and miserably conscious that I was suffering under mental derangement … The sensation was as if I was lost in a fog, and was cut off from all my past life and belongings, and it was an exquisitely painful sensation, indeed, as terrible a nightmare as I think anyone ever experienced. To become conscious of the failure of any of our powers – hearing, seeing, or any other faculty – is always the cause of sadness, mainly because the mind recalls the memory of its former enjoyment, and contrasts it with its present loss. But that mind should realise the loss of mind, should retain the power of being conscious of the loss of itself … was the cause of the most acute suffering.

The dream was prescient, for Fitz was now experiencing the early stages of dementia. On one occasion, he arrived for dinner 'at the wrong hotel, at the wrong time, on the wrong day'. On another, he returned home later than usual to inform Fanny that he had been having a long conversation with an old friend, a friend who – as she pointed out – had been dead for three years.

'I am much too old and infirm to do the work of my office properly,' he wrote to Amy on 8 July:

> My memory is going fast, yet all whose opinion I value from the Governor downwards beg me not to resign. It is not a pleasant position to be in and I have no other call to stay as my pension would be about £550 a year … I am getting through the winter so far very well so far as coughs go … My memory is going so fast I shall soon forget who I am – and shall probably be taken up for the commission of some crime which I shall be unable to deny.

He added a postscript: 'We lunched at Government House on Monday. The Governor says I must not think of retiring. It is rather hard on me.'

Fitz spent four more days in the audit office. His bronchitis returned and his colleagues remarked that he looked 'very ill'. On 15 July, he retired to bed. His lungs became congested and by the 23rd, a day when gales buffeted the house on the clifftop, his condition was 'giving rise to considerable anxiety'.

On the 28th, telegrams were sent to Lyttelton (now a vicar in Auckland) and Eva (in Masterton where her husband was a bank manager). Both of them hurried home to Wellington. Fitz rallied on the 31st, but 'the improvement was only temporary'. At four o'clock in the afternoon of 1 August, Fanny sent a telegram to John Hall (who had asked for news): 'UNLESS CHANGE IN TWENTY HOURS HOPELESS.'

That evening and through the early hours of the night, Fanny and five of her children (Gerald, Lyttelton, Eva, Geraldine and Edward) clustered around the bed as Fitz lay struggling for breath. Towards midnight, he drifted into unconsciousness. At four o'clock in the morning, he took his last laboured breath.

'There is grief over the city from end to end today,' wrote the Wellington correspondent of the *Star* a few hours later:

> The cause is the death of James Edward FitzGerald, whose name has been a household word in the colony since the early fifties, when he landed at Lyttelton a passenger in one of the historical first four ships … The number of the brave and true who landed on that famous occasion is sadly diminished. Full of hope and strength and talent they landed; earnestly they set about the work that was before them, and well they did it. Nearly half a century has gone, and where are they? Some perished among the pioneers who made bridges into the wilderness; some have achieved competence and a few have obtained imperishable fame. Of the last, the greatest remaining example was James Edward FitzGerald, who joined the majority this morning.

On the afternoon of 3 August, a large number of carriages gathered at Clyde Cliff: the premier and his ministers, the Speakers of both Houses, the mayor and city councillors, Fitz's friends and colleagues. Government offices had closed for the day and flags flew 'at half-mast on the shipping and above the principal mercantile establishments'.

Inside the house, Fitz lay in a coffin of 'beautifully mottled kauri wood'. At three o'clock, the coffin was loaded into a hearse and, to the tolling of the bell of St Mark's church, the funeral procession wound its way down the hill to the city, followed by large numbers of mourners on foot. Fitz was carried into the church on the shoulders of the assistant comptroller-general and four clerks from the audit office.

After a service conducted by the bishop, the bell tolled again as the cortège made its way to the Bolton Street cemetery. Three of Fitz's sons followed the coffin, but his son-in-law James Brandon was missing (he blamed his absence on 'an unfortunate miscarriage in the telegraph department'). And while Fanny's sons watched their father being laid to rest alongside six of his children, she and her two daughters stayed home in Clyde Cliff, the house filled with floral tributes, the curtains drawn against the winter light.

The following day there were tributes in parliament, before the assembly was adjourned as a mark of respect. In the Legislative Council, Charles Bowen – whose friendship with Fitz began at the cuddy table in the *Charlotte Jane* – gave a moving tribute:

> Like many generous-minded men, and men of great aspirations, he has from time to time in his public career been the champion of lost causes and impossible loyalties; and his attitude naturally aroused vehement opposition. But the hostile feelings which he may have sometimes evoked have all died long ago, and I am quite sure no one lives who does not rather remember his great ability, his public spirit, the chivalry and generosity of his character, his genial disposition, and the charm of his society …
>
> I remember, when I was a boy, how he, then a young man of exceptional promise, attracted the best of those around him by his brilliant conversational powers, his genial wit, his artistic and literary taste, and his wide and varied knowledge … He has left to us a great legacy – perhaps the greatest that can be left to a country – the memory and example of a great and upright man, who did his duty to the best of his power throughout life, whether in the public arena or in private life.

Meanwhile, in the House, Premier Richard Seddon was choosing his words with care:

> As a pressman and writer he had no superiors and few equals. His writings were brilliant … and proved him to be endowed with very great power indeed … He was a real orator. I have had the pleasure, years ago, of listening to him, and I may say that I have heard very few equal to him … He possessed very great natural abilities, and it followed that he was self-confident; and I attribute a great deal of the good that was done by him to that fact alone. It was necessary in the position which he held, as Comptroller and Auditor-General, that he should have self-confidence, because in a great measure

it depended upon him, and him alone, to decide what was right, proper, and in accordance with the law.

Robert Stout now rose to his feet and asked to say a few words about his old friend:

> He was a giant in the days when New Zealand had giants in this House ... He was an orator, and some of the speeches which he made in the New Zealand Parliament can hardly, I think, be surpassed by those delivered in any Parliament in the world ... He was not only a great orator and a great statesman, but he was a great man in every walk of life ... and the one thing which, perhaps, stands out stronger than anything was his desire to do what was right and just in everything which he undertook.

'When the history of this colony comes to be written,' he concluded, 'there will be no name amongst the great names we have had in New Zealand that will stand out so bright as that of James Edward FitzGerald.'

CHAPTER THIRTY-FIVE

A Pilgrim Mother

1896–1901

Mrs FG ... is certainly a woman of a great deal of spirit.
Richard Harman, 24 September 1857

My mother was a woman in a thousand.
Amy Levin

*I*n Canterbury, the 'Pilgrim Fathers' who arrived in the first four ships had acquired the status of legend. Why, asked one of Fanny's friends, was 'nothing said about the Pilgrim Mothers? Yet they bore the same discomforts, hardships and privation and in addition had to put up with the Pilgrim Fathers.'

Fanny had arrived in New Zealand prepared to '*rough*' it for a few years (as advised by Wakefield); in the event, she had to rough it for much longer because of Fitz's inability to make money. But her marriage was (in Fitz's words) 'fortunate and happy and prolonged', providing them both with an 'immense sum total of happiness'.

She was 64 when she lost the man whose sparkle and wit made every day worth living: 'Those who knew her best felt that she never got over the death of her husband ... She still did her accustomed work, but it was more and more an effort, and though she clung to those she loved with all the strength of her affectionate nature, life was not the same to her since he was gone.'

For some years, Fanny had devoted her time to voluntary work. She was a foundation member of the Alexandra Home and the Levin Home for Orphaned Girls (founded by Amy in memory of her husband), and president of the Ladies Christian Association and Girls Friendly Society. As one of her colleagues put it, 'all this hard work, voluntarily undertaken, and her many sorrows were a great strain upon her'.

Fitz had written his will during an official visit to Timaru in 1874, a few

Fanny, photographed after Fitz's death. 'She still did her accustomed work, but it was more and more an effort ... life was not the same to her since he was gone.'

Private collection

lines scribbled on a sheet of paper which he took to the Post Office to be witnessed by the postmaster and counter clerk: 'I leave all property of which I shall die possessed, or to which I may be entitled at the time of my death, of every description whatever ... to my dear wife, Fanny FitzGerald. I appoint her my sole executor and the guardian of my children.'

Fanny obtained probate on 21 August – but not until the counter clerk in Timaru confirmed that the will had indeed been signed in his presence. A few weeks later, she decided to sell four acres of land at Clyde Cliff, retaining only the house and the garden. This 'Valuable Freehold Land' was divided into four lots which offered a 'delightful situation, commanding an uninterrupted view of the city and harbour ... an unequalled opportunity for subdivision into convenient building sites in a healthy and central part of the city'.

The auction was held on 18 December. As surveyors set to work in the grounds, Fanny lived on in Clyde Cliff – at first with only Edward and Geraldine for company. Edward worked as a clerk in Levin & Co. Geraldine taught at the Sunday school and was Fanny's devoted companion; she and her mother were a familiar sight in Wellington, 'driving around town in the family gig'.

Otho arrived home in 1897 to become vicar of Newtown, a parish close to the city. The following year, Eva returned to Wellington when her husband was appointed secretary of the Electric Light Syndicate. And in 1899, Lyttelton resigned his parish in Auckland, returning to Clyde Cliff a few days after the Boer War began.

. . .

The declaration of war in October 1899 led to an outbreak of jingoistic fever in Wellington. Richard Seddon, a staunch imperialist, offered support to the mother country, and recruiting officers toured the colony in search of volunteers. They came to the Star Boating Club in December where several members, including Edward FitzGerald, signed up to fight for Britain. Edward took extended leave from Levin & Co. He was given the rank of volunteer corporal, and his contingent embarked for South Africa on 20 January 1900.

Thirty thousand people gathered to see the volunteers leave, 'the whole of the reclaimed land a living mass of humanity'. The crowds sang along as Edward's contingent marched down the quay to the steamship. As the ship moved away from the quay, the band struck up 'Soldiers of the Queen' and once again the crowds began to sing, 'the song taken up by the voices in a swelling chorus, the volunteers firing their rifles in reply'.

From the garden at Clyde Cliff, Fanny watched the ship steam out of the harbour, taking her youngest son to fight in a distant land. A few weeks later, she resigned as president of the Girls Friendly Society, complaining of 'failing health'. She was suffering from abdominal pains and was diagnosed with gallstones.

'The many friends of Mrs J.E. FitzGerald,' wrote the *Weekly Press* on 13 June, 'will regret to hear that she is very ill. Her illness began after eating some oysters. Others have lately been affected from the same cause.' It was not the oysters, for Dr Fell now diagnosed a more serious condition: suppurative cholangitis. Gallstones had blocked her bile ducts, bacteria had multiplied, infection had spread. Fanny had septicaemia.

Early on the morning of Sunday 8 July, Otho left Clyde Cliff to walk the four miles to his parish:

> After a long illness of very much suffering one could see that the
> end was near ... In the early morning I went off to my church
> which was some distance away to take the early communion. When
> I started off again for the mid-day service there was the thought
> in my mind. 'Will she be alive when I return?' I do not think many
> could realise what a strain I was under while preaching that morning
> when all the time I was thinking, 'Will I see her again?' But she lived
> just long enough for me to return to say 'Good-bye' before God
> called her Home.

Two days later, Gerald, Lyttelton and Otho followed their mother's coffin to St Mark's church. It was another well-attended funeral, 'indicating the great respect in which the late Mrs J.E. FitzGerald was held by all sections of the community'. The cortège, according to the *Evening Post*, 'was about a

The FitzGerald family plot in the Bolton Street cemetery, photographed in the 1960s before the graves were removed to make space for a motorway.

Alexander Turnbull Library, Wellington (P.J.E. Shotter Collection, F-25517-35mm-19)

quarter of a mile in length, and included the Governor's carriage'. The bishop conducted the service, after which Fanny joined her husband and children in the Bolton Street cemetery.

The following day, Charles Bowen paid tribute to 'one of the best and bravest of the first settlers in Canterbury':

> The light girlish figure that was a tower of strength to many a wavering soul in the difficulties and hardships of the early days; the attractive young matron who was as ready to spend her time in helping the afflicted as she was to charm society by her accomplishments and her ready wit … Many charitable institutions will miss her firm guiding hand, and many a sorrowful heart will yearn for the cheerful presence and kindly help. Honest and straightforward as she was in thought, word and action, she occasionally startled strangers by her very downright expressions of opinion, which her wit now and then sharpened into something like an epigram. But those who were at first offended became often her firmest friends.

Fanny's estate was valued at £9746 (almost £600,000 today), partly because the Draper trust had appreciated in value, partly because Clyde Cliff was now unencumbered by mortgage, and partly because the four acres sold in December 1896 had raised more than £5000. The estate was divided equally into eight portions – one each for her seven surviving children, and the eighth to be held in trust for Willy's three children until they reached the age of 21.

In England, Amy made preparations for a visit to New Zealand, booking a cabin on the steamship *Gothic* which left London on 22 November. She arrived in Wellington on 5 January 1901 and moved into her old home in Tinakori Road.

Seventeen days later, the death of Queen Victoria brought Wellington to a standstill: church bells tolled; flags flew at half-mast; windows were draped in black. Fanny was five years old when Victoria came to the throne. Six months after she died in Clyde Cliff, the long Victorian era came to an end.

CHAPTER THIRTY-SIX

An Unfinished Tale

1901–1933

And though I shall die,
From my seed shall grow
An endless progeny
On the earth to blow.

Fitz, 'The Flower', July 1888

Clyde Cliff was put up for sale after Fanny's death. It was described as a 'magnificent and valuable property ... the substantially built two-story family residence containing 14 rooms, with verandah, wash-house and stable, formerly occupied by the late Mrs FitzGerald ... The grounds are tastefully laid out and planted with a large number of imported and native plants, and command an unequalled view.' The auction was held on 28 January 1901, and 'after some competition' from other bidders, Amy bought the FitzGerald family home for £2550.

She returned to London six weeks later, followed by her brother Lyttelton. 'The rev. gentleman's health,' explained the *New Zealand Freelance*, 'has been giving his relatives much concern, and it is thought a twelve months' visit to England will set him up again.' A few weeks after arriving in London, he attended a family wedding where he took a shine to the bride's widowed mother. In November, the London correspondent of the *Evening Post* reported that 'The Rev. Lyttelton FitzGerald is still in England. A rumour has reached me that he will not return to New Zealand a bachelor.'

Edward returned from South Africa in May 1901. Otho resigned his parish three months later, after which he too embarked for England. He joined the Central Africa University Mission and arrived in London in time to officiate at Lyttelton's marriage on 28 December. Otho was as unprepared for Africa as he had been for Australia. He caught malaria and resigned after a few months.

He returned to New Zealand, where he married a rector's daughter and settled down as vicar of Avonside in Christchurch. He died in 1947.

Lyttelton's wife was unenthusiastic about living in New Zealand, so he accepted a perpetual curacy in Devonshire. She left him in 1912, after which he was diagnosed with a nervous breakdown. Sent to recuperate at a 'hydropathic establishment' in Ilfracombe, it was soon discovered that he was suffering from heart disease, 'the revival of an old malady'. He died in March 1913, with Amy at his bedside.

Gerald's wife died of tuberculosis in October 1900, leaving three young daughters. He married again five years later, by which time he had made his name as a civil engineer in Wellington. He administered Willie Levin's estate for more than a quarter of a century. And following the traditions of his family, he wrote poetry and composed music, songs for his children to sing around the piano. He died in Wellington in 1937.

Geraldine was her father's daughter, inheriting his mental condition as well as his intellect and facial features. After her mother's death, she enrolled at Canterbury College, and completed the first year of a Bachelor of Arts degree. In 1917, she founded Chilton Saint James, a school for girls in Lower Hutt. With a zeal for education (and a laugh like a hyena), she was an inspiration to many of her pupils; a source of terror to others. She enjoyed woodcarving and – like her father – was often seen whittling a piece of wood, a man's handkerchief on her lap to catch the shavings. She died unmarried in 1955.

Amy continued to live in style on the Levin wealth: she rented a small stately home south of London, employed several servants, and spent most of her winters in the south of France or in Egypt. In 1905, she sold Clyde Cliff to the Catholic Redemptorist Order, which demolished the house and built a monastery in its place. Amy's two sons returned to New Zealand after completing their education (one was killed in the First World War). When she died in 1925, her personal wealth was divided into equal shares and held in trust for her elder daughter, her sisters Eva and Geraldine, and her brother Edward. And by this time, both Eva and Edward were much in need of her largesse.

James Brandon had proved an unsatisfactory husband, 'going through money like water'. His appointment as secretary of the Electric Light Syndicate was short-lived. After this, he moved his family from one place to another, sometimes in employment, sometimes not (at one stage he ran a chicken farm near Lyall Bay). In 1919, he and Eva settled in Otaki. They died in 1937, six months apart, leaving a family of six daughters.

Edward became a farmer after he returned from South Africa. He acquired land in the upper Retaruke valley, inhospitable country described as 'very rugged, a maze of steep hills'. He cleared the land of bush and, with a loan from the government, built a homestead, planted orchards and bought sheep. He was turned down for service in the First World War ('not passed fit enough to go'). More than a decade later, when the Great Depression hit farmers particularly badly, Edward had no choice but to simply 'walk off the land'. He moved with his wife and three daughters to Auckland, where he scratched a living as a door-to-door salesman.

He became increasingly estranged from his wife and, one morning in 1933, he disappeared from the house, 'taking with him only a small hand-bag'. A few days later, his wife received an envelope with a money order and a scribbled note: 'the last of the money and the last of me'. Another letter was addressed to Gerald in Wellington: 'The receipt of this by you will be positive evidence that I am dead, by my own hand.'

Edward's body was never found; twelve years later, the Supreme Court declared death by suicide. But shortly before he disappeared, he wrote an enigmatic letter to his favourite daughter: 'I have come to the conclusion that it would be great fun to try the experiment of seeing how far "the necessities" could be done without altogether … go into the bush and build a hut of saplings and bark, then live on what you could kill or grow, clothed chiefly in skins. What do you think of this idea?'

So perhaps, instead of drowning himself in the ocean (as his friends surmised), Edward returned to the upper Retaruke and lived out his days as a hermit in the bush.

...

Almost 70 years after the last burial in the FitzGerald family plot, mechanical diggers arrived in the Bolton Street cemetery to remove several thousand graves to make room for a motorway. And so that cars can speed easily into the city centre, the bones of Fitz and Fanny and six of their children were dug up and reinterred in a common vault, their tombstones moved elsewhere in the cemetery.

Simple memorials in the form of a cross, they no longer stand over the bodies of those they were erected to commemorate. You can hear the cars coming and going as you stand beside them and reflect on the events that brought Fitz and Fanny here, to this green resting-place in the centre of a modern city.

Fitz did not foresee the advent of the motorcar – but he understood the pace of technological change. 'The world has got so small since I was a boy,' he wrote in 1892. 'The two sides of it have shrunk into a tenth of the former distance. Humanity is changing under the influence of telegraphs, telephones and the development of electricity. We shall soon be breakfasting in New Zealand and dining in England.'

Postscript

I have enjoyed my journey through the life of James Edward FitzGerald, following 'the flash of a meteor' through 50 years of New Zealand history. Fitz stood tall in provincial and general politics, but his true legacy is the *Press* – founded to oppose the construction of the Lyttelton tunnel. The newspaper and the tunnel both thrive today, one disseminating news and opinions throughout the country, the other allowing swift and easy travel through the Port Hills: the great opposing projects of Fitz and Moorhouse united by posterity.

Fitz was indeed a man of many talents – but as I read through the volumes of his correspondence, it soon became clear how much these talents were compromised by his mental condition. He was not responsible for his mood swings. He could not prevent the months of hyperactivity when his mind raced from one idea to another at breathtaking speed; when he contradicted himself almost by the sentence; when only he knew the answer to every question. That is the nature of the disorder. Nor could he prevent the months of lethargy, depression and perceived ill health.

Today, these mood swings can often be controlled by medication. Fitz had no such opportunity. So instead of feeling exasperated (as I sometimes did when reading his letters), we should sympathise with a man of intelligence and talent whose potential was destroyed by a condition over which he had no control. As William Gisborne described it, 'either too jubilant or too depressed, he never knew that "golden mean" of temperament which moderates elation in victory and sustains hope in defeat'.

In 1867, after his near-bankruptcy at the *Press*, Fitz insisted that he was not downhearted at the course of events that led to his move to Wellington. This is belied by the expression in his eyes. The photograph taken by Alfred Barker on the morning of 6 February 1868, the day of the 'welcome breakfast' for Lord Lyttelton and Henry Selfe, the day Fitz gave one of his most moving speeches, is an image I find particularly painful. There is such a deep sense of loss and disappointment in those pale grey eyes.

…

Fitz lived and worked in Wellington for almost 30 years. And during these years, he began to fabricate the past. His ambition thwarted by uncontrollable changes of mood, he looked back on his life in England and tweaked the truth.

There was a pattern to these inventions. As an academic, he could have achieved 'a very high position' at Cambridge if his health had not broken down. He was rejected by the Royal Engineers because of poor eyesight. He was personally responsible for the reorganisation of the British Museum in 1849, happily arranging for the abolition of his own position as assistant secretary. He would have shone in the English political world, 'only weak lungs forbade him to live in England'. He gave up a brilliant career in London to become a Canterbury Pilgrim. He was offered two colonial governorships in 1858–59, both of which he rejected because of ill health.

None of this is real. And the invention of youthful walking tours in Ireland and Scotland (during which – he said – he stayed with peasants in hovels and paid for his board and lodging with sketches) is particularly revealing. He wanted to be perceived as a thoughtful young man who made these journeys to see for himself the condition of the 'common man'. John Godley, his 'one hero', did exactly this (in Europe, the United States and Canada) – an embarrassing contrast to Fitz's years of aimless inactivity in Bath.

The best decision he ever made was his choice of wife – and I have her betrothal ring, so tiny it barely fits over my little fingernail. Fanny was, in his own words, 'one of the rarest companions God ever gave a man for a wife'. A woman of courage and spirit, intelligent, witty and sharp, her life in New Zealand was never easy. I am angry at Fitz's thoughtlessness; I grieve with her at the deaths of so many of her children. Despite the exhaustion and pain, despite Fitz's blindness to her problems, she loved her husband, a man who inspired and exasperated her in equal measure. She understood his mood swings; and I share with her a sense of what might have been, what Fitz could have achieved if his brain chemistry had allowed him to harness his undoubted gifts.

I have learned that Fitz was not the legendary hero of my youth. He was too changeable, too arrogant when his mood was high, too obsessed with health when he was down. But infuriating as he could often be, he inspired real devotion in his family and friends. Most of all, I shall remember his mischievous sense of humour, his 'ready wit', his 'fondness for a joke', his 'delightful fund of anecdotes', and how his home life – at least until the dark days of the 1880s – was 'so full of joy'.

Timeline

1818	4 March	Birth of James Edward FitzGerald (Fitz) in Bath
1819	24 April	Death of Fitz's mother
1832	21 March	Birth of Frances Erskine Draper (Fanny) in Odessa
1842	January	Fitz graduates from Cambridge
1844	26 February	Fitz begins work at British Museum
1845	8 April	Death of Fitz's father
1846	18 February	Rose Paynter marries Charles Graves Sawle
1848	27 March	First meeting of Canterbury Association
1849	13 January	Vancouver Island granted to Hudson Bay Company
	15 December	Fitz appointed secretary of Society for the Reform of Colonial Government
	25 December	Fitz made redundant from British Museum
1850	6 March	Fitz appointed emigration agent for Canterbury Association
	25 April	First meeting of Society of Canterbury Colonists
	30 July	Farewell breakfast on board the *Randolph*
	22 August	Fitz and Fanny marry in St George's church, Bloomsbury
	7 September	*Charlotte Jane* sails from Plymouth
	16 December	*Charlotte Jane* arrives in Lyttelton
	17 December	Fitz appointed immigration agent and (temporarily) sub-inspector of police
1851	11 January	First edition of *Lyttelton Times* (edited by Fitz)
	7 February	Fitz's half-brother Gerard arrives on the *Castle Eden*

	6 June	Fanny's brothers William and George Draper arrive on the *Duke of Brontë*
	23 June	Death of the Ward brothers
1852	January	Fitz gives up editorship of *Lyttelton Times*
	19 February	First child (Amy) born in Lyttelton
	30 June	Passing of New Zealand Constitution Act in London
	August	Fitz resigns as immigration agent
	22 December	Godleys embark for England
1853	24/25 January	Fitz and Fanny move to Springs station
	April	Death of Fanny's brother William on the plains
	20 July	Fitz wins election for superintendent of Canterbury
	10 August	Fitz and Fanny move to Christchurch
	15 August	Fitz elected to represent Lyttelton at general assembly (parliament)
	27 September	First meeting of provincial council
	12 October	Birth of second child (William) in Christchurch
	17 October	Death of Fitz's brother Robert on P&O steamer
1854	11 May	Fitz and Fanny embark for parliament in Auckland
	24 May	First New Zealand parliament opens in Auckland
	14 June	Fitz asked to form a ministry (the 'mixed ministry')
	2 August	Fitz and his ministry resign
	16 September	Parliament prorogued
1855	7 June	Birth of third child (Robert) in Christchurch
	10 July	Canterbury Association wound up
	8 Aug–15 Sept	Short parliament in Auckland. Fitz does not attend
	21 December	General election. Fitz re-elected to represent Lyttelton
1856	15 April	First 'responsible parliament' opens in Auckland
	17 June	Fitz and Fanny leave for Auckland. He is unwell and can take no part
	16 August	Parliament prorogued
1857	2 April	Fitz opens last session of his provincial council
	26 June	Birth of fourth child (Gerald) in Christchurch
	29 June	Fitz accepts position of emigration agent in London
	30 June	Fitz's provincial council dissolved. Fitz too ill to attend
	July	Fitz resigns from general assembly
	24 August	Fitz opens Sumner Road in the circulating medium
	30 September	Fitz and family leave for England
1858	19 February	Fitz and family arrive in London
1859	1 June	Birth of fifth child (Lyttelton) in London

1860	21 August	The New Zealand Bill withdrawn
	3 September	Fitz and family leave for New Zealand
	11 September	Death of Fanny's father in London
	2 December	Fitz and family arrive in Lyttelton
1861	8 April	Birth of sixth child (Maurice) at Springs station
	16 May	Fitz elected to represent Akaroa on provincial council
	25 May	First edition of the *Press*
	17 July	First sod turned on railway project
	22 October	New session of provincial council opens
	17 November	Godley dies in London
1862	10 June	Fitz elected to represent Ellesmere in parliament
	30 June	Fitz embarks for parliament in Wellington
	29 July	Governor Sir George Grey asks Fitz to form a government. Fitz declines
	July–August	Fanny's illness at the Springs station
	6 August	Fitz's speech on Maori affairs
	31 August	Fitz embarks for Lyttelton
	16 October	Farm sale at the Springs
	17 November	Fitz and family move to Christchurch
	18 December	Fitz resigns from provincial council
1863	9 February	Birth of seventh child (Evangeline) in Christchurch
	17 March	The *Press* becomes a daily paper
	9 October	Fitz signs power of attorney for Harman & Stevens
	10 October	Fitz embarks for parliament in Auckland
	19 October	Parliament opens in Auckland
	25 November	Fitz moves motion to move seat of government
	1 December	Opening of railway from Christchurch to Heathcote
	8 December	End of parliamentary session. Fitz embarks for Lyttelton
1864	16 November	Fitz embarks for short parliament in Auckland
	24 November	Parliament opens in Auckland
	13 December	Parliament prorogued. Fitz embarks for Lyttelton
1865	15 January	Birth of eighth child (Selwyn) in Christchurch
	1–13 April	Fitz's expedition to find alternative to Arthur's Pass over the mountains
	22 July	Fitz embarks for parliament in Wellington
	12 August	Fitz accepts position of minister for native affairs in Weld government
	12 October	Weld's government resigns
	20 October	Fitz leaves parliament before end of session
1866	12 February	General election. Fitz returned as member for Christchurch

	28 June	Fitz embarks for parliament in Wellington
	14 August	Fitz proposes vote of no confidence in Stafford; his motion defeated the following day
	17 August	Fitz leaves parliament early and embarks for Lyttelton
	6 September	Fitz re-embarks for Wellington
	24 September	Fitz again leaves parliament before end of session
	29 September	Harman & Stevens terminate contract with the *Press*
	6 October	Birth of ninth child (Katherine) in Christchurch
	14 December	Gold transport from Hokitika fails
	30 December	Fitz accepts position of comptroller-general in Wellington
1867	2 January	Fitz resigns seat in parliament
	28 January	Fitz leaves for Wellington
	4 April	Farewell dinner for Fitz in Christchurch
	9 April	Fitz and family leave Christchurch for Wellington
	November	Fitz makes plans for settlement of Taupo lands
	9 December	Opening of Lyttelton railway tunnel
1868	6 February	Welcome breakfast for Lord Lyttelton and Henry Selfe in Christchurch
	May	Fitz gives up Taupo scheme
	15 June	Fitz gives lecture on 'Religious Teaching'
	July–August	Fanny's illness in Karori
	18 August	Fitz gives lecture on 'The Nature of Art'
	16 September	Birth of tenth child (Otho) in Karori
	1 December	Press Company formed in Christchurch
1869	14 May	William's leg injured in accident in Karori
	13 December	Death of Fanny's mother in London
1870	March	Publication in London of 'The Self-Reliant Policy in New Zealand: A Letter'
	5 July	Julius Vogel introduces public works policy
	6 June	Fitz accused of trying to influence Colonial Office
	June	Fitz awarded CMG in Queen's Birthday Honours
	6 September	Death of Henry Selfe in London
	29 September	Fitz gives lecture titled 'On Government'
	November	Fitz forms plans to buy Pitt Island in the Chathams
1871	Jan/Feb	Fitz gives up Pitt Island scheme
	15 September	Birth of eleventh child (Geraldine) in Wellington
1873	14 August	Birth of twelfth child (Edward) in Karori
	15 December	Death of Fitz's eldest half-brother (Gerald) in England
1874	5 January	Fitz writes will in Timaru
	April	Fitz and Fanny move to Clyde Cliff

1875	October	Engagement announced between Amy FitzGerald and W.H. Levin
1876	18 February	Birth of thirteenth child (Mabel) at Clyde Cliff
	19 April	Lord Lyttelton commits suicide in London
	20 May	Amy marries W.H. Levin in Wellington
	1 November	Abolition of provinces
1877	Autumn	Civil service moves into new government buildings
1878	25–26 January	Fitz travels overland from Christchurch to Hokitika
	15 July	Death of Robert (aged 22) of pneumonia
	October	Fitz appointed auditor-general
	13 December	William marries Ella Smith in Taranaki
1879	September	W.H. Levin elected to parliament
1880	16 May	Death of Selwyn (aged 15) of diphtheria
	29 June	Death of Katherine (aged 13) of diphtheria
	21 August	Death of Mabel (aged 4) of meningitis
	Sept–Dec	Fitz and Maurice in Australia
1881	23 March	Death of William's wife Ella at Clyde Cliff
1882	12 April	William marries again, to Frances Featherston
	19 June	Gerald marries Esther Budge in Picton
	15 November	Fitz gives lecture on 'The Possible Future Developments of Government in Free States'
1883	22 February	Fanny and Maurice embark for London
1884	15 January	Fanny and Maurice return to Wellington
	April	Engagement announced between Evangeline and James Poole Brandon
1885	8 February	Evangeline marries James Poole Brandon in Wellington
1886	11 April	Fitz's sister-in-law Jane dies in wreck of *Taiaroa*
	10 July	Death of Maurice (aged 24) of tuberculosis
1887		Fitz's essay on 'Imperial Federation' published in *England and her Colonies* in London
1888	2 June	Death of William (aged 34) of kidney disease
1889	July–Nov	Fitz and Fanny visit London

1893	30 March	Gladstone reads Fitz's letter in House of Commons in support of the Government of Ireland Bill
	15 September	Death of W.H. Levin in Wellington
	19 September	Electoral Act passed allowing for female suffrage
	8 November	Fitz gives inaugural address at opening of Wellington Citizens' Institute
1895	29 August	Fitz gives address at second annual meeting of Incorporated Institute of Accountants
1896	8 February	Amy leaves for England
	2 August	Death of Fitz at Clyde Cliff, aged 78
1900	20 January	Edward sails for Boer War in South Africa
	8 July	Death of Fanny at Clyde Cliff, aged 68

Notes to the Text

PART I: FITZ FINDS A VOCATION
Quotations from contemporary accounts
Manuscript sources
FitzGerald family papers (BL, Mss Eur D.1171)
FitzGerald papers (ATL, MS–Papers–0064): letters from Robert FitzGerald,
    W.S. Landor, W.E. Gladstone, Lord Lincoln, Lord Lyttelton, Lord Naas
FitzGerald (J.E. and Fanny), letters to William Vaux (ATL, qMS–0792)
Gladstone papers (BL, Mss Add 44367–44368): letters from FitzGerald
Godley papers (CM, 131/39): letters from FitzGerald, Wynne
Lyttelton papers (CM, 79/50): letters from FitzGerald

Published sources
Landor, W.S., *The Letters of Walter Savage Landor: Private and Public*
Wakefield, E.G., *Founders of Canterbury*
Wakefield, E.J., *The Hand-Book for New Zealand*
Canterbury Papers
New Zealand Journal

1 The Maternity

'In the midst of domestic enjoyments': *Derby Mercury*, 15 April 1819

'The mobs of poor men': FitzGerald, MS lecture, Christchurch Mechanics Institute, 1864 (CM, O'Neill papers)

'It was almost an unknown topic': J.S. Bartrum, www.bartrum.net

'Often roar with laughter': Augustus Hare, *The Years with Mother*, p. 58

'Much distressed … walked straight from the Senate House': 'Dreams', *Monthly Review*, January 1890, p. 4

2 Pride and Poverty

'Even gentlemen of the first station': Charles Buller, 1843 (*Illustrated London News*, 7 September 1850)

'There was seldom an evening': Graves Sawle, p. 56

'The Scinde horse took the enemy's camp': Sir Charles Napier, Hyderabad, 18 February 1843

'Now for the first time': W.S. Landor, July 1843 (*Letters and Other Unpublished Writings of Walter Savage Landor*, pp. 108–09)

'Going from port to port … a dance at a friend's house … had the boat broached-to': 'Dreams', *Monthly Review*, January 1890, p. 3

3 Coins and Catalogues

'Powerfully moved … strange monuments … the hard and brittle material': FitzGerald, 'The Nature of Art', 18 August 1868, pp. 6–7

'A special gift for repartee': the *Press*, 25 May 1911

'I had lately a delightful letter': W.S. Landor, 17 January 1845 (*Letters of Walter Savage Landor: Private and Public*, pp. 139–40)

'Walked together, and sketched': MS chapter of novel (CM, O'Neill papers)

'None of these four sons': will of Gerald FitzGerald, proved London, June 1845

'Who can describe the parting scene?': MS chapter of novel (CM, O'Neill papers)

'Is it possible': W.S. Landor, 15 March 1846 (*Letters of Walter Savage Landor: Private and Public*, p. 152)

4 The Colonial Microbe

'I know not what language to use': Irish Migration: A Letter', p. 19

'My Lords and gentlemen': 'A Letter to the Noblemen', pp. 3, 6, 11, 13

'Went unheeded': 'Irish Migration: A Letter', p. 22

'Infected with the colonial microbe': attributed to William Rolleston (Stout, p. 3)

'The shocking distress': 'Irish Migration: A Letter', pp. 14, 21

'Be ready to consider any practical plan': Hawes to FitzGerald, 24 February 1848 ('Vancouver's Island, the Hudson's Bay Company …', p. 9)

'England ought to know': 'Vancouver's Island: The New Colony', p. 3

'What is to become of them? … The great emigration': 'Irish Migration: A Letter', pp. 4–5, 20

'The enterprise of young men': 'Vancouver's Island', pp. 3, 7

'This work was on the point': *An Examination of the Charter and Proceedings of the Hudson's Bay Company*, p. 294

Report of the Commissioners (British Museum), Parliamentary Papers, Vol XXIV, Session 1850

'The Principal Librarian reported': quoted in letter from British Museum to R.B. O'Neill (CM, O'Neill papers)

5 A Slice of England

'There is in a colonial life': Canterbury Association, prospectus, June 1848 (reprinted in
    Canterbury Papers, no. 1, 1850)
'That the recent attempt ... the evils inflicted ... the tide of young': MS draft speech
    (CM, O'Neill papers)
'Simmering with discontent': Gladstone to Adderley (Childe-Pemberton, p. 70)
'A despotic and irresponsible ... the town of Manchester': article reprinted in *The Times*,
    2 January 1850
'The rare enjoyment of an evening': FitzGerald, obituary of Edward Gibbon Wakefield,
    Press, 21 June 1862
'Let anyone put an advertisement': Hawkins, *Canterbury Association, A Full and Accurate
    Report*, p. 24
'Had a conversation with Hutt ... *professedly* on the score of ill health ... If the scheme
    succeeds': Wynne to Godley, 29 March 1850 (CM, Godley papers)
'Appearing before him ... His Lordship came up': 'Speech delivered at the Breakfast by
    the Early Colonists', 6 February 1868, p. 7
'We have perhaps been rather late': Adderley, *Canterbury Association, A Full and Accurate
    Report*, p. 21
'The Canterbury colony will open': FitzGerald to unidentified peer, 2 April 1850 (NLW,
    MS 2572 E)
'One of the best of our colonists': J.R. Godley to his father, 20 January 1851 (CM,
    Godley papers, 131/39)
'To meet and discuss ... illustrating his remarks': *Ipswich Journal*, 25 May 1850
'It is within your power': FitzGerald to intending colonists, 10 July 1850 (CM, Barker
    papers, 12/49)
'Intriguing and without scruple': Adderley (Lord Norton), (Childe-Pemberton, pp. 69,
    70, 87)

6 Just a Schoolgirl

'I've lain beneath the feet': FitzGerald, 'The Flower', 1888 (ATL, FitzGerald papers,
    MS–Papers–0064)
'The best house in the town': Morton, p. 13
'The very temple of hospitality': Holman, p. 20
'The timid lively child of twelve': MS chapter of novel (CM, O'Neill papers)
'Nothing is more graceful': 'Gymnastic Training', *New Zealand Schoolmaster*, 1886
'Those mysterious stirrings': John Henry Newman, *Sermons ... Preached Before the
    University of Oxford*, 1843 (excerpt in private collection)
'FitzGerald is engaged to be married': Wynne to Godley, 5 July 1850 (CM, Godley
    papers)
'Heaven speed you, noble band!': G.W. Martin, words by Martin Tupper (Amodeo,
    p. 312)
'Good old English fare': *London Examiner*, 7 September 1850
'We sail at daybreak': FitzGerald to Lord Lyttelton, 3 September 1850 (HHA, 10/19/4)
'We awoke very early': Dr Alfred Barker, diary (Burdon, p. 16)
'Sternly real did I feel my position then': Ward, pp. 17–18

PART II: FITZ STARTS A NEW LIFE
Quotations from contemporary accounts:
Manuscript sources
Barker papers (CM, 12/49): transcripts of diaries and letters
Bishop, Mary Ann, diary September 1850–May 1851 (CM, ARC1900.38)

FitzGerald family papers (BL, Mss Eur D.1171)
FitzGerald papers (ATL, MS–Papers–0064): letter from Sir George Grey
FitzGerald (J.E. and Fanny), letters to William Vaux (ATL, qMS–0792)
Godley papers (CM, 131/39): letters from FitzGerald, and from Godley to his father
Lyttelton papers (CM, 79/50): letters from FitzGerald
Selfe papers (HC): letters from FitzGerald
Published sources
Deans, Jane, *Letters to my Grandchildren*
Godley, Charlotte, *Letters from Early New Zealand*
Gundry, Dr J.S., *Dr Gundry's Diary*
Innes, C.L., *Canterbury Sketches*
Jackson, Thomas, 'In the days of our youth' (*Press*, 16 December 1911)
Ward, *The Journal of Edward Ward*
Canterbury Papers
Lyttelton Times
New Zealand Journal

7 The *Charlotte Jane*

'A fussy, methodical red-tapeist': Pratt, p. 210
'Oh, no you don't!': *Press*, 25 May 1911

8 The Cabin on the Hill

'The most affecting moment of both our lives': Godley, *Writings & Speeches*, p. 252
'Perfectly inaccessible except by a crane': Sewell, Vol. I, p. 126
'Imported cattle are more liable': Wakefield, E.J., p. 148

9 A Bigger Fish

'It was absolutely necessary': Wakefield to Godley, 17 August 1850 (Wakefield, E.G.,
    p. 318)
'Been up and down … He is nearly the most provoking man': ibid. pp. 318–19
'Who can ever forget': quoted in Carrington, p. 114
'It is only colonists who have any idea': Georgiana Bowen, 12 March 1851 (Ell,
    pp. 30–31)
'A slice of England … It is difficult to glance': *The Times*, London, 5 July 1851
'It did not appear to him': Grey, June 1852 (Bohan, *To Be a Hero*, p. 124)
'We have heard no very remarkable': Charles Torlesse (CM, Lyttelton papers, 79/50)
'We each went in our turn': Dr A.C. Barker (Andersen, *Old Christchurch*, p. 68)

11 Sheep, Sheep, Sheep

'I long to be off to a sheep station': FitzGerald to Rintoul, 6 July 1851 (Gardner, p. 32)
'I venture to hope': FitzGerald to Gladstone, 19 December 1851 (BL, Gladstone papers,
    Mss Add 44371, f. 92)
'Tell Mrs FitzGerald': Godley to FitzGerald, 24 February 1852 (CM, FitzGerald,
    transcripts of inwards correspondence)
'Step by step it grew enfeebled': Thomas Cholmondeley, 5 May 1852 (*Lyttelton Times*,
    8 May 1852)

PART III: FITZ BECOMES A POLITICIAN
Quotations from contemporary accounts
Manuscript sources
FitzGerald family papers (BL, Mss Eur D.1171)

FitzGerald (J.E. and Fanny): letters to William Vaux (ATL, qMS–0792)
Lyttelton papers (CM, 79/50): letters from FitzGerald
FitzGerald papers (ATL, MS–Papers–0064): letters from R. FitzGerald, Gladstone,
    Godley, Lord Lyttelton
Godley papers (CM, 131/39): letters from Bowen, Cookson, FitzGerald, Hamilton,
    Harman, Sewell, Watts Russell, Weld, and from FitzGerald to Hamilton (1856)
Selfe papers (HC): letters from FitzGerald, Godley, and from FitzGerald to Hamilton
    (1854)
Stafford papers (ATL, MS–Papers–0028): letters from FitzGerald
Published sources
Cox, C.P., *Personal Notes and Reminiscences of an Early Canterbury Settler*
Deans, Jane, *Letters to my Grandchildren*
FitzGerald, letter to 'a friend', 13 August 1854 (*Daily Southern Cross*, 27 October 1854)
Innes, C.L., *Canterbury Sketches*
Monro, Dr David, diary entries quoted in Wright-St Clair, *Thoroughly a Man of the
    World*
Sewell, Henry, *The Journal of Henry Sewell 1853–1857*, Vols I and II
Lyttelton Times
New Zealand Parliamentary Debates

12 A Boy out of School
'Unreasonable and inconsiderate ... inexpressively comic': Godley to Adderley, 22 May
    1851, 20 January 1852 (Godley, *Extracts*, pp. 176, 183)
'Speaking with much humour': Gundry, II, p. 67
'The people here are so anxious': Godley to Adderley, 11 November 1852 (Godley,
    Extracts, p. 190)
'For the last five years': Godley, *Writings & Speeches*, pp. 167–68, 169, 173–74
'As level as the sea ... there was nothing between us': Stack, p. 6
'The office which you are about to confer': FitzGerald, 18 July 1853 (Gardner, p.16)
'Go back to your sausage machine ... Is thy servant a dog?': Alpers, p. 88

13 Dignity and Decorum
'There is a certain solemnity': 'Address of His Honor the Superintendent', pp. 2, 12
'When Captain FitzGerald joined the ship': Captain Moresby to Lucius FitzGerald,
    1 November 1853, FitzGerald family papers (BL, Mss Eur D.1171)

14 A Restless Husband
'The officials who formed the old executive': Weld to Scrope (Lovat, p. 92)
'The difficulties that would arise ... enormous discrepancy': FitzGerald, 'Official
    Memoranda', p. 16
'Forbidden by honour and duty': ibid. p. 18
'I myself would continue': ibid. p. 22
'Went wild': Weld to Charlotte Godley, 12 January 1855 (CM, O'Neill papers, folder
    17, item 261)
'A man incapable of speaking': FitzGerald, letter to *Daily Southern Cross*, September
    1854 (reprinted in *Lyttelton Times*, 2 December 1854)

15 A Beast with a Bill
'The reception of the ex-ministry': *Daily Southern Cross*, 10 November 1854
'Placing it at the disposal': FitzGerald to Lyttelton Colonists Society, 6 October 1854
    (*Daily Southern Cross*, 10 November 1854)

'I ask you not to despair': *Lyttelton Times*, 11 October 1854
'Inordinately vain ... thoroughly heartless': Wakefield to *New Zealander*, September
    1854 (reprinted in *Lyttelton Times*, 2 December 1854)
'Drove home in an open chaise': Jerningham Wakefield, 8 May 1855 (Temple, p. 517)
'His passion for work ... a parliamentary platypus': Cox, Alfred, *Recollections*, p. 115

16 Spasms of the Heart
'If I am wanted': FitzGerald to Stafford, 5 December 1855 (ATL, Stafford papers,
    MS–Papers–0028)

17 A Missed Opportunity
'I wish FitzGerald had been here': Cargill to Hamilton, 28 May 1856 (CM, Godley
    papers, 131/39)
'I wish indeed FitzGerald were with us': Sewell to Hamilton, 11 June 1856 (ibid.)
'Had I been sufficiently recovered ... The whole colony': FitzGerald, Address to the
    Electors of Lyttelton, 17 November 1856, pp. 3, 5
'The delight of small boys': Cox, Alfred, *Recollections*, p. 118
'Bundles containing our best bonnets': Tripp, p. 2
'So rough was the road': Purchas, p. 61
'It must be admitted': ibid. p. 62
'To till the land': FitzGerald, address to provincial council, 30 June 1857 (*Daily Southern
    Cross*, 21 August 1857)
'Will not wholly deprive us': provincial council to FitzGerald, 3 May 1857 (ATL,
    W.J. Hunter papers, MS 1777–01, f. 148)
'I confess I am greatly mortified': FitzGerald to provincial council, 20 June 1857 (ibid.
    f. 150)
'I certainly did not think it worthwhile': FitzGerald, address to provincial council,
    30 June 1857 (*Daily Southern Cross*, 21 August 1857)
Opening of the Sumner Road, reported in *Lyttelton Times*, 26 August 1857

PART IV: FITZ STARTS A NEWSPAPER
Quotations from contemporary accounts:
Manuscript sources:
Burke, E.J., 'Reminiscences of Old Canterbury' (CM, ARC1900.109)
Canterbury Provincial Government Archives (ANZ, CH287): letters to Moorhouse
    from FitzGerald, Selfe
FitzGerald papers (ATL, MS–Papers–0064): letters from Lord Carnarvon, Godley,
    Grey, Harman
FitzGerald (J.E. and Fanny), letters to William Vaux (ATL, qMS–0792)
Godley papers (CM, 131/39): letters from Bowen, Cookson, FitzGerald, Harman, Weld
Hall papers (ATL, MS–Papers–1784): letters from FitzGerald (J.E. and Fanny), Selfe
Levin, Amy (née FitzGerald), biographical notes
Lyttelton papers (CM, 79/50): letters from FitzGerald, Hamilton
Selfe papers (HC): letters from Bowen, FitzGerald (J.E. and Fanny), Harman,
    Hamilton, Moorhouse
Sewell, Henry, diary 1859–66, TS, Vol 3 (ATL, qMS–1788)
Published sources:
Carter, C.R., *Life and Recollections of a New Zealand Colonist*
Chudleigh, *Diary of E.R. Chudleigh 1862–1921*
Cox, C.P., *Personal Notes and Reminiscences of an Early Canterbury Settler*

Innes, C.L., *Canterbury Sketches*
Scholefield, *Richmond–Atkinson Papers*, Vols I and II
Lyttelton Times
New Zealand Parliamentary Debates
Press

18 An Influential Colonist
'I sent you a parting shot': FitzGerald to Stafford, 24 October 1857 (ATL, Stafford
     papers, MS–Papers–0028)
'Great regret at the stoppage': *London Examiner*, 14 November 1857
'An eloquent and glowing ... where the position of the labouring': *Otago Witness*,
     1 January 1859
'Mr FitzGerald was the first who landed': Godley, *Writings & Speeches*, pp. 252–53, 254
'Taking a final survey of the ship': Butler, p. 1
'I am quite persuaded': FitzGerald, 30 June 1857 (Andersen, J.C., *Jubilee History*)
'If young men want to go out': *Otago Witness*, 1 January 1859
'But still ill ... grown much': Edward Stafford travel diary, 11 April, 12 May 1859
     (Bohan, *Blest Madman*, pp. 178, 179)
'I want to ask you to be Godfather': FitzGerald to Lord Lyttelton, 22 June 1859 (HHA,
     10/19/6A)
'It is only recently': FitzGerald to Carnarvon, 19 May 1859 (BL, Carnarvon papers, Add
     MS 60782, f. 32)
'I wish to say a word ... You seemed to think': FitzGerald to Lord Lyttelton, 20 August
     1859 (HHA, 10/19/30)
'I can't tell you how I long': FitzGerald to Nina Gresson, 15 September 1859 (private
     collection)
'A Bill has been brought ... although acting ... a great step ... simply praying':
     FitzGerald to Richmond, 17 August 1860 (*Otago Witness*, 14 November 1860)
'Superfluous, dangerous ... As one who has taken a share': FitzGerald, Memorandum,
     5 July 1860, p. 10
'The policy of this bill': FitzGerald, Memorandum no. 2, 30 July 1860, pp. 17–19
'With an indifference ... When I recollect': FitzGerald to Richmond, 17 August 1860
     (published in *Daily Southern Cross*, 30 October 1860)
'The Bill is opposed by ... all the Tory party': FitzGerald to *The Times*, 17 August 1860
     (*The Times*, 20 August 1860)
'An obstinate opposition': Fortescue to Gore Browne, 27 August 1860 (Bohan, *Blest
     Madman*, p. 183)
'No labour, time or money': FitzGerald to Richmond, 17 August 1860 (*Otago Witness*,
     14 November 1860)

19 Without Fear or Favour
'FitzGerald! Once again we meet!': Crosbie Ward, *Lyttelton Times* (Reeves, *Canterbury
     Rhymes*, pp. 70–71)
'Among other ideas': FitzGerald to Gladstone, 3 October 1849 (BL, Add MS 44368,
     f. 257)
'Come over to Christchurch tomorrow morning': Raven to Watson, 14 May 1861
     (O'Neill, p. 13)
'I want your regular assistance': FitzGerald to Jacobs, 15 May 1861 (ATL, FitzGerald
     papers, MS–Papers–0064)
'The present crisis ... If the railway be made': FitzGerald to electors of Akaroa, May
     1861 (CM, O'Neill papers, item 404)

'A newcomer with no knowledge ... only nominal': George Sale, quoted in a cutting
from *Press*, c. 1928
'There is no honest man but FitzGerald': *New Zealand Chronicle*, 13 July 1861
'The sod which has been turned today': Archdeacon Mathias, 17 July 1861 (Reed,
p. 168)

20 No Common Man
'Always hung loosely': E.J. Burke (CM, MacDonald Dictionary of Canterbury
Biographies)
'The worst of our rivers': Sewell, Vol. II, pp. 208, 210
'I well remember what a serious expenditure': Cox, Alfred, *Recollections*, p. 115
'Looking at him as he sits': *Lyttelton Times*, 4 January 1862
'The Hippopotamus ... There is a class of human beings': 'Cadets', *Press*, 8 March 1862

21 The Grand Demonstration
'The people are dying out': Trollope, p. 124
'Raising the expectations': FitzGerald to Gore Browne, 11 August 1856 (Evison, p. 254)
'Convoke the greatest alarm': FitzGerald to McLean, 16 August 1856 (ATL, McLean
papers, MS–Papers–0032–0272)
'One thing is clear': FitzGerald to Stafford, 27 July 1857 (ATL, Stafford papers,
MS–Papers–0028)
'The Natives are not represented in the Assembly': Memorandum no. 2, 30 July 1860,
p. 12
'The most eloquent of our public men': *Daily Southern Cross*, 6 September 1862
'By far the finest piece of oratory': FitzGerald, MS lecture (CM, O'Neill papers)
'Mr Speaker, if I were to say': FitzGerald, 'The Native Policy of New Zealand, a speech
delivered in the House of Representatives', 6 August 1862, pp. 4, 32, 33–34, 35
Farm sale at the Springs: *Lyttelton Times*, 11, 22 October 1862, Chudleigh, pp. 62–63

22 Friend Whititera
'FitzGerald ... is an architect': Gore Browne to Adderley, 15 June 1858 (Bohan, *Blest
Madman*, p. 173)
'They sang together and separately': C.W. Richmond, 7 December 1862 (CM, O'Neill
papers, folder 17)
'Remarkable for its spirit': Charles Darwin, 24 March 1863 (Darwin correspondence
project, letter 4058)
'Sweet Maid Marian': FitzGerald to Miss Raven, 1 January 1863 (ATL, FitzGerald
papers, MS–Papers–0064)
Celebrations for marriage of Prince of Wales, 9 July 1863, Andersen, *Old Christchurch*,
pp. 344–49; Pratt, p. 274
'He was quite ignorant of the whole facts': Weld to Godley, October 1861 (CM, Godley
Papers)
'Our attention has been called': *Taranaki Herald*, 8 August 1863
'The present suspicious and sulky attitude': FitzGerald to Adderley, 13 October 1865
(*The Times*, London, 20 December 1865)
'Moved [them] again ... an impracticable dream ... Do you think I am': *Press*,
9 September 1863
'Out of the 51 persons qualified': *Lyttelton Times*, 9 September 1863
'Enormous crime ... to be committed': *Daily Southern Cross*, 7 November 1863
'I do appeal to the House': *Daily Southern Cross*, 19 November 1863

'The whole colony is made to suffer': Address to the Electors of Lyttelton, 17 November
    1865, p. 22

23 A Prophet in the Desert
'Took a great deal of trouble ... massive strength': FitzGerald to Hamilton, 14 August
    1895 (Christ's College Archives)
'Rather sublime than beautiful': Jacobs (quoted in Hamilton, p. 12)
'The great complaint, the never-ending subject': Barker, pp. 42, 59
'The management or disposition of my property': power of attorney, 9 October 1863
    (ATL, FitzGerald papers, MS–Papers–0064)
'You are not using me well': Selfe to FitzGerald, 14 April 1864 (HC, Selfe papers)
'Paying a very high ... we should have felt it necessary': memorandum, 5 November
    1864 (ATL, FitzGerald papers, MS–Papers–0064)
'We may say': Harman & Stevens to FitzGerald, 14 November 1864 (CM, O'Neill
    papers)
'Bitter and unseemly ... utterly – I am not afraid to use': FitzGerald, 'The Self-Reliant
    Policy', p. 6
'I, together with others': FitzGerald to Adderley, 14 November 1864 (*Weekly Press*,
    1 April 1865)
'Sacrificed every principle ... irretrievable mischief ... disgracefully ... it takes ten
    Englishmen ... the real truth': speech reprinted in 'The Military Defences of
    New Zealand', 1864
'We trust that our ... citizens': *New Zealand Herald*, 27 July 1864
'The soldiers, having heard': advertisement in *Daily Southern Cross*, 9 December 1864
'Conveying to you': FitzGerald to Cameron, 9 December 1864 (*Wellington Independent*,
    17 December 1864)
'A grand public demonstration': *Press*, 15 December 1864
'Don't let this business cause any coolness': Selfe to FitzGerald, 20 September 1864
    (HC, Selfe papers)

PART V: FITZ GOES TO WELLINGTON
Quotations from contemporary accounts:
Manuscript sources
Atkinson, Arthur, MS diary 1865–66 (ATL, MS–0110)
FitzGerald family papers (BL, Mss Eur D.1171)
FitzGerald papers (ATL, MS–Papers–0064): letters from Gladstone, Lord Lyttelton,
    and Harman & Stevens correspondence
Gladstone papers (BL, Add MS 44403, 44405): letters from FitzGerald
Hall papers (ATL, MS–Papers–1784): letters from FitzGerald (J.E. and Fanny)
Levin, Amy (née FitzGerald), autobiographical notes
Lyttelton papers (CM, 79/50): letters from FitzGerald
McLean papers (ATL, 1551–272, 0032–0272): letters from FitzGerald
Rolleston family papers (ATL, MS–Papers–0446): letters from FitzGerald (J.E. and
    Fanny)
Selfe papers (HC): letters from Bowen, FitzGerald, Moorhouse
Sewell, Henry, diary 1859–66, TS, Vol 3 (ATL, qMS–1788)
Published sources
Chudleigh, *Diary of E.R. Chudleigh 1862–1921*
FitzGerald, Otho, *Leaves from the Life of a Colonial Parson*
Innes, C.L., *Canterbury Sketches*

Scholefield, *Richmond–Atkinson Papers*, Vols I and II
Evening Post, Wellington
Lyttelton Times
New Zealand Parliamentary Debates
Press

24 The Road to Hokitika
'Make the road, Johnny': poem titled 'A Road Song' published in *Punch in Canterbury*,
    1865 (Reeves, *Canterbury Rhymes*, p. 94)
'As speedily as possible': Hall to Dobson, 14 March 1865 (Dobson, p. 14)
'It is clear that the right pass': FitzGerald to Bealey, 29 March 1865 (Logan, pp. 39–40)
'The farthest point … We start at nine o'clock': FitzGerald to Bealey, 31 March 1865
    (ibid, p. 40)
'A kind of roofed van': Harper, p. 93
'Bend and twist about': Lyttelton, *Two Lectures*, Lecture 2, p. 26
'Swinging, rocking motion … creaking and rolling': Courage, pp. 37–38
Description of 'picnic party' expedition: *Lyttelton Times*, 15 April 1865; *Press*, 15 April
    1865
'I had previously examined': Dobson to Hall, 11 April 1865 (Dobson, p. 15)
'The most practicable pass': Dobson to Hall, 5 April 1865 (ibid.)
'I would have had far less pleasure': *Weekly Press*, 27 May 1865
'But are *different* … be glad to work': 'Memorandum on a proposal': MS draft, 16 July
    1865 (CM, O'Neill papers)
'FitzGerald considers himself a man of genius': *Southern Monthly Magazine*, January
    1864

25 An Ordinary Rooster
'An experiment, the result of which': *Wellington Independent*, 15 August 1865
'It is if a notorious poacher': *Lyttelton Times*, 14 September 1865
'I like FitzGerald exceedingly … but I was amazed': Fenton to Rolleston, 7 November
    1865 (ATL, Rolleston papers, 82-355-09/1)
'Of mushroom growth … vowing vengeance … the members of the Government':
    Lyttelton Times, 6 September 1865
'To guide and moderate … language calculated': *Press*, 15 September 1865
'The full and cordial support': Frederick Weld, 11 October 1865 (Lovat, p. 133)
'He did not propose to alter': FitzGerald, 'The Self-Reliant Policy', p. 8
'The question which will be put': speech, 2 November 1865 (reported in *Press*,
    4 November 1865)
'We are having such public meetings': FitzGerald to Rolleston, 10 November 1865
    (ATL, Rolleston papers, 82-355-09/1)

26 A Painful Parting
'A good many people think': Filumena Weld, 12 February 1866 (Bohan, *Stafford*, p. 218)
'Feeling that he had been made a tool of': *Evening Post*, Wellington, 17 August 1866
'Mr FitzGerald, who had retired in a sulk': *New Zealand Herald*, 28 September 1866
'The following quantity of gold': *West Coast Times*, 12 December 1865
'Gold escort arrived here': 14 December 1865 (Logan, p. 59)
'The House of Representatives is a body': 'Address to the Electors of Lyttelton',
    17 November 1856, p. 10
'Very bitter consequences … the best of women … conveyed to her': Wakefield, Edward,
    p. 25

'There would be nobody to look after the *Press*': fragment of a letter (O'Neill, p. 89)
'Mr FitzGerald walked into the office': Wakefield, Edward, p. 26
Farewell dinner to FitzGerald, 4 April 1867, reported in *Press*, 6 April 1867

27 Chesney Wold

'Up steep, steep hills': Mansfield, 'Prelude'
'A great old rambling house': Mansfield, 'About Pat', Queen's College magazine,
    December 1905, p. 5
'Manner is gentle and amiable', J.C. Richmond, 28 June 1865 (Porter, p. 231)
'Recording my earnest protest': FitzGerald to Fitzherbert, 12 September 1867 (ATL,
    FitzGerald papers, MS–Papers–0064)
'Such cataracts of water': Barker, 15 February 1868 (Burdon, p. 80)
'My pretty garden': Barker, 4 February 1868 (ibid. p. 79)
'We had a very pleasant meeting': Barker, 15 February 1868 (ibid. p. 81)
'It is a sort of return match': 'Speech delivered at the Breakfast by the Early Colonists of
    Canterbury', 6 February 1868

28 A Rigid System of Economy

'Poor FitzGerald writes in very low spirits': Bowen to Lyttelton, 1 June 1868 (HHA,
    10/19/19)
'The standard of public life ... I could not reconcile': FitzGerald to Grey, 9 September
    1868 (ATL, W.J. Hunter papers, MS–Papers–1777–4)
'Very seriously ill ... Had it not been for my husband's': Fanny FitzGerald to Lord
    Lyttelton, 7 December 1868 (HHA, 10/19/24)
'Going on satisfactorily ... composed a very pretty hymn ... a new accomplishment':
    ibid.
'Just now we have a sick house': Barker to his brother, 17 December 1869 (CM, Barker
    papers, 12/49)
'An inalienable provision ... to pay the dividends': will of Mary Draper, proved London,
    4 January 1870

29 An Island in Sight

'It seems an unusual course': Bell and Featherston to Fox, 15 March 1870,
      'Correspondence relating to a letter by J.E. FitzGerald Esq', Wellington, 1870
    (ATL, FitzGerald papers, MS–Papers–0064)
'The opportunity of offering': Fox to FitzGerald, 6 June 1870 (ibid.)
'Great regret ... the principle that any such attempt ... I was only speaking': FitzGerald
    to Fox, 9 June 1870 (ibid.)
'More an appeal to the snobbish': FitzGerald, 'Imperial Federation', *England and Her
    Colonies*, p. 71
'My dear Stafford, I told you one day': FitzGerald to Stafford, 24 November 1870
    (ATL, Stafford papers, 0028-34)
'With regard to taking refuge elsewhere': Rolleston to FitzGerald, December 1870
    (Stewart, p. 40)
'His duty to sustain running paper warfare': Vogel (Dalziel, p. 129)
'A very jolly dinner party': Monro, 25 September 1871 (Wright-St Clair, p. 261)
'The taking of the whole Pacific islands': FitzGerald to Grey, 3 December 1883 (Bohan,
    Blest Madman, p. 321)

30 FitzGerald's Folly

'A house for Mrs Fanny FitzGerald', specifications and contracts (ATL, Swan family
    papers, fMS–3928–12)

'I confess that I have long looked': Sir George Arney to Fanny FitzGerald, 28 March
    1874 (Macalister, p.16)

'We had a very pleasant visit from Mrs FitzGerald': Jane Atkinson to Anna Richmond,
    26 October 1875 (Porter, p. 304)

'One thing is quite obvious': FitzGerald to Selfe, 3 September 1856 (HC, Selfe papers)

'The vessels at the wharf': *Evening Argus* (Gore, p. 48)

'A long and animated ... looked much like bribery': House of Representatives,
    28 October 1876 (*Otago Witness*, 4 November 1876)

'With such sharp turns': Harper, p. 96

PART VI: FITZ GROWS OLD

Quotations from contemporary accounts:

Manuscript sources

FitzGerald family papers (BL, Mss Eur D.1171)

FitzGerald papers (ATL, MS–Papers–0064): letters from Gladstone, Grey, Hall

Gladstone papers (BL, Add MS 44498, 44507): letters from FitzGerald

Hall papers (ATL, MS–Papers–1784): letters from FitzGerald (J.E. and Fanny)

Levin, Amy (née FitzGerald), autobiographical notes

Rolleston family papers (ATL, MS–Papers–0446): letters from FitzGerald (J.E. and
    Fanny)

Published sources

Chudleigh, *Diary of E R Chudleigh 1862–1921*

FitzGerald, Otho, *Leaves from the Life of a Colonial Parson*

Gore, Ross, *Levins 1841–1941*

Scholefield, *Richmond–Atkinson Papers*, Vols I and II

Evening Post, Wellington

Lyttelton Times

New Zealand Parliamentary Debates

Press

Levin, W.H., obituaries

FitzGerald, J.E., obituaries

31 An Afflicted Family

'A more disconnected, disunited, ill-assorted party', Captain Russell, NZPD (Bohan,
    To Be a Hero, p. 264)

'With a view to assisting the enquiry': Hall to FitzGerald, 3 September 1880 (ATL,
    W.J. Hunter papers, MS–Papers–1777)

'Recording all the chief decisions': *The Star*, 4 June 1888

'In his beloved canoe, took many a long': *Press*, 11 June 1888

'Wretched night, no sleep ... large body of water': Sir John Hall, diary entries, 4, 13,
    14 March 1883 (Terrace Station Archives, Hororata)

'Was beguiled by dancing': *The Star*, 24 July 1883

'We could hardly see ... had most narrow escape': Sir John Hall, diary entries, 4, 8 June
    1883 (Terrace Station Archives, Hororata)

32 The Flash of a Meteor

'I was only a day or two ago': FitzGerald to Domett, 19 May 1883 (ATL, Domett
    papers, MS–Papers–1632)
'The praises of his contemporaries': *Taranaki Herald*, 13 July 1886
'She had seen the roses fade': MS chapter of novel (CM, O'Neill papers)
'Singularly sweet temper ... Great sympathy is felt here': *The Star*, 4 June 1888
'This is the seventh child': Sir John Hall, diary entry, 4 June 1888 (Garner, p. 229)
'The doctrine of competition ... These colonies': 'The Possible Future Developments of
    Governments in Free States', pp. 12–13, 18, 30
'No ordinary man ... The pity of it': Gisborne (1897), pp. 80–82
'Much time and labour have been bestowed': FitzGerald to Jervois, 12 July 1888 (ATL,
    W.J. Hunter papers, MS–Papers–1777)

33 White Azaleas

'I toil on amidst figures': FitzGerald to Domett, 19 May 1883 (ATL, Domett papers,
    MS–Papers–1632)
'Mr J.E. FitzGerald, who has been ill for some time': *Otago Witness*, 18 July 1889
'Letters received by the last mail': *West Coast Times*, 30 October 1889
'His innocence and simplicity': FitzGerald to Amy, 1892 (private collection)
'Sorr, I want to collogue': FitzGerald to Bottomley, 2 March 1891 (ATL, FitzGerald
    papers, MS–Papers–0064)
'Matters of local and transient interest': FitzGerald to Grey, 14 April 1892 (ATL,
    W.J. Hunter papers, MS–Papers–1777)
'Not lost but gone before': Margaret Gatty, *Parables from Nature*, second series, 1859
'When I think of those who never more': FitzGerald, 'Unpublished Thoughts in Verse',
    1893
'If I were called on to make a speech': FitzGerald to Norton, September 1892 (Childe-
    Pemberton, pp. 289–90)
'Certainly if it can help': telegram, FitzGerald to Gladstone, January 1893 (Bohan, *Blest
    Madman*, p. 328)
'Will the House forgive me': Gladstone, House of Commons, 30 March 1893 (*New
    Zealand Herald*, 19 May 1893)
'It is admitted on all hands': *New Zealand Herald*, 19 May 1893
'Socialistic philosophy ... We live in an age': Wellington Citizens' Institute, inaugural
    address, pp. 4–5, 10
'I shall require a little assistance': *New Zealand Graphic*, 5 August 1893 (Martin, p. 113)
'Mr FitzGerald will become entitled': FitzGerald, 23 October 1894 (ATL, FitzGerald
    papers, MS–Papers–0064)
'This is a portrait of one who was said': FitzGerald (private collection)

34 Joining the Majority

'The old man would be much pleased': FitzGerald, 28 February 1895 (private collection)
'Our old man is also in bed': Fanny to Emily Richmond, 3 July 1895 (ATL, Richmond
    family papers, 77-173-09/1)
'Minister of Lands Attacks the Auditor-General': *North Otago Times*, 3 August 1896
'The honour you have done me': 'Incorporated Institute of Accountants in New
    Zealand, Address delivered by J.E. FitzGerald', pp. 1, 5–6
'The spectacles are not mine': FitzGerald to Amy, 11 May 1895 (private collection)
'Conveyed her interest as executor': W.H. Levin probate papers, 1893 (ANZ Wellington,
    AAOM 6029 78/4215)

'If I should die tonight': FitzGerald, printed poem (private collection)
'I dreamt … that I was *Mad*': 'Dreams', *Monthly Review*, January 1890, pp. 1–2
'I am much too old and infirm': FitzGerald to Amy, July 1896 (private collection)
Tributes to J.E. FitzGerald, New Zealand Parliamentary Debates, Vol XCIV, 4 August
    1896

35 A Pilgrim Mother

'Nothing said about the Pilgrim Mothers': Mary Rolleston (Rolleston, p. 117)
'Fortunate and happy … immense sum total': FitzGerald to Selfe (Bohan, *Blest
    Madman*, p. 312)
'Those who knew her best': Charles Bowen, *Press*, 11 July 1900
'I leave all property': J.E. FitzGerald, probate papers, 1896 (ANZ, Wellington, AAOM
    6029 97/5234)
'Driving around town': Geraldine FitzGerald obituary (unattributed press cutting)
'The whole of the reclaimed land … the song taken up': *Hawere and Normanby Star*,
    22 January 1900
'The many friends of Mrs J.E. FitzGerald': *Weekly Press*, 13 June 1900
'One of the best and bravest': Charles Bowen, *Press*, 11 July 1900

36 An Unfinished Tale

'Magnificent and valuable property': advertisements in *Evening Post*, January 1901
'The rev. gentleman's health': *New Zealand Freelance*, 9 March 1901
'The Rev. Lyttelton FitzGerald is still in England': *Evening Post*, 14 November 1901
Disappearance of Edward FitzGerald: Edward and Florence FitzGerald probate papers
    1944/45 (ANZ, Auckland, BBAE 1570 557/1944, 241/1945)
'I have come to the conclusion': Edward FitzGerald to Amy FitzGerald (private
    collection)

Bibliography

Manuscript sources
Alexander Turnbull Library, Wellington (ATL)
Atkinson, Arthur S., MS diary, 1865–66 (MS–0110)
Domett, Alfred, papers (MS-Papers-1632)
FitzGerald, J.E., papers (MS–Papers–0064)
FitzGerald, letters from J.E. and Fanny FitzGerald to William Sandys Wright Vaux
(qMS–0792)
Hall, John, papers (MS–Papers–1784)
Hunter, W.J., papers (MS–Papers–1777)
McLean, Donald, correspondence with J.E. FitzGerald (MS–Papers–0032–0272)
Richmond–Atkinson family papers (MS–Papers–4298)
Richmond family papers (77–173)
Rolleston family papers (MS–Papers–0446)
Rolleston, William, papers (77–248, 82–355)
Sewell, Henry, Journal, typescript, 1859–66 (qMS–1787–1788)
Stafford papers (MS–Papers–0028)
Stafford, Edward, travel journal, ed. Edmund Bohan (MS–Papers–6593)
Swan family papers (fMS–Papers–3928–12)

Archives New Zealand/Te Rua Mahara o te Kāwanatanga (ANZ)
Auckland office: probate papers, defence files
Christchurch office: Canterbury Provincial Government Archives
Wellington office: probate papers

British Library, London (BL)
Carnarvon papers (Add MS 60782)
Gladstone papers (Add MS 44367–68, 44371, 44403–05, 44498, 44507)
Papers of Captain Robert FitzGerald, Bombay Army, and James Edward FitzGerald of
New Zealand (MSS Eur D.1171)

Canterbury Museum, Christchurch (CM)
Barker papers (12/49)
Bishop, Mary Ann, journal (ARC1900.38)
Burke, E.J. (ed. J.C. Andersen), 'Reminiscences of Old Canterbury (ARC1900.109)
Draper, Dr William, 'Memoranda of Hospital Stores and Medical Comforts', *Duke of Brontë*, 1851 (Canterbury Association papers, box 2, folder 9)
FitzGerald, J.E., Inwards correspondence, typed transcripts
Godley papers (131/39)
Lyttelton papers (79/50)
MacDonald Dictionary of Canterbury Biographies
O'Neill papers

Christchurch City Libraries, Aotearoa New Zealand Centre (CCL)
Minutes drawn up by the First Body of the Canterbury Colonists
Jackson, Thomas (bishop-elect), Report to Archbishop of Canterbury, 1851 (serialised in *Christchurch Star*, c. 1932)

Guildhall Library, London (GL)
Diocese of London, Cronstadt chaplaincy records

Hagley Hall Archives (HHA)
Letters to Lord Lyttelton (folder 10/19)

Hocken Collections/Uare Taoka o Hakena, University of Otago (HC)
Selfe papers (MSS 0046/001–2, 0047/001–2, 0167–002)

Hororata, Terrace Station Archives
Hall, Sir John, diary, February–June 1883 (Group 1, Series D)

National Library of Wales, Aberystwyth (NLW)
Pennant MSS (MS 2572 E)

Private Collections
Levin, Amy (née FitzGerald), autobiographical notes

Official publications
London
British Museum: Report of the Commissioners, Parliamentary Papers, Vol XXIV, Session 1850

Wellington
Hansard (New Zealand Parliamentary Debates), 1854, 1862–67, 1896

Publications of J.E. FitzGerald
'On a Coin of Guy de Lusignan, King of Cyprus', *Numismatic Chronicle*, 1846
'A Letter to the Noblemen, Gentlemen and Merchants in England', 14 October 1846, London
'Proposal for the Formation of a Colony in Vancouver's Island on the West Coast of North America', London, May 1847
'Vancouver's Island, the New Colony', reprinted from *Colonial Magazine*, August 1848

'Vancouver's Island, the Hudson's Bay Company, and the Government', reprinted from
    Colonial Magazine, September 1848

'Irish Migration: A Letter to W Monsell Esq, MP', 25 September 1848, London

'Vancouver's Island', reprinted from *Colonial Magazine*, c. November 1848

An Examination of the Charter and Proceedings of the Hudson's Bay Company, London,
    1849

'The Society for the Reform of Colonial Government', *Colonial Magazine*, January 1850
    (reprinted in *The Times*, London, 2 January 1850)

Society for the Reform of Colonial Government, manifesto, London, 29 January 1850

'Address of His Honor the Superintendent at the Opening of the First Legislature',
    27 September 1853, Christchurch

'An Address to the Provincial Council of Canterbury ... upon the financial
    arrangements between the general and provincial governments', 1 November 1853,
    Christchurch

'Official Memoranda', letters to Colonel Wynyard, 9 August 1854, Christchurch, 1855

'Address to the Electors of Lyttelton', 17 November 1856, Christchurch

'Letter from J E FitzGerald Esq. on the Waste Lands Act, 1858 and the New Provinces
    Act, 1858', 12 March 1859 (reprinted from *Canterbury Standard*, Christchurch,
    1859)

'Memorandum relating to the Conduct of the Native Affairs in New Zealand, as
    affected by a Bill now before Parliament', 5 July 1860, London

'Memorandum no. 2 relating to the Conduct of the Native Affairs in New Zealand, as
    affected by a Bill now before Parliament', 30 July 1860, London

'The Native Policy of New Zealand: A Speech delivered in the House of
    Representatives', 6 August 1862, Wellington

'The Representation of New Zealand', 1864 (reprinted from *Press*, Christchurch, 1864)

'A Tale I Heard in the Bush', published in *Literary Foundlings: Verse and Prose*,
    Christchurch, 1864

'Letters on the Present State of Maori Affairs' (correspondence between
    J. E. FitzGerald and Aterea Puna, 16 November 1864 and January 1865),
    Christchurch 1865

'The Military Defences of New Zealand: A Speech delivered in the House of
    Representatives', 5 December 1864, Christchurch

'Speech on the Native Affairs of New Zealand', 18 August 1865 (reprinted from *Press*,
    26 August 1865)

'Speech delivered at the Breakfast by the Early Colonists of Canterbury', 6 February
    1868, Christchurch

'Religious Teaching: A Speech delivered at the Presbyterian Church', 15 June 1868,
    Wellington

'The Nature of Art: A Lecture', 18 August 1868, Wellington

'The Self-Reliant Policy in New Zealand: A Letter', 26 December 1869, London, 1870

'On Government: An Address delivered at the schoolroom of the Presbyterian Church',
    29 September 1870, Wellington

'A Strange Story – if True', short story published in *Daily Southern Cross*, 31 May 1873

'Darwino-Theology', article published in *New Zealand Magazine*, January 1876

'The New Zealand University', article published in *New Zealand Magazine*, 1877

'The Constitution of Second or Upper Chambers in Colonial Legislatures', article
    published in *Victorian Review* (Melbourne), October 1882

'A Speech on the Possible Future Developments of Government in Free States',
    15 November 1882, Wellington

'Public Debts and Sinking Funds', article published in *The Victorian Review* (Melbourne), July 1885

'Gymnastic Training', lecture published in *New Zealand Schoolmaster*, April 1886

'Imperial Federation', essay published in *England and Her Colonies* (five best essays submitted to the London Chamber of Commerce), London, 1887

'On the Fourth Dimension', article published in *Monthly Review*, 1889

'Dreams', article published in *Monthly Review*, January 1890

'Shakespeare', two articles published in *Monthly Review*, July 1890

'Unpublished Thoughts in Verse', Wellington, 1893

'Inaugural Address delivered at the opening of the Wellington Citizens' Institute', 8 November 1893, Wellington

'Address delivered by the President, Incorporated Institute of Accountants of New Zealand', 29 August 1895, Wellington

Unpublished Work of J.E. FitzGerald
FitzGerald papers (Alexander Turnbull Library)
'The Flower', printed poem, July 1888

R.B. O'Neill papers (Canterbury Museum)
Speech on the motion that the recent attempt to force convicts on the Cape Colony is tyrannical and unconstitutional, 27 November 1849

Speech on economics delivered to the working men in Christchurch, 1864

Memorandum on a proposal ... for the purpose of determining the best form for ships propelled by machinery, 16 July 1865

Lecture on 18th-century British politics (incomplete)

A Dialogue concerning the Exchequer, Book 1

Paper on Home Rule for Ireland, c. 1893

The Mixed Marriage, A Farce in One Act, play (in the style of Restoration comedy)

Chapter 3 of a romantic novel

Private Collections
'A Galopade', by G.J. Gollop, 1842 (illustrations)

Some Notes on the FitzGeralds of the Queen's County, c. 1889

Letters, Memoirs, Reminiscences, Essays, Contemporary Reports
Adams, C. Warren, *A Spring in the Canterbury Settlement*, Longman, Brown, Green and Longmans, London, 1853

Alpers, O.T.J., *Cheerful Yesterdays*, John Murray, London, 1928

Barker, Lady, *Station Life in New Zealand*, 1883. Reprinted by Golden Press, Christchurch and Auckland, 1973

Bruce, A. Selwyn (ed.), *The Early Days of Canterbury*, Simpson and Williams, Christchurch, 1932

Butler, Samuel, *A First Year in Canterbury Settlement* (1863), The Echo Library, Teddington, 2006 (reprint)

Canterbury Association, *Canterbury Settlement: A full and accurate report of the public meeting held in St Martin's Hall on 17 April 1850*, London, 1850

——*Canterbury Papers*, London 1850–52

Carter, Charles Rooking, *Life and Recollections of a New Zealand Colonist*, 2 vols, R. Madley, London, 1866–75

Chudleigh, E.R. (ed. E.C. Richards), *Diary of E.R. Chudleigh 1862–1921*, Simpson and Williams, Christchurch, 1950

Courage, Sarah Amelia, *Lights and Shadows of Colonial Life*, Whitcoulls, Christchurch, 1976

Cox, Alfred, *Recollections: Australia, England, Ireland, Scotland, New Zealand*, Whitcombe & Tombs, Christchurch, 1884

——*Men of Mark in New Zealand*, Whitcombe & Tombs, Christchurch, 1886

Cox, C.P., *Personal Notes and Reminiscences of an Early Canterbury Settler*, Canterbury Publishing Co., Christchurch, 1915

Deans, Jane, *Letters to My Grandchildren*, 3rd edn, Cadsonbury Publications, Christchurch 1995

Deans, J., *Pioneers of Canterbury: Deans Letters 1840–1854*, A.H. & A.W. Reed, Dunedin, 1937

Dobson, Edward, 'Report upon the Practicability of Constructing a Road through the Otira Gorge', Provincial Government of the Province of Canterbury, Christchurch, 15 May 1865

FitzGerald, Otho, *Leaves from the Life of a Colonial Parson*, privately printed, Christchurch, 1943

Fry, Margot, *Tom's Letters: The private world of Thomas King, Victorian gentleman*, Victoria University Press, Wellington, 2001

Garner, Jean and Foster, Kate, *Letters to Grace: Writing home from colonial New Zealand*, Canterbury University Press, Christchurch, 2011

Gatty, Mrs Alfred (Margaret), *Parables from Nature*, second series, Bell and Daldy, London, 1859

Godley, Charlotte, *Letters from Early New Zealand*, Kiwi Publishers, Christchurch, 2000 (reprint)

Godley, John Robert (ed. J.E. FitzGerald), *Writings and Speeches of John Robert Godley*, Press Office, Christchurch, 1863

Godley, John Robert (ed. C.B. Adderley), *Extracts from Letters of John Robert Godley to C.B. Adderley*, Savill & Edwards, London 1863

Graves Sawle, Lady Rose (née Paynter), *Sketches from the Diaries of Rose Lady Graves Sawle 1833–1896*, printed for private circulation, 1908

Gundry, Dr J.S., *Dr Gundry's Diary*, 2 vols, Nags Head Press, Christchurch, 1982–83

Hare, Augustus, *The Years with Mother* (abridged edition of first 3 vols of *The Story of My Life*, 1896), Century Publishing, 1984

Harper, Henry W., *Letters from New Zealand, 1857–1911*, Hugh Rees, London, 1914

Hart, George R., *Stray Leaves from the Early History of Canterbury*, Press Office for Canterbury Caledonian Society, Christchurch, 1889

Hill, S.S., *Travels on the Shores of the Baltic*, A. Hall, Virtue & Co., London, 1854

Holman, James, *Travels Through Russia, Siberia, Poland…*, G.B. Whittaker, London, 1825

The Illustrated Handbook to Bath, Simms & Son, Bath, 1843

Innes, C.L. (Pilgrim), *Canterbury Sketches; or Life from the Early Days*, Lyttelton Times Office, Christchurch, 1879

Jackson, Thomas, 'In the days of our youth', published in the *Press*, 16 December 1911

Kilbracken, Lord Arthur Godley, *Reminiscences of Lord Kilbracken*, Macmillan, London, 1931

Landor, W.S. (ed. Stephen Wheeler), *Letters of Walter Savage Landor: Private and public*, Duckworth, London, 1899

——*Letters and Other Unpublished Writings of Walter Savage Landor*, R. Bentley & Son, London, 1897

London Chamber of Commerce, *England and her Colonies*, Swan, Sonnenschein, Lowrey, London, 1887

Lyttelton, Lord George William, *New Zealand and the Canterbury Colony* (lecture given on 11 January 1859), W.H. Dalton, London, 1859

——*Two Lectures on a Visit to the Canterbury Colony in 1867–8*, T. Mark, Stourbridge, 1868

——*Ephemera*, 2 vols, John Murray, London, 1865, 1872

Mansfield, Katherine, 'Prelude' from *Bliss and Other Stories*, Constable, London, 1920

——'About Pat', published in *Stories*, Queen's College magazine, London, December 1905

Marshman, John & Henry Selfe Selfe, *Canterbury, New Zealand in 1864*, New Zealand Examiner Office, London, 1864

Meredith, G.L. (ed. A.J. Harrop), *Adventuring in Maoriland in the Seventies*, Angus & Robertson, Sydney, 1935

Morton, Edward, *Travels in Russia and a Residence at St Petersburg and Odessa in …* *1827–29*, Longman, Rees, Orme, Brown and Green, London, 1830

Paul, Robert Bateman, *Letters from Canterbury, New Zealand*, Rivingtons, London, 1857

Pratt, W.T., *Colonial Experiences or Incidents and Reminiscences of 34 years in New Zealand by an Old Colonist*, Chapman and Hall, London, 1877

Reeves, William Pember (ed.), *Canterbury Rhymes*, Lyttelton Times Company, Christchurch, 1883

Scholefield, G.H., *The Richmond–Atkinson Papers*, 2 vols, R.E. Owen, Wellington, 1960

Sewell, Henry (ed. W.D. McIntyre), *The Journal of Henry Sewell 1853–1857*, 2 vols, Whitcoulls Publishers, Christchurch, 1980

Society of Land Purchasers in the Canterbury Settlement, 'Report of the Special Committee … to take into consideration the best means of improving the communication between the port and the plains', Lyttelton, 1851

Stack, J.W., *Through Canterbury and Otago with Bishop Harper in 1859–60* (1906), reprinted by Nags Head Press, Christchurch, 1972

Stout, Sir Robert, *Our First Premier, James Edward FitzGerald: A lecture*, 31 July 1906, New Zealand Times Co., Wellington, 1906

Torlesse, C.O. (ed. Peter Bromley Maling), *The Torlesse Papers*, Pegasus Press, Christchurch, 1958

Tripp, Ellen Shephard (née Harper), *My Early Days*, Christchurch, 1917, reprinted by Kiwi Publishers, 1929

Trollope, Anthony (ed. A.H. Reed), *Anthony Trollope in New Zealand*, A.H. & A.W. Read, Wellington and Auckland, 1969

Waitt, Robert, *The Progress of Canterbury, New Zealand: A Letter Addressed to Joseph Thomas Esq.*, Sumfield & Jones, London, 1856

Wakefield, Edward Gibbon (ed. E.J. Wakefield), *Founders of Canterbury*, Stevens & Co., Christchurch, 1868

Wakefield, Edward Jerningham, *The Hand-Book for New Zealand: Consisting of the most recent information*, John W. Parker, London, 1848

Ward, Edward (ed. Sir J. Hight), *The Journal of Edward Ward 1850–1851*, Pegasus Press, Christchurch, 1951

Secondary sources

Acland, L.G.D., *The Early Canterbury Runs*, 4th edition, Whitcoulls, Christchurch, 1975

Alington, Margaret, *High Point: St Mary's Church, Karori, Wellington 1866–1991*, Parish of St Mary, Karori, 1998

——*Unquiet Earth: A history of the Bolton Street Cemetery*, Wellington City Council (Ministry of Works and Development), Wellington, 1978

Amodeo, Colin, *The Summer Ships*, Caxton Press, Christchurch, 2000

Andersen, Johannes C., *Old Christchurch*, Simpson and Williams, Christchurch, 1949

——*Jubilee History of South Canterbury*, Whitcombe & Tombs, Auckland, 1916

Bohan, Edmund, *Blest Madman: FitzGerald of Canterbury*, Canterbury University Press, Christchurch, 1998

——*Climates of War: New Zealand in conflict 1859–69*, Hazard Press, Christchurch, 2005

——*To Be a Hero: A biography of Sir George Grey*, HarperCollins, Auckland, 1998

——*Edward Stafford: New Zealand's first statesman*, Hazard Press, Christchurch, 1994

Burdon, C.C., *Dr A.C. Barker 1819–1873: Photographer, farmer, physician*, John McIndoe, Dunedin, 1972

Canterbury Old and New, 1850–1900: A souvenir of the Jubilee, Whitcombe & Tombs, Christchurch, 1900

Carrington, C.E., *John Robert Godley of Canterbury*, Whitcombe & Tombs, Christchurch, 1950

Childe-Pemberton, William S., *Life of Lord Norton (Right Hon. Sir Charles Adderley, KCMG, MP)*, John Murray, London, 1909

Crean, Mike (*Press*), *First with the News: An illustrated history*, Random House, Auckland, 2011

Cresswell, Douglas, *Early New Zealand Families*, Pegasus Press, Christchurch, 1949

——*Canterbury Tales*, Bascands, Christchurch 1951

Cyclopedia of New Zealand (Wellington edn), Cyclopedia Company, Wellington, 1897

Dalziel, Raewyn, *Julius Vogel: Business politician*, Auckland University Press, Auckland, 1986

Deans, John, *Pioneers on Port Cooper Plains: The Deans family of Riccarton and Homebush*, Simpson and Williams, Christchurch, 1964

Ell, Sarah (ed.), *The Lives of Pioneer Women in New Zealand*, Bush Press, Auckland, 1993

Evison, Harry C., *The Long Dispute: Maori land rights and European colonisation in southern New Zealand*, Canterbury University Press, Christchurch, 1997

Gardner, W.J. (ed.), *A History of Canterbury*, Vol. II, Whitcombe & Tombs, Christchurch, 1971

Garner, Jean, *Sir John Hall: Pioneer, pastoralist and premier*, Dryden Press, Hororata, 1995

Garrett, Helen, *Henry Jacobs: A clergyman of calibre*, Shoal Bay Press, Christchurch, 1996

Gisborne, William, *New Zealand Rulers and Statesmen* (1886), revised edition, Sampson, Low, Marston & Co., London, 1897

Gore, Ross, *Levins 1841–1941: The history of the first hundred years of Levin & Company Ltd*, Levin & Co., Wellington, 1956

Hamilton, Don, *The Buildings of Christ's College 1850–1990*, The Caxton Press, Christchurch, 1991

Hankin, C.A., *Life in a Young Colony*, Whitcoulls, Christchurch, 1981

Hight, James, & Straubel, C.R. (eds.), *A History of Canterbury*, Vol. I, Whitcombe & Tombs, Christchurch, 1957

Irvine, R.F. & Alpers, O.T.J., *The Progress of New Zealand in the Century* (The Nineteenth Century Series), W. & R. Chambers, London, 1902

Karori Historical Society (eds. Judith Burch & Jan Heynes), *Karori and its People*, Steele Roberts, Wellington, 2011

Katieke School Committee, *Katieke: The district, the people, the schools*, Taumarunui, 1985

King, Michael, *The Penguin History of New Zealand*, Penguin Books, London, 2003

Logan, Robert, *Waimakariri: An illustrated history*, Phillips & King, Christchurch, 2008

Lovat, Lady Alice Mary (Fraser), *The Life of Sir Frederick Weld, GCMG*, John Murray, London, 1914

Macalister, John, *William FitzGerald 1853–1888*, Balinakill Press, Wellington, 2011

Manson, Cecil, *Pioneer Parade*, A.H. & A.W. Reed, Wellington, 1966

Martin, John E., *The House: New Zealand's House of Representatives 1854–2004*, Dunmore Press, Palmerston North, 2004

May, Philip Ross, *The West Coast Gold Rushes*, Pegasus Press, Christchurch, 1962

Moar, Neville, *FitzGerald's Town: Lincoln in the 19th century*, privately published, Lincoln, 2011

Morrell, W.P., *The Provincial System in New Zealand, 1852–1876*, Longmans, Green & Co for Royal Empire Society, London, 1932

Mulcock, Dr Anne, *A Quite Original Type of School*, privately printed, Christchurch, 1992

Oakley, John, *Paintings of Canterbury 1840–1890*, A.H. & A.W. Reed, Wellington and Auckland, 1962

O'Neill, R.B., *The Press, 1861–1961: The story of a newspaper*, Christchurch Press Company, Christchurch, 1963

Patrick, Margaret G., *From Bush to Suburb: Karori 1840–1980*, Karori Historical Society, Karori, 1990

Percival, John, *The Great Famine: Ireland's potato famine 1845–51*, BBC Books, London, 1995

Phelps, Jim, M.D., *Why Am I Still Depressed? Recognising and managing the ups and downs of bipolar II and soft bipolar disorder*, McGraw-Hill, New York, 2006

Purchas, H.T., *Bishop Harper and the Canterbury Settlement*, Whitcombe & Tombs, Christchurch, 1903

Porter, Frances, *Born to New Zealand: A biography of Jane Maria Atkinson*, Allen & Unwin/Port Nicholson Press, Wellington, 1989

Reed, A.H., *The Story of Canterbury*, A.H. & A.W. Reed, Wellington, 1949

Reeves, William Pember, *The Long White Cloud: Ao Tea Roa* (1898), reprinted by Golden Press in association with Whitcombe & Tombs, Auckland and Christchurch, 1950

Rice, Geoffrey W., *Lyttelton: Port and town, an illustrated history*, Canterbury University Press, Christchurch, 2004

Rogers, Anna, *Illustrated History of Canterbury*, Reed Publishing (NZ), Auckland, 2007

Rolleston, Rosamond, *William & Mary Rolleston: An informal biography*, A.H. & A.W. Reed, Wellington and Auckland, 1971

Scholefield, G.H., *Notable New Zealand Statesmen*, Whitcombe & Tombs, Christchurch, 1946

Scotter, W.H., *A History of Canterbury*, Vol. III, Whitcombe & Tombs, Christchurch, 1965

Singleton, George, *Ellesmere: The Jewel in the Canterbury Crown*, Selwyn District Council, Leeston, 2007

Stewart, William Downie, *The Right Honourable Sir Francis H.D. Bell ... His life and times*, Butterworth & Co., Wellington, 1937

Stewart, William Downie, *William Rolleston: A New Zealand statesman*, Whitcombe & Tombs, Christchurch, 1940

Stocker, Mark (ed.), *Remembering Godley: A portrait of Canterbury's founder*, Hazard Press, Christchurch, 2001

Stuart, Peter, *Edward Gibbon Wakefield in New Zealand*, Price Milburn for Victoria University of Wellington, Wellington, 1971

Temple, Philip, *A Sort of Conscience: The Wakefields*, Auckland University Press, Auckland (second edition), 2003

Wakefield, Edward, *Sir Edward William Stafford GCMG, A Memoir*, Walbrook & Co., London, 1922

Wigram, Henry F., *The Story of Christchurch New Zealand*, Lyttelton Times Co., Christchurch, 1916

Wilson, A.N., *The Victorians*, Hutchinson, London, 2002

Woodhouse, A.E., *George Rhodes of the Levels and his Brothers*, Whitcombe & Tombs, Auckland and Christchurch, 1937

Wright-St Clair, Rex E., *Thoroughly a Man of the World: A biography of Sir David Monro*, Whitcombe & Tombs, Christchurch, 1971

Unpublished theses

Greenaway, Richard, 'Henry Selfe Selfe and the origins and early development of Canterbury', University of Canterbury, 1972

Simpson, Eila G., 'The history and development of the *Press* ... 1861–1876', University of New Zealand (Canterbury College), 1942

Smith, Ngaire Steventon, 'James Edward FitzGerald,' University of New Zealand (Canterbury College), 1932

Websites

Archives New Zealand (www.archway.archives.govt.nz)

Australian newspapers (trove.nla.gov.au/newspaper)

British Newspaper Archive (www.britishnewspaperarchive.co.uk)

Department of Internal Affairs, New Zealand (www.dia.govt.nz/births-deaths-and-marriages)

Dictionary of New Zealand Biography (www.teara.govt.nz/en/biographies)

Encyclopedia of New Zealand (www.teara.govt.nz)

New Zealand newspapers (paperspast.natlib.govt.nz)

Index

Page numbers in **bold** refer to illustrations.